THROUGH THE READING GLASS

Women, Books, and Sex in the French Enlightenment

SUELLEN DIACONOFF

STATE UNIVERSITY OF NEW YORK PRESS

cover art: Louis-Léopold Boilly, *A Young Painter and His Model*, ca. 1788–1792,
printed with permission from Smith College Museum of Art, Northampton, Massachusetts.

Published by
STATE UNIVERSITY OF NEW YORK PRESS, ALBANY

Printed in the United States of America

For information, address the State University of New York Press,
194 Washington Avenue, Suite 305, Albany, NY 12210-2365

Production, Laurie Searl
Marketing, Fran Keneston

Library of Congress Cataloging-in-Publication Data

Diaconoff, Suellen.
Through the reading glass : women, books, and sex in the French Enlightenment / Suellen Diaconoff.
p. cm. — (SUNY series in feminist criticism and theory)
Includes bibliographical references and index.
ISBN 0-7914-6421-0 (hardcover : alk. paper) — ISBN 0-7914-6422-9 (paperback : alk. paper)
1. French literature—18th century—History and criticism. 2. French literature—Women authors—History and criticism. 3. Women—Books and reading—France—History—18th century. 4. Women and literature—France—History—18th century. I. Title. II. Series.

PQ265.D52 2005
028'.9'0820944—dc22 2004015116

10 9 8 7 6 5 4 3 2 1

THROUGH THE READING GLASS

SUNY series in Feminist Criticism and Theory

Michelle A. Massé, editor

CONTENTS

ACKNOWLEDGMENTS

In addition to all the people with whom I am not personally acquainted but who helped make this book come to pass—writers and critics, both past and present, librarians, and museum personnel—I would especially like to offer sincere thanks to the following: Jennifer Voter, *secrétaire extraordinaire*; Andrea Breau and Maria Thompson, research assistants; Peggy Mencham, Colby College reference librarian; Margaret Erickson, Colby College art librarian.

Over the years it took to complete this book, my work has been supported by research and travel grants from the U.S. National Endowment for the Humanities and from Colby College to conduct research in the libraries of the Bibliothèque Nationale and the Bibliothèque de l'Arsenal in Paris.

I am grateful to the following museums and collections for granting permission to reproduce the images in this book: National Gallery of Art, Washington, D.C.; Union Centrale des Arts Décoratifs, Paris; Bibliothèque Nationale de France, Paris; Wallraf-Richartz-Museum and the Rheinisches Bildarchiv in Cologne, Germany; Smith College Museum of Art, Northampton, Massachusetts; Wrightsman Collection, New York; Frick Collection, New York; Réunion des Musées Nationaux/Art Resource, New York; Staatliche Kunsthalle, Karlsruhe, Germany; Museum of Fine Arts, Boston; Toledo Museum of Art, Ohio. Thanks to financial support from the Colby College Humanities Division, I have been able to include these illustrations.

Finally, I dedicate this book to my parents, who taught me through example the pleasures of both the book and of reading.

INTRODUCTION

THE READING GLASS AND THE POLITICS OF VIRTUE

"Does she read, your little granddaughter, Mlle Rotisset?"

"Reading is her greatest pleasure. She spends some time reading every day."

"Oh! I can see that; but take care that she does not become a scholar. That would be a thousand pities."

—Manon Roland, *Mémoires*

We have not often recognized that it is as lovers of print culture and knowledge that eighteenth-century women participated in and contributed to the intellectual vitality of the Enlightenment. As a result, the story of their relationship to books and the development of a reading culture for their sex has received relatively little attention despite its potential to reveal the ways in which women envisioned the remaking of society. For reading, it has been said, is at the beginning of the social contract, and at no time is such an affirmation more important than in a century that characterized itself as devoted to the goals of universal enlightenment. As the single most important sign of a literate society, reading is an essential rite of passage by which people create links with one another and by which individuals develop a sense of cumulative time. It is the primary skill required in the extension of literacy within a culture and exchange between cultures, and it is the principal yardstick by which to measure the intellectual progress of a society and specific groups—such as women—within that society.

A veritable thematic structure of Manon Roland's *Mémoires*, reading is the narrative center post of her text, as of her life. From earliest childhood, her favorite hours were those spent in the cozy recesses of her *cabinet paisible*, where she would happily retire with a volume surreptitiously borrowed from her father's atelier. The book might be by her favorite author, Plutarch, or one of the other critics, philosophers, moralists, or metaphysicians whose texts she discovered and consumed with pleasure. For her, personal reading was both an assertion and organization of her private space. In her *petite*

FIGURE 1. Jean-Honoré Fragonard (1732–1806), *A Young Girl Reading*, ca. 1776, oil on canvas. Gift of Mrs. Mellon Bruce in memory of her father, Andrew W. Mellon, Image Copyright 2003 Board of Trustees, National Gallery of Art, Washington, D.C.

retraite, removed from the agitation of normal household activities and a society that she often found unpleasant or unjust, she took pleasure in the beauty of books and the nobility of ideas. Here she read, reflected, meditated, and wrote, and in, the process of this journey through words, made the evolution to a female intellectual, a path she traces, step by step, in her memoirs through the history of her reading.

Reading is also centerpieced in many paintings by eighteenth-century artists who are intrigued by the stasis of the reading subject in intimate relationship with a book. The female reader of Fragonard in *A Young Girl Reading* (Figure 1), dating from 1776, is an exquisitely feminine creature of refined sensitivity, engaged in an act of private reading and transported into a world unseen but wonderfully imagined. This reader, seen in profile, is a young, fresh beauty, seated on a chair with a long armrest, and leaning against a very large pillow. She is beautifully though simply dressed in a lemon-yellow gown with a frilled white collar and cuffs and a bow at her bodice. Her hair is drawn back into a loose chignon, with a mauve ribbon in it. Head slightly bowed, she holds a small volume lightly in one hand, and is deeply engrossed in her reading.

Even though the exact locale of the room is unidentifiable—there are simply two plain walls—the scene nonetheless conveys a feeling of softness and sensuality, particularly underscored by the comfortable plumpness of the pillow and the pert, nubile roundness of the contours of the girl's face and body. While the book is often used iconographically in painting to indicate knowledge, power, or intellect, here, and especially because there is no paper or pen or desk nearby, we conclude that it is of the lightweight variety, probably a fiction in which the reader is uncritically immersed, carried away in a reverie of desire. Though this woman is not the eroticized reader of a Baudouin (Figure 2), languorously sprawled in a chair, an open book at her side, and equivocally self-involved, she has nonetheless been caught in a private act of reading. We can speculate that what intrigues the artist is the quality of her femininity or feminine nature in general, as he invokes in his viewer questions about what she is reading and how it may be impacting her fantasies, longings, and behavior.

While such questions might not carry the same dramatic and negative extravagance as expressed by Father Charles Porée, a Jesuit preacher, who some forty years earlier had warned about the sin and moral evil to which novel-reading would lead women, they nonetheless arise from the same mind-set that genderizes the reading experience. For his part, Porée had indicted both the novel and the woman reader in the most unequivocal of terms when he had charged that woman's reading of novels would lead to the loss of three precious feminine virtues—simplicity, modesty, and reserve—and that she would ineluctably be led down the path from moral to social to political evil.[1]

With these three views of reading—real, pictorial, and moral—we have ample proof that books and sex are intricately and evocatively intertwined

FIGURE 2. Pierre-Antoine Baudouin, *La Lecture*, Union Centrale des Arts Décoratifs, Paris.

in the eighteenth century. For Manon Phlipon, the future Madame Roland, reading is a means toward personal fulfillment and gives access to what Pierre Bourdieu has called cultural capital.[2] It is a way of experiencing the world and coming to find one's place in it. For her, the book, which is enduring when so much else is impermanent, is simultaneously a pleasure and a challenge. She will spend her life reading seriously and will ultimately use all she learns in books to "read" and write—create and record—her self. For Fragonard's reader, on the other hand, reading is a private leisure activity, offering escape from the present, a suspension of the self, coupled with the opportunity to be transported into and transformed by a fictional world of otherness in terms of space, time, and companions. Finally, for Porée, the female consumer of novels is dangerous not only to herself and her family, but also to society and the very moral and political fabric of the nation.

The investigation into these divergent images and what they imply regarding women's reading, writing, and sexuality in the eighteenth century is the subject of this book. More specifically, it is the politics of women's reading acts that constitutes my focusing optic. I will argue that for them reading and its mirroring activity, writing, are key processes through which they seek, create, and confirm individual identity, and that, in those processes, issues of sexuality play a central role. Indeed, I would agree with Terry Eagleton that reading, writing, and sexuality share a number of interlinking characteristics that invite us to study them together. For, as Eagleton has said, each is conducted in private spaces that are always violable; each is shaped by desire, and all three carry for women, in particular, danger and risk.[3] It will, furthermore, be my argument that eighteenth-century women's acts of reading and writing are characterized by an underlying awareness of sexuality that finds expression in the sustained tension between virtue and *volupté* (sensual pleasure) characterizing their works, though muted by their commitment to produce the kind of writing that leads to ethical reading.

A POLITICS OF VIRTUE

Women's ideal of ethical reading is grounded in their more general adherence to a politics of virtue, which I believe they adopted in order to respond to the contradictions of a society that cast them simultaneously as *assujeties* and *souveraines* (ruled or ruler).[4] In fact, the challenge for intellectual women in the eighteenth century was to find a means of accommodating both the abstract Cartesian split between mind and body ("the mind has no sex") together with the real fact of their exclusion from universalist discourse, and the Enlightenment ideal of equality.[5] Their challenge was to rearticulate for their purposes the Cartesian dualism that split mind *and* body, intellect *and* emotion, the mental and material, while promoting a view of woman as both mind *and* body, both intellect *and* sexuality. Cartesianism notwithstanding, popular perception had tended to ascribe to females only one-half of the equation—body, emotion, material—while rational, universalist discourse had simultaneously absorbed and excluded them, acknowledging women as potentially intellectual equals, but physical creatures of difference, diametrically opposed to men. The delicate problem for women intellectuals was to incorporate both female sex and rationality into their discursive practices, and to reposition themselves vis-à-vis the new abstract ideal of equality, without at the same time causing undue anxiety in society at large. Their strategy was, I believe, to adopt a *politics* of virtue, which was a way of using the Cartesian method for their own purposes, and to speak in an approved idiom—that of revolutionary virtue—with universalist underpinnings.

As women of reason, they may have concluded that more prestige could be won not through unseemly battles that they were destined to lose, but through a discourse that positioned them as champions of virtue. By joining in the national discourse promoting virtue, and at the same time seizing hold of the least contentious of revolutionary objectives—broad universal culture—through programs of reading and writing, eighteenth-century women strove to participate in the groundwork of the Enlightenment. It was likewise the most efficacious means of advancing themselves individually and collectively. By allying themselves with virtue, they sought to counter both popular anxieties about female aspirations to learning and arguments by the contemporary medical and philosophical establishment, which had made, as Anne C. Vila declares, the quest for enlightenment natural to man's constitution, but pathological to woman's.[6] Hence, by advocating what we might call "feminized" virtue, which they defined as courage, conviction, and integrity, the women of this book sought to carve out a place for themselves in the revolutionary remaking of society.[7]

Dorinda Outram has suggested that the revolutionary discourse of virtue was actually highly problematic for women's advancement because that discourse was internally contradictory, since it dismissed all that was wrong about the "evil" ancien régime, including, importantly, the role of women.[8] It is in part for this reason that I emphasize their *politics* of virtue, which suggests both genuine conviction and a strategy. To gain entry into discourse, female intellectuals needed to use current language of culture, but at the same time they also sought to establish a new and efficacious ideal for women. Hence, they, too, would dismiss the old corrupt model of the aristocratic society woman (an object of scorn for men and women alike), while proposing a more accessible and democratic ideal, that of virtue. Social standing would not depend on money or title or background, but rather on the belief in values of goodness, fortitude, and commitment (rather than selfishness, privilege, and inconstancy). The path to this new ideal would be charted through a new consciousness and a revised notion of the female self that did not depend on men or on religious practice—though neither was disqualified—but rather on education and particularly a self-education that began with reading.

All the writing subjects of this book had a passion for learning, a number were self-taught, and several were professional pedagogues. Some, like Félicité de Genlis, were eager to teach and illustrate a form of empowered virtue in their texts, while others such as Madame de Graffigny used a new definition of virtue as independence and self-esteem to liberate heroines from conventional plots and lead them to a new valorization of themselves and their right to happiness. Women like Mesdames de Villeneuve and Leprince de Beaumont chose to revision virtue in their fairy stories and sometimes even to write surprisingly feminist stories, while an intellectual such as Isabelle de Charrière set virtue in creative dissonance with erotic urgency in letters and fiction to produce both art and artful readers.

By laying claim to a heterogeneous politics of virtue redefined and in incorporating it into their discourses of reading, writing, and sexuality, these women made unique contributions to Enlightenment objectives and ideals and to the liberal agenda aimed at reworking the social contract. In examining both their experience and their texts, readers today will come to understand not only how eighteenth-century women differ from us—while also offering firm but quiet strategies for renewal—but also why they were to feel so betrayed by the revolution itself. For, as historian Joan W. Scott has shown, the outcome of the French Revolution did little to advance the cause of women, let alone open up new possibilities for them.[9] Those new possibilities had been sketched out by Madame de Lambert in the early part of the century and further elaborated in a number of important pieces of fiction. In 1727, she had encouraged women to value themselves and to envision new personal autonomy. Seeking to embolden them, she wrote, "One of the greatest of happinesses is knowing how to be sufficient unto one's self,"[10] an objective that would be illustrated in fiction by Madame de Graffigny's female protagonist, Zilia, in *Les Lettres d'une Péruvienne* (1747), and by Madame de Genlis's heroine in *L'Histoire de la Duchesse de* C*** (1782), to cite just two examples. We can speculate that such stories of virtuous and independent female protagonists struck a chord with contemporary female readers, since in the period from 1786 to 1800, it was *Les Lettres d'une Péruvienne* (1747), whose heroine plots out a new role for herself without a husband, that was vastly more popular than the more conventional love story of disorderly passion followed by the heroine's death in *Manon Lescaut* (1731).[11] Because women were the primary consumers of novels, it seems reasonable to speculate that there was something about stories of female self-sufficiency and virtue that they found particularly appealing and inspiring.[12] Their enthusiasm may well have been based on this image of empowering virtue, so unlike the modest and self-effacing virtues typically attributed to or preached to women. With the new model of virtue forefronting female protagonists of sensitivity and reason, will, and stamina, women were neither victims nor revolutionaries, but rather individuals capable of demonstrating that the battle for legitimacy and respect could and should be waged on the grounds of virtue redefined.

They were, indeed, the moral sex, as Liselotte Steinbrügge entitled her study of women in the Enlightenment. But I would suggest that it is unlikely that they would have concurred that the epithet was a cynical or clever ploy by which they would be denied roles of importance in society.[13] For in truth, these women were not aspiring to the same positions in the public sphere as those held by men. What they wanted was equal respect in their different domains. Having absorbed the lessons of Cartesianism that reason could be used by either sex and that the mind had no sex, they sought to join universalist discourse through the promotion of virtue. What I am calling their "politics" of virtue is simultaneously an expression of sincere Enlightenment idealism, combined with strategies of "moral" self-promotion. It is on these grounds of a bivalent politics of virtue that I seek to establish a new view into women's discursive practices in the eighteenth century. In this sense, my argument both builds on and diverges from the work from the past two decades devoted to women under the ancien régime.

No scholar of early women's culture today works without paying an enormous debt to Nancy K. Miller, Joan DeJean, Erica Harth, Dena Goodman, Joan Landes, Joan Hinde Stewart, and many others both in and out of the field of French cultural studies.[14] Quite simply, these scholars were responsible for such original, groundbreaking work on women's writing that they virtually created a new field in French literary studies. By the power and quality of their analysis, they made woman-oriented scholarship not only respectable but exciting and a force to deal with. Those of us who have been in the field for several decades have no trouble remembering when panels on women's writing at national conferences were at best tolerated, or when Ph.D. candidates who chose to work on women's topics did so at their own peril, given the disregard that doctoral committees and many potential employers had for such work. So, there is no doubt that these scholars have made it possible for subsequent critics to continue the work on women, even while perhaps mapping the terrain differently.

The challenge in studying the condition of women and their writing from more than 200 years ago is neither to undervalue voices from the past, nor to overread their texts as deliberate demonstrations of *our* political and social battles. In the endeavor to forge links, to validate, and to reclaim, the critic always risks reading and understanding from an overly contemporary standpoint, making the women of the past resemble us, our struggles, and our resistance. It is perhaps a particularly "readerly" move, for, as Roland Barthes suggests, all reading tends to rewrite the text of the work within the text of our lives.[15] But since neither the politics nor the poetics of eighteenth-century female expression is co-determinate with present context or needs,

I have not situated my study in a vocabulary of radical protest, nor do I concentrate on what happened *to* women from a retrospective perspective. Instead, my focus is on the recuperation of virtue in their works and reading, in order to take eighteenth-century women at their word and to place them within *their* century. What this means is "listening" carefully to what they said, trying to use words with the meaning they gave them, while at the same time being aware that I cannot totally divorce myself from the culture in which I live.

Aside from Madame Riccoboni, none of the writers of this book was primarily a novelist, but they were practitioners of the word: readers, essayists, memoirists, short story writers, letter writers, fabulists, poets, and journalists. In other words, they cover a wide variety of registers and a broad swath of discursive practices, which would seem to throw into doubt the charge that early women writers suffered in silence. For some of these women, the embrace of virtue was a narrative move, not reflected in their own lives, but deliberately chosen as the best way to promote women's interests, while for others it was a personal choice, not without its own contradictions and revealing the conflict between liberal impulses and individual reserve. But for all, the adoption of the strategies of virtue, whether politically, esthetically, or ethically motivated, was the specific means through which they sought to negotiate for themselves new positions of authority and to integrate social responsibility with competing Enlightenment principles of individualism in sexual and personal affairs. Virtue is the word they use, and it behooves us, when reading them, to use it and to understand it as they did. For the definition of virtue that women posit and which becomes for many the directing force of their reading and writing is both a calculated strategy and a measure of their genuine belief in female worth and their determination to demonstrate that value. Hence, when they rally other women to virtue, it is not to exhort them to be demure, retiring, or uncoy, but to urge them to be courageous, resolved, and responsible.

Though their notion of virtue is in no way exclusively synonymous with sexuality in the narrow sense of the erotic body, issues of sexuality factor in their writing, because, as Michel Delon writes, a new awareness of sexuality in the mid- to late eighteenth century was unavoidable, given the philosophical and cultural currents of the period represented by materialism, sensualism, and the regency.[16] Whether in the memoir or fairy tale, the love letter or essay, the epistolary novel or historical romance, eighteenth-century women's writing carries a discourse on sexuality, showing that despite the protocols of silence that society imposed on them, they were neither voiceless nor inarticulate about matters of sexuality. Among the topics that women wrote about were not only courtship, marriage, maternity, sickness, and health, but also desire, adultery, psychological and sexual violence, including rape, menstruation, childbirth, breastfeeding, menopause, the aging body, masturbation, lesbianism, and bisexuality. I will not argue that they dealt in great depth with some of these issues, but the very fact that they did at all challenges preconceived notions about women in the eighteenth century and suggests that they are less prudish than we might at first have thought.

One finds in Madame Riccoboni, for instance, a rescripting of boudoir rape, while Manon Roland remembers a brush with sexual assault, that probably more than she knew helped to determine her feelings about sex. Madame de Charrière problematizes sexuality, especially in working-class girls who are at once more natural about sex and more vulnerable to being abandoned, but she also estheticizes desire, turning it into a thing of art and producing through it a work of art. Félicité de Genlis chooses to show a female protagonist abjuring sexuality for a new kind of empowerment through chastity regained, while both she and Madame de Graffigny reveal that "choice" in the eighteenth-century literary vernacular means choosing not to marry. The periodical press written by and for women frequently received letters from subscribers querying society's assumptions about women or asking for sexualized advice on how to keep husbands faithful or rewin their passion. Even the writers of fairy tales, Madame de Villeneuve and Madame Leprince de Beaumont, incorporate the problems of female sexuality with eroticism and enlightenment into their tale of Beauty and the Beast.

Yet while treating issues of sexuality in their works, they are also convinced that the female writer carries a special responsibility toward her readers. These women know that storytelling is important in the creation and conduct of gender, and they often choose to tell stories that seek to rethink issues of sexuality and women's responsibility, thereby inviting or challenging their readers to do likewise in their own lives. In writing their texts of virtuous reconfiguration, they are motivated by the conviction that reading is the route not only to knowledge and understanding, but also to self-improvement. Their new stance of idealism and self-promotion—this politics of enlightened virtue—calls on women to find and create themselves within a process that starts with reading and evolves into writing, in an unclosed and ever-renewed circle that forms a new kind of female autobiographics.

READING AND POWER

As contemporary reading theorists such as J. A. Appleyard assert, becoming a reader is a complex process,[17] complicated yet further, historians of women would argue, by considerations of gender. Hence, reading and the issues that surround books become the site for yet one more struggle for authority. Similarly, cultural critic and historian Pierre Bourdieu stresses that reading, like writing, involves questions of power, since the book carries with it the potential, first, to act on the reader's mental structures and through them on societal structures.[18] As a consequence, not only can the book, read and written, transform the reader's vision of the world and the world itself, but both reader and reading can be endowed with revolutionary potential.

Yet, historically, the woman reader has been denigrated, on the one hand, for being an inconsequential, passive, and vulnerable reader of lightweight subject matter, and, on the other, for reading with the absurd and inappropriate pretentions of the bluestocking. In the eighteenth century she was told not to read novels because of the deleterious effects they would have on her innocence and not to read science or philosophy because they were not made for her delicate fibers.[19] According to a popular view in the eighteenth century, advanced by the medical establishment represented by men such as S. A. Tissot and D. T. Bienville, the reading of novels by women was a kind of quasipathological stimulus giving rise to episodes of panting, insomnia, nervousness, languor, and tears.[20] But because most women were neither educated for, nor judged capable of dealing with demanding, intellectual material, they were rarely encouraged to engage in more meaningful kinds of reading.

Still, as the calls for educating women's minds increased in number, the subject of women's reading gave rise to discussions often fueled with gender-loaded questions. In this new angle on the war between the sexes and the politics of reading, questions were posed concerning *what* women should read, and *who* should decide what they read. Commentators warned about the social, sexual, religious, and even health dangers that lay in women's reading. In 1766, Doctor Tissot wrote, "Continuous reading produces . . . nervous illnesses" and he asserted that "of all the causes that have harmed the health of women, the main one has been the infinite increase in novels over the past hundred years. . . . A girl who reads rather than running at the age of ten, will be when she is twenty a vaporous woman and not a good wet nurse."[21]

Indeed, the emergence of philosophical medicine in the mid-eighteenth century and the writings of physician philosophers provided the justification for suggesting that woman's sensibility as well as her physiology were different from man's and that therefore reading would affect the two sexes differently. In the 1780s, the physician Edme-Pierre Chauvot de Beauchêne studied in *De L'Influence des affections de l'âme dans les maladies nerveuses des femmes, avec le traitement qui convient à ces maladies*, the cause and effects of vapors, a well-known malady that began with feelings of languor or melancholy, leading to swooning, inexplicable floods of tears, nervous convulsions, and loss of consciousness. The primary causative agent of vapors, which he considered a serious public health problem, was none other than the novel. Presenting a notion of female reading that was sensationist and corporeal in nature, and that involved the interlocking of specific physiological and psychological factors so that women would literally and physically experience the effects intended by the text, Chavot de Beauchêne and other commentators, sometimes including women themselves, conventionally issued warnings about the dangers of reading and offered the eroticized woman reader as a negative model. For some commentators, the novel seemed literally to possess a phallic quality, while for others it was a contagion that infected the body as much as the mind. Rousseau had opined in his first preface to *La Nouvelle Héloïse* that chaste girls do not read novels, thereby implicitly chiding Richardson for promoting the idea that novels could have an educative effect. He develops the idea in the second preface, through the memorable image of a house on fire. If the objective is to educate a young person, he warns, do not expect the reader to learn virtue by reading a novel, which is tantamount to setting a house on fire in order to put the pumps in action ("c'est mettre le feu à la maison pour jouer les pompes").[22]

The women writers of this book, on the other hand, offer an alternate view. Indeed, one can discern in their works a set of basic principles that suggests an implicit theory of "right" and useful reading, including of the novel. Like Robert Darnton's example of Jean Ranson, who "entered into parenthood through reading and relied on books to make his offspring into so many Emiles and Emilies,"[23] these women believed that reading was an important resource, especially for their sex, which had been sidelined from other realms of intellectual or cultural exchange. Since "right" reading was neither a passive nor mechanistic skill, but rather an active construction of the mind, they saw its primary purpose as an educative goal and the improvement of the moral self. Indeed, they would agree with Rousseau's Julie who tells St. Preux that she can scarcely imagine "what sort of goodness a book can have if it does not carry its readers to practice good."[24] For them, this educative function of the written page would be extended to all kinds of texts, from novels to fairy tales, essays to memoirs. Hence their emphasis on printed narratives that lead to the discovery of and commitment to moral values; hence their belief that reading is a vehicle through which intelligence is honed and an individual's sense of identity modified and improved; hence their endeavors to write works that might be described both as "esthetic" and "efferent," meaning that the reader should experience the text fully, living through its events, but also carry away something valuable from the experience that she will be able to make use of in her own life.[25] And, hence, also, the ethic of responsibility that arises from so many of their texts. This is, I believe, a significant development in the relationship between reader and reading, presenting a new rhetorical situation that women writers will endeavor to use to the advantage of their sex.

It is not generally acknowledged that it is as readers that eighteenth-century women participated in the intellectual vitality of the Enlightenment, even if their acts of reading were largely confined to domestic spaces and private collections rather than the *cabinets de lecture* and so-called public libraries being established in Paris. In fact, of course, we know very little about early women's reading practices—how they read, where they read, and why they read. There is no monograph on the subject, and the records of statistics and facts that would nourish such a volume do not exist.[26] Early in the twentieth century, in an effort to recover general reading practices from the past, historian Daniel Mornet studied the inventories of some 500 private libraries in Paris from the period 1750 to 1780. But as critics, including Robert Darnton, have observed, such listings only show which books people possessed and not which books they actually read or how they read them.[27] Nor do they, we might add, include any information specifically about women's reading.

While early female bibliophiles have been acknowledged in French history, they tended to be cast as *collectors* rather than *lovers* of books. Joannis Guignard, for instance, writing in the late nineteenth century, was convinced that women collected books in the eighteenth century in order to demonstrate a sense of style.[28] "Our great ladies would have felt they were failing their duty," he says "if they hadn't been able to show off in their richly decorated salons books beautifully bound by the likes of Derome or Padeloup," two of the most famous bookbinders of the eighteenth century (74). And while this may have been true, it certainly requires some further substantiation—such as, for instance, that the pages of all those books in their libraries had never been cut. But many antiquarians of the book, like many early commentators on reading, scarcely needed those proofs, for in their minds, the idea that women could be lovers of books and serious readers was a contradiction in terms. One early historian of women's reading, Albert Cim, quotes various misogynist judgments concerning the relationship of women and books, including one of the kinder pronounced by a M. Porel who said, "The love of books is a mark of delicacy, but it is a delicacy of men."[29] Cim will dismiss that judgment as outrageous, but his own text often veers toward the conclusion that women of the ancien régime looked upon books as objects of beauty to admire passively upon their shelves rather than to consume with passion.

It is against such portrayals that I situate this study and its reflections on how various figures of reading infiltrate, shape, and define the discourse and processes by which specific eighteenth-century women endeavored to give sense to and make sense of female experience.[30] Even the casual reader should be struck by the special place reserved in these women's writing for the act of reading and the spaces of reading. For the double power and pleasure of the book, which speaks to both hearts and minds, impels them, in their fiction, to present the female reader as a sympathetic and valued character, and, in their nonfiction, as a model to emulate. Certainly their decision to emphasize reading is related to their desire that females be better educated, both in classical and practical ways, but it also bespeaks their aspirations for women to become and be accepted as active consumers and producers of culture. Reading is, indeed, at the beginning of their new social contract.

⁂

In the following chapters, I will consider reading as a trope through which to examine the cultural project of women laying claim to Enlightenment society. While I will investigate how reading functioned in the lives, texts, and society of my female subjects—despite the paucity of hard information we have on this subject—my intention is not to discern who read which works or how many books were sold, or to determine the quality of reader response to their works—which are valid but difficult questions outside the purview of this study. Rather, my objective is to consider how women's reading was viewed and constructed in letters and fiction and memoirs and book lists by intelligent women in the eighteenth century who saw it as key to woman's moral self-enlightenment. Toward that end, I have specifically chosen to deal with a wide variety of their texts, from fairy tale to journalism, fiction to memoirs, the essay and the love letter, in order to show how women used writing of all kinds for the same purposes of recuperating virtue through reading. Finally, while my discussion of their works will be informed by a variety of ideas from contemporary reading theorists, it will not be driven by any one approach. Hence, in several respects, my approach is heteroclite, as befits a period as multifaceted as the eighteenth century.

To situate the issue of women's reading, chapter one on "Female Readers and *l'espace du livre*," discusses the rites and protocols of reading and literacy in eighteenth-century France. It also studies visual representations of women's reading and looks at the problem of gendered reading practices and the prohibition of women from reading spaces in the public sector. In casting the history of women's reading in terms of a spatial metaphor of movement from the *boudoir* to the figurative *bibliothèque*, I wish to show that the women of this book sought to replace the erotic power granted them in the boudoir with the intellectual power to be gained in commerce with books and ideas. The kind of cultural knowledge represented by books—the synedochical *bibliothèque*—would subsequently permit women to extend their objectives and stake out new claims to artistic and intellectual property. Reading would be the original impulse for writing, and reading and writing would become mutually reflected activities.

For two women, in particular, Manon Roland and Félicité de Genlis, who are the subjects of chapters two and three, this is particularly true. An examination of their lives as set forth in their memoirs reveals how their reading served as an apprenticeship for their writing. Contrary to expectations concerning female readers, these two women defy the definition of and protocols surrounding women's reading. Neither was a lightweight, romantic reader, who lost herself in books for escapist reasons; nor was she a bluestocking misfit with no outlets for her erudition. Largely self-educated, each used reading to better herself, and, with the aid of various mentors, during her adolescence and young adulthood, embarked on a conscious reading program that was serious, demanding, and largely classical in nature. Throughout their lives and in conjunction with their reading, these women wrote, first, copying out or keeping journals of their readings, and then, once they had served the reader's apprenticeship, writing texts of their own. In consequence of their self-training and in defiance of protocols, each used her writing in ways not expected of women. Madame Roland participated actively in political discussions, even if through the signature of her husband, and ultimately was to produce one of the most affecting texts of the revolution when she wrote her personal memoirs, while Madame de Genlis quite literally abandoned the accouterments of her sex to adopt pen and ink and produce a body of work including ten volumes of memoirs, fiction, historical romance, pedagogical treatises, fairy tales, and theater that rivals in types of genre and in volume the most prolific of male writers at any period in France.

From the politics and protocols that ruled women's reading, as related in chapter one, chapter two will concern the actual reading practices and the birth of one remarkable eighteenth-century female intellectual, Manon Phlipon Roland, for whom reading is a refuge from the vulgarities of the world, but also the means to survival. In her *Mémoires*, composed in prison while awaiting a sentence of death, she relates her coming-to-self in large measure through the processes of her own reading. Far from representing a mere defense of her life, this extraordinary autobiographical text is a compelling demonstration of how reading, which had formed her life and will, is part of a collective continuum of future readers and writers. For, it is by *our* acts of reading and writing, in response to hers, that we actualize her unenunciated goal, which is to trump the executioner's blade.

In opposition to Manon Roland who left behind this single text, Félicité de Genlis wrote ceaselessly for publication throughout her long life, in large measure because she sought to provide female readers with the kind of books that would allow them to make ethical readings. Dedicated to producing an oeuvre totally grounded in a new vision of women's reading and the woman reader, Madame de Genlis reworked an ostensibly frivolous genre—the romance— to produce in *L'Histoire de la Duchesse de La Vallière*, an uplifting story that would force women readers to rethink what it meant to be happy. In relating the true story of Louise de La Vallière as a triumph over romance, Madame de Genlis used one of the most popular forms of women's reading for the dual purposes of teaching history and inspiring women to reconceptualize their own personal history. In moving the affective pleasure of reading to another, more engaged level, and constructing a model for both an esthetic and efferent reading, Madame de Genlis reveals that the objective of reading, as of life itself, is for self-improvement. As a result, *la romance genlisienne* becomes an invitation to read not through the lens of romantic sensibility but through the intellect framed by moral conscience. Chapter three examines how remapping the romance leads to reading as a transforming experience.

If reading has practical and moral functions for Félicité de Genlis, with Isabelle de Charrière it will have artistic and intellectual ones. Her fiction calls for what could be considered an antiRousseauist reading in that Charrière does not seek to create a bond of sentimental dependency between reader and writer, as Rousseau had done, but rather to intellectualize and estheticize the reading experience, and to reconfigure desire—that key component of fiction that had caused such alarm over woman's consumption of novels. Yet while Charrière does, indeed, posit desire as the primary explanatory mechanism of human behavior and a key element in reading, she transforms it in her fiction while retaining it in her own love letters. In chapter four, I examine the differences in the projects of desire that characterize her love letters to Baron d'Hermenches and her short epistolary fictions (*Lettres neuchâteloises* and *Lettres de Lausanne*), and argue that paradoxically her scripting of both desire and her reader in the love letters is more consistent with conventions of fiction than the fiction itself, which endeavors to deny all conventions. In counterdistinction to those who claim that the novel is the site of troublesome erotics, Charrière's project of desire in fiction has less to do with eroticizing desire than with neutralizing it through the intellect. Thus, while her novellas, which are windows into the internal mechanisms of desire and thought processes, may be read privately, they will never have to be read secretly. What Charrière does, in fact, is to change the definitional basis of reading for pleasure, showing how the project of desire need not always be sexual, but rather can be esthetic and intellectual, producing not what Claude Labrosse has called an *érotisme d'âme* but an *érotisme d'intellect*.[31] In this sense, her texts work to produce an antisentimental ideal of reading in which the reader's pleasure derives not from "redemptive sentimentality," but from the ability to intellectualize and estheticize desire into a work of art.

For Marie-Jeanne Riccoboni, on the other hand, the project of fiction is more pragmatically located in the responsibilities of the writer toward her reader. Through the lens of gender and the metaphoric interplay of rape and reading, chapter five investigates opposing notions of esthetics and reading as represented by Madame Riccoboni, the most popular and best-selling novelist of the eighteenth century, in contrast with the master of ironic eroticism, Choderlos de Laclos, whose publication of *Les Liaisons dangereuses* leads to a brief but important argument between them. Though Riccoboni does not accuse Laclos of "raping" his reader in the same way that many moralists accused the novel of doing, she nonetheless implicitly charges him with ironizing the corporeal notion of reading and explicitly assails him for giving female readers negative models of womanhood. While accepting the idea of a sexualized reading, she refuses, nonetheless, to ratify the principle whereby the reader is made complicitous with rape. Through her rearticulation of a rape scene in *Les Lettres de Juliette Catesby*, she both de-eroticizes the rape and the reading, in support of her guiding principle that reading relations, like human relations, should inspire and not degrade.

The same objective is a vital part of the fairy-tale genre, which by its very nature is optative, presenting what "should" be. Chapter six examines two versions of the eighteenth-century fairy tale, "La Belle et la Bête," written by Madame de Villeneuve in 1740–1741 and Madame Leprince de Beaumont in 1758. Remarkably, this ostensibly simple tale becomes the unexpected site for a discourse on books and the skills of reading. Acts of reading abound, whether in the power structure of the fairy universe—a veritable *cité des dames*—where fairies become rival readers of *le grand livre*, or in the library of the Beast's palace where Belle is dazzled by the book treasures that await her. Fairies consult manuals for recipes that will help them prevail, and Belle is called upon to read both her dreams and the painting of a prince imprisoned in the frame who implores her to free him. In fact, as the fairy tale shows, acts of reading in multiple varieties are the principal ways we gain knowledge. Furthermore, the linking of reading, books, and sex constitutes real female empowerment. In that respect, one might suggest that critics from Jean-Jacques Rousseau to feminist scholars have missed this embedded message that makes the fairy tale not only a schooling in reading—instructing young readers in techniques of negotiating and deciphering meaning from the text—but also the very site for warranting women as readers, keepers, and creators of knowledge through the book.

The final chapter examines the development of a completely new kind of reading experience for women with the birth of the female periodical press. For the first time, women are identified as a separate interest group and a type of periodic literature is established specifically for them. In opening a forum for women, this press—written by, for, and about women—will, moreover, play a role in redrawing the boundaries of a changing community moving toward greater democracy. Significantly, the relationship between reader and writer will be far closer than in a book culture and also far more fluid. Readers could and did become published writers in periodicals like the *Journal des dames*, which encouraged them to practice their voices and their rights on the pages of the press intended for their "glory." In giving women both voice and a sense of proprietorship, the female periodical also allowed the fair sex to exercise a kind of market power that went beyond writing letters to the editor to agree or disagree, because now they could express dissatisfaction by withdrawing their economic support and canceling a subscription. The birth of the female periodical press marks not only a new chapter in the history of print culture, but also a capital moment in the history of women's reading in France.

⁂ ⁂ ⁂

Historians of reading tell us that the practice of reading is not an invariable in history and that its development and practices depend very much on time and place. Furthermore, they say, as reading engages with issues of access and education, the politics of canon formation, and other cultural modes of domination and morality, the story that emerges reveals a society's values, its successes and failures, plus, inevitably, the role of the sexes within it. Thus, in eighteenth-century Europe, the explosive growth of reading, together with the development of two new literary forms—the novel and the periodical press—would have profound emancipatory consequences for women, according to reading historian Matei Calinescu.[32] On the one hand, women's consumption of print culture would lead to the spectacular expansion and diversification of their own written production and, on the other, the extension of an increasingly sophisticated female reading public.

Yet to assume that eighteenth-century women read as we do three centuries later would be in error. It would also be to overlook the ways in which their discourses on reading and empowering virtue would modify the social contract. In view of my desire to give full weight to these differences, while at the same time probe them more fully, I will take up the reading glass, that venerable tool that simultaneously suggests earlier times and a closer look. The objective will be to examine how a reading culture for women was being constructed, one in which books, sex, and acts of reading are richly and evocatively intertwined. My choice of the reading glass—the reader's emblem par excellence—is predicated not only on its figurative and symbolic properties, but also on the object's literal and historical status in the eighteenth century.

As we know from historians who have traced the invention and evolution of optical devices, the reading glass was both a social and cultural object in eighteenth-century Europe, alongside other vision aids, including eyeglasses, which had been in use since the thirteenth century.[33] In their earliest form, *besicles*, as the first eyeglasses were known, were composed of two convex lenses with a rivet pivot. Like the reading glass, they could be held by hand, either by the lens frame or an attached handle. Or they could be perched on the nose. It was not until the eighteenth century that a pair of temples was fastened to eyeglass frames made of steel, silver, gold, or tortoiseshell, an invention that enhanced the comfort of wearing glasses and made them less prone to slippage.

As for the reading glass itself, also called a loupe, it appears to be related to the reading stone, a segment of a glass sphere, dating back to 1000 A.D. and laid over reading materials by presbyopic monks to magnify the letters of their manuscripts. Over time, the reading stone evolved into a reading glass, so that by the time of the eighteenth century, it was an object of beauty as well as utility, as handsome museum collections of early reading aids in Paris, Bern, and West Germany bear witness. Typically, its single, round lens is encased in a silver, wooden, or brass frame, which folds back into a plain or decorated case of similar materials, attached to a handle made of enamel, leather, mother of pearl, or horn. In Paris, readers and others such as jewelers and watchmakers, seamstresses and tailors whose work required magnification and detail, could purchase their reading glass or eyeglasses, from lens and mirror makers who either peddled their wares on the street or offered them in their place of business. One famous shop on the quai de l'Horloge was presided over by a well-known craftsman, Louis-Vincent Chevalier, who in 1765 earned the status of master optician, a term adopted in 1720 by those who specialized in the fabrication of eyeglasses.

In W. Poulet's *Atlas on the History of Spectacles*, illustrating the incorporation of early optics in painting, engravings, and caricatures from the thirteenth through the nineteenth centuries, the vast majority of subjects wearing or utilizing vision aids are men. This is not surprising, given that from the beginning vision enhancers were associated with book learning, which meant with monks and scholars. However, not all uses of eyeglasses were serious. As early as the fifteenth century, spectacles were used to poke fun at the intellectual or those with intellectual pretensions, and, in the eighteenth century, optical aids sometimes made their way into erotic caricature, as in one image showing two men—one holding a pair of *besicles* to his eyes and the other equipped with a magnifying glass—peering at the genital area of a young woman asleep on a bed.[34] Relatively few women are represented using reading aids, perhaps because fewer of their sex were readers or because they avoided being painted with objects that were thought to block the beauty or sensuality of the face or that suggested inadequacy in any way. Poulet's volume does, however, depict several older eighteenth-century women with optical aids, including Caroline Hershel (1759–1848), known for her discovery of eight comets, who is shown wearing a pair of spectacles on a cord around her neck as she studies a chart on a table, a book under her hand. And there is the curious self-portrait by Anna Thurbusch (1722–1782), also with book in hand, who has fastened a large monocle, arranged to a scarved coiffure, over one eye. A third woman, old and unidentified, holds a pair of *besicles* in her hand, almost as though she were looking for something to read. What these several examples suggest is that while it would be difficult to assign a clear gender component to the portrayal of early optical aids, vision tools had a real and historical presence in eighteenth-century French culture. Which makes them, I think, a particularly apt metaphor to use in a book on reading.

As William R. Paulson, who writes on the eighteenth-century's fascination with blindness, says, sight has always occupied a dominant conceptual place among the senses in Western culture, since it is widely assumed to be the primary sense capable of probing the presence of a world exterior to the self.[35] That this world might be in a text makes it no less relevant and, indeed, only underlines the importance of an optical aid that helps us enter and analyze the inner vision of a writer. In that sense, the reading glass seems to me to be the epitomical Enlightenment tool.

ONE

FEMALE READERS AND *L'ESPACE DU LIVRE*

A QUIET REVOLUTION

> The only place where I stopped was a rather large chamber surrounded by a delicately worked grille that held countless books of all colors and all forms, in admirable condition; I was in such a state of enchantment that I hardly thought I would be able to leave without having read them all.
>
> —Zilia, *Les Lettres d'une Péruvienne*, Lettre 35

In 1919, Albert Cim published *Les Femmes et les livres*, which gives an account of important private library collections held by early modern French women.[1] The women who figure in his book are both known and unknown and include individuals as different as Charlotte Corday, who is said to have given away all her books, except her Plutarch, before leaving for Paris to assassinate Marat; Louise-Diane-Françoise de Clermont-Gaillerande, Duchesse de Brancas ou de Villars-Brancande (1711–1784), whose library was composed of 3000 to 4000 volumes; and Mademoiselle le Duc, marquise de Tourvoie, identified as a "danseuse à l'Opéra, maîtresse puis femme de Louis de Bourbon, comte de Clermont," who possessed a personal library consisting of an astonishingly large number of books on theology. Also on this list of early women bibliophiles is the name of one of the most visible and controversial women of the late eighteenth century, Marie-Antoinette, who, according to inventories possessed two different collections of books. The first, catalogued as "La Bibliothèque de la Reine Marie-Antoinette," was located in the Château des Tuileries, while the second, under the title "Livres du Boudoir de la Reine Marie-Antoinette," was her private collection kept at the Petit Trianon.

The holdings of the first library, transported in 1793 to the Bibliothèque Nationale, are, one assumes, the officially sanctioned library for public display. At the royal palace, this library had occupied ten armoires, identified by letters of the alphabet and arranged by the king in the following categories: *religion*, *histoire*, *art* (*sciences et arts*), and *belles lettres*. Below the royal coat of arms, each volume bore on its spine or cover the initials "CT" for Château des Tuileries. The largest number of volumes of this collection belonged to the category of history, while the second most numerous were shelved under belles lettres, including a number of works by women, such as *Les Femmes illustres* by Mademoiselle de Scudéry, Madame de Lafayette's *La Princesse de Clèves* and *Zaïde*, fairy tales by Madame D'Aulnoy, and almost all of Madame Riccoboni's novels.

The second library of the queen—those"livres du boudoir"—was catalogued by order of the Convention and sent in 1800 to the Bibliothèque publique de Versailles, after duplicate copies of its holdings were sold. Rumor quickly had it that this library was composed of books "of an ultralight kind," an insinuation only partially contested by another nineteenth-century bibliophile, Ernest Quentin-Bauchart, who opined that in his judgment the queen's personal library was no more morally disreputable that those of many other "great ladies of the time." In fact, there was "nothing at all scandalous about it," he added.[2] Nonetheless, the charge stuck: "the books from the boudoir" were exactly the type of reading that the moral police might expect from a discredited queen.

It is the distinctly different names given to these two collections of books that arrests my attention: *bibliothèque* and *boudoir*. For this choice, it seems to me, is dictated less by the architectural structure in which the books were found than in what is implied about the quality of the works and their putative reader. Any book characterized as belonging in the boudoir automatically is deemed suspect, assumed to be of lightweight, frivolous nature, in the libertine or erotic mold. The sniff of disapprobation implicit in the very naming of this collection serves to censure the queen through her reading material. On the contrary, by identifying the books of the other collection as a *bibliothèque*, the cataloguers bestow a legitimacy on those holdings, rendering them honorable reading, since reading that takes place in the *bibliothèque*, undertaken for serious purposes, carries prestige and dignifies both text and reader. Underscoring the principle whereby certain spaces are associated with body or mind—*boudoir* or *bibliothèque*—and are further associated with female and male respectively, Madame de Genlis expressed considerable disapproval of the fad among early nineteenth-century women who, she acerbically observed, had taken to referring to their *cabinet* —a sex-neutral space, in her view—as their *boudoir*, thereby reinvoking a space of sexual intrigue and moral laxity. "This strange words," she caustically objects, "formerly was used only by courtesans."[3]

It is the tradition of associating female reading with a particular morally compromised space that disturbs her. For, to characterize women's reading as that derived from or involved with the boudoir was both a spatial marker and totalizing shorthand, which not only eroticized the reading act and the reader, but essentialized the woman as pure sexuality. To evoke the woman reader as easy prey, victim, or unthinking consumer by associating her with a particular space is a reminder that, as Robert Scholes has written, the human condition is often looked upon as one of textuality filled with tropes and traps.[4] It was a view that Madame de Genlis and other women challenged. In an age in which female literacy was low, and even more so when the fair sex was so often not given credit for having brains, she had concluded that reading idly and for pleasure, as one might do in the boudoir, was a luxury her sex could not afford. Embracing a model of telic reading, defined by critic Matei Calinescu as reading for a goal external to itself, Madame de Genlis also knew that such reading could always become paratelic or autotelic—a goal in itself, an intrinsically motivated process—which is her objective.[5] However, reading in the boudoir was antithetical to this goal because space is neither innocent, nor has it been used innocently against women.

QUESTIONS OF SPACE: DISCURSIVE, POLITICAL, AND CULTURAL

Indeed, as psychologists and cultural anthropologists tell us, space is not a neutral philosophical concept, but rather an ideological structure and an iconographic language offering provocative insights into both the construction and the representation of identity. Not surprisingly, it has also been a concept central to scholarly arguments framed around issues of private and public space and the transformation of those spaces as the institutions and practices of a new bourgeois society were established.[6] In the last decades of the twentieth century, a number of women scholars, including Dorinda Outram, Joan Landes, Dena Goodman, Joan DeJean, and Erica Harth, used the notion of space to retell or explain the story of women, choosing to examine discursive, political, or social spaces, in the effort to say what happened to women and women's works under the ancien régime.[7] While my intention is to focus on another kind of space—*l'espace du livre*—it is nonetheless useful to rehearse their arguments.

In 1988, at the height of academic feminism, Joan Landes published an important feminist study in which she argued that ironically the collapse of the ancien régime led to even "more pervasive gendering of public space." Speaking of the paradoxical relationship between feminism and republicanism that resulted in feminism adopting a "highly gendered bourgeois male discourse that depended on women's domesticity and the silencing of the 'public' woman of the aristocracy and popular classes,"[8] Landes set forth the major themes of women's disenfranchisement, which most subsequent commentators have renewed, agreeing that when social or political arbiters dismiss, disqualify, or deal with female speech as inherently contradictory, women end up by being treated as second-class citizens.

Dorinda Outram has written that eighteenth-century women were excluded from speech even when they adopted the revolutionary discourse of virtue, since their enterprise turned into a futile attempt to legitimate themselves and establish a new identity in society.[9] Hence, while acknowledging that many women did speak out in the public domain, she underscores the point that their speech failed to carry weight in public discourse. In part, this was because the universalistic rhetoric that women adopted carried such internal contradictions that they were ultimately ensnared in a catch-22 position. The paradox was that the woman who spoke publicly could not be considered virtuous, but if women did not speak, they had no chance of gaining respect for their minds. Quite simply, female virtue and speaking publicly were incompatible, according to Outram, because virtue was defined differently for the two sexes. For males, she says, virtue meant putting the state above personal or sectional interests, whereas for women, virtue was personal, revolving almost exclusively around the question of chastity.

While one might object that women themselves were redefining virtue, away from sex and meaning something more like self-esteem and self-improvement, it is nontheless true that Outram's main point about public space and the exclusion of women's voices in political matters is accurate. More interesting and more relevant, however, are several other points she makes. The first concerns her own demonstration of caution about treating "women of the eighteenth century" as a single category and undifferentiated whole. And the second, associated point is her critical observation that feminist historians have tended to forefront only left-wing female political activists, thereby ignoring the masses of uninvolved or even counterrevolutionary women. Arguing for the inclusion of more "registers" of women's expression and particularly of more nonpublic texts, such as diaries, personal letters, and autobiography, Outram makes the very important point that "normal female response to the Revolution" was not to embrace but rather to reject it.[10] Moreover, as she concludes, the vast majority of women in the future would be adopting another universalistic, highly conservative rhetoric—that of the Church. In persuasively arguing that women's most enduring role was in the counterrevolution, she declares that it was female devotion to throne and altar during the revolution that would, in the course of the following century, ultimately determine two sex-differentiated spheres of politics, with women adhering in greater numbers to the right-wing interests of the Church and men to left-wing republicanism.[11] Her cautionary statements about equating eighteenth-century women's political identity with twentieth-century feminism's goals are, in my view, salutary. They also support a more focused speculation about the specificity of the cultural project for and by women, such as will be undertaken later in this chapter through an investigation of the protocols and principles of female reading in eighteenth-century France.

In another approach to women under the ancien régime, Erica Harth examined the interplay of gender, space, and speech in order to reveal how women had been excluded from all the new discursive spaces of power—the café, the club, the journal, the *conférence*, and especially the Paris *académies*—which led, in her judgment, to the development of a modern rational discourse of inquiry and progress wholly shaped by a single sex.[12] Even in the salon, that ambiguous space, that is not quite public or quite private, Harth says, women were not much more than hostesses who merely brought together the men who were to write the treatises and essays that would found the Enlightenment. To be sure, she acknowledges, the boundaries of the salon, the *académie*, and the *conférence* as gendered spaces were not always absolute, since salons sometimes crossed the line into *académies* and *conférences* occasionally had mixed audiences. But the primary meeting spaces open to the two sexes were those within private dwellings—the *alcôves*, *ruelles*, *cabinets*, and *chambres*. Indeed, this leads Harth to set the bed (*le lit de repos*, similar to a reclining sofa) and the library in juxtaposition, calling them emblematic of two different spaces and two types of discursive practices—a notion that likewise underlies the thematic focus of this chapter. For whereas *le lit de repos* was situated next to a *ruelle*, or conversational space, where visitors, either male or female, would sit, and was associated with inconsequential speech, the library was a place, described by Antoine Furetière in his *Dictionnaire universel* (1690), where male scholars and humanists would gather in an informal academy. As Harth writes, "The library, where in general rules of censorship were suspended, was a privileged space for research and discussion. There, scholars of different religions, beliefs, and interests, and social backgrounds agreed to disagree and to air their questions as openly as possible. The conditions of freedom for this embryonic republic of letters were discipline and order in the proceedings [and] mutual trust."[13] Hence, the *ruelle* was the place of casual conversation, while the library was the space giving rise to the production of written texts. It is a distinction that effectively reveals the phenomenon of gendered spaces, as Harth understands them in the mirror images she establishes, with the triangle of bed-speech-woman, on the one hand, and, on the other, library-writing-male.

In the eighteenth century, these two spaces were transmuted into two separate views of the woman reader. Both the medico-philosophical establishment and visual artists of the rococo tradition imagined the woman reader primarily in the boudoir, where all activities, including reading, are frivolously self-involved. Women of ambition, on the other hand, provided an alternative vision of the enlightened and responsible woman reader, which sought to conjoin her reading with the notion of the library and all it implied about the seriousness and usefulness of purposeful activity. Their objective was, in fact, to break out of the gendered opposition, as identified in

Harth's paradigm, and to move from the boudoir—that corrupted space associated with ancien-régime politics and in which the female principle is embodied in the devalued "speech" of the body—to the realm of the *bibliothèque*, which they envisioned as an ideal and nonpoliticized place of objective knowledge and liberating truth. This is the move that Madame de Genlis makes when she gives up the paints and pomades of the boudoir for the books and paper and pen of the *bibliothèque/cabinet*, as described in chapter 3. And this is the ideal of the library as a shelter for the mind, which Madame Roland in chapter 2 evokes when, while awaiting a sentence of execution, she uses the memories of a life filled with books to help her put aside "the injustices of men, their follies, and my own wrongs."

The focus on two discrete spaces that oppose body and mind should illuminate why women adopted a *politics* of virtue as a means of repositioning themselves through textual representation and language, as they sought to offer a new idea of the sensitive yet responsible woman to their readers. For their goal never was, I believe, to set women's aspirations at the level of political participation in the business of the nation, but rather, much more modestly, but nonetheless historically important, to begin the work of encouraging female confidence by asking women to commit themselves to a new view of their own capacity for courage and moral action, and to begin this task by reading excellent authors. For, as the *Journal des dames* said, "The best refutation that one can give to the prejudice that refuses Women the pleasure of cultivating Belles-Lettres is the Catalogue of all those ladies who have distinguished themselves in this career (of reading books)" (June 1764). Thus despite Landes's negative assertion that reading would become for women "an element in the process in which life was remade along domestic and virtuous grounds,"[14] and Outram's judgment that the very idea of virtue, so crucial to revolutionary discourse and so absent during the ancien régime, would be the very element that would bring down even the most committed of women, such as Manon Roland,[15] it is, I submit, women's embrace of book culture that is the most important arena in which to judge their contributions to social change. For them, political invisibility was not particularly a liability, because it was not the issue. If the paradox for women was that they were simultaneously absorbed into and excluded from rational universalist discourse, then the way out of the dilemma was to redefine the terms and to discard the male definition of female virtue concerned with body and chastity, replacing it with a new, enlightened vision of female virtue through the pursuits of the mind and the exercise of reason.

While I am aware of the dangers of appearing reductive by invoking two specific spaces—the boudoir and the library, representing the dichotomy between body and mind—in fact, I believe that by doing so we avoid the problem of overreading women's objectives and will be able simultaneously to argue that women *did* participate in a revolution. For, as Chrétien-Guillaume Lamoignon de Malesherbes, Directeur de la Librairie from 1750 to 1763, observed in a speech in 1775, the world of the ancien régime was being transformed through a significant shift in the structure of communications. Whereas previously people had needed to assemble to receive news and ideas, now the literate had their primary information sources in books and other printed materials. Thus, a formerly *aural* public was becoming a *reading* public.[16] With the publication of a veritable tidal wave of reading materials, from novels to journals to political and philosophical tracts, reading became the principle means of staying abreast of the flood of new ideas. Women, as well as men, were reading in ever greater numbers, with female literacy growing faster than male literacy in the eighteenth century, despite a continuation of absolute differences.[17] In turn, women writers, whether novelists, journalists, or fabulists, were increasingly inclined to consider that female education was a *textual* undertaking, in which reading was the most potent force in the enlightenment and self-improvement of the individual woman to whom they directed their ideology of virtue. As a consequence, in promoting *l'espace du livre* these women were in the forefront of a cultural revolution, one that would pit two views of the woman reader, as of the reading act, in opposition.

In the pages ahead, I will first consider the trope of the woman reader as presented by a number of eighteenth-century visual artists, many of whom built on the discourse of the antiwoman reader by locating her reading in the boudoir and stipulating the boudoir as a space of desire. Against those playful or ironic images of the embodied and eroticized reader, based on a notion of consumption—woman consumed as object, woman as consuming subject—women themselves tried to place the ideal figurative space of women's reading and the production of work outside the boudoir. Or, as Madame de Genlis did, in the *cabinet*, which represented for her objective knowledge, reason, and the unsexed mind. As the single discursive space to which large numbers of women, from intellectuals to pedagogues to bourgeois mothers, laid claim, the room-of-their-own was to become *l'espace du livre*, which in the broadest sense means books and access to knowledge, personal, moral, and learned. Reading was the bridge between the private–domestic spaces to which they were confined and the public spaces which they were denied. Books blurred the lines between those spaces. Reading, then, rather than speech, became the focus of women's cultural and prefeminist agenda, as the most accessible means by which female lives could be improved. It is through the issues of reading, I believe, that today we may come to understand the real quality of woman's consciousness in the eighteenth century and to discover how in fact and despite conventional assessment to the contrary, many women did participate in a revolution—a *reading* revolution.

VISUAL REPRESENTATIONS AND THEORIES OF GENDERED READING

Since works of art provide what Linda Docherty has called a window on ideology, it is not surprising that historians of reading so frequently use visual interpretations of women as readers to help establish the past.[18] For, as Docherty points out, the mental and temporal aspects of reading make it an activity particularly amenable to interpretive manipulation (338). Thus, literary and social critics study painting as a complement to statistical research. The latter seek to answer questions about the economics of book publishing and reading, distribution, and the development of venues for obtaining reading material—bookstores, reading rooms, subscription services, libraries.[19] Literary critics examine how pictorial representation dialogues with or resists contemporaneous reading theory and practice. The visual arts, then, supplement economics, sociology, and history, bringing in the psychological dimension, since painters often seek to penetrate the interior monologue taking place between reading subject and object read. At times, they use the book to symbolize power and the pursuit of knowledge by the subject–reader, and at other times to signify leisure, escapism, imagination, sexual readiness, contemplation, isolation, pleasure, desire, concentration, absorption, virtue, vice, vulnerability, separation. Consequently, the book is almost never a simple sign.

In eighteenth-century rococo art, for instance, the trope of the woman reader offers some of the clearest evidence of gendered thinking about reading in the age of the Enlightenment. Roger Chartier has written that reading in the painting of that period signifies differently for the two sexes, with women's reading commonly being shown as an act of private pleasure, while men's is the pretext to reveal status or social condition, or a more reflective and meditative state of mind.[20] In demonstration of the first proposition, illustrators of the rococo show the woman reader in feminine spaces, the *boudoir*, the *cabinet privé*, the *chambre à coucher*, which is often slightly to considerably in disarray, suggestive of the effects that reading has on her. Such paintings seem to show that women read with their bodies, and that the act of reading produces in them physiological effects having moral and behavioral consequences. When the artist does show her in the library, it is with what might be described as an ironic leer.[21] Jean-Marie Goulemot suggests that irony was precisely the goal of Emmanuel de Ghendt in his intentionally mistitled sketch, *Le Midi* (Figure 3), depicting a young woman in the grip of an erotic reverie, including the suggestion of masturbatory behavior. The title, Goulemot proposes, should more rightfully be *The Effects of Reading* or *The Influence of Wicked Books*, because the illustration emphasizes the physical consequences of the book on the female reader.[22] In this view of the woman reader experiencing the effects of the book, de Ghendt playfully depicts the idea that a woman's reading encounter with a text of desire leads to guilty behaviors.

FIGURE 3. Emmanuel de Ghendt, *Le Midi*, Cliché Bibliothèque Nationale de France, Paris.

If the visual artist takes an ironically humorous view of the woman reader "under the influence," both the Church (through a representative such as Father Porée) and the male medical and philosophical establishment, with doctors such as S. A. Tissot and D. T. Bienville, or their colleagues Pierre Roussel, Pierre-Jean-Georges Cabanis, and Paul-Victor de Sèze, produced theories of behavior that were corporeal in nature with far more negative consequences for the promotion of women's reading.[23] For these men, who built on the approach of moral anthropologists for whom sexual difference was located in no specific organ, but rather in the entire "sensible system," the female reader was like a vessel waiting to be filled. Her reading encounters became "invasions" by the aggressive (male) text; she was either the seduced victim or in guilty and criminal collusion with an anthropomorphized "predator" text. Such anthropomorphizing is, of course, something of a convention of rhetoric, since the book is often attributed with the physical characteristics of the human being, possessing a spine, divided bilaterally into left and right sides, having voice and soul, and also intentions.[24] But it takes on an insalubrious role when the female reader becomes the hunted prey or gullible victim, though never the independent consumer of a text, capable of asserting mastery over the book and/or of appropriating it for herself.

While most antiwoman reader commentary in the eighteenth century is less direct about the effects on woman's sexual behavior than de Ghendt, the primary fear alluded to again and again in conduct books, and often ironized in prefaces to novels such as *Les Liaisons dangereuses*, is that the text will engage the female reader in a dangerous process of fantasy construction. Since the text "forms" the reader, and not vice versa, the woman who reads a fiction of desire will be modeled like clay by her reading and subject to uncontrolled desire. Her reading will be a "priming" activity, nicely ripening her for seduction. In agreement with Rousseau's idea that no honest girl would read a *roman d'amour*, the male author of the *Manuel de la toilette et de la mode*, a conduct book for women in the 1770s, railed against novels, which he called "contemptible" and whose single merit was in his view to flatter "the depravity of the reader."[25] "There are books," he weightily opined, "that one must not read in order to remain virtuous and out of respect for public opinion, which quite correctly esteems that a young woman should remain ignorant about certain things." The problematics of female ignorance and whether it should be equated with innocence and virtue is, of course, one of the many issues that Diderot explores with erotic intent only partly veiled through the body of Suzanne Simonin in *La Religieuse*, and the subject equally attracts the rococo artist who trades heavily in erotic equivocation.

The charms of the questionably innocent female are the subject of another representation of the female reader as vessel or victim of the text, when Pierre-Antoine Baudouin portrays in *La Lecture* (Figure 2) a female subject who appears "at risk" from a text conceived as both carnal and phallic. Located in the *cabinet cum boudoir*, Baudouin's woman reader is half-lying in her chair, head back and resting against the cushions, her limbs limp, an open book at her side. It is doubtful that her reading matter is a volume of religion or history; rather, it must be a novel, which has exercised its power on her delicate fibers and exquisite sensibility. The viewer's intrusion at a very private moment upon this woman in a swoon or intense reverie is all the more unsettling because she is not situated in a sexually neutral place, but rather in a coquettishly appointed boudoir. To be sure, the room contains writing table, globe, maps, books, and a musical instrument, but it is nonetheless a boudoir with its bed-drapery, a dressing screen, the erotically charged and ubiquitous lapdog. If not Boucher's frankly sexual and disheveled boudoir of Figure 4, Baudouin's boudoir is presented unambiguously as the space of woman's guilty pleasure through reading. Boucher's subject, of course, evokes much more explicitly, through form and position, a voluptuousness that seems at first only tangentially associated with reading. However, the open book next to the nude woman suggests another possibility and potential pun on the idea of reading as unveiling. For rather than the truth being unveiled by the book, it is the female reader herself who is unveiled. It is as though her reading has been a sensual preparation, an erotic primer, similar to what Peter Brooks calls a kind of forepleasure that "could include both delay and advance in the textual dynamic . . . the creation of . . . 'dilatory space' through which we would seek to advance towards the discharge at the end, yet all the while perversely delaying, returning backwards in order to put off the promised end."[26]

FIGURE 4. François Boucher (1703–1770), *Ruhendes Mädchen (Louise O'Murphy)*, 1751, Wallraf-Richartz-Museum Köln, Repro: Rheinisches Bildarchiv Köln, WRM 2639.

Such images that visually textualize the woman reader may reveal, as art historian Michael Fried has suggested in another respect, the invention of man and of his need. In describing the asymmetrical relationship between man and woman, he said, "The woman is made a reader and consequently a text only in response to an initial act of textual self-representation on the part of the man; the successful lover is the author, at one remove, of the text woman becomes." [27] That is, she becomes the sensitive and sexually vulnerable reader, because such is *his* desire.[28] In Fried's interpretation, the woman subject in the painting is the "text" of male psychology in which he creates the female reader according to his needs and, through that image, can observe her, again and again, for his pleasure.

Something similar transpires in a painting by Louis-Léopold Boilly, *A Young Painter and His Model* (Figure 5), though this time both male and female are shown in contemplation of a painting that is the *mise-en-abyme* representation of their mutual desire created during the sittings. Reading from left to right across the painting, as one does the page, we see on the table the box of sundries with lid askew, a glass jar, an alabaster nude sculpture of a woman, a canister, salmon-colored ribbons and sashes—one on the table, the other flung over a background easel, as though denoting "untied," "opened," "revealing." Draped on the table somewhat precariously is a rich tapestry cloth, perhaps earlier used by the nude model to cover her body during rest periods. On this fabric sit two books, while the model, her bosom awash in the same light as the sculpture, holds a third dog-eared volume, as though interrupted in her reading. Seated behind her is the young painter, one hand on her arm, the other pointing to the completed work of art in the far right. As the woman model gazes upon it, head tilted back and lips parted in surprise and pleasure, she sees not the image she was expecting, but rather one of the painter's erotic desire, which has painted her asleep and him at her bedside, a hand cupped over her breast. This silent *déclaration d'amour*, a text within a text, or painting within a painting, duplicates the *mise-en-abyme* aspect of the reading act in which the reader of the romance not only reads herself into the text of the protagonist but mirrors the same erotic pleasure in being chosen and desired and imagining herself "there."

Another visual textualization of the woman reader that focuses on the interdependency of sex and reading is a 1988 film called *La Lectrice*.[29] In this intelligent, yet playful and ironic confection, part fairy tale, part spoof, part celebration of reading, harking back to the spirit of the rococo, Deville presents brilliantly the topoi and lieux communs of reading: stories within stories; visual puns and intertexts; reading a life and living a reading; superimposed acts of reading on acts of sex; reading as reading-in-the-mind or reading between the pages; reading as a protosexual activity, and the dangers that accompany it.

Appropriately for a text that focuses on the relationship between book, sex, and reader, the action begins in the Lectrice's bed. Her live-in partner

FIGURE 5. Louis-Léopold Boilly, (1761–1845), *A Young Painter and His Model,* ca. 1788–1792, oil on canvas, 18 1/8 x 14 7/8 in. (46 x 37.9 cm), Smith College Museum of Art, Northampton, Massachusetts, purchased with the Beatrice Oenslager Chace (Class of 1928) Art Acquisition fund, the Madeleine H. Russell (class of 1937) Fund, and the Hillyer / Mather / Tryon Fund, 1996.

pleads tired eyes and asks if she will read aloud to him a novel called *La Lectrice* by Raymond Jean.[30] At that moment a wonderful new *métier* is born, and the female protagonist becomes a professional reader, who will advertise her services and offer housecalls to a variety of clients who for one reason or another need or wish to be read to. Deville's reader, played by the actress

Miou-Miou, is nothing if not the essential sensual reader—kittenish but also sensitive and intelligent—and in short order, her clients include a wheelchair-bound young man whose mother wishes to divert him with readings by Maupassant and Baudelaire; a blind widow of a Russian general who wants to delight once again in the words of Tolstoy and Marx; a child to whom she reads *Alice au pays des merveilles* and with whom she cavorts at a traveling fair; a wealthy président–directeur–général who does not understand the pleasures of slowness (such as Milan Kundera has described them, one might add[31]) until she reads to him while langorously and sensuously engaging in sex; a retired judge who has her read to him, in his book-lined library, explicitly sexual scenes from Sade's *Les 120 Journées*.

Although one might normally think that as a static subject reading would be uncinematic, Deville shows that it is in fact a dynamic process. The reader, the text, and the client become involved in complex relationships with one another that take them to "places" they otherwise never would have visited. When the Lectrice reads, she mediates the text for her client/viewer involving him in what has been called a performative reading.[32] For instance, the sexual tension that exists between reader and text takes shape in actuality in the scene in which the Lectrice brushes her skirt in such a way that it exposes her bare thigh to the eyes of the invalid youth. As she reads aloud "La Chevelure," Maupassant's short story of displaced eroticism, her visual appearance and voice cause the youth to experience frightening feelings of arousal. By staging the reader's response, making it a visual phenomenon, a merging of reader and text takes place. Before our very own eyes we have ample proof of the pleasure of the text, and it is a pleasure that at base is sexual, involving the woman reader who fulfills a male's fantasy. Reader of the text, she is also the performer of his fantasies through the mediation of a text he asks her to read.

While this film is at once a genial satire of the professional reader (interpreter, reviewer, theorist), it is also a reader's delight celebrating the seductive pleasures of reading at all ages. But, as the film shows, being a reader is a "profession" requiring art, intelligence, talent, and feeling. And it is also a craft, in danger of becoming lost or of consuming itself. What makes the film so delightful and so French is its very rococo mixture of whimsy, intelligence, and sex.

Reading a film, like reading a text, other theorists say, functions primarily through a sexualized notion of vision. In developing her notion of sexuality and the reading encounter, critic Emma Wilson, for instance, concludes that the pleasures of viewing and of reading are coextensive, both located in a sexualized notion of vision.[33] Reading texts of desire, whether the printed word or the visual text, as in the image of the woman reading in her boudoir by Baudouin, might depend, then, in Wilson's view, on an economy of vision that engages the reader of the text or image in a complicit or potentially voyeuristic encounter. Further, the woman presented in the image is not only the subject of the artist's work, but also, in a type of *mise-en-abyme* structure of desire, the constantly replicated object of desire of each successive viewer. Hence the artist's desire for the woman is reproduced through the female subject in collusive relationship with a text of desire, and yet again when the viewer is invited to assume the spectatorial position of his (or her) own desire, in endless replication. In this approach, the spectator/reader becomes a kind of voyeur who engages in a type of violation or transgression in an erotic encounter with the woman–reader subject.

This is the subject of an exquisitely painted work of equivocal content by François De Troy, *The Garter* (Figure 6), which should perhaps more

FIGURE 6. Jean François de Troy (1679–1752), *The Garter*, 1724, Private Collection, New York. Photograph courtesy of the Metropolitan Museum of Art, all rights reserved.

appropriately be called "the reading encounter." This scene shows a young woman who had been reading prior to being interrupted by the approach of an entreating male. Unlike the typical rococo image, this picture places the subjects in an aristocratic salon with gilded mirror, Louis XV table, a luxuriously sculpted clock, and a piece of furniture called a *bibliothèque*. As we know from historians of eighteenth-century culture, books were precious items, due to their substantial cost, and were frequently kept behind lock and door. In fact, they could be stored in a variety of pieces of furniture from the humblest *tablette à livres*, a small locking cabinet that might contain other objects, to more substantial pieces such as the *buffet grillé*, the *bibliothèque à deux battants grillés*, the *buffet en forme de bibliothèque*, or the *armoire à deux portes*—all of which would typically be locked between uses.[34] In this painting, the *bibliothèque* of the salon, abundantly filled with books behind glass doors, has both a decorative and practical function, signifying wealth and knowledge.

The viewer will note that the book has been closed and is lying on the table, suggesting that the female reader—a strikingly modern figure with her short and curly coiffure—has been surprised or caught off-guard by the visitor, and has rapidly put down her reading. An aristocrat by his clothes, sword, and properly pigtailed hair, the male is nonetheless portrayed as an intruder. Both man and woman are locked in gaze—she, startled, and he with imploring, doe-like eyes, as he gestures with one hand. The equivocal morality of the woman reader is proposed by her double action: with one hand she brazenly raises her skirts, revealing a bare calf, while with outstretched arm she pushes away the man's advances. She is alarmed by his demeanor; her lips are tightly pursed, while his seem slightly apart. The erotic implications of the scene may suggest that a woman who has the impudence to have intellectual pretentions and reads novels or philosophical tracts or scientific treatises opens herself to such attacks on her chastity (hence her unseemly display of so much leg), or, alternatively, that a woman who reads will not be exercising sufficient vigilance against attacks on her virtue, both from within the book and from men. Perhaps this man is only asking for what he might reasonably believe he can expect from a woman indulging in reading, which he may presumptuously assume deals with "forbidden" material.

By entitling his painting *The Garter*, and combining it with a female reader, De Troy plays the book against the garter, so to speak, thereby evoking the intertextual relationship of reading and sex. Since women's reading had conventionally been proposed in antiwoman rhetoric as a "priming activity," one in which she seeks escape—perhaps from domestic responsibilities and/or in sexual release—it is possible to read this scene as showing a woman who has been surprised in a guilty activity, since reading for pleasure is often seen as tantamount to pleasuring oneself. The male intruder may either be proposing himself as a more appropriate partner or, on the other hand, may be presented by the painter as the figurative consequence of woman's reading. The fact that the woman is in a salon and not the intimate and private boudoir suggests that if she has been engaged in guilty behavior caused by her reading, she has truly "forgotten herself," for this is a semipublic room. From an antiwoman reading stance, the transgression may be hers, for she has scorned both sexual and gender protocols to indulge in a potentially dangerous pastime. Though not a rococo painting, De Troy's portrayal clearly shows, as much as those of de Ghendt and Baudouin, that reading and sexuality *are* intertwined in provocative ways.

The sense of transgression in De Troy's picture recalls an episode in Manon Roland's *Mémoires* that deals provocatively with a similar violation of woman's privacy, this time by a father. In the *septième cahier*, Manon describes how one day, during her absence, Monsieur Phlipon took it upon himself to bring a visitor, the worthy Monsieur de Boismorel, into his daughter's *petite retraite* and permitted him to leaf through her *Oeuvres de jeune fille*. [35] Upon learning of this invasion of her domain, Manon is furious. In describing her bitter resentment at the assault on her privacy by two men, one a parent, the other a "voyeur" of sorts, Manon uses the verb *violer* (violate, break faith, rape, ravish). That which is dearest to her—that private nook, those books she loved, the pages on which she wrote her thoughts—has been profoundly violated. Her space, she objects angrily, had been trespassed, in an abuse of her trust.

When her father tries, ineffectively in Manon's assessment, to explain and justify his act, she retorts that it was nothing short of an assault on freedom, independence, and property. The choice of words is deeply significant, revealing true Enlightenment concerns on the part of the young woman. Manon is offended because the physical and spiritual space she had created for herself in the retreat of her *petit cabinet* has been casually invaded. Monsieur Phlipon had literally led another man into his daughter's inner sanctum, exposing what is most intimate and private in her life to the eyes and touch of an outsider. Manon's reaction of outrage comes both from her own inviolable sense of personal and private boundaries and from her republican ideas about the sanctity of property. If the ultimate result of this specific trespass will be positive—Monsieur de Boismorel invites Manon to make use of his library, and the two of them begin what for her will be a developmentally very interesting correspondence—the fact remains that the whole episode is cast under the equivocally sexual sign of violation.

What these two examples of spatial transgression—one recounted in memoirs, the other in a painting—reveal is that the protocols of woman's space are quite different from those of men. We cannot imagine an eighteenth-century woman boldly intruding upon the male and making assumptions about his activities and his space, for his private space is assured and legitimized by both convention and prejudice, and his study is off-limits because of the serious nature of his work. To achieve similar respect for their space and work, according to Madame de Genlis, women needed to set their sights on the ideal figure of the library, which represents not only a refuge of the mind, a safe harbor and a retreat from the material and emotional vulgarities of the world, but also a space endowed with the ability to confer a quiet sense of power through commerce with books. To associate women's reading with the mind required equal access to the library and changing society's mind about women's activities and mental capacities. It meant opening the spaces of knowledge–the *universités*, *collèges*, and *académies*, those "lieux masculins du savoir," as Linda Timmermans has called them.[36] But first it required a desexualizing of the process of reading women and the recasting of the female reader not as some delectable, mysterious, or vulnerable essence, but as a person with a serious claim to *l'espace du livre*. It would be through this space and all that it implies that a connecting bridge between two spheres as between the two sexes could be achieved. If the mind really had no sex, equal access to knowledge and equal respect for learning were not only eminently suitable to both sexes, but absolutely necessary.

To be sure, not all visual representations of women reading should be cast in a negative light. The book can, for instance, be merely a prop for the portraitist, as in Boucher's pleasing painting of Madame Boucher (Figure 7); or in Nonnotte's portrait of the comfortable-sized and middle-aged Madame

FIGURE 7. François Boucher (1703–1770), *Madame Boucher*, 1743, oil on canvas, Copyright The Frick Collection, New York.

Nonnotte (Figure 8), which shows the homey pleasant view of woman's reading; or in Vigée-Lebrun's famous painting of Marie-Antoinette (Figure 9), in which the written text is used to counteract the public's image of the queen as frivolous, morally corrupt, and lavishly self-indulgent. But the real staple of rococo depiction tends to equate woman's reading with her sexuality as shown in the anonymous engraving of *Amynthe à son lever* (Figure 10). Seated on a bed and still wearing her sleeping cap, Amynthe holds a book in her left

FIGURE 8. Donat Nonnotte (1708–1785), *Madame Nonnotte*, Copyright Réunion des Musées Nationaux/Art Resource, New York.

FIGURE 9. Elisabeth Vigée-Lebrun (1755–1842), *Marie-Antoinette*, Copyright Réunion des Musées Nationaux/Art Resource, New York.

FIGURE 10. Anonymous, *Amynthe à son lever*, ca. 1750, engraving, Cliché Bibliothèque Nationale de France, Paris.

hand and appears both dreamy and distracted from the task of dressing. Her morning gown thrown open and her pert breasts spilling out from their chemise, she is at once the woman reader-under-the-influence and the woman to be read.

Other images of women readers may carry cautionary subtexts without the sly erotic wink that the subject woman and books so often evokes. For instance, in *A Girl Reading* (Figure 11), Alexis Grimou shows a female figure caught in a strong, masculine gesture, slightly hunched over her book, jaw firmly planted on her hand, another hand (*not* characterized by slender fingers) poised to turn the page, expressing her impatience to be left alone. The

FIGURE 11. Alexis Grimou (1679–1752), *A Girl Reading (La Liseuse)*, 1731, Staatliche Kunsthalle, Karlsruhe.

image, while not explicitly negative, also is not particularly attractive. One might question if with the loss of sexuality, this woman reader has gained legitimacy, or whether instead there resides an admonitory message about female reading within the portrayal. What is implicit in Grimou becomes more explicit in a pair of paintings by Jean Raoux that contrast the occupations of women, in *The Vestal Virgins* (Figure 12) and *Modern Virgins* (Figure 13). Whereas vestal virgins have a common purpose and work in unison,

FIGURE 12. Jean Raoux (1677–1734), *The Vestal Virgins (Vierges antiques)*, 1727, oil on canvas, 92 x 72.5, Musée des Beaux-Arts, Lille, France, Copyright Réunion des Musées Nationaux/Art Resource, New York.

FIGURE 13. *Modern Virgins*, 1728, oil on canvas, 92 x 72.5, Musée des Beaux-Arts, Lille, France, Copyright Réunion des Musées Nationaux/Art Resource, New York.

modern women all move in their separate pursuits. The lack of shared goals and clear evidence of disarticulated female existence in Raoux's contemporary world are suggested by the number of figures looking out from and leaving the picture and by the total self-absorption of the female reader. She is lost in a hefty tome, an indirect suggestion that the woman who reads separates herself from those traditional female endeavors that hold a community together. Such images might reasonably be seen as expressing ideas similar to those of Doctor Cabanis, who had argued that women who wish to succeed in scholarly endeavors are not truly women, but rather "ambiguous beings who are, properly speaking, of neither sex" and who "will fail at wifely and maternal duties."[37]

In distinct opposition to Cabanis's warning, Jacques-André Portail's pen sketch entitled *Woman Reading* (Figure 14) marries woman, book, and femininity through the subject's total absorption in the printed word and her

FIGURE 14. Jacques-André Portail (1695–1759), *Woman Reading*, undated, black, red, white chalk with touches of blue watercolor, 46.4 x 36 cm (18 1/4 x 14 3/16 in.), Museum of Fine Arts, Boston. Bequest of Forsyth Wickes Collection; 65.2597. Photograph Copyright 2003, Museum of Fine Arts, Boston.

exquisitely beautiful lacy gown. This *liseuse* is not merely posing with a prop, nor lost in contemplation and offering herself to the lascivious spectator. Rather, she is a participant in the culture of the book, only a step away from Vigée-Lebrun's *Comtesse de Cérès* (Figure 15) who takes pen in hand to create her own text. Directly engaging the viewer with her look, almost as though she were inviting us to try to call into question her activity as thinker

FIGURE 15. Elisabeth Vigée-Lebrun (1755–1842), *Comtesse de Cérès*, 1784, oil on canvas, 36 3/4 x 29 3/8 in. (93 x 75 cm), Toledo Museum of Art, Purchased with funds from the Libbey Endowment, Gift of Edward Drummond Libbey.

and writer, the Comtesse de Cérès is comfortable with the instruments of expression and uses them with grace and force. Together, these images of women offer an alternative to the vision of rococo painters, who so joyfully and ironically had located their meaning and significance in the boudoir of their imagination. For in the images by Portail and Vigée-Lebrun, *féminité* is combined with *savoir, culture*, and *créativité* and their subjects represent a new ideal of women bred on an alternative dream as consumers and producers in the world of words.

In that sense, one might conclude that at last the real textualization of woman into *l'espace du livre* has begun. It is a view that will be adopted by nineteenth-century realist painters from Manet to Daumier, Fantin-Latour to Bonvin, who will demonstrate an extraordinary fondness for the theme of the reader, with the vast majority of their tableaux depicting the reader as woman—*la lectrice*—but no longer with the sly winks of their rococo predecessors.[38]

THE PRACTICES AND PROTOCOLS OF READING IN EIGHTEENTH-CENTURY FRANCE

While Robert Scholes says that the human condition can be seen as one of textuality, Robert Darnton reminds us that nothing could be more misleading than to assume that people in the past have always read as we do, or that their approach to the printed word and the book as object resembles our own.[39] Indeed, it is not only in matters of style and taste that readers of the past differ from us, but also in the very practices and protocols that surrounded their reading. It is for that reason that prior to exploring in subsequent chapters the figures and culture of reading that reside in women's writing, it is necessary to evoke what we know and do not know about women's reading in actual practice. That means looking at issues of female literacy and the protocols of reading—the conventions, rules, and standards—that had an impact on how and where women read in early modern France. An examination of this kind of information is necessary, first, to understand how ancien régime women read differently from us and, second, to see whether, or to what extent, it is possible to speak of a revolution in women's reading in the late eighteenth century.

Female literacy

Rates of literacy in early modern times are extremely difficult to determine with accuracy because in good part there is little agreement about how literacy should be defined. Is literacy the ability to write and, if so, to write something other than one's name? Is it the ability to read and, if so, to read what kinds of texts? To be literate, must the individual be expected to read *and* to write or does the mastery of only one skill confer the status of literacy?

The situation is further complicated in eighteenth-century France because, as Abbé Grégoire said, at the time of the revolution at least six million Frenchmen were not francophone.[40] What that means, Martyn Lyons points out, is that for nearly a quarter of French people, the revolution was conducted in a foreign language. Moreover, since it was only from among the ranks of the French speakers that one might find people knowing how to read and write, the overall rates of literacy, even without speaking of women specifically, represented a minority of those living in France. Promotion of mass literacy, which in practical terms necessitated the use of a single language, would take several generations to achieve, especially in the rural areas where the use of Breton or various patois dominated daily life.

To be sure, the classical syllabus of primary education in France has always given reading first place, followed by writing and numbers.[41] But in ancien régime France, who would be schooled? And how did geography and social class play into issues of literacy? One can say that in general the northern half of the nation was more literate than the southern part, the towns were in advance of the countryside, and that members of the elite classes were much more able to write as well as to read than those of the lower classes.[42] Nonetheless, we should not assume that only the elite classes could read, because, according to most recent historians of culture, reading as a passive skill was more widespread than formerly assumed. Roger Chartier corrects a common misperception by pointing out that there was, in fact, an educated servant class in ancien régime France.[43] Furthermore, he observes that typically women outside the privileged classes might learn to read, but not to write, since writing was considered by many to be a suspect and noncollateral skill for women.[44] When the Church at last came to encouraging reading so that the faithful could have ready access to the Bible and other sacred texts, it still drew the line at writing, which it feared would lead to too much independence.[45] Thus while *writing* was an ability developed primarily among the elite, *reading* was a skill that enjoyed a larger and wider participation.

Clearly, the determination of the actual rate of literacy is highly inexact and extremely relative. In the introduction to their collection of essays in *Going Public*, Dena Goodman and Elizabeth Goldsmith state that the most generous estimates of general literacy at the end of the eighteenth century place the figures at 27 percent of Frenchwomen and 47 percent of Frenchmen.[46] But those figures refer to the percentages of the two sexes capable of signing their names, and, as most critics now agree, simply being able to sign one's name does not imply a very expressive level of literacy. The ability to form the letters of one's name says nothing about the ability to write in any meaningful way, nor to read any word other than one's own name. Hence, cultural historians now generally conclude that while percentages of signers constitute some kind of "rough composite index," typically such figures underestimate reading skills, while exaggerating those capable of writing.[47] In addition, they contend that for females even more than for men, the percentage of signers is in no way a reliable indication of the percentage of readers.

Furthermore, we must realize that signers are not necessarily either writers or readers, nor are readers automatically writers. In other words, the possession of one skill does not imply the equal possession of another. Many a simple housemaid, for instance, could read the equivalent of dime-store novels or a volume from the *bibliothèque bleue* without being able to write so much as a moderately literate letter. As we know from myriad accounts in eighteenth-century texts, the chambermaid or servant girl was often accused of "polluting the mind" of her young female charge by passing on to her some "suspect" reading material, but she almost never was capable of composing a written text to plead her innocence.

For reasons of simplicity, when I refer to female readers in general, I am speaking of any and all of them, while the writing subjects of this text come primarily from the upper bourgeoisie. There are no adequate figures that would suggest the exact dimensions of literate women—meaning those capable of reading a wide variety of texts and of writing at least a letter—in the eighteenth century. But if we use Goodman and Goldsmith's figures, it is safe to say that we are talking about a percentage somewhere between a quarter and upwards of a third of all Frenchwomen. By the end of the century, this would mean roughly some three and a half million potential female readers, based on a population of twenty-six million, according to the figure generally attributed to the France of 1789.

Access to Reading: Libraries, Both Public and Private

There have not, of course, always been libraries, and certainly not public libraries providing readers, regardless of status or sex, with easy access to books. In France the first so-called public library was established by Mazarin in 1644, with some 40,000 books. By 1689, that library was open two days a week for readers who were obliged to be unusually self-sufficient and even hardy, since there was no catalog to consult and the library appears to have been neither heated nor lighted.[48] By the mid-eighteenth century, the royal family became interested in establishing its own libraries for personal use, an act soon emulated by aristocrats. According to Madame de Genlis, who had ties to the royal family and who loved libraries, *la bibliothèque du roi* was the most beautiful in the world with its rare books, manuscripts, and medals. By the end of the century, according to her figures, with which L. S. Mercier agrees, it consisted of some 300,000 volumes of printed books, plus 70,000 manuscripts, 200,000 prints and engravings, 400,000 bronze medals, and 300,000 medals in gold.[49] It was, however, a pity, she opined, that this august library contained a copy of anything an author wished to deposit because, given the amount of poor writing, the result was a diminished collection. It is an opinion shared by Mercier, who began his chapter on the "Bibliothèque du roi" by saying, "This monument to genius and to foolishness proves that the number of books is not a gauge of the riches of the human spirit. It is in but a hundred volumes that its wealth and real glory reside."[50] The ideal library, both he and Madame de Genlis agree, should be constructed on a model of expurgation, meaning a small collection of only *good* books, whereas the architect Etienne-Louis Boullée defined the library's function as being the *summa* of human knowledge, declaring that it should be destined for everyone's disposal. A modern reader, however, is aware that Boullée's inclusive pronoun "everyone" probably did not mean women.

In addition to the royal library, which few would visit, libraries in the eighteenth century were also maintained by religious orders, although their holdings were limited in subject matter, and user privileges were restricted. In the more public domain, there were *chambres de lecture*, or private reading clubs, with initiation and yearly fees, where male members came to read and converse in comfortable, well-lit surroundings.[51] And in Paris, the 1700s saw the establishment of eighteen *bibliothèques publiques*, most of which had very limited hours of public access.[52] But the eighteenth-century practice that truly increased the consumption of books in the public arena was the extension and establishment of the much frequented *cabinets de lecture*, located on the same premises as a bookseller's main commercial enterprise. Dating from 1756, some *cabinets* defined their prospective users as "hommes de lettres" or scholars, and offered to these patrons, in return for a monthly sum of about three *livres*, the opportunity to read novels, travel books, philosophical essays, political pamphlets, or erotic works.[53] With a particularly popular book, like *La Nouvelle Héloïse*, a common practice was to divide the text into sections and demand an hourly rental fee of 12 sous, per volume.[54] In addition to these standard sources for formal and public reading, male readers also had the opportunity during their perambulations in town to come into contact with a great deal of unofficial printed materials, such as the "portable" book or document—the *canard*, *libelle*, or *placard*—that were passed out on the street corner or nailed onto a wall.

These were, however, the public spaces of *male* reading. Woman's opportunities for reading were vastly more circumscribed in the public domain. Indeed, her reading would almost necessarily be restricted to the private holdings in her own home, whose size and makeup depended on the family's fortune and general level of cultivation. Or she might borrow books from friends or extended family, a particularly important means of obtaining reading materials, given the cost of books.[55] Chartier observes that during the second half of the seventeenth century in Paris, the threshold of 100 works was rarely reached by merchants or bourgeois, whereas one out of every two noblemen had such collections, and the libraries of *gens de robe* were at least this large.[56] In the case of Manon Phlipon, whose reading habits will be the subject of the next chapter, we never learn how many books her father owned (except that she characterizes his collection as a "petite bibliothèque"), nor, once she was married, how many volumes might have constituted her own private library, but we do know that she had access to books throughout her life, obtained, as she says, occasionally through rental, but primarily from various benefactors who invited her to borrow copiously from their private collections.

Furthermore, unlike their male counterparts, women readers rarely had the opportunity to belong to a community of readers or to enjoy the kind of intellectual camaraderie (or competition) that access and membership in such institutions bring. Few women had the opportunity to discuss their reading with qualified tutors, though some tell us that they might engage a father or a priest or perhaps a visiting guest in such discussions, but rarely, it appears, another woman, except possibly a mother. We do not know of any exclusively female literary societies, such as proliferated among male readers, from mid-century forward, though it is possible that some of the prerevolutionary women's clubs may have done group readings. But for the most part, these *clubs patriotiques de femmes* were primarily for political discussion and action, not for reading, and in any event they were dissolved after the revolution since women's clubs were judged to be discordant with the new civil society envisioned by male authorities. Unlike men's reading, women's was private, nearly exclusively domestic, and accessed largely through the resources of family or friends.

One might speculate, however, that it is precisely this private, intimate aspect of woman's reading that would make it easier for the journalists of the feminine press and writers like Madame Riccoboni and Madame de Genlis to win their female reader's attention and respect. It does not, however, necessarily follow that women reading in the privacy of their homes were the silent, isolated readers of times past. For a new relationship of reader to book was being developed, one that had been initiated by Rousseau who had asked people to read with heart and soul. Once that happened, once readers discovered that books could offer wise counsel about the world, as well as self-knowledge through Proust's "poetry of the inner life," they also came to understand that thousands of others like them were having similar experiences with printed culture. Shared interests through reading would create new communities that would have a major impact on the social contract.

Progressive women of the eighteenth century were persuaded that reading could play a major role in the promotion of a new vision of the self-empowered woman. This is why, in opposition to the gendered theories of reading in vogue, women writers would propose models of ethical reading in which the female reader would no longer be the guilty or docile recipient of male ideas—the one who read passively for mere pleasure—but rather the responsible consumer and, ultimately, producer of texts and ideas. Woman's *reading*, then, was important not so much because political speech was forbidden to her, but because reading was perceived as the primary activity by which women's self-education would take place. Domestic reading did not have to be trivial. Instead, it could be empowering, a means of finding friendship, joining a community, and of being challenged to improve. For women to read in this way, was revolutionary.

A READING REVOLUTION

When historians have used the notion of a revolution in reading, they have referred to a number of major changes in the way people have read in the past. They have pointed, for instance, to the passage from oral reader to silent reader as an important milestone, which brought about the privatization of reading.[57] Others, such as a number of German scholars, have argued that as of 1750 there was a *lese revolution*, consisting in a change from the tradition of *intensive* reading—reading few books, but reading them again and again, as one might with the Bible—to *extensive* reading—reading widely, given the growing availability of reading materials including the chapbook and almanac, in addition to novels, periodicals, and philosophical and political works.[58] And finally, scholars have studied how a single influential writer, like Jean-Jacques Rousseau, brought about profound changes in the way people read by calling on them to approach the printed page with an open heart and soul and in total absorption, so that they could bring the text of their reading into the text of their lives.[59]

But no one has spoken of the possibility of another more specific revolution—that of the role that reading was to play in the lives and ultimate empowerment of women. And yet to do so may be to avoid the horns of the dilemma for scholars of eighteenth-century women's history who must refrain from merely reinscribing the futility of the efforts to advance the cause of women under the ancien régime, and from overplaying the role of women as subversive *résistantes* to the status quo. By concentrating, instead, on the culture of women's reading and its issues, I believe that we may both recapture the concerns of a sizeable group of women—far more than those relatively few involved in political action or resistance—and tap into some important ways in which eighteenth-century women were different from us. We may also recenter the argument of women's history by suggesting how reading and the rhetorical spaces of reading will play a major role. To address women's history from within the specific frame of reading has the benefit of including a far greater proportion of the female population in eighteenth-century France—even while admittedly not the majority—and of joining eighteenth-century women's concerns with the most universalistic of Enlightenment aims: the promotion of literacy and education.

All the women of this book read and wrote throughout their lives; indeed, one might conclude that, based on their own experience, they could not imagine living without these two activities. In the following chapters, we will see how two individual women became readers and in fact made themselves into female intellectuals. And we will consider how they came to see reading and writing as interrelated activities, each honing the skills of the other. These women wrote letters and essays, and fiction and fairy tales, memoirs and history, texts they intended to publish and texts that were meant for themselves. And they read. Inveterate practitioners of the "reader's craft," they did not reject male models of good writing, but they did reject the view of reading in which women were cast either as seductresses or the seduced. For reading, they believed, should be neither a seduction, nor a voyeuristic spectacle. It should enlighten and, when possible, ennoble rather than exploit the reader. It should help women live by promoting virtue and responsibility. Because reading was so important to them, they could not help writing texts in which structures and figures of reading play essential roles.

In their fiction, they did not always provide their heroines with new possibilities for adventure. And it is true that their female protagonists are often much less adventurous than they themselves, and do not, like Isabelle de Charrière or Madame Riccoboni, take on lovers twenty years younger or, like Madame de Genlis, have extramarital affairs. But this, I believe, is directly related to their sense of responsible reading. Most female writers inscribe an ideal of feminine virtue in their texts, not because they are dim-witted or hopelessly idealistic, but because they consider that the objective of women's reading should be for self-improvement and enlightenment. The models they present to women within their texts are intended to help the reader cope with life and also to bring out the best in herself. These writers did not aim to incite their readers to demand new public roles in the public sphere, but to come to value themselves as autonomous individuals, who live in intimacy with others to whom they have responsibility, but for whom they do not have to sacrifice their own sense of self. That is certainly an important message. Simply because eighteenth-century women were not a part of the political fabric, and did not have the kinds of public roles of women today, does not mean that they had no role in remaking society or contributing to Enlightenment ideals.

The women writers of this book did not define their struggle for respect in terms of access to public spaces and participation in policy-making; they did not see the politics of state and society as their highest calling. But they are, nonetheless, part of a quiet revolution. Their revolutionary project was focused on centerpiecing a program of moral improvement through acquisition of a new kind of knowledge, including self-knowledge, through reading. It was a project that would have revolutionary impact on the culture of the book. More women would read more books, and as accounts from Mesdames Roland and Genlis show, their reading would be both intensive (favorite authors were read again and again) and extensive (they were voracious readers of everything they could get their hands on). It would be women readers, moreover, who would turn novels into bestsellers and make publishing into a reader-driven business. And they would participate in the early development of reading for practical knowledge in everyday life, as, for instance, when teachers such as Madame Leprince de Beaumont and Madame de

Genlis answered the public's developing thirst for books that would help parents educate and raise their children with volumes or essays on pedagogical theory.

The history of women's relationship to *l'espace du livre* as readers and consumers has often been overlooked in Enlightenment history. Yet the evidence suggests that many thousands of eighteenth-century women had integrated the Enlightenment ideal of self-enlightenment into their lives and acted on the belief that the written text was important not merely as entertainment, but as a practical resource in structuring a meaningful life and in living in relationship to family or friends and the larger society. Surely, then, it is possible to speak of a revolution—a quiet one, perhaps, but a revolution, nonetheless.

TWO

AUTOBIOGRAPHY AND REREADING

MANON ROLAND, 1754–1793

> Farewell, my child, my husband, my maid, my friends. . . . Farewell peaceful cabinets where I nourished my spirit with the truth, controlled my imagination by study, and learned in the silence of meditation to govern my senses and scorn vanity.
>
> —Manon Roland, *Mes Dernières Pensées*

In the last lines she commits to paper before going to the guillotine, Madame Roland pays homage to books and a lifetime of reading in a letter-text entitled "Mes Dernières Pensées," written from the Conciergerie only days before her execution. Appended to her *Mémoires*, also composed in prison, these texts, less than 200 pages in length and one of the most powerful and poignant books of the eighteenth century, must be studied under the sign of rereading. For they are an essential expression of remembering, re-evoking, retracing, rethinking, and rediscovery.[1] Rereading her life through the memoir provides Manon Roland escape from the present, reconciliation with the past, and the means to achieve continuing life in the future through her unknown readers. Thus her *Mémoires* demonstrate that just as reading had been the primary intellectual passion of her life, so would it be the resource of her last days and the means by which she would ultimately trump time and the finality of death.

But however positively Madame Roland characterizes the lifelong passion that had disciplined her mind and shaped her thinking, this same reading has been used by critics to indict her for imitating literary heroines and theatricalizing her death.[2] Indeed, it has become common to assert that Manon plundered her reading for the roles she would adopt in life: supportive wife, devoted mother, tragic heroine who chose death to remain virtuous, much as did the Princess of Cleves or Julie. And she is further charged with never having played those roles from fiction nobly. For it is said, she was a cruelly faithful wife to a man to whom she had confessed her passion for another, a reluctant mother to a child who did not make her proud, a female incapable of sisterly solidarity, and a woman whose taste for suffering borders on the emotionally unhealthy. When at last she was imprisoned, she chose one last dramatic role and played it to the hilt: the condemned heroine who must perish in the only heroic way a woman might during the revolution—by the guillotine—even if it was not for political beliefs as much as to resolve an otherwise impossible contradiction between love and duty.

Such accusations offer clear evidence that Manon Roland presents a problem for many contemporary scholars. More than any other female figure of the eighteenth century, she has inspired the least empathy and the most skepticism. She is found to be extravagant in her willingness to suffer and insufferable in her self-righteousness; too much the virtuous victim and too masochistically self-involved. As a result, critics have sought to attach labels to her behavior, which they attribute variously to the rule of repressed sensuality, a mother complex, domestic heroism, or arrested individuation and imitative behavior based on reading. While on occasion, she may elicit their reluctant admiration, she has clearly for many been a hard woman to like, perhaps because, as Lesley Walker insightfully suggests, Manon simply was not enough of a rebel.

In several ways, she is an ideal subject for a study on women, books, and sex, and especially one that seeks to take eighteenth-century women on their own terms. In trying to diagnose the negative reactions that she has produced in critics, I have concluded that the reasons may be threefold and that each could be thought to bear upon a separate aspect of reading. I would categorize them as involved with issues of difference, literature, and virtue.

To begin, Manon Roland is different from the woman many people expect to find. She does not act in compliance with our expectations. A female intellectual of the eighteenth century, and as such out of step with her times, she is even more removed from ours because of rigid idealism coupled with the embrace of victimhood. We do not understand how an intelligent and committed woman would make the choices she did and especially the decision to give up on living when she was in the prime of life. Moreover, she did not act consistently enough, or control her negative impulses adequately, or do what was necessary in order for us to enshrine her. But, dare we forget, she was a product of different times and different conflicts. Like another self-proclaimed sensitive woman of the eighteenth century, also a voracious reader and driven intellectual—Isabelle de Charrière—Manon had been inspired by classical texts that taught the superiority of reason over the disorder of the passions. Yet at the same time she, like Belle de Zuylen, was subject to personal impulses and social strictures that ensnared her in a double bind. Caught in these constraints, both women explored in writing the problem of integrating *sagesse* (wisdom) and sensitivity, reason and passionate longing. But while Charrière would write her life like a novel and her novellas as muted inquiries into displacement, Manon in a single text written for publication, an abbreviated autobiography, would reread her life not in romantic imitation of heroines from literature, but through the lens of idealism tempered by bitter disappointment and in demonstration of what she saw as courage in the face of moral corruption. In reading her, we need to retain a keen sense both of a different moral culture and the tumultuous times in which she lived.

At the same time, Roland's memoirs are a form of literature—not in terms of being a work of the imagination, but in their self-conscious use of literary style and structure, including dialogue and other narrative techniques. In fact, they are a hybrid, early form of literary female autobiography, with as their model, the *Confessions* of Jean-Jacques Rousseau. At once confessional and consciously selective, she, like the master, endeavors to capture a portrait of her youthful self and reveal through key episodes the foundational bases of her character that would continue into adulthood. Choosing to cast her text as *mémoires particuliers*, a form that William Zinsser says, "assumes the life and ignores most of it,"[3] Manon focuses primarily on her premarriage years and a handful of specifically vivid memories. She chronicles her journey of personal identity through family, education, and childhood experiences, carefully selecting those that shape her vision of herself and the world. She describes the presence and absence of friends in her life, the evolution in her personal relationship to religion, the men who pressed their suit for her hand, and she devotes many pages to expressing her own very different feelings toward and relationship with each of her parents, dissecting their marriage and implicitly suggesting that its failings are related to her own austere notions about the wedded state.

But this text, unlike her letters, also includes gaps where readers today expect fuller discussion: on being a wife, on the birth and upbringing of her daughter, on why she has only one child, on the changes in the quality of life when the Rolands became public personages, on falling in love with Buzot and the constraints of her decision to be a virtuous republican wife. Despite a highly charged physical portrait of her self, Manon does not feel called on to present a full anatomy of her every thought and motive.[4] Indeed, her notions of privacy and appropriateness prevent her from indulging in the rhetoric of confessional intimacy that characterizes much modern autobiography. Nonetheless, she does write about some unusual personal details of her intimate life, and their presence shows that *self*-censorship is not an issue in her writing, while the actual style of presentation is highly literary. To be sure, she does not develop at length this commentary, but, unlike Félicité de Genlis in her memoirs, Manon does incorporate subject matter that is extraordinarily personal and sexual. No other woman writer of her time wrote of her first menstruation, of the adolescent stirrings of sexual feeling that caused such guilt, of being the probable object of lesbian attraction, of the unpleasant "surprises" of her wedding night. These subjects are all the more extraordinary because in memoirs in which brevity is a requirement, the author must make deliberate choices about what to include and what to cast aside, particularly, in the eighteenth century, if its inclusion suggests a lack of virtue.

It is, I think, this last word that is the lynchpin of the problem that readers have with Madame Roland—virtue. Our definition of her understanding of virtue depends in large part on our assessment of her as a woman, though it should be vice versa. If we describe her notion of virtue as self-serving and hypocritical, masochistic and self-righteous, we shall scarcely be able to sympathize with her. But if we define it as committed idealism, subject to the frailties of human nature, we are much more likely to feel that it is okay to like Manon and write about her sympathetically. This, in fact, is how I believe Manon viewed her early years in particular and why she devoted so many pages to bringing out both the seriousness and the carefree illusions of that little personage who charms, amuses, and delights her as she looks back over her life. For young Manon, virtue was courage and resolve, industry and intelligence, justice and truth. If she did not always demonstrate these characteristics, they were, nonetheless, always her clear objective, as they would continue to be in her adulthood.

To write a literary account of her life, Madame Roland had to reread that life and analyze its underlying structures, themes, and tensions. It was a salutary exercise. For in reviewing both its pleasures and the struggles between intense feeling and sentiment, in conflict with self-control and containment, she reasserted authorial control over the past as over the page, and used the act of rereading for the purposes of recovery and renewal and, ultimately, of liberation. In the following pages, I would like to retrace that journey, first through the reading that formed her, then the writing she undertook, and finally the role that sexuality played in her life through her text.

BECOMING THROUGH READING: THE MAKING OF A FEMALE INTELLECTUAL

As she sits in her prison cell in the fateful autumn of 1793, Manon Roland takes pen in hand, in order not once, but twice, to trace her memories, both private and public. Fearful that her first texts, secreted out by acquaintances who visited her in prison, had been destroyed when her friend, the liberal lawyer Luc-Antoine Champagneux, had hurriedly burned every paper in his house that the revolutionaries might find incriminating, Manon began again, in a kind of second rite of self-reading, to set forth a life that would shortly, at age thirty-nine, be extinguished. She had spent the first five weeks of her incarceration composing a document entitled *Notices historiques*, by which she hoped to set the political record straight, but the last weeks of her life were devoted to reconnecting with her self and leaving an accounting of that early person. In part, her purpose in writing was to make a textual gift to her twelve-year-old daughter, who within one year would lose both parents, one to the guillotine and the other by his own hand, and in part, as Manon frankly admits, to distract herself, shore up her courage, and deny the finality of the executioner's blade. "It is to live a second time to come back through . . . all the steps of my life," she wrote.[5]

Significantly, for the first time in her life, she openly seeks a public of readers in her own name. Repeatedly she evokes or addresses her unknown reader, as though by creating a relationship through narrative with that person she reconfirms or reassures herself of the basic ties that bind humankind. One of the ways she endeavors to create a bond with her reader is by tracing her own development as a reader. In fact, considering the large number of pages in the *Mémoires* devoted to books, it is clear that Manon felt she could not give an accurate account of herself without tracing her reading history. Reading was something almost as natural as breathing and grew out of who she was. She writes that she does not remember the actual process of learning to read, though she was told that she knew how to read by age four, and she learned to write at five. Books were her friends, in a literal sense as well as a figurative one, since we do not hear about any playmates during her youngest years. Instead, as she says, "Under my father's tranquil roof, I was happy from childhood with my flowers and books" (205).

What drove her was what she called "the rage to learn," and because of it she became an insatiable reader, who from a very early age consumed the most serious literature. Indeed, if anything should convince us that people were different in the eighteenth century, it ought to be this chronicle of Manon's reading habits and of her preferred texts. For here was a young girl of eight years of age whose favorite author was Plutarch and whose other reading consisted, somewhat implausibly, we may judge, of works by philosophers, moralists, and metaphysicians. We do not hear that she read fairy tales or children's stories or imaginative literature of any kind. But she read omnivorously whatever was at hand, and in a proper bourgeois home that meant largely classical or religious texts. She describes reading the lives of saints, a Bible in early French, an old translation of the civil wars by Appien, theatrical works from Turkey, Scarron's *Roman comique*, memoirs including those of Mademoiselle de Montpensier whose pride she greatly admired, and even a treatise on *L'Art héraldique* whose colored plates and figures she found entertaining (211). Need one add that this is scarcely the reading of even the most precocious children today.

As a clever and self-disciplined child, Manon rapidly decided that reading was her favorite activity and, like all young readers, had a special private refuge where she would snuggle up with a book. Her reading nook was a cramped, recessed space off the salon where she would go with a prize volume, secretly borrowed from a bounty hidden by one of her father's pupils in the master's workshop. To retreat to her cozy hideaway was to enter a world of her own. There, she spent many wonderful hours of clandestine pleasure, nourishing her spirit with travelogues, theater, *histoires tendres*, and translations of Plutarch, readings, which, as it turned out, her mother was also secretly borrowing.

This love of reading, developed in childhood, continued into Manon's adolescence and young adult years. She generally undertook several kinds of reading at the same time, some serious and some for relaxation, and especially valued long historical works that her mother would read aloud and that the daughter would study more closely the next day in the solitude of her *cabinet*. Though in the *Mémoires* she never talks about a trip to a bookstore or a bookbinder, she does mention that her father occasionally gave her gifts of books, and that she sometimes commissioned him to borrow for her works by Pascal, Montesquieu, or Locke (245; 248–249). Once she described how she was so fascinated by a book (on geometry, no less) that she decided to copy it out in longhand so that she would have a copy of her own (262). She laughs about having had the patience to reproduce it in the format of "un petit in-8 " and about the fact that it had never occurred to her to consider buying the book. But of course, books were expensive, and a young girl would have had few means with which to buy them.

When she had exhausted her father's small collection of books and her mother's various religious works (becoming, in the process, as she humorously described it, successively a Jansenist, Cartesian, stoic, and deist), she was fortunate in finding other benefactors who put their libraries at her disposal. There was Abbé le Jay who opened to her his library of historians, mythologists, church fathers, and literary men, including Condillac, Voltaire, Bossuet, and *Don Quixote*. And Abbé Morel who lent her volumes by second-rate Christian apologists, intended to bolster her weakening faith, but that actually supplied Manon with the names of the atheists and materialists or deists—d'Holbach, Helvétius, Diderot, and D'Alembert—whose works she was then eager to procure. There was the blind Abbé Legrand who liked to talk with her and brought her books of philosophy to read, and the Genevese clockmaker, Monsieur Moré, who promoted her reading of philosophical mathematicians, physicians, and naturalists such as Buffon. Later on, there were several older gentlemen, widowers, who, charmed by her intelligence and physical attractiveness, became reading mentors with whom she conducted "correspondences of the mind." Monsieur de Boismorel invited her and her father to his country home and opened his library to her, lending her many volumes, including Bayle, she recalled. And it was he who kept her current about what was happening in the world of savants and literature. Her last reading mentor before her husband, with whom she formed a veritable reading and writing partnership, was the fifty-five-year-old Monsieur Sevelinges d'Espagny, who was smitten with her and with whom she even proposed a "mariage blanc," according to Paul de Roux.[6]

Because her reading was not the result of a careful progression designed by a professional educator, Manon read whatever was available, even including various works on agriculture and economy, because, as she puts it, "I always had to be learning something." (277). At one point she describes how, in her early reading, she would be transformed into the person with whom she most identified in the story or turned into a clone of one opinion or another, until she did a new reading.[7] But at other points she exercises, even as an adolescent, clear, critical distance. Thus she was thrilled to read of virtuous republics, because this helped to undermine the cynicism expressed by Helvétius, whose works she consumed, probably to the consternation of her mother. As she tells it, it was not because of personal observations that she became a republican, or that she was first able to focus on *les vices de l'organisation sociale*, but rather, she explains, as a result of her reading, which subsequently confirmed what she observed in society. Indeed, at one point she even gives us the idea that she found books more appealing than life because the latter was so often ugly. Speaking of society, she says, "What I had seen made me happy [to stay] in my *cabinet* and read the great books of the masters, savoring at my leisure all their beauties." (282). It was not until after the death of her mother that she read and reread Bossuet and Fléchier and Bourdaloue and Massillon, combining such reading with their opposites, she says, and taking wicked pleasure in putting her Paw, Raynal, and *Système de la nature* on the same bookshelf.

Her reading, as presented in the *Mémoires*, mentions relatively few women writers. Manon does observe that she read Madame de Sévigné and the memoirs of Mademoiselle de Montpensier, and she refers to Madame de Puisieux in a wholly disparaging way, noting that while she had imagined a woman writer to be a very respectable person, in fact, "at age sixty she still preserved, along with a bent back and toothless gums all those childish airs and pretensions that are hard to forgive even in the young" (278). The only other contemporary woman writer to whom she makes reference is Madame Benoît, a prolific writer whose works and personage Manon discredits as loose and facile. Introducing her subject, she says, "I'll have to say a word about her for those who have not read her novels, entirely forgotten since long before the Revolution, and upon which heaps of dust will have settled when my Memoirs are discovered" (280)—an indication that she expects her work to have a longer shelf-life than Madame Benoît's. And then in one of her finely chiseled and piquant portraits, Madame Roland presents a rather naughty recollection of this *grande voluptueuse*, whose bosom right down to "the little rosette" was so often bared and "heaved so invitingly" that men of questionable taste and morals would have been "churlish" to refuse its beckoning call.[8] As such instances reveal, Manon did not feel it necessary to promote other women writers. Nor did she feel obliged to promote the reading of women's texts.

Nowhere does she discuss doing lightweight reading, such as novels or periodicals like *Le Journal des dames*, let alone volumes of *la bibliothèque bleue*, but this does not necessarily mean that she never did. When studying the autobiographer's self-generated reading lists, Roger Chartier counsels prudence in accepting everything that a writer says about his or her reading, because, he writes, when we want to construct a conscious identity, we remember only "legitimate literature" whose invocation is related to our attempt to underscore a particular notion of personal history.[9] Perhaps Manon did not consider casual reading worthy of inclusion in her memoirs or perhaps as a young girl she had scant chance to develop a taste for that literature, for, she tells us, her mother unobtrusively oversaw what she read and was careful that no book of questionable morals would fall into her hands. In consequence, Manon indirectly attributes maternal surveillance for developing in her a taste for only "good" literature.[10] Still, we wonder if she had read *Les Lettres d'une Péruvienne* or *Lettres de Mistress Henley*, to say nothing of infamous works like *Les Liaisons dangereuses*.[11] We do know from an inventory of the Rolands's belongings that they had a library composed nearly entirely of nonfiction works, but also including at least two volumes of erotic literature, one an edition of the Italian Renaissance poet, Tasso, whose works are marked by a melancolic disposition and sensuous inspiration, and the other *Les Aventures du chevalier de Faublas*, the picaresque and erotic novel by Manon's friend, Lovet de Couvray.[12] To be sure, she, like Madame Riccoboni, would quite likely have found Laclos's tale of cynical seduction and his portrayal of women a discredit to their sex, but it is puzzling why she does not mention in the *Mémoires* some of the most popular novels of her times, especially when we know from her letters that she was an active consumer of novels by Richardson. Furthermore, given the striking similarity between the virtuous end that she chooses for her life, so similar to the decision of the Princess of Cleves, it is surprising that she makes no reference to that novel here, though she does in her letters.[13]

But, of course, she does not have time to discuss all important books, only those that had produced the greatest *conscious* impact on her. Hence, the most important discussion of her reading is that which concerns Rousseau, whom she first read following the death of her mother. In fact, it was another man of the church, Abbé Legrand, who, seeking to distract her from her sorrow, brought her *La Nouvelle Héloïse*, which was to deeply affect her. At one point, she acknowledges that had she been introduced to Rousseau's works much earlier, she might have read no one else, since she found his appeal so compelling. When she muses as to why her mother allowed her to read the skeptical or materialist works of Voltaire, and Boulanger, and the marquis d'Argens, and Helvétius, despite her disapproval of their anti-religion stance, but kept Rousseau from her, Manon concludes that it probably was because her mother did not want her reading works that might appeal too much to the senses as opposed to the intellect. The distinction is as interesting as it is typically eighteenth century. For it is not works that challenge religion or the political and social status quo that concern a parent, but those that bear on the child's moral life. Not surprisingly, mothers have tended to be less worried about intellectual seductions than seductions of the senses.[14] Like Madame Phlipon, eighteenth-century mothers may have felt that reading Rousseau was risky because his writing exposed their daughters to a sensitive, romantic, and tortured soul that would enflame their imagination. Perhaps such mothers had read Madame de Lambert, who in 1737, while refusing to forbid novels because interdiction would only increase their desirability, had warned against the dangers of female imagination "which invests things that please with the charm and illusion that make their appeal, but for a pleasure of this kind, what damage is done!" Imagination, she charged, blocks reason, adding "nothing is more opposed to happiness."[15]

This fear of imagination may appear puzzling unless we distinguish between the creative imagination and the use of imagination as the excuse for conduct. The young woman nurtured on the unrealistic dreams of penny romances or who seeks to live out in Emma Bovary style her fantasies was not applauded in the eighteenth century any more than in the nineteenth century. Quite simply, *boyarysme* is not an admirable model for a life. The argument against it derives not from the same kind of criticism raised by Father Porée who claimed that novels give rise to imagination and that imagination kills off modesty, but rather from the quality of irresponsibility that characterizes a person whose guiding principle is the imagination.[16] Imagination as the inspiration for moral behavior is a risky affair. For every young woman whose imagination is inspired by a Joan of Arc or a Sister Bernadette, there are hundreds of others for whom imagination links only with sex or pleasure. That, it seems, is the core of the issue for mothers.

But for us, there is also the matter of reading tastes. Readers today are bewildered by the appeal that Rousseau exercised on eighteenth-century women—both why they adored him and why the reading of his *Héloïse* could be considered perilous.[17] But precisely because of the difference between contemporary and earlier readers, it is all the more important that we try to understand, since, if nothing else, women's admiration for Rousseau undeniably underscores that eighteenth-century women were different from us, and in ways that should not be erased. Two hundred years ago women found in Rousseau a soulmate on issues ranging from his empathy for victims, to his enthroning of mothers and domesticity, to his argument for marriages based on love, to his criticism of novels driven by the passions. They did not feel they had to follow slavishly every one of his dictums.[18] But in Rousseau they found an emotional sensitivity at sharp variance from that of most men, and it is this openness and vulnerability and courage, despite the odds, that appeals to them. He was, as Manon Phlipon said, the interpreter of feelings, able to express what she had felt, but had not yet put into words: "Rousseau made on me . . . an impression comparable to that Plutarch had exercised on me at age eight; it seemed that he was the nourishment I needed and the interpreter of feelings that I had before reading him, but that he alone knew how to explain to me" (302). Rousseau read into her soul. He expressed what she felt inchoately and made her aspire to live with beauty and grace and sensitivity; he gave her a calling and in so doing ennobled her life. Moreover, he set for women a standard far more attractive than that which filled the typical conduct books of the day, like the *Manuel de la toilette et de la mode* and *La Bibliothèque des femmes* and *La Bibliothèque des dames*, each so imitative and moralistic. Women's enthusiastic support of Rousseau, unlike the hacks of the volumes just referred to, was first, for the positive and genuine value that he gave to emotion (the ostensible female "domain"), and, second, for inspiring them to feel deeply but to live through virtue and sagacity. They did not need to admire all aspects of his writing to be able to experience an emotional resonance with Rousseau's kindred spirit whose writing urged them to celebrate feeling but also to temper the passions through the sixth sense that required sensitivity to be channeled by virtue.[19] In that they could recognize what was admirable in Rousseau simultaneously with expressing specific reservations suggests an intellectually nuanced critical position on their part that does them credit.[20]

The specific notion of virtue that women writers embraced was, in fact, bolstered by their reading of Rousseau and has, I suggest, more to do with self-esteem and personal responsibility than with sexual chastity. Nonetheless, it was a convention, as much in the eighteenth century as in contemporary feminist argumentation, to lament the cultural prejudice against the woman writer who was charged with compromising her sexual virtue by publishing her writing. Manon herself says, "I saw early on that a woman who won this title lost much more than she acquired. Men do not like her and she is criticized by her own sex; if her works are bad, she is made fun of, which is only right; if they good, they are attributed to someone else. If people are forced to recognize that she produced the best part, they sift through her character, her manners, her conduct, and her talent so that the qualities of her mind are offset by the glare of her shortcomings" (304).

Indeed, there is very little that suggests that Manon Roland let public prejudice determine what she would or would not write. On the contrary, what is striking in her *Mémoires* is the boldness of her prose, the trenchant—even tough-minded—quality of her opinions, and the firmness of her grasp on herself.[21] She exhibits no fear of her enemies, nor hesitancy about speaking candidly. Indeed, I would suggest that based on her example and the fact that so many women of the eighteenth century were writing and publishing in every genre and domain—misogynist commentary notwithstanding—we need to reexamine the real impact of such commentary on women's writing.[22] Could it be that the very claim of beleaguered status and apprehension about self-expression worked in women's favor? For it strikes me that, given the existence of hundreds of female writers, women were neither so timid as they or others have often wanted to portray them, nor so silenced as is frequently asserted. It is, of course, quite another thing to acknowledge that very little of their writing would *subsequently* make it into the canon. This leads me to suggest that eighteenth-century admonitions about women's writing need to be placed within the grammar of Enlightenment politics and cultural life in which criticism and protest were both an expression of authentic opprobrium and a rhetorical tool. We should not forget that while the Enlightenment was a censorious period, it was also a period of intense self-questioning. Hence, for women to write, despite or perhaps because of conventional denunciations about compromising their sexual chastity, was to demonstrate in that highly articulate and articulated age their own contrary principle of virtue as courage.

Writing was an integral part of the self-discovery and the self-education of Manon Roland. Her early correspondence with Sophie Carnot, for instance, is not only a precious source of information on how girls in the ancien régime spent their daily lives, but also a record of the developing writing skills of one young intellectual.[23] Speaking of the circularity of letters and observation, she says about her epistles to Sophie, "My letters . . . fed themselves; I learned how to reflect more through communicating my thoughts; I applied myself to study with greater ardor because I found pleasure in sharing what I had acquired, and I observed things with greater attention because I took pleasure in describing" (248). Writing was key to who she was and how she constructed meaning. As the intimate companion of her reading, writing not only consumed a considerable portion of her daily activities, it was also one of the most important measures of her self-worth. "I liked making an account to myself of my ideas," she says, "with a pen in my hand I was able to clarify them; when I wasn't writing, I dreamed more than I reflected; with the pen, I controlled my imagination and followed a line of reasoning" (303). The phrase is revealing, for writing, following on reading, was the way by which she disciplined her mind, brought order to her life, and counteracted any tendency toward letting her imagination take her into dangerous bypaths.

Both reading and writing likewise shaped all her relationships, from simple friendship to the more intimate and enduring union of marriage. We recall that she first met Jean-Marie Roland when he delivered a letter to her from Sophie Cannet, during one of his trips to Paris,[24] and that the subsequent friendship and courtship of Manon and Roland was due in large part to the fact that he left his manuscripts with her during an eighteen-month stay in Italy. As she asserted in her memoirs, it was through her reading of these manuscripts, which contained his travel writing, personal reflections, *projets d'ouvrages*, and personal anecdotes, that she got to know him better than had he paid her frequent visits in person. Despite her later statements concerning a lack of amorous passion in the marriage, it is clear that reading and writing were a shared intellectual passion, for Manon and Roland formed a partnership and collaborated with one voice, she says, on the many letters, *mémoires*, and proposals that issued forth under the Minister of Interior's signature. Yet this domestic collaboration in which she had been deeply invested was profoundly shaken when Manon fell in love with their mutual friend and fellow traveler, François Buzot. Virtually every historian of her life has offered the specter of a guilt-torn Manon who regards prison as a sort of salvation, since even she herself had confessed in a letter, "I owe to my executioners the reconciliation of duty and love."[25] But in postreading her life in the *Mémoires*, Manon proposes more mixed motivation. There, in presenting her decision to replace her husband in prison, Manon wrote "my only ambition was to keep my soul pure and to see the glory of my husband intact," for she explains, "my persecuted and proscribed husband will not die for the future" (277). Even more important, nor will she. "And I myself will have some existence for the future generation," she adds, thereby establishing in that single sentence undeniable proof that the real motivation of her memoirs is to live beyond death by dint of her pen.

As her life hangs by a thread and she invokes her readers, Manon Roland is not playing the role of heroine. She *is* a heroine. She is a woman inspired by high-mindedness, but surrounded by political expediency. For her to adopt romantic irresponsibility when she has the opportunity to set an example is unthinkable. What she learned from her reading, she incorporates into her final narrative. "One is wise," she had written, "for oneself and virtuous for others" (258). Hence, at this capital and complex moment in her life, as in that of the nation, she melds wisdom with virtue in an act of extraordinary courage, for which the reading of a lifetime—of moral and philosophical texts more than of novels—had prepared her. Whether, in the final analysis, her *Mémoires* are viewed as a legacy of ethics in action or a problematic psychology in which the struggles of *volupté* or sensuality and virtue remain unresolved, depends to considerable extent on whether the reader can make the same moves as Manon, who recuperates virtue for her own purposes and redesigns *volupté* into a positive value even when it is ultimately repressed.

VERTU AND *VOLUPTÉ* IN POSTREADING A LIFE

We accept as commonplace today that those who write their memoirs will inevitably resurrect their sexual coming-of-age, but two centuries ago when Manon did so, she was breaking new ground for French women writers. Some critics, like Elissa Gelfand, have argued that in writing of her sexual identity, Madame Roland sought to defend herself against the political charges that she was a monster and a nonfemale who had forgotten she was a woman and a mother.[26] But I would submit that the discourse of sexuality in her text is motivated primarily, if not exclusively, by the politics of literary confession rather than by slander and the politics of the street. My argument is not, however, that Madame Roland uses books to discover the roles she will play in her life, but rather that she uses literature as inspiration and the source for techniques, devices, and structures that will allow her to appeal to her reader. In this particular narrative project, her literary touchstone will be *Les Confessions* more than *La Princesse de Clèves* or *La Nouvelle Héloïse*, and using Rousseau's confessional model, she will seek her way to the reader's heart and mind by means of humor, self-revelation, and, most important, breaking silence.

So when Manon tells her "story of her suitors," when she talks of being the object of possible lesbian attraction,[27] when she discusses her intellectual and literary relations with many men, she does so with a sense of humor. In the story of the trials and tribulations of finding a husband—a long, drawn-out affair covering several years—which Manon entitles, *l'histoire des prétendants*, she reveals this period of her life as imbued with such animated good humor and so many literary elements—a whole troupe of frequently comic and implausible characters, masked identities and impersonated voices, plot turns and *mésententes*—that we are struck by the incongruous fact that this text of pleasure is written from prison.

In narrating the story of her suitors, Madame Roland reveals herself as alternately high-spirited and mocking, rational and romantic, practical and philosophic. But always, she is perceptive, intelligent, and sprightly. As she parades before her reader the bevy of suitors, old and young, moderately well-born and petit bourgeois, rich and poor, all of whom consider themselves to be eminently worthy—even if this confident young woman does not—the reader is amused to find her life resembling that of so many of Jane Austen's heroines. Getting oneself appropriately situated—*établie*—was a singular, time-consuming activity, fraught with risks and ripe with opportunities for clashes, especially between strong-willed daughters and often ineffective fathers.[28] Monsieur's Phlipon's ideal candidate was a wealthy man involved in commerce; Manon's was not, and she used reconstructed and extended dialogue to pursue the argument and develop the differences between herself and her father (284–287). Suitor after suitor (whom Manon compares to "bees buzzing around a newly opened flower") presents himself, most often pressing his cause in letters sent to her parents, which, typically, were answered by Manon who sketched out for her father an appropriate reply. She seemed to enjoy this game of counterfeiting the male voice, something she did numerous times during her lifetime. In recounting the ghostwriting of these "Dear Johns," she says, "Every time that it was question of writing, my father was of a charming docility and copied what I wanted without difficulty," adding, "I got great amusement out of playing the papa" (286). Despite the reservations that her father articulated about her remaining an old maid, he would simultaneously, nonetheless, dispatch the letters and the would-be suitors, seemingly unaware of the ironic exchange of sexual roles in which the daughter adopted through her pen "the style of paternal wisdom" and the father, the behavior of the submissive female.

Typically Manon takes recourse to a certain jocularity, frequently using humor in telling her stories, whether in relating the tale of all those feckless suitors, who presented themselves at her father's door and had to be discouraged, or in musing over her youthful anxiety concerning sexual stirrings. In a remarkable effort to give an intellectual and physiological baring of herself, Manon opens her *quatrième cahier* with a lighthearted reference to her first menstruation, as nature declares itself on the first of May (she actually remembers the date!) in her fourteenth year when she is "like a young and fresh rose which is opened to the powerful rays of the spring sun" (251). She recalls that the event, for which she had been prepared, even if in somewhat imprecise terms by her mother, was a joyful one and marked, she had felt, her "initiation into the class of adults." Despite this unusual indication of eighteenth-century sex education, the event subsequently is treated as a pretext for her to tell a rather charming and humorous, but also highly revelatory, story about herself, one she never confided to her mother, but which now she tells a public audience.

Referring to sexual stirrings so strong and unusual that they awoke her, she recalls how, as a good reader of *Philotée*, her first feelings were those of fear, for she knew "that it is not permitted to us to take from our bodies any kind of pleasure, except in marriage" (251–252). Guilt, shame, and sorrow succeeded one another, all the more so because what she had felt was a sensation of pleasure. In the shorthand style Madame Roland uses to reproduce the immediacy of her earlier self, she writes, "I felt I must be horribly guilty . . . and in a way that displeases the Holy Lamb! Great agitation in my poor heart, prayers, and acts of mortification." Hence her subsequent vigilance so as not to be caught unawares again; hence penances of various kinds—such as mixing ashes with her bread, and salty tears, for good and dramatic measure. Tracking the movements of an adolescent conscience overly sensitized by vague religious admonitions, the adult Manon recreates her young self's anxious search for explanations. Were her feelings some type of religious testing, was she experiencing the same demons as those of which Saint Paul had to rid himself, was it because of *that* that Saint Bernard had thrown himself into the snows, that Saint Jerôme mortified himself with hair shirt and whip, and that those who wished for perfection were told to fast? Reviewing the mixture of fears that assailed her, Madame Roland observes tongue-in-cheek, "In truth, I am almost happy to be in prison in order to recall these piquant episodes," which, at present, she declares, "entertain me greatly."

Conscious again of her reader, she says, "I already see the curious worrying about what I might say in confession," which provides her with a convenient transition to further develop the cunning that the young Manon was to exercise. Baffled as to whether her feelings were not in fact *a test*, Manon (like a Madame de Merteuil—though a most unlikely comparison!) decides to address her *directeur* with her concern. But how was she to do it, what was she to describe? The writer's delight in relating this episode is shown when once again she uses imaginary interior dialogue to replicate the anguish of the young adolescent. "What could I say? 'Father, I am guilty . . . '

And then? What to say next? My heart beat, my face turned beet-red, I began to perspire." And then she finds the perfect phrase, again so redolently literary: " 'I am guilty . . . of having had feelings contrary to Christian chastity.' Ah! the perfect phrase!" she exults. Though she immediately thereafter worries, "But what if he should ask for more elucidation?" In exasperation, she concludes, "Well, that's for him to decide; as for myself, that's all I can say."

This is a thoroughly delightful scene, one in which Madame Roland can reveal both the troublesome silences of the Church so eager to punish sins and the clever deceits of youth seeking either forbidden knowledge (as one has frequently seen in literature) or absolution (as is the case with the young Manon). Once again she narrates the action through dialogue, using both reconstructed interior dialogue and two-way dialogue with a real and weary Abbé de Morel, who, ascertaining that the young confessant had not explicitly sought to feel the pleasures of the flesh ("Did you do anything to contribute to it?" and "You haven't engaged in any wicked reading, have you?") ends the interview with a dismissive "Okay.What else?" In view of this, Manon concludes that what she had experienced was, indeed, "a test" which demands only that she be "vigilant" in the future.

This is, of course, precisely the sort of episode that libertine or protolibertine literature is filled with in the eighteenth century. But for her part, Madame Roland brings to it both a freshness, through genuine first-person narration, and an originality whose purpose is not erotic titillation, but humorous reflection on pubescent guilt and innocence. While the young Manon may have been almost as deviously motivated as Madame de Merteuil, who in taking recourse to her confessor had said, "I didn't so much want to enjoy [those sensations]; I wanted to know; and the desire to instruct myself suggested the way of going about it" (Lettre 81), the outcome for Manon has a different result. This is in part because Manon comes up against a more sophisticated *directeur* than the Marquise's, for Abbé de Morel who hears Manon's confession seems to have been "wise" to the ploys of the young seeking forbidden knowledge. Consequently, the denouement of her tale is less erotically and morally compromising than the one in which Merteuil quips that the *directeur* "made the evil so great that I concluded that its pleasure must be intense." Manon, we might judge, was not so lucky, but rereading herself and her first awkward discovery of sexuality, more than twenty years later, is a way of attaining another objective—that of recalling to the reader the pathos of her present situation.

Manon's second memory is likewise concerned with guilt and innocence and occurs when she was not more than ten or eleven (217–223). It is, however, far more traumatic, less for actual physical violation than for the extraordinarily strong impression it left on her because in several ways Manon is victimized and betrayed, not only by the perpetrator but also by her parents, particularly her much beloved mother. The episode concerns a young apprentice of her father's, several years older, who takes liberties with her, first forcing her to hold his penis (which the young Manon describes as "this strange thing"), and, on a later occasion, having an orgasm in her presence. Both are clearly troubling events for the young girl. It is her very first experience with sexual difference and it is deeply disturbing. Her reaction on the first occasion, as she recounts it, is anger in the presence of the young man, and haughty dismissal of his attempts to goad her into accepting that her mother engages in similar activities with her father. In private, she is upset and confused, but also curious. "I would have liked to know what the other wanted me to learn," she admits, but adds, "I would have liked to hear about it without being myself the person to whom he said it."

A second encounter is more problematic. Once again she is alone in her father's atelier with the young man. At one point, in order to observe a ruckus that is taking place out on the street, she climbs on a table for a better view, but when she comes to dismounting it, with the young man's "help," she falls into his arms and ultimately lap. She immediately feels his *chose extraordinaire* poking into her back, and struggles to free herself, though not before the fully aroused young man manages to caress her "there where nothing else had reached." When she finally manages to break free, she is horrified to see that he is in the throes of some "crisis" or what we assume is orgasm. She writes, "I was horrified. His eyes seemed to be popping out of his head, he was breathing hard. I was on the point of fainting. He noticed me, and his crisis no doubt ended, he took on a gentle air." This time repugnance takes the place of curiosity. She is shocked, worried, sad, and offended. This time she spills the beans to her mother.

Though Manon does not overtly ill judge her mother's reaction, the modern reader certainly will. For the mother reacts so emotionally and interrogates her daughter with such circuitous intensity—"she asked me a thousand convoluted questions, in order not to teach me more than I already knew and to assure herself that I had not been more instructed"—and raises so dramatically the specter of religion, virtue, honor, and reputation that the poor young girl feels even more confused and convinced that she is the sinner rather than the victim. Perhaps at some level she does fault herself for being alone in the father's atelier with the pupil; certainly she seems to buy the notion, as did Madame de Genlis's heroine in *L'Histoire de la Duchesse de C****, that if a daughter confided everything to her mother in the first instance, her conscience would be clear and her purity would remain intact. In fact, in a summing-up of the incident, Manon seems to imply that one of a mother's most important duties toward a daughter is to preserve her from "corruption" by all and any means. Religion is, of course, a natural *préservatif* or contraceptive. Thus, convinced that she is somehow terribly guilty, Manon hurries off to confession, for despite her disinclination to retell the terrible events, she knows that expiation comes only with confession. Looking back thirty years later, the memoirist comments only with partial irony, "So there I was, a penitent before having been a sinner."

What is most curious about the conclusion of this episode is that Madame Phlipon decides not to tell her husband or have the youth punished, but simply declares that henceforth she and her daughter will take their meals apart from Monsieur Phlipon and his pupils. For a modern reader, this reaction is sadly inadequate. The child, after all, has been violated by the actions of the youth and has been made to feel uncomfortable in her own home. Yet both she and her victimizer remain under the same roof, and she is merely swept into closer embrace by her mother, who seems by her own actions to suggest that silence and greater self and maternal surveillance are the best responses. To be fair, Madame Phlipon may have felt that had she confided the incident to her husband, he may have held her personally accountable, for by tradition a child's moral safety was the mother's responsibility. She may have concluded that in allowing the young man to remain in the home, while exercising more loving but vigilant supervision of her daughter, she would both be avoiding several unpleasant scenes (with her husband and with the husband and pupil) and satisfy herself that she was indeed a good and proper mother capable of preserving her daughter's virtue. We might ruminate as to how typical this maternal reaction was at the time, but, however that may be, it is hardly surprising to learn that Manon is so marked by these events that in the same paragraph in which she writes that henceforth she regarded men "with a sort of terror that grew especially if they seemed in any way friendly," she also links her fear of anything sexual, including knowledge of sex, so that for her "the events of the first night of my marriage were as surprising as they were disagreeable."

What is striking in Manon's recounting of this event is first the amount of space she allots it—some five pages, which makes it one of the longest narratives of her memoirs—and second, how she *narrates* it, using dialogue, description, moral commentary, and even once briefly, ironic humor (her "So there I was a penitent . . . "). In other words, she does not just give an account, but turns it into a narrative story, with an anticipatory lead to fix the reader's attention ("An event too important by its influence on my future conduct for me to pass over in silence . . . "); a preliminary and neutral preparation of characters and the scene (the young man had been singled out to join the Phlipons for dinner occasionally); and a development through dialogue of ensuing events and the resulting ambiguous feelings evoked in her, which she recounts through recreated interior monologue, as she tries to decipher whether or why the event should have any consequences for her: "I had a great deal of difficulty trying to decide what impression this scene had made on me. Every time I tried to think about it some concern or distraction broke in. After all, what harm had he done? None. Should I tell? The very thought of having to decide how to talk about it prevented me from doing so. Should I hold it against him? Even that seemed doubtful." Narrative intensity is further developed in the second encounter with the young man, as the story figuratively reaches its climax at the same time the young man literally does so. The effort toward moral and narrative resolution begins with narrator's account of the event to her mother, whose emotional reaction is presented in a kind of *discours indirect libre*.

The immediate effect of this trauma is to throw Manon into the arms of religion. In terms of her subsequent behavior, it made her fearful with men, it caused her to repress her emotions, to flee all mention of sex or reproduction—even in her reading of Buffon.[29] Seven or eight years later, she once again sees her victimizer, whose conscience, it appears, does not prevent him from bringing his new wife to the Phlipon home for a very proper round of introductions. For her part, Manon remains deeply affected, and her memoirs bear witness to the continuing negative emotional consequences she feels from the episodes with this young man..

However, in the end, she is able to make these unfortunate events serve her literary purposes, for she now takes the opportunity in her memoirs to let the reader know that what she has just done—tell this story—is an act comparable to Rousseau's famous story of the stolen ribbon. This is a meditated and writerly move on her part that simultaneously underscores the *littérarité* of her text and puts her in the company of the great *moraliste*, Jean-Jacques. The comparison, however, is inexact, if fascinating, for what it may imply. When Rousseau chooses in his *Confessions* to relate his tale, he is coming clean. He *had* stolen the ribbon, but had accused another of doing it and was believed. The innocent party, "a friendly, honest, good girl who was surely worth a great deal more than me," he relates in Livre II, was punished and dismissed, and Rousseau felt great remorse all his life for having gotten off scot-free. Forty years later his conscience is still heavy, his guilt bitter and discomfiting. Confessing this crime for the first time in his life—even Madame de Warens had never heard it—does not deliver him of his pain and self-condemnation, but it does permit him to claim transparent and complete honesty in his confessions. Can Manon make the same claim? Is the twinning of her story with Rousseau's accurate? The point, after all, of Rousseau's story was to reveal himself as the moral criminal. He accuses himself of the sins of lying and ruining a young woman's life, and, in his inimitable way, delved into the complicated set of motivations and spontaneous utterances and actions, which, he had concluded, only made his crime more heinous. This was a determining event in his life, at the origin both of his decision to write his confessions and to atone for the sin by committing his life to the pursuit of justice for the poor and disadvantaged.

In comparison, Manon's story, while possibly as defining in terms of her future psychosexual development, is not the key motivating factor behind her decision to write her memoirs. The real relationship between her text and his has to do with breaking the silence and dealing with shame—of the wrongdoer in Rousseau's case and the ambivalent victim in Manon's. He had not told anyone of his action, before writing his *Confessions*, because he was ashamed of himself. She had not told anyone (aside from her mother)—

no intimate friend or even husband, from whom, she says, she hid almost nothing—because she is uncertain about the quality of her own absolute innocence with the apprentice and because of another kind of shame, the kind that comes when an intelligent and capable female, regardless of her age, breaks the silence and speaks of victimization, especially of sexual victimization. Now, in composing her *Mémoires* for a public of faceless readers, Manon risks further humiliation, but emulates the master and reveals for the first time painful memories. In this sense, she endeavors to liberate herself through confession to a reader.

Ironically, while Rousseau was applauded for his honesty, Madame Roland would be accused by Sainte-Beuve of an act of *impudeur*.[30] In part, it is because she is writing in a time before the victim's rights were recognized and, in good part, because she is a woman and has broken the rule by which women are not to speak of their own sexuality or sexual experience. In her self-portrait, Manon had said of *volupté*, "I doubt that another was made as much for *volupté* and yet tasted it so little," a phrase which has been cited by her critics who accuse her of being both too bold and too boastful (254). Yet it was a common dilemma for women whose lives in society as in fiction were constructed through those two opposing poles of virtue and *volupté*. For her part, Manon solves the conflict by an oxymoron, saying that in situations dangerous to her morality she remained *sage par volupté*, or virtuous through sensuality.[31] To be *sage par volupté* is rendered intelligible only when read in context with the sentences that surround it: "I remained the mistress of my imagination by constantly chiding it" and "I see pleasure, like happiness, only in what charms the heart as much as the senses and does not cost any regrets." What she endeavors to create is a resolution between the two oppositions through a kind of standoff, in which *volupté* becomes a mental construct, tamed and mastered through careful dosages, with her mind regulating desire through the imagination. She is *sage* or virtuous because *volupté* takes place in her head or imagination and she tightly controls it. Furthermore, pleasure, which is an intellectual and moral concept for Manon, requires that the heart and the senses be united in acts that will cause no regrets. Hence, she will not consummate her love with Buzot, for to do so would be to lose both intellectual and moral control. She will be *sage* (or virtuous) through the exercise of the mind that can contain and accommodate *volupté*.

In Manon's rereading, there is no necessary conflict between virtue and *volupté*. She has bared her sexuality and done so without compromising herself. Indeed, she has used these episodes of sexuality to underscore both her humanness and sincerity, and furthermore to point up the difference between her and *les grands voluptueux*, such as Madame Benoît or Danton, whose appetite for power, either sexual or political, is both vulgar and corrupt. As a true daughter of the Enlightenment, Manon uses her intellect to resolve contradictions and reaffirm a belief in the power of the mind to transcend them. For Manon, virtue is not merely sexual chastity (though she does not dismiss its importance), but rather personal honesty, commitment, and the resolve to live up to one's ideals. In that sense one could say that she returns to the etymological roots of the word—*virtuosum*—implying valor and courage. When virtue is defined in that way, it is no longer the polar opposite of *volupté*, but a quite different value. In that sense, her death can be read as an act of political and personal courage that likewise bespeaks a particular self-interest—one that can be identified as authorial in nature. Instead of placing all value in an impossible and passionate love for one man, Manon, at the end of her life, seems to conceive of and at last permit herself another relationship. Having spent her entire life as a reader, now, in rereading herself, she produces a memoir not just for her family and friends but for all those faceless readers she had addressed in friendship throughout her text and who will live in the centuries ahead. If earlier in her life she had abjured the role of writer—something of a ritual disclaimer, to be sure—now, in the most propitious of circumstances for an author who wants to be read, she embraced the opportunity that history provided to survive through her text into the future.[32] She may have deemed it a fine foil, indeed, to the executioner's design.

CONCLUSION

As the only one of her parents' seven children to survive, Manon is clearly and literally a survivor. In describing certain qualities of temperament that she possessed from youngest childhood and that often brought her in direct confrontation with her father, with whom she shared neither taste nor philosophy of life, Manon reveals obstinacy, resistance, and the unshakable determination to prevail. Early in the memoirs she recalled a scene in which, at age six, she angered her father by being unable to swallow a medicine (209–210). He spanked her for disobedience and when she still refused the dosage, threatened to begin again. Ceasing to cry, she recounts, how she silently presented him with her backside, not in submission to his superior strength or out of respect to him, but from her own sense of pride. In this episode, Madame Roland captures something revealing both about the poignant injustices that mark children so deeply and her own clear-eyed resolve and courage that will remain with her to her death.

For in the end, she does not die as a character from fiction, but *in character* with herself. Rational choice had always determined her decisions. She does not choose *when* to die so much as she chooses *how* to die—which is both heroic and political, as contemporary reports of her trial and trip through the streets to the guillotine make clear. The argument that Manon could have saved herself is too facile and too romantic, for she did not have control over her freedom and, moreover, continued throughout her imprisonment to object to the injustice of her arrest. Nor does the quality of her death reflect either the fictional (and very nonpolitical) heroines to whom she is usually compared, for she does not die as the Princesse de Clèves, who makes her love into an *objet d'art*, nor as Julie in the knowledge that her heart had won out over her mind.

Instead, Manon dies as part of events beyond the individual life. Her disgust with the spectacle of political betrayal and corruption is voiced throughout the *Mémoires*. "Our government is a kind of monster," she writes, "whose form and actions are equally disgusting; it destroys all that it touches and devours itself" (234). She is sickened by the "desolation of the country" and the "degradation of its citizens" (237), feelings that contributed fundamentally to her depression about the future and her decision to relive "the sweet impressions, the pleasant memories, and the happy feelings" of her past in her writing, before her execution. Hence her text arises from personal depths plus political anger at the squandered idealism of the revolution and scorn for those who have put themselves above moral law. It is a personal and political text written from prison, whose bars are physically real and not merely the externalizations of internal constraints that prevented her from achieving happiness with Buzot. It is both disturbing and presumptuous to arrogate to ourselves the power to decide that there is something inauthentic about the way this woman faced death. But, regardless the point remains that as a result of the choice she made in those last weeks in prison, we have a document of remarkable originality: for the first time a woman traces the evolution of her own mind and matter in an autobiographical text intended for the public.

In many ways, the project of reading and writing that Manon had conducted throughout her life was a rehearsal for this last and most important act of rereading her self and writing for publication in her own name. The solitude she experiences in prison is not unfamiliar; indeed, it is something she had always cherished. Years before she had written to Sophie, saying, "I am alone and I like being alone. . . . Today everything is closed and I am inaccessible to others." Seclusion is a privileged condition because, as she continued, "There are so many things to say to oneself that can be done only in solitude. It is in seclusion that one understands oneself and gathers strength."[33] Some sixteen years later in prison, she would surely have said the same thing.

Madame Roland did not write in a vacuum or merely in soliloquy. Rereading her life had another objective beyond merely running the clock by writing the past. For just as throughout her life, reading had been the quest to make intellectual connections between truth and ideas, now, at the end of that life, it would represent the intense effort to connect with the future, to leave a legacy, through a flesh-and-blood reader. Seeking to engrave her self on the world as much as to bequeath a memory, Manon created an empathetic autobiography, one that demonstrates in its text and subtext Philippe Lejeune's assessment that "autobiography . . . is a mode of *reading* as much as a type of writing."[34] For, in fact, the autobiography of the intellectual represents a continuum of reading. Born in the love of books and taking written shape in the rereading of a life, then passed on to a new reader, autobiography represents both the multiplicity and mutuality of reading. From Manon's foundational and formational reading, to her rereading, and ultimately our reading, there is a constant renewal as the contract between book and reader is continuously reenacted.

THREE

THE ROMANCE AS TRANSFORMATIVE READING

FÉLICITÉ DE GENLIS, 1746–1830

> . . . women must understand under what conditions it is permitted that they become authors. (1) They must never be overly anxious to have their work published; (2) proper behavior requires them to show . . . the deepest respect for religion and for the principles of austere morality; (3) they must only respond to critics when incorrectly cited or when the criticism is founded on an imaginary fact. . . . [However] I definitely do not urge women to play the role of victims.
>
> —Madame de Genlis, *De L'Influence des femmes sur la littérature française*

A WOMAN OF CONTRASTS

On her thirtieth birthday Madame de Genlis received an unusual surprise from the Duc de Chartres that she describes in the third volume of her *Mémoires*: "25 January: I found in my *cabinet*, seated next to my desk, a life-sized doll, coiffed in feathers, a pen in hand."[1] Accompanying this gift were "a ream of superb paper, thirty-two large blank books bound in green leather, and twenty-four smaller ones bound in red." At the feet of the doll was "a carton filled with letter-writing paper, envelopes, sealing wax, gold and silver powder, a knife, scissors, a ruler, compass, etc." This gift, it turns out, was conceived in response to a vow made earlier by Madame de Genlis in the company of the Duc and other women at Palais Royal, when, to distinguish herself from the gussied-up women or "painted dolls" who surrounded her, she asserted that *she* would be able to give up wearing rouge at age thirty without considering it a sacrifice. As a reminder of that vow, the Duc de Chartres sends his gift, which both challenges his former lover and captivates her imagination. From this point on, she no longer wears rouge, and her fifty-year-plus career as a writer is consecrated.

It is a graphic illustration of a woman's exchange of forms of self-presentation—from paints and pomades to pen and paper—and it is a capital moment in Madame de Genlis's life. Though she had been writing since her youngest years, now that her status as writer was so demonstrably authorized and approved by the man who would later name her *gouverneur* of his children, she would henceforth devote herself exclusively to a career of writing and teaching and, in the course of the next several decades, publish more than 140 volumes of letters, essays, fairy tales, pedagogical manuals, theater, memoirs and *souvenirs*, novels and historical romances. With indefatigable energy, she produced an oeuvre that outrivals in sheer number of printed pages nearly every other writer, male or female, of her period. Even at seventy-five years of age she was planning a major new undertaking—this time to redo the entire *Encyclopédie*, so as to make it into an ethical work that would, in her view, be more useful, once cleansed of its immorality and impiety. Mercifully, according to her critics, given both the amount she had already written and the nature of the task as she conceived of it—so antithetical to the original purposes of the *Encyclopédie*—ill health prevented her from realizing her plans, although she continued work on her multivolume memoirs, even when she could no longer wield a pen and had to dictate them to a secretary.

Looking back on her long life, Madame de Genlis judged that whereas she might, if given the chance, change certain elements of her personal life, there was practically nothing she would alter about her literary career. Critics today, being less forgiving about the kind of open moralizing and repetitiousness that characterize much of the Genlisien corpus, have not shared the latter part of her assessment. Still, nearly everyone agrees there are gems in this plentiful oeuvre, and when all the individual choices of her best work are put together, the result is a not inconsiderable achievement. Some value most highly her novels, others her memoirs, still others her personal correspondence.[2] As for her personal life, majority opinion has tended to cast it as a problematic mixture of pride, hypocrisy, and ambition, while more recently there has been a growing minority who applaud her passion and incisive intellect and say that she had the kind of talents and instincts that would have made her an effective politician, had such a role been possible.

No one can deny that Madame de Genlis was an extraordinary woman, nor that she was well placed to report on the extraordinary times during which she lived—under some eleven different political regimes, from Louis XV to the reign of Louis-Philippe, her former pupil. She knew nearly everyone of importance, in political as well as literary circles, and her accounts of encounters with such men as Rousseau and Voltaire are fascinating for what they reveal both about the great men themselves and about the confidence of the young woman who met them. If she ultimately judges Jean-Jacques to be insincere and difficult (*Mémoires*, I, 1–18), she is put off by the malicious impiousness of the writer of *Candide* (II, 314–330). A lifelong opponent of the *philosophes*, Genlis found their skepticism distasteful, but insisted that while her experience made her sympathetic toward the royalists, she was in fact of "no party except that of religion" (III, 260). Indeed, her commitment to a life consistent with Christian morality is one of the constants of her writing (if not always of her life) because she believes that the writer bears a responsibility to produce texts of moral usefulness. She is critical of much and of many people in her memoirs, but insists, "I have never permitted myself to criticize except in the interests of religion and morality," the two goals of all writing, she steadfastly maintained (I, 4).

Possibly because of this current of self-righteousness that flowed from her pen as from her lips, and certainly because of her strong opinions, which she never hid, Madame de Genlis provoked strong feelings in many who either knew her or knew of her. The calumny of some nineteenth-century commentators is, however, especially offensive because it is so overwrought. For a more balanced assessment, we might consider the words of Louis-Philippe, as reported to Victor Hugo. In a description that reveals both reservations and grudging admiration, her former pupil underscores how Madame de Genlis was at once systematic, severe, and seductive. He describes her as something of a martinet, "a tough preceptor," saying that she raised his sister and him *"avec férocité."* She was, he reacalls, a demanding task-mistress, requiring that they sleep on boards and rise at dawn. She oversaw every detail of their life from their daily diet ("never a tasty tidbit, never a sweet," he notes) to the scheduling of every hour with useful activity—"copious work and no pleasure," he quips. In addition to school subjects, she also taught manual crafts, and thanks to her he says, "I can perform all kinds of trades. . . . I can bleed my man, just like Figaro. I am a carpenter, groom, mason, blacksmith." When he was young he admits to having been afraid of her, but as he grew into his teenage years, he fell in love with her, without realizing it. She, however, "understood and saw right through him," he notes. With grace and wit she defused what could have been an awkward situation, laughingly dismissing him, "Come now, Master Chartres, big boy that you are, why do you always want to be in my skirts!"[3]

In a real sense, Louis-Philippe captures what was remarkable about this seductive yet difficult woman, who had spent her life struggling not only with others but also with two very opposing sides to her own nature. On the one hand, as a young woman she was impetuous and very *romanesque*, drawn to adventure and extravagant disguise, while, on the other, she exhibited a clear tendency toward austerity and authoritarianism.[4] She admits that even into her twenties she was simultaneously "very reasonable" and given to extravagant actions (I, 120). Once, for instance, on an outing she swallowed a fish whole to prove that she was no "Paris society lady" (I, 197–198). And frequently she rode her horse with wild abandon, eager, she said, to happen upon a strange château where kind strangers would receive her (I, 239). Commenting about one of her escapades that scared everyone in her entourage, including her husband, she says, "I loved placing myself in the most extraordinary situation and triumphing over the obstacles of adversity" (I, 214). She was attracted to extremes, to the melodramatic, and to the life of the imagination, admitting, "I have always preferred occupying my time with what I was creating" (I, 214) rather than with what was already there. This may explain her taste for the *roman noir* and for the supernatural element or incident in her own fiction. As she grew older, however, she tried consciously to tame such extravagances, specifically, I believe, by redirecting or disciplining them through her writing and reading.

Attracted to the unusual and to proving to herself and to others that she was intellectually, emotionally, and even physically capable of dealing with any problem, Madame de Genlis often expresses overweening confidence bordering on arrogance—a charge that has traditionally been made against other strong women. Her biographer, Gabriel De Broglie, suggests that her life was a struggle precisely because so much was stacked against her—first, the relative poverty of her family after her father lost his fortune, then the vehement disapproval of her husband's family to their marriage, her own lack of formal education, and finally, one might add, her fundamental conservatism—intellectual, moral, and political, as the century moved toward greater liberalism. In contrast to her expressions of conservative morality, however, are examples of behavior that at best could be defined as morally ambiguous, and that quite possibly relate to that pole of her personality drawn to drama and extravagance. How else, for instance, to explain her presence at Palais Royal in the 1770s and 1780s, when it was a hotbed of corrupt politics and morals—she who said she loved virtue? Or, what to think of her adulterous affair with the Duc de Chartres, at the same time she served his wife as lady-in-waiting? And how to square insensitive treatment of her second daughter with her assertion of protective maternal instincts and repeated pronouncements about virtue and morality?

In the memoirs, where Madame de Genlis makes the ritual claim to truthfulness, she never admits to having had an affair with the Duc de Chartres, and she disingenuously suggests that the coldness of the Duchesse de Chartres (who learned of her husband's affair with Genlis only much later) was both inexplicable and a "tremendous injustice" (IV, 13). Her complicated relations with her aunt, Madame de Montesson—who led a very disorderly life and at one point was married to a man fifty years older than herself, and eager to replace him after his death by the very fat and thoroughly corrupt Duc d'Orléans—are duly noted by Madame de Genlis, but most often without comment or even the pretense of probing her own feelings or motivations. A striking exception to the silence concerning her own lapses comes in the third volume of the memoirs, when she describes the marriage of her second daughter to Madame de Montesson's lover, the corrupt Comte de Valence, who was double the age of his bride but half that of his mistress. To Madame de Genlis's credit—though still without admitting the whole truth—she does agonize over her own role in arranging that marriage (III, 324–328), which, unsurprisingly, turns out disastrously—so much so that Madame de Genlis tries to distance herself from, and refuse any responsibility in, what her daughter became: more or less a high-society whore (de Broglie, 180).

The separation between the image of herself that she wants to convey and the one created by her various silences, evasions, or partial confessions opened the door to her detractors, who described her in the blackest of terms as a cold, personally ambitious, and self-serving woman. For Genlis, such criticism was explained by the fact that she was breaking gender expectations. "People want to persuade us," she wrote, "that as soon as a woman leaves the usual route . . . she must no longer be considered to be anything but a man, and deserving of no particular respect."[5] Underscoring this point, Genlis commented insightfully on the quality of difference between the two gendered pronouncements, "Il a fait parler de lui" ("He got himself talked about") and "Elle a fait parler d'elle" ("She got herself talked about"), observing that while the first refers to the male's talents or actions, the second carries with it negative moral judgment.[6] Rejecting such sexualized thinking, she set her own course, one that endeavored to show that women could be feminine and strong, controversial, and intellectual. What more is required to call her a feminist?

Two positive character traits that her critics rarely mention are the courage and resourcefulness that she demonstrated throughout her life. During the revolutionary years, for instance, when aristocrats went into exile, she lived by her wits, sometimes traveling and living incognito, in England, Belgium, Germany, and Switzerland, always aware that any group might be infiltrated by spies. It was in exile that she learned that her husband, with whom she had not lived for many years, but with whom she appears to have remained friendly, had been executed for refusing to vote for the king's death, and she admitted in her memoirs to feeling both sorrow and guilt at that point for not having convinced him to leave France. Interestingly, she turned this drama into a written work entitled *Les Parvenus* (1824), thereby attempting, as she often did, to resolve in her art what was unresolved or problematic in her own experience.

Though she succeeded in living an independent life, she was never financially secure. Late in life, she regretted her former disdain of money, saying, "it is absurd to reject out of vanity payment of a debt, something I did a thousand times" (VI, 309). But financial gain was never her primary motivation. Writing was. "I was born to write," she says, "to cultivate the arts and literature" (VII, 76), and until her death in 1830, she did just that, living by her teaching and writing, including paid work on the periodical, *La Bibliothèque des romans*. Her profession as a writer enabled her to deal with what in her own life was sometimes messy or ambiguously motivated; it permitted her to restructure life—both the life already lived and the one she encouraged of her readers. Whether she was writing to applaud the role of women in literature (*De L'Influence des femmes*, 1811), or to relate the fictionalized life of an admirable woman in *L'Histoire de la Duchesse de C****** (1782), or to present fairy tales or pedagogical essays, it was the desire to teach better ways of finding happiness that informed her enterprise. The creation of text, the telling of stories, even the historical romance, functioned for her as the means by which to reassess and rewrite problems or conflicts in her own life or in the lives of other women. It is this refracted experience and the interweaving of ethics and esthetics that I will investigate, first by tracing her "coming to" reading and writing, then by scrutinizing her reading philosophy and program, and finally by examining closely one of her most successful historical novels, *La Duchesse de La Vallière* (1804).

READING AND WRITING: COMPLEMENTARY ACTS

In proof of the defining role that Madame de Genlis gives to reading and writing in her memoirs, she even lets these activities have equal billing with the announcement of her first pregnancy, delivering the news of impending motherhood—normally a capital event for a first-time mother—in this way: "The idea that I was going to become a mother made me much more reasonable. For several months I worked on writing 'Reflections of a Twenty-Year Old Mother,' although I was only nineteen at the time" (I, 266). In the next breath, she lists the books she is reading, history, theater, poetry, and "the voluminous travels of Abbé Prévost," creating the impression that pregnancy, writing, and reading—each a gestational act in itself, and together signs of a busy and productive life—are coequal and interconnected activities.

With what often appears to be total recall in her memoirs, Madame de Genlis not only catalogues all the titles and authors she read during her early years and adolescence, but also provides details on how reading and writing became the defining characteristics of her identity. As a child she learned to read and write at home, acquiring those skills in the classical order, first reading, then writing.[7] When she was five or six, her father hired the village *maîtresse d'école*, Mademoiselle de Mars, as a private instructor to teach her reading, a skill the young child easily acquired. Later, it was the *femme de chambre* who supplied her with reading material, a risky proposition for the novice reader, Madame de Genlis judges in her 1790 text on the *Suppression des couvents*, in which she argued the benefits of convent libraries and nuns as guides to proper reading.

As for writing, she composed her first romance when she was six, even though she did not yet know how to manipulate a pen and had to ask

Mademoiselle de Mars to write out the story under her dictation. Madame de Genlis considers the lack of even a single lesson in penmanship another shortcoming in her formal education, musing that it "is rather odd that a person who has written so much never learned how to write [proper penmanship]" (I, 85). She recalls with some distaste that even at age eleven, when she addressed New Year's greetings to her father, "never having held a feather pen," her missive with its "big and ugly letters," was something of an embarrassment. If the enterprise was saved, it was only because her spelling was excellent, she observes with almost audible relief, "because reading . . . had engraved in my head all the words and how to spell."

Endowed with an active imagination and decidedly curious about everything, the young Félicité borrowed books from her father's library, sometimes taking them to bed when she was supposed to be sleeping. In the first volume of her memoirs, she relates one such episode with its nearly disastrous results. Having carried off to bed the Gascon opera, *Alcimadure*, she fell asleep before putting out the candle, which subsequently caught on fire, engulfing her bed in flames. Fortunately, she recalls, her mother chose that evening to tiptoe into her daughter's room to leave a surprise gift of a bracelet, and was thus able to save Félicité's life. As modern readers, we might make two observations in regard to this episode. The first is an ironic comment that the incident illustrates the *actual* danger of reading during the Enlightenment, rather than those moral ones, trumpeted by the *Mémoires de Trévoux*, which preached against immoral reading and "l'école des romans." The second more serious one concerns the remarkably mature reading engaged in by Félicité, much like Manon Phlipon, which leads me to reflect on how different and more serious adolescent readers were during the Enlightenment period.

Another way in which Madame de Genlis is like Manon is that she traces in her memoirs the people she knew and the places she visited through her use of their libraries. Whether at her brother-in-law's château of Genlis, or at Sillery where her in-laws resided, Palais Royal or Versailles, or during travels abroad, she never fails to mention the libraries she visited and the books she borrowed. She also describes how her taste in both literature and philosophy was influenced by a number of modestly successful literati, who attended dinners at the homes of friends and relatives and whose conversation she listened to with fascination. From them she acquired a dislike for *les philosophes* and anything that suggested irreverent skepticism about the church or government. One of her early mentors was the writer Sauvigny, who later introduced her to Rousseau, and she recalls the pleasure she took in reading aloud with him Pascal's *Lettres provinciales*, Corneille's theater, and Madame de Sévigné's *Lettres*, which Genlis calls "the perfect model of epistolary style" (*De L'Influence*, 178). It was, moreover, Sauvigny who helped her hone her writing style by directing her toward writers such as Buffon, Massillon, and Fénelon, from whom she says she learned the value of *le naturel*, *la clarté*, *la précision, l'harmonie, la correction, et la propriété d'expression*—the very characteristics that do, in fact, describe her literary style.

For her, reading was to the mind what exercise was to the body. Energetic about acquiring instruction and committed to never losing a minute of her day, she devoured books wherever she was. By example she showed that reading was the only art needing no special paraphernalia or place and could be practiced at any time of night or day. Whether at her *toilette* or in a carriage on the way to Versailles, she would have a book in her hand and a notebook in her pocket for recording reflections on her reading. "I wrote resumes of everything I read," she says, "a habit I have kept throughout my life" (I, 209). These reading journals were, she asserted, as vital to the process of reading as the book itself, adding, "Nothing attached me more to my reading than this collection of notes, excerpts, and reflections that consumed a huge number of notebooks" (I, 376).[8]

For her, as for Manon, reading and writing were complementary activities. Similarly, modern reading-theory research confirms the beneficial effect of combining writing with reading, promoting their complementarity as key to the processes of analytic thinking. When the reader steps back from the text and reconceptualizes content through writing in ways that cut across ideas and disciplines, she engages in complex thought. Writing becomes the powerful expression of reflection, one of the most disciplined forms of thinking, requiring precision, careful examination of language, and tough judgment on whether an argument can stand up and make sense to the critical eye. Writing, like reading, is the active search for meaning, knowledge, and understanding.[9] The two in tandem form the bedrock of Madame de Genlis's pedagogical fictions and essays.

READING ADVICE

Recalling that her own introduction to reading had been highly unstructured and seriously unguided, she lays out a reading program for girls in volume four of her 1782 text, *Adèle et Théodore, ou Lettres sur l'éducation.*[10] The program was to begin at age six and continue to age twenty-two, or later if scheduled *re*readings of important works are counted. Reserving a key role for mothers in mentoring the child's reading, Madame de Genlis deems it their responsibility to select suitable books and to see that only they are read.[11] In fact, by denying children the right to choose their own reading materials, the effect will be to increase their desire for books, according to Genlis. Mothers must also insist that their children apply themselves seriously to their books. For whenever we are bored with our reading, Genlis admonishes, it is because we are not addressing the book in earnest—though she also stipulates that a writer should not seek to fatigue a reader through gratuitous complexity.[12] She further suggests that reading can be used to counter bad behavior, without a parent's direct intervention. Hence, when

Adèle is naughty, her mother gives her a book about a child close to Adèle's age, whose story demonstrates why and how a little girl should behave.

As for the question of novel reading, Madame de Genlis's mouthpiece and Adèle's mother, Madame d'Almane, judges that only three novels—*Clarissa, Grandisson,* and *Pamela*—meet the test of being truly moral. She does, however, allow her daughter to read her first novel, *Robinson Crusoe*, at age ten, and three years later, *La Princesse de Clèves, Zaïde, Cleveland*, and *Le Doyen de Killerine*. Such novels are permissible, it appears, if mother and daughter read together, so that the mother can supervise her daughter's understanding. The most dangerous age for reading novels, Madame d'Almane asserts, is sixteen or seventeen—interestingly, the very age at which Félicité was married, as were both her daughters, Caroline and Pulchérie.[13] Hence, a novel like Rousseau's *La Nouvelle Héloïse*, which contained what Madame de Genlis thought were "revolting details" " (*Adèle et Théodore*, xii)[14] was too dangerous to read, a view seconded by Manon Roland's mother who feared the effect that novel could have on her sensitive daughter. Madame de Genlis was critical of romantic love and questioned why it alone should satisfy the human heart. Thus she has Madame d'Almane say, "The heart is made for love, I agree; it needs a sentiment that keeps it engaged and occupies it," but she adds,"does it always have to be love?" (I, 415) It is a question Madame de Genlis asks repeatedly through heroines like the Duchesse de C*** or the Duchesse de La Vallière whose stories prove emphatically that romantic love is neither the only, nor the best love with which to fill a life.

Continuing this critique of romantic literature, Madame d'Almane faults *La Princesse de Clèves*, because women readers learn from it that passion is out of their control, that it is "useless to oppose its progress, and that under its influence virtue becomes one more torment" (*Adèle et Théodore*, I, 415–416). Anything that so transforms virtue is a problem, according to Genlis, because virtue is intended to make life more beautiful, not more painful. Moreover, the princess has not been sincere in fighting her passion, for as Madame d'Almane says, "she who fights in good faith will never be vanquished." Instead, by looking for all the ways to keep passion alive, while trying not to lose her virtue, the princess so denatures passion and virtue that they destroy her.

Madame de Genlis's objection to women's consumption of the popular novel derives neither from a desire to assert her intellectual superiority, [15] nor from her own often affirmed (if not necessarily practiced) religious convictions.[16] Rather, I suggest that her critique of the novel derives from her belief that the primary function of all reading must be to construct the moral individual. Reading should contribute to the bank of knowledge that opens the way to a better self and hence a better society. An ethical reading, such as the one she proposes in *La Duchesse de La Vallière*, participates not only in instruction about the past, but will involve the reader in the process of constructing new knowledge about herself and conceiving new alternatives for her future. Thus Madame de Genlis will not refuse to write of women in love, but she will take them *beyond* romantic love, a journey that she herself had likewise made.

For her, honorable, ethical reading will solidify virtue, meaning strength and integrity. In a chapter devoted to reading in *Le Petit La Bruyère*, Genlis states that "any book that does not develop feelings that support virtue, or that does not offer useful ideas, is nothing but a frivolous work that does not merit rereading regardless of its style and ability to please" (24). Interestingly—and problematically—since in her view the objective of all writing and reading is to bring the reader to virtue, neither the ethics nor the esthetics of writing are served by the revelation of that which is ignoble. A respect for the *bienséances* or proprieties, together with a particular vision of morality, is, consequently, more important than absolute veracity. Hence, if Madame de Genlis is untruthful or incomplete in her memoirs about certain episodes in her life, it is because, in her view, that kind of untruth is as beneficial to the reader as to the writer. She believes that the reader should not read to discover the ugly; nor should the writer compromise her authority by displaying her shortcomings.[17] Of course, it could be objected that in equivocating or leaving in silence certain issues, even if in the interests of virtue, the writer risks undermining the very foundation of the virtue she promotes.

It is noteworthy that in both *De L'Influence des femmes sur la littérature française* and *Annales de la vertu*, she sought to reclaim a place in literary history for female writers whose names had been erased in the process of canon formation. In *De L'Influence*, her objective was to give women a positive history of themselves, starting with Radegonde, born in 519 and wife of the Merovigian king, Clotaire I, and progressing to Sophie Cottin (1770–1807), primarily remembered as the author of *Claire d'Albe* (1799). The purpose of this pantheon of female creators and protectresses of letters was to offer "an unbroken line, from the beginning of the monarchy to the present, of queens and princesses who encouraged and protected talents and who even successfully cultivated literature" (1–2). Likewise in the *Annales*, Madame de Genlis set forth a history of some fifty early women writers, accompanied by her judgment of their novels, poetry, opera librettos, and other writing.[18]

In publishing these pro-woman treatises and her own reading suggestions, she is part of a long line of women who, since Christine de Pisan in the fifteenth century, have taken pride in recalling the specificity of female production in literary history. Christine had also established reading advice to young noblewomen in both *Le Livre des Trois Vertus* and *Le Trésor de la Cité des dames*. And like Félicité, Christine believed that early reading exerts an especially strong influence on the impressionable young child, which is why the child's first books must be carefully chosen. For, she said, "the doctrine and teaching that the child receives will remain that to which s/he returns throughout life."[19] Christine had also questioned whether or not the romance genre could be recommended reading, especially when the primary purpose of reading is moral self-improvement. The perennial argument from the Middle Ages well into the nineteenth century would thus revolve around the issue of whether literature can teach by telling a story through a "bad" or fallen female protagonist or whether only a positive role model would be acceptable.[20]

Madame de Genlis solves the problem of whether the novel or romance is moral reading by choosing from the pages of history a protagonist whose story will be both a romance *and* a triumph over romance. What attracts her to the story of Louise de La Vallière's life is its potential for instruction and because in it Genlis finds a *thématique* that illustrates her own reading ideology, and a *problématique* that is central to the lives of women, bearing on affective relationships. Thus, the author is able both to assert the worthiness of her text, because it derives from the "heritage model of instruction," which is based on real history, and to satisfy her own ideological imperative that a reading be morally uplifting. If her historical romance initially puts into conflict the competing needs of *volupté* and virtue, in the end it shows that real happiness for a woman depends on the respect she has for her self. This is, according to the author, what makes her romance both ethical writing and reading.

REMAPPING THE ROMANCE: *LA DUCHESSE DE LA VALLIÈRE* (1804)

Published four years after Madame de Genlis's return from her *exil d'émigrée* to a Paris she hardly recognized, *La Duchesse de La Vallière* is a striking variation on the romance and a provocative example of the creative negotiation that can take place between fiction, history, and personal ideology. Situated in the seventeenth century, in the splendor of the court of Louis XIV, and arising both out of Genlis's nostalgia for a more noble France and her attraction to an unusual female heroine who will ultimately take charge of her destiny, the novel recounts the life of Louise de La Vallière, one of the royal mistresses, who distinguished herself in her early thirties by abjuring the court and becoming a nun.[21] Based on memoirs from le grand siècle, Genlis' novel teaches about the past, but it is also a fictionalized recreation of an intimate relationship whose power comes from overcoming (or remapping) romance in the very romance itself. To understand this, we need to examine several interlinked aspects of the author's own reading of both history and of the novel grounded in history, together with the reasons that motivate her choice of a female protagonist with whom she identified so closely.

History and the Novel

The remapping of the romance begins with history. In her "Réflexions préliminaires sur les femmes" in *De L'Influence des femmes*, Genlis observed that few women incorporate history in their writing because they lack the education to do so. Without proper instruction in history, women writers have had to confine themselves, instead, to "real acts," showing a kind of "sublime heroism" (x). This is exactly what Félicité de Genlis does in *La Vallière* with the story of one woman who achieves glory not by imposing herself on events of national import, but by removing her self from the national scene. But Genlis will claim to have written a *roman historique* rather than an historical romance, arguing that in preparation for writing the novel, she read historical texts and documents, particularly Dangeau's memoirs (which she criticizes Voltaire for not having consulted for his *Siècle de Louis XIV*). To be sure, she does demonstrate a considerable concern for historical veracity, frequently adding notes or indicating the source for a particular element recorded in historical fact. In her preface to the novel, she boasts that while she invented some things—specifically, interior dialogue and motivation for certain acts—she neither took recourse to the imagination nor left out anything of consequence. She asserts, "I believe I have invented nothing; instead, I have merely guessed it " (I, xxxviii).[22] This suggestion that she creates history through intuition and reflection implies the less demanding standard of history writing, as set forth by the seventeenth-century *honnête homme* and author of *L'Art poétique*, Nicolas Boileau, who required only that characters be socially and psychologically true.[23]

Nonetheless, Madame de Genlis will claim to write history more successfully than someone like Mademoiselle de Scudéry whose novels are historical only in their purely external choice of theme and costume. And she distinguishes herself from another predecessor, Madame de Lafayette, whom she nonetheless admires as France's foremost novelist of either sex. Still, she critiques *La Princesse de Clèves* not in terms of its literary qualities, but rather Lafayette's vision of woman's destiny. To begin with, Genlis observes that Madame de Lafayette used history merely as a source from which to pluck secondary characters and create atmosphere. Furthermore, history was a pretext to the love story of a *fictional* woman who by that fact carries diminished legitimacy for the reader since she comes from the imagination. (Madame de Genlis, on the other hand, chose a real person whose impact had been recorded in history by both Madame de Sévigné and the seventeenth century's most famous preacher, Bossuet, who had pronounced the sermon when Louise took her final vows.) Genlis faults Lafayette for a denouement that offers no positive resolution for the heroine. And finally, she believes that without the opportunity for the princess to be profoundly transformed, the novel cannot have a positive impact on the reader or lead to a useful and efferent reading.[24]

While Madame de Genlis is greatly influenced by Lafayette's artistic vision and the quality of her psychological analysis, she steadfastly claims that her own work represents an example of a more integrated use of history within fiction. Furthermore, by concentrating her resources on the essential nature of Louise's own story, she also "improves" on Lafayette by eliminating the extraneous (in her view) interpolated stories and a whole host of historical personages, named but rarely developed.[25] In sum, by focusing the reader's interest on the fateful story of one real woman, and providing an ending that inspires admiration and respect for an act that is emphatically not ambiguous, Genlis believes she has given women a powerful example of behavior to emulate.

If Genlis chose to write about the seventeenth century, it was because she believed that le grand siècle represented a grander, better time in French history. "How one loved, how one thought, how one wrote, how one told stories at that time! So much wit, reason, naturalness, grace. What worthy sentiments, what sensitivity, shorn of ostentatious window-dressing! That's what it meant to be French then!" (II, 131) Invoking the past, she reads into it a nobility of spirit, and applauded its potential to carry lessons for the present. It was the perfect period for her to write about, as was Louise the perfect heroine. In chronicling the life drama and inspiring example of her heroine, Genlis aimed to use the historical romance to reveal ethics as a living narrative, and to persuade readers that they, like Louise, could reshape their lives through the power of virtue reasserted.

Reading the Romance and Its Intertextualities

In remapping the romance, Madame de Genlis will demonstrate the key role of reading *within* the text, and make intertextual use of *La Princesse de Clèves*. In fact, she begins by making Madame de Lafayette's novel a real part of the seduction of Louise, describing how Madame de Lafayette's work in progress, making the circuit of the court, is a beautiful but dangerous tale. Hearing everyone speak of the novel (which historically would have required that it be in circulation more than fifteen years before it was published), Louise succumbs to its vision. "She believed that a grand passion is an inevitable and invincible sentiment," explains Madame de Genlis, and that "one never triumphs over true love" (I, 58). This intertextual literary reference merits our attention, first, because for the most part the author respects historical chronology. But, second, by motivating Louise's fall through a novel of romantic love, Madame de Genlis seems to confirm the old stereotype about the dangers of such novels.

Her intertextual use of *La Princesse de Clèves* continues with a number of direct borrowings, but in that many, if not all of them, are based on known facts of the affair between Louis XIV and Louise, it is difficult to decide when historical romance (*La Vallière*) is imitating fiction (*La Princesse*) and when actual history imitates the art of romantic fiction. The borrowed incidents or scenes include letters penned by someone other than the signator; key moments of indiscretion or chance that convince the male he is loved; flights from the court by a young woman dangerously in love; portraits given, stolen, or made; ingenious pretexts by the heroine to keep alive her passion; mistakes by the court as to who loves whom; impudent confessions that come back to haunt; scenes from a court at play in which the lover is wounded and the lady reveals her love in spite of herself and *bienséances*. To be sure, *La Princesse de Clèves* was a key text for large numbers of women writers whose works would subsequently be compared with it, and, as I have indicated, nearly all the "borrowings" were based on historical fact. Still, the interweaving of Lafayette's fiction into historical "fact" is a striking characteristic of Genlis' work.

To complicate the issue of intertextuality yet further, I believe that Genlis's novel constitutes a remarkable rereading of herself. In fact, I would argue that if Genlis is successful—and I believe she is—in her story of La Vallière and in reproducing the internal thought processes of the Duchesse, it is because she relates to Louise personally, having herself, though much less innocently and nobly, experienced a similar drama at court. It is this intratextuality, between romance and history, between an historical/fictional protagonist and her self, that makes possible a double-reading of the novel, revealing it as a site for exploring seventeenth-century woman and for rewriting the "long" eighteenth-century self.

With retrospective regret, Madame de Genlis refers in her memoirs to the "jour fatal" when she went to live at Palais Royal, a dangerous place, though she admits that at the time she was very excited about taking up residence at court. With the pain of hindsight, however, she recalls that if she came to Palais Royal with an "irreproachable reputation," it was there that she began "a new career." Writing with rare candor, she looks back, saying, "I saw the brilliance of the court . . . and let myself be carried away by vanity, curiosity, and over confidence." Furthermore, she revealingly continues, "In making decisions in one's life, it is pernicious to consider an act as isolated from other considerations and to reassure one's conscience by repeating that there is nothing reprehensible in it" (*Mémoires*, II, 164–166). This is precisely the mechanism that she treats in Louise de La Vallière's story, and the same one that she sees governing too many women's actions. For Louise knows what is right, yet she searches to justify and rationalize her passion, convincing herself that it would be cruel to leave the man who loves her and who, she tells herself, depends on her love of him. Only after a long struggle with her conscience, during which Genlis shows how easily hope is reborn when one is in love, will Louise be able to demonstrate strength and in a sublime act of sacrifice, make of renunciation not a failure of passion but a triumph of will.

Certainly what attracts Félicité de Genlis to Louise de La Vallière is, first, her profound respect for any woman able to overcome her own weaknesses, and second, and perhaps even more important, the many resemblances between their life stories. Both women came from noble families—though Louise's was more distinguished and not quite as impoverished—and they both were daughters who had good but emotionally reserved mothers. Genlis writes, for instance, that Louise was the only daughter of an "excellent" mother who was not, however, "what we would call today a passionate mother," a reference to the new ideal of motherhood sweeping society in the early 1800s and to her own experience with a good but distant mother.[26] Both Louise and Madame de Genlis shared an unusually strong attraction to the reassuring eternities of religion and communal life. Yet each would, notwithstanding her ideals, become involved in a problematic intimate relationship with a member of the royal family, and in the process of making the husband an adulterer, betray the wife with whom she lived in close proximity. Félicité, in fact, owed her position at the court of Palais Royal to the Duchesse de Chartres, whom she served as lady-in-waiting, while Louise (who was a *fille d'honneur* to Louis XIV's sister-in-law, Henriette d'Angleterre) professed to feeling genuine friendship for the repeatedly deceived Marie-Thérèse. Félicité de Genlis came to court as a twenty-six-year-old married woman and the mother of three children, whereas Louise arrived as a charmingly shy seventeen year-old virgin. Neither, however, was prepared for the kind of raw ambition and ferocious jealousies that raged in the hothouse of court intrigue, and each exhibited too much trust in others whom they expected to show their same generosity of spirit. Both women, furthermore, unwisely attached themselves to more experienced and cynical mentors—Mademoiselle de La Vallière relied on Mademoiselle d'Artigni, who had all the vices of the court, while Madame de Genlis followed her aunt, Madame de Montesson, a lady of few principles and much ambition. In the end, both Louise and Félicité would ultimately lose favor with her protector and be replaced by a new "confidante." Madame de Montespan took Louise's place in the king's heart, while Choderlos de Laclos replaced Madame de Genlis as the intimate political counselor of the Duc d'Orléans. Each left the court in order to free herself. In a final move of self-liberation and salvation, Louise abandoned the palace to find peace in a Carmelite convent, while Félicité requested permission to leave court and live at Belle-Chasse so that she could devote her time completely to the education of the royal children.

In the final analysis, both women had the courage to live their lives in uncommon ways. It is that recognition of similarity with Louise de La Vallière that inspires the admiration of Madame de Genlis and her identification with Louise. She, too, aspires to the image of moral balance and beauty achieved by Louise, for therein lies moral and intellectual strength. Consequently, she casts Louise's decision to leave court as a positive step, or a coming-to-self, since like other fictional heroines created by Genlis, Louise achieves through what would normally be considered a negative decision, the kind of personal empowerment that will bring her the truest happiness.[27] It is important to underscore that for a Genlisien heroine, withdrawal does not imply defeat, but rather reassessment and realignment of what is important in a life—similar to when Madame de Genlis had accepted both the Duc de Chartres's gift and challenge. Though the heroine's decision may mean leaving a man, whether a faithful or unfaithful lover, it is a choice she makes for, and which represents her right to, true happiness. Moreover, it is she, and not society, who defines what constitutes happiness, which does not necessarily have to be the heterosexual couple. Instead, like Félicité de Genlis herself, her heroines—most notably, Louise and the Duchesse de C***—propose alternative definitions of happiness and female worthiness. Their message is not that independence should be forced on every woman, but rather that self-autonomy is an alternative route that may offer greater possibilities of fulfillment than male–female relationships. In this respect, the image of a new kind of heroine—surprisingly located in the romance—challenges society and the traditional view of Genlis as ideologically conservative.

The Romance and Issues of Genre

It is common to associate women with the reading of the romance, whether the chivalric romance of the Middle Ages, the romantic text of sublime courage written by Balzac, the gothic romance, or the Harlequin romances in the United States. And it is just as common to censure the reading of romance, since it is equated with escape and irresponsibility. Because Madame de Genlis accepts such criticism as valid, she writes a different kind of romance in order to inspire a new kind of pleasure. Her romance, which will partake of many of the same structures and plot elements as the popular and formulaic genre, will aim to entertain and please, but also to edify. An investigation into the ways in which her tale relates to other forms of the romance will help to understand these similarities and differences.

To begin with, like the modern popular romance, defined by Janice Radway, her novel is first and foremost about a female protagonist, unlike the medieval romance that focuses primarily on the knight's desires and exploits.[28] Moreover, it chronicles not merely the events of a courtship, but what it *feels like* for a woman to be intensely sought after. As a consequence, Madame de Genlis's romance invites a special kind of emotional collaboration on the part of the female reader to follow the heroine through a long struggle, against herself and the pursuing male, taking her through a journey of amorous longing and regret before coming to recognize where true happiness lies. In respect to the development of the *liaison amoureuse*, Genlis adheres to the basic pattern of the romance, skillfully building the anticipation, excitement, and sexual tension, before bringing the affair to the point of physical consummation. She also gives emotional satisfaction to her female reader in several ways, particularly by showing that the male pursuer is passionately in love with the heroine, whom he courts with chivalrous but single-minded purposefulness. Like male lovers from courtly literature to the romantic novel of the nineteenth century, he will protest the innocence of his intentions and a noble lack of sexual intent, while aiming to get the heroine to bed. And he will, once she finally cedes to his passionate entreaties and her own desires, continue to cherish her for many years—if not the "forever" of the fairy tale.

In sharp contrast with the modern romance, though consistent with historical fact and the author's own emotional grammar, the consummated love in *La Duchesse de La Vallière* will not result in a conventional happy ending. Instead, Madame de Genlis underscores how passion leads Louise into a humiliating loss of self-respect, which she subsequently must correct by abjuring her love and repudiating the power of sex. Only then will she be able to reclaim her center, discovering in a recommitment to chastity a new kind of empowerment. Given this denouement, readers might even conclude—in demonstration of Janice Radway's suggestion that the romance gives the reader instruction about patriarchy and the role of women in society—that Genlis's novel could be interpreted as revealing the inability of patriarchal culture to satisfy its female members. Arguably, when Louise de La Vallière withdraws from court despite the king's efforts to retain her presence, when she chooses religion over passion, and the convent over the court, she is, in fact, not only choosing herself, but also rejecting both royal volition and the virility of the most powerful man of Europe. I would not make the claim that it was Madame de Genlis's intention to challenge the edifice of patriarchy in her historical romance, but I would point out that she is undeniably enamored of heroines who make this choice, possibly because it was one that she herself had made. In a creative turn on the romance, then, Madame de Genlis combines history, gender, and genre to serve her own purposes and write a story of virtue and woman triumphant.

Sexuality and Body in the Romance

One of the most intriguing aspects of the text of *La Duchesse de La Vallière* is that it is simultaneously a historical romance and the site of a discourse on female sexuality and behavior. In choosing to recount the story of this particular protagonist, Madame de Genlis presents a classical grammar of sexuality that underscores what she sees as the destructive power of sex "on the destiny of a sensitive woman born for virtue." Characterizing her protagonist by two highly prized features of womanhood—*volupté* and virtue—she shows her subjected to the ravages of sexual passion, torn between ecstatic joy and even stronger humiliation that accompanies a forbidden sexual relationship, hiding from friends, making convoluted alibis to herself, foreseeing the deep shame she will feel when she tries to explain her life and actions to her children. But if Louise is conventionally weak in that she caves in to the power of desire, she will also become unconventionally strong. For while *La Duchesse de La Vallière* is clearly a text of powerful female desire and sexuality, it is even more so a text of overcoming desire—recognizing it, living it, but going beyond it. Genlis believes, and Louise de La Vallière's story shows, that it is never too late to choose to live with honor, and that women can do so by redirecting their libidinal energies to the process of realizing individual potential. Significantly, Madame de Genlis's interest is not like our contemporary concern with legitimizing female desire. In fact, the real triumph of Louise's story, as perhaps of Félicité's, is in reassessing the body and rising above desire, opting instead for reason, which becomes the vital principle of life. In the end, it is not sex that counts, but soul. Nonetheless, much of Louise's story must be recounted through the body. When she comes to court, Louise is a virgin both sexually and emotionally, and it is this very chastity, coupled with her physical and moral beauty, that the king finds irresisible. By valorizing her heroine's physical and personal attributes at the same time that she presents her as "untouchable," Genlis shows how the woman's desirability is heightened and her chastity is eroticized.

This is signaled first through the physical beauty of the female protagonist, which Janice Radway has theorized is one of the givens of the romance, inextricably associated with sexuality, and a sign both to the hero and to the reader that the heroine is ready for and capable of carnal pleasures. Physical beauty enhances the value of the character, not only within the text and for the male suitor, but also for the reader, who reads beauty as the sign of a special worthiness with which to identify or to which to aspire. Genlis understands that while objectively the female reader may not be as beautiful as the heroine, and may even be insecure in her own attractiveness to men, she may nonetheless feel justified or validated in her femaleness through the heroine's ability to excite the passions of a man who represents exemplary virile power. By identifying with the feelings and struggles of the female protagonist, the woman reader experiences through her what it is like to feel passionately desired by a man. Having identified herself so intimately with the physical and psychological feelings of the heroine, the reader will quickly recognize and feel attuned to the painful pleasures and struggles of illicit love that will be channeled through the heroine's body.

A common topos of the romance heroine requires that she speak her passion through the body long before her voice utters a confession of love. Thus, in the presence of the king, Louise's body speaks a treacherous language of blushes, awkwardness, and shy nervousness that only conspire to intensify his ardor. Like the Princesse de Clèves, she tries to remove her body from moral danger. But wherever she goes, her suitor also goes, even when it is only the regal image of His Royal Highness, displayed in public squares and private quarters, that follows and penetrates her with his gaze. Her second retreat is to a convent, a refuge and metaphor of the virgin's body. It will not, however, be a barrier to an amorous king. Thundering up to the convent doors on a galloping horse, the king, as the secular representative of the divine, gains entrance despite the ineffective objections of the frightened nuns, and, in a wonderfully melodramatic scene, literally pulls his beloved away from the cross around which she has flung her body, in one last desperate attempt to save herself from her own raging desire.

By keeping her heroine so long unyielding, the author conserves the sympathy and identification of the reader, who finds in Louise's long resistance sufficient justification to refrain from impeaching her virtue. But, of course, in the end, the protagonist does cede. And in the instant of her physical consent, she loses, Genlis writes, "the happy right to respect herself" (I, 153). By acceding to her own sexual urges, Louise falls into the abyss, despite the worthiness of her lover and the genuineness of her love, and she will be "saved" only by a new battle with the body.

Genlis prepares this crisis by revealing that even from the beginning Louise's pleasure was mixed with anguish. Subsequently, as pervasive guilt begins to affect her mental and physical health, her body becomes a virtual text of shame and torment, first through a pregnancy that she attempts to hide and then through the hideous agonies that she experiences during labor and childbirth when she turns her guilty conscience against her physical body. Deeply ashamed to be giving birth to an illegitimate child, and believing that somehow the court may still be unaware of her pregnancy, Louise represses her cries of pain, which only redoubles them (I, 172). Heightening her dishonor, two days after giving birth, she is forced to rise from her bed to dress and properly receive the queen, who, incredibly, apparently did not know that Louise had just put into the world another illegitimate child fathered by the king. In these scenes, Louise's body acts both as the sign and as a form of punishment, at once signaling her guilt and taking its revenge on her.

As such incidents suggest, Madame de Genlis had a marked interest in the links between body and mind and in analyzing the behavior of women who in the grip of bizarre or romantic excess punish themselves through their bodies. In *De L'Influence*, for instance, she discusses how Louis's next mistress, Madame de Montespan (who would in turn be dismissed some years later when the king became attached to Madame de Maintenon), sought, once she was no longer at court, to atone for her crimes of the flesh, by macerating her own body, wearing against her skin iron-studded necklaces, bracelets, belts, and garters (218). It is a behavior that likely appealed to Madame de Genlis's inclination toward the *romanesque*.[29]

But in *La Vallière*, her interest is in showing that women can be specially gifted to demonstrate sublime heroism. Unlike Balzac, however, who also was attracted to showing this capability in his female characters, Madame de Genlis did not restrict women's sublimity to a single moment of superhuman physical strength. Instead, the sublimity that she enshrines is that which permits women to overcome the contingent, the physical, the body that betrays and destroys and ultimately perishes itself. The most noble and beautiful part of woman, then, is not her physical beauty, but her effort toward transcendence. It is this part of Louise's story, the triumph over the physical, that constitutes for Genlis the ethical center.

ENNOBLING CHASTITY

Objecting that men create heroines of extreme sensitivity but no energy, Madame de Genlis moves to correct that lack in her heroines. In *La Vallière* she writes the tortuous struggle of a female character who after arduous combat will mobilize all her powers of self-discipline to give up the man she still loves, not in an expression of self-punishment or hopeless resignation, but in positive triumph over the contingent, physical self. Louise does not abandon love, but rather, like the Duchesse de C***, will change the object of her adoration: from the secular king of France to the spiritual king in heaven. In the second half of her novel, Madame de Genlis undertakes to show a new struggle taking place in a character who though passionately in love had been recklessly indiscreet, and now increasingly is mortified by the reproaches, silent or voiced, of her friends as of her enemies, and especially those of her own conscience. Ineluctably, Louise comes to realize that to refind her equilibrium, she must regain her self-respect. Dispossessing herself of nearly all the material wealth that the king had lavished on her, and that she feared gave her the appearance of having been bought like a whore ("All this luxury that surrounds me, announcing my shame, strips me of what could excuse it. *Hélas*! I had given myself, but the entire universe may well believe that I had been bought" I, 187), she realizes that she must dispossess herself of a passion that is ruining her. She will not be a Nouvelle Héloïse, but a *newer* Nouvelle Héloïse, because if Julie's story was one of sublimation and unhappiness, despite her heroic embrace of self-denying virtue, leading to death, the Genlisien heroine in choosing a Carmelite convent will prove that chastity and the conventual life can be a form of self-empowerment and the beginning of a new and more satisfying life. In point of fact, the historical Louise spent exactly half of her long life in the convent, entering it at age thirty-four and remaining there until her death at sixty-eight.[30]

In a study about nuns who throughout history have viewed their apartness as an opportunity to transform themselves, Jo Ann Kay McNamara has described the cloistered life as a haven that privileges the development of the individual whose contemplative and creative energies are liberated, focused, and intensified by the "spiritual stillness and repetitive rhythms of communal religious life."[31] For such women, there is a kind of feminist empowerment in dedicated chastity. This is not power in the conventional sense, but rather power over the self and in freeing the self. It is a liberation from all that weighs down and denies the individual woman in society. In entering the convent and leaving behind the constraints of court life, Louise de La Vallière would at last be free. As she tells the young postulant nun, Emmeline, "this gate that is going to close on you permanently will separate you forever from seducers, ill-doers and the envious. . . . Never look upon these sacred walls as a prison! It is only here that we can enjoy real freedom . . . and follow . . . the principles we revere and the inspiration of our conscience" (II, 93). Where others might see unnecessary rigor in her choice, given the austerities of the Carmelite order, Louise envisions only happy consolations and advantages.

Physically vulnerable but strong in will, the ideal woman, illustrated in Louise, is capable not only of a kind of ennobling sacrifice that will lead to salvation, but of feminine courage and self-determination. According to Genlis, that sacrifice must be public, it must be brillant and genuinely motivated. The sublimity of the sacrifice depends on giving up what is truly wanted for something even more precious. By elaborating this kind of *sacrifice sublime*, Madame de Genlis succeeds in presenting a heroine who is both psychologically true and motivationally inspiring. Thus, when Louis proposes that Louise remain at court and triumph over her enemies by giving the court a virtuous example, she rejects that worthy project for one even worthier. By leaving the man she loves, she chooses not continuing hope for a temporal and fleeting passion, but a relationship with the Almighty that will have everlasting value.[32]

For Madame de Genlis, therein lies the distinction between Louise and the Princesse de Clèves, for the former does not choose self-exile and virtual obliteration, but the embrace of a new community. In place of the empty, or at least unwritten, horizon that opens before the princess, resulting in her premature death, Madame de Genlis's heroine has a future that will include good works, meditation, and personal development through faith. In Louise's story, reason triumphs over passion, and if reason cannot temper the violence of the sorrow caused by the sacrifice required, and if it leaves a "terrible emptiness in her heart, which had renounced what it loved," that emptiness will be filled by faith that will preserve, exalt, and raise the soul. Sister Louise de la Miséricorde, who pronounced her vows on June 4, 1675, would spend thirty years repairing her soul, and by the time her life came to an end, as Madame de Genlis writes in the final phrase of her book, her death would offer a sublime spectacle: "her soul, purified, separated without violence from the mortal body to receive the glorious prize due to her generous sacrifice and many good works."

However the reader feels about the choice made by Louise, it *is* an uplifting story of an exceptional woman who ultimately understands, as had Madame de Genlis, that the most worthy life is not made by affairs of the heart and body, but by the heart that listens to the mind. Turning the romance on its head, Madame de Genlis in fact restores the primacy of the head to the female protagonist of the romance.

CONCLUSION: TRANSFORMING THE READER

In terms of women's writing of the eighteenth and first third of the nineteenth century, Madame de Genlis should be an imposing figure. If there is little about her that is profound, there is much that is energetically engaging. And while she may have written too much and too repetitiously, there is nonetheless a significant part of her vast oeuvre that deserves to be better known, both for the texts themselves and the role she sought to play in the history of women's reading.

In Madame de Genlis's pragmatic philosophy, reading books—even the romance—is valuable because the primary purpose of reading is for self-improvement. Since she is persuaded that a true story can more successfully inspire the reader, she is attracted to history with a capital "H" in Louise de La Vallière, and to history with a small letter in the real-life Italian duchess on whom *L'Histoire intéressante de la Duchesse de C**** is based. For she sees in these women's lives the quality of dramatic, personal decision-making that moves them beyond romantic passion into role models of female self-realization. Thus, in retelling their stories, Madame de Genlis's novels serve the woman reader who is supposed to lay down her book exhilarated by an alternative vision of herself as a rational, ethical, and moral individual capable of making difficult choices. To read thusly represents a dynamic concept of the reading act and of the woman reader, both oriented toward the power of change.

Indeed, I would argue that the central principle of Genlisien philosophy concerns *transformation*. According to Madame de Genlis, each human life is centered on a principle of energy that can be dissipated or productively channeled. When human energy is properly understood and used, it permits us to gain control over the contingent and realize our own potential. But to arrive at that point, we must learn a high level of self-discipline. Thus a Genlisien text does not emphasize repression, but rather the redirection of our emotions into positive energy outlets. Whatever helps the individual to exercise discipline and live in accordance with higher aims is that which will, in her estimate, allow women to achieve self-esteem and transcendence. Hence, both religious principles (she is rarely more precise) and reading (and here she is very precise) should be our guides because they help us determine the ideals toward which we should strive and strengthen us to resist challenges to our integrity.

A determined pedagogue, Madame de Genlis believes that if the best and most heroic part of life is in transcending expectations—one's own and society's—women need good stories in which to find role models. This is precisely the use she makes of Louise de La Vallière, who, as a real person, carries the authority of history, and, as a figure in a fictional drama, sweeps the woman reader into a collaborative relationship. Always the pedagogue, Félicité de Genlis constructs her text with a view toward the relationship between teacher and student. As teacher/writer, she guides the reader toward greater wisdom, teaches moral principles, and helps the reader avoid or overcome the disaster of unleashed passions. In *La Vallière* she provides her female readership with a romantic story, while leading her beyond the romance, and helping her to understand that she alone bears responsibility for the quality of her life. For this reason Jenny Mander is correct to situate much of the Genlis corpus in the tradition of Fénélon, from Télémaque to Mentor, and to see in it a pedagogical relationship between reader and text that resembles a "cercle pédagogique."[33]

Even in a genre like the romance, Genlis's approach is to offer a prescriptive narrative. By revising key elements of the romance in the second half of *La Vallière*, she moves the woman reader from a conventional and superficial reading of the romance as a text of pleasure, into an esthetic and "efferent" reading. This is done through the enactment of a principle of a *lecture intimiste*, a kind of heart-to-heart reading, in which the author's narrative skills and literary talent together with the choice of an appropriate heroine lead the reader to feel she has a close and individual relationship with a flesh-and-blood woman.[34] When such a relationship is established, and when the heroine in the text makes the right moves—"beautiful" or ethical choices, according to the writer—the reader is likewise inspired. In the case of *La Vallière*, the very romance itself becomes the site of an ethical *lecture intimiste*.

Madame de Genlis's commitment to producing useful, engaged, transforming reading does not in itself make her a feminist, but the quality of the stories she tells may reveal her to be far more feminist than has generally been acknowledged.[35] For while she says that she would educate women differently from men, that the two sexes have separate social roles to play, and that women have no business in affairs of the state, she provides examples of autonomous decision-making both in her own life and in her fiction.[36] Moreover, she decries any notion of the double standard in behavioral expectations, morality, or financial affairs, saying, "The moral precepts traced by a divine hand do not form two different codes, one for men and the other for women."[37] In fact, she continues, "the Supreme Legislator prescribes the same virtues and the same duties to the two sexes. . . . He asks of us all the same courage of mind, because our souls are equally capable of noble, elevated, and generous feelings." Perhaps because of her own example, she is convinced that when a woman focuses on what truly is important and is indefatigable in her efforts to attain excellence, she will prevail, if not by the standards of her society, then by those of justice and morality, which should be more important to her. In the final analysis, the primary and constant message that Madame de Genlis communicates to women throughout her works is their capacity as rational, rather than emotional, beings. Indeed, for her, rationality and responsibility are women's new virtues.

Linda Timmermans has argued that eighteenth-century feminism is respectful of a social order in which women were excluded from various "fonctions viriles," but that while accepting the limits placed on them by social and church structures, women learned to make those difference turn to their advantage. Playing the card of sexual difference, she says, they accepted the distinctions drawn between the sexes, and exploited their apartness, introducing themselves into many domains from which they were a priori excluded, including writing and literary criticism. By assuming the limits imposed on them, they better achieved their ends, she states.[38] To a very large extent, this is true of Madame de Genlis, who does not lose energy fighting the battle of the sexes, and who outwardly respects bifurcated thinking about the roles of the sexes; at the same time she does exactly what she wants and becomes a *femme auteure*.

When Madame de Genlis accepted the Duc de Chartres's gift and abandoned cosmetics for new tools of expression, she was not disavowing her femininity, but rather the prejudice that a woman could not or should not practice a man's profession. She was eager to show that her greatest asset was her mind, with her body being merely its "charming vessel." Similarly in her texts, her favorite heroines were those like herself, who used their bodies as vehicles of encyclopedic or cultural rather than carnal knowledge, or like Louise, who disavowed carnal pleasures for spiritual ones. Her novel of the Duchesse de La Vallière was both a romantic story from the pages of French history, and a cautionary tale about the struggle between heart and ethics. But it was also, in her mind, a challenge to the woman reader to do as she had done. That is, just as Madame de Genlis had forsaken paints and pomades, just as she had forged her own identity as a writer, and transformed the romance genre, so did she charge the women who came to her text to become not only responsible readers, but readers virtuously transformed by their reading and productive in their own right.

FOUR

THE PROJECT OF DESIRE: CONSTRUCTING READER AND READINGS

ISABELLE DE CHARRIÈRE, 1740–1805

> You asked me, Momma . . . if I could bear not to marry. . . . I think that if I am always with you and busy and never have the time to go out and about, nor to read novels, I would neither desire nor regret anything.
>
> Cécile, *Lettres de Lausanne*

READING DESIRE

Disheartened by the inferior quality of gentleman suitors who pass through their salon, Cécile declares to her mother in *Lettres de Lausanne* that were the two of them to pursue life together, she might be able to accept being an unmarried woman, provided that she did not socialize with those having husbands, wives, lovers, or children, and—most pointedly—that she did not read novels. The reason for the last proviso is clear: the novel is the site of desire, which the youthful Cécile equates exclusively with romantic desire. As a highly sensitive reader who identifies with the typical heroine in fiction whose sole objective is to achieve a marriage of love, Cécile is fearful about the feelings of inadequacy and incompleteness that she would suffer after reading the story of someone else's happiness. For her, reading fictions of desire will be not an escape-through-the-romance, but an unhappy confrontation with her own lack of romantic fulfillment—a risky path leading to depression.

Cécile's apprehension about fictional texts of desire has affinities with reading reception theorists or phenomenologists, both modern and from the eighteenth century, who construe and construct reading as a desiring activity. Indeed, the leading metaphor for describing reading relations is one derived from a discourse on sexuality, in which desire is posited as the decisive energy emanating from and flowing into a text, and in which relations between reader and writer are proposed as a coupling.[1] For some critics such as Roland Barthes, all reading requires and produces a mobilization of desire; we do not read without projecting desire onto a text, and our interactions with a work are inseparable from the desire that we turn onto and receive from the pages of a book. I would suggest that Charrière understands the concept of desire as central to the reading experience, and she will make full use of Barthes's "hedonistic project" or project of desire within her love letter, but deals differently with desire in her fiction. There, if desire remains the mediator of exchange within all reading, not all desire in her writing will be sexual.

Focusing on what critic Emma Wilson calls the illusory space of the reading encounter between reader and writer,[2] I would like to show that while it is desire that shapes the project within Charrière's love letters and short fiction, that desire is exploited and estheticized differently in the two forms. For, curiously the love letters of the clandestine and chaste affair she has with the Baron d'Hermenches rely much more on Belle's reading of fictions of desire, and on the narrative conventions of desire in fiction, than the novellas she writes. In consequence, her love letters become art by imitating fiction, while her fiction withdraws into a kind of minimalist space of understatement. In this curious reversal of play between fiction and life, we see not only how Isabelle's writing both preforms and performs desire, but also how she endeavors to make reading not the risky and romantic business that Cécile thinks it is, but rather the pursuit of an artistic and cerebral experience. In estheticizing desire and deromanticizing it, Charrière shows how the art of fiction can become the means of reassessing reality and rethinking desire. Reading, then, will no longer be the dangerous seat of women's aspirations with regard to erotic desire, but rather the opportunity for esthetic and intellectual pleasure or, as Isabelle Vissière calls it, a kind of *volupté intellectuelle*.[3] In this sense, her fiction carries women's reading to another level, at far remove from the practical function it played for Madame de Genlis, while her love letters embrace all the *lieux communs* of epistolary romance that make reading so dangerous, according to eighteenth-century critics.

In the following pages, I will explore these ideas on the interplay of reading and desire, first by examining how Belle constructs her reader in a real-life epistolary romance in which expressions of sexual desire are at the pulse of her writing,whose purpose, nonetheless, is to keep her at remove from the loved one; and next by looking at issues of the psychological and artistic displacement of desire onto both the internal and external spaces and structures in which her fictional characters live. My ultimate objective is to suggest how the pleasures of reading desire in Charrière are more than anything else related to the mind and its potential to create tiny jewels of uncommon beauty.

READING THE LOVE LETTER

The very idea of the letter, real or in the epistolary novel, depends fundamentally on the notion and action of reading. Letters are written to be read by a reader, or, as with the love letter, by a lover/reader. But the reader can also be the writer/self, the one who has read enough to know that love is a story that tends to be told, structured and reenacted with recurring elements and leitmotifs. I do not mean to imply that the desire thus written is not real or that it is only a by-product of imagination, but rather to suggest that love letters in the hands of twenty-two-year-old Belle de Zuylen take up all the *lieux communs* of the dangerous liaison because she understands how desire, which is essential to exchange, is constructed.[4] Reading desire through the lens of fiction in her love letters, Belle will emphasize danger while exploiting the distance that separates her from her beloved; she will portray herself as exquisitely sensitive, yet fearful of giving in to the senses; she will evoke the contradictions of *vertu et volupté*, while fetishizing all the objects of epistolary commerce.[5]

Since the first order of business is to make sure that she has a reader, Belle seeks to captivate the dashing, forty-year-old (and married) Constant d'Hermenches whom she met at a ball in The Hague. Thus in an initial letter (9 September 1762) Belle sets the conditions for a thrilling erotic adventure: a correspondence between them would be "very pleasant," she says, but it must be clandestine; the risks are so great, she observes, that reason counsels her not to write, but her heart will not renounce the project; however, he must use a "safe address" to which to send his missives and within a specific time frame; for this correspondence is dangerous, but, she adds, the accompanying *frayeurs* (of both fear and pleasure, we may assume) are worth it if he will promise sincerity.

For the reader (both d'Hermenches and us), Belle has clearly just demonstrated that despite her inexperience she knows how to portray and inspire desire. Challenging a man to prove his mettle is not only a flirtatious tactic, but also a stimulant within the narrative scheme of the epistolary form: if an initial letter is to become a correspondence, it depends on her reader accepting the gauntlet and responding to the call. Her letter serves as a springboard to a man who can scarcely resist when she tells him in the same letter that he is like "those rare and precious things one has the folly to want to acquire and to conserve at any cost, even though one can make no use of them." Interestingly, through this choice of words, she reverses the tradition and objectifies the *male*, revealing that she will assume the dominant role in their relationship—she will write it, he will read it—while likewise evoking the idea that like a collector and conservator of desire, she will make an art of their affair.

During the most intense period of their love affair-through-letter, 1762–1764, we see how much the affair is presented and conducted through the prism of fiction, and how her discourse of desire is alternately rhetorical, erotic, spontaneous, and calculated. She is a young woman who loves literature, discovering self-expression at the same time as the world of the senses, struggling with the contradictions of heart and reason, desire and duty, virtue and *volupté*. Belle is in love with words, with expression, with the pleasure that comes from circling, capturing, or creating a thought, wrapping words and sounds and rhythms around ideas or feelings, teasing out or inventing original or tender insights.[6] To write one's impulses is to tame them provisionally, but also to make them into small works of art, which means that by giving them sensuous shape in language, the writer/reader can subsequently, time and time again, return to them, caressing them with mind and lips. The delicious utterance of words and images in the mind, as in vocalization, is an important part of the pleasure of textually creating both self and desire in the letter. Thus, she writes to be read by another, but also to read/create herself.

Liberated by distance, Belle speaks with youthful passion and uses a language of appealing frankness, which certainly must have engaged and even enthralled the somewhat jaded d'Hermenches. With deliberate suggestiveness, she evokes her own sensual nature, telling him in a 25 July 1764 letter that if she were free to decide her own fate, it would be difficult to remain chaste, for she says, "My senses are like my heart and mind, avid for pleasure, and susceptible to the most lively and delicate impressions." Reading her self as exquisitely responsive to all sensory phenomena, she implies an image of herself quivering under his touch. Another time she speaks of how her imagination searches for him and how her desires caress him before she falls asleep, concluding, "believe me, a man and woman of feeling can never trust themselves to be just friends" (25–27 December 1764). Often she writes to him just before retiring, which leaves her, she confesses guilefully, in a state of arousal. "Goodnight," she writes in an entry from 13–18 September 1764, "I am going to bed in a state of agitation, which writing to you gives me." She admits to sleeping with a pair of his gloves, to kissing his letters, that if she had neither father nor mother, she would be like the celebrated *amante*, Ninon de Lenclos (1620–1705), "but more delicate and constant" (25 July 1764). Underscoring the inevitability of her passion, she tells him, "if I continue to think about you always, I will one day be your mistress, unless we live at opposite ends of the world or you no longer care for me at all" (13–18 September 1764). She can, of course, allow herself to be so sexually frank and aggressive, precisely because there is scant chance that her desire, real or artistic, will be acted on. But it is also exciting to propose her capacity for the sensual and the forbidden.

Understanding the dramatic potential of evoking danger and either genuinely disturbed by her own scripting of desire, or enamored of this convention of the romance, Belle counsels d'Hermenches to burn her letters. "In the name of God, Sir," she says in an early communication, "burn my letters and do not ask me for others" (15 or 22 September 1762) and, at a later point, she inquires with anxiety, "what are you doing with my letters? Are you burning them? . . . They should perish in flames" (25–27 December 1764). Of course this does not happen, since love letters are rarely destroyed when the passion is still strong, and as Belle herself admits, "I shall not destroy your letter; I too much like its scintillating ardor" (2 March 1765). But the repeated exhortation to burn her letters in this *correspondance de feu*, as she terms it, serves the purpose of stoking the imagination of her reader while increasing both the value of the letter and its erotic intensity.

As in the best epistolary novels, it is the letters themselves, in fact, that both structure and give texture to what happens. Like the female protagonist of fiction, Belle focuses nearly the entire early narrative drama between them on the letter itself, as though it and not their mutual erotic attraction were the affair. As Ruth Perry has shown, such insistence on the production, significance, and eventual disposition of the letter is one of the plot devices of the epistolary novel, in which the problems of a clandestine correspondence and the letters themselves become the focus of the novel instead of merely the frame of the story.[7] Belle recognizes this, even saying at one point that all their exchanges "up to now have spoken only of the letters themselves" (9–10 October 1762).

Likewise, and in another bow to literature, the separation of the two lovers not only explains why they write, but becomes the necessary condition to their affair. Indeed, consistent with fictional epistolary romance, their relationship depends and thrives on physical separation. In all the years they corresponded, they saw each another in person no more than a handful of times, and then in public gatherings, not only because such meetings were difficult to arrange, but because, one suspects, it suited Belle's literary needs to have a relationship predicated on writing. Written words let her maintain the erotic equivocation: to be "at once virtuous and voluptuous."[8] Hence on one occasion she begs d'Hermenches not to respond to all that is "licentious" in her letter, for she admits to being "ashamed" by what she has written. But by opting to send her missive, after confessing that she was unable to tear it up, she makes sure that he receives her revelations. Simultaneously underscoring the intimate nature of her disclosures and promising that it will be, she hopes, the last time she dares to show herself as she is, she throws into high relief her eagerness to have sensual contact with the world and with a reading lover.[9]

There are, of course, real perils in committing words to paper, as tragic heroines of the epistolary repeatedly discovered. Indeed, it would become almost an ironic convention of the epistolary romance to have the resisting woman acknowledge the danger of writing, even to her would-be seducer.[10] But by continuing to write, despite an awareness of its dangers, the real woman, like the fictional one, demonstrates to her reader her powerlessness over passion—which is a powerful way of keeping the reader's desire aflame. Hence, Belle writes, "The confident air of virtue that I take in speaking of our liaison and our correspondence is hypocritical; in point of fact, all is not so innocent" (25–27 December 1764). Perhaps she is recalling her disingenuousness in granting him permission to write (she *herself* had initiated the correspondence!) when, sounding like the artless ingenue, she had asked: "After all, why go against my will and refuse you an innocent thing that you have seemed to desire so ardently and that by that very fact I have pleasure in granting you?" She had even added, "You swore to me that I ran no risk, that there would be no more danger in speaking to you or in writing than in thinking; and I so want to believe that" (23–24 July 1764). Neither Cécile de Volanges nor Madame de Tourvel could have revealed themselves more. As Belle must know, protestations of this kind in fiction are used to indicate a breach in the woman's armor of self-awareness. The fictional heroine's evocation of the dangers of epistolary discourse is always a part of the scheme, signaling her ambiguous willingness to be further drawn into the snare. Nonetheless, she will not be any less inclined to plead with her lover to prevent her from doing exactly what both he and she would like to happen. But when, like the heroine of dangerous liaisons in fictions, Belle implores her correspondent, saying, "I beg of you, d'Hermenches . . . keep me from doing anything that might cause me shame" (3–4 August 1764), we have to ask: Is she playing the game, or playing at playing the game? In making her own self-assessment and suggesting that she knows that their correspondence is not, after all, so innocent, Belle points to the power of a reader who possesses "dangerous secrets" that could destroy her. "Do you not tremble at the consequences of this correspondence?" she asks with breathless anticipation, underscoring yet again the affinity of danger and passion, and her pleasure in suggesting that they are living a novel.[11]

Whether her relationship with d'Hermenches has truly placed her on a perilous path, Belle is infatuated by the suggestion that it has. Her desire for evoking danger, just like her desire for d'Hermenches, has both a real and literary function.[12] She knows that she is being extraordinarily assertive, that she is enflaming d'Hermenches, and that such behavior is dangerous, but she cannot, *will* not stop. As the written word fills the void of absence, the act of writing becomes for Belle more than a substitute for presence, more than a remedy to absence; it is an addictive necessity. Frequently there are "bunchings" of letters, sent as a package and covering the space of several days. While such *lettres-fleuves*, as the Vissière editors call them, may result from the inability to find a reliable source to deliver them, they may also be the consequence of a compulsion that is at once literary and sexual.[13]

For his part as reader, d'Hermenches is charmed and enamored. He finds her exquisitely sensitive, but also seems to understand that it is not the realness of his caresses that she craves and needs, but the praises of his love (20 October 1764). Perceptively, he suggests that Belle's fire goes into her writing: "your imagination is everything," he tells her, "that's what carries the fire . . . you will see that when we meet." The test will occur, he says, if he kisses her hand in a stolen moment or holds her closely while dancing and she feels nothing. For, he tells her, "the most beautiful [love] letter typically produces the coolest meeting, just as the most tender rendezvous is followed by the briefest of notes" (13 November 1764). He is responding to her apprehension about a rare meeting that is to take place between them. She is nervous about being with him, quite likely because she fears disappointing him. "Do you know what I fear," she asks d'Hermenches, and then provocatively suggests that her anxiety about seeing him is based on a fear of wantonly giving in to passion. "Be careful not to enflame my senses," she warns, "you know me so well, and there would be little glory in exciting a guilty emotion" (8–9 November 1764). Yet at the same time, she underscores distrust of herself in the company of an attractive man with the reputation of a libertine and who possesses "all the secrets of my heart." She could scarcely be more laudatory to male ego or more literary, though events will show that it is d'Hermenches who made the more accurate prediction. Following their meeting, which is a disappointment precisely because nothing happens, she laments "I don't know how to speak to you in the way I know how to write you" (4 or 5 December 1764).

In the cross section of reading, writing, and sexuality that is this affair, the older and more experienced d'Hermenches may have understood that Belle's letters, despite their discourse of desire and intent to inflame through word and image, actually are a kind of barrier for Belle, who is as much an apprentice in the erotic endeavor as in the literary one. Letters keep Belle chaste if not innocent and become for her a protosexual substitute for a real lover. Cast in the role as the reluctantly chaste participant–spectator, d'Hermenches becomes the essential but distant lover/reader of Belle's desire. As the reader, he is always "other," but the necessary other; he is the reader she wants and needs. We are accustomed to the idea of the female reader being constructed by others, but here, in a turnabout of the convention, it is the woman who creates the male lover/reader. In her letters, she flirts, compels, and even manipulates him, seeking to seduce, to tease, to involve him in erotic but safe play. And he complies with her wishes: he reads her as she wishes to be read.

Belle, the reader of French, the language of love, uses her readings of the epistolary to shape both her desires and her writing of desire. In privileging bodily emotion and sensation, her letters, which possess a vibrant carnality, are in large measure performances in which she writes and views herself as would a spectator/reader. Indeed, one might say that her very notion of reading relations in the letter is hierarchical and only outwardly collaborative between the real reader and writer. This is so, because the reader she may be most interested in pleasing is the artist who resides within herself. Belle addresses her letters to a man/lover very much present in her mind, but he is not the only reason that these letters exist. Similar to Madame de Graffigny's heroine, Zilia of the *Lettres péruviennes*, Belle is equally the *narratrice* and *lectrice* of her letters. She writes to find herself, but perhaps even more so to create a reading of the desiring self. For this reason the role of lover and reader in her letters shifts back and forth between man and woman, writer and consumer, text and self.

READING MADAME DE CHARRIÈRE'S FICTIONS OF DESIRE

LOCATING DESIRE

To this point, I have looked at the love letters of a correspondence and examined how Belle de Zuylen exploited the verbal and affective structures and conventions of epistolary fiction as she conducted a love affair in writing and in the process turned it into a work of art. As we saw, the love letter for Belle was both an expression and a representation made for her actual reader, d'Hermenches, whose participation she needed in the ongoing creation of her self as artist–lover. In that the desire that informs her letters is at once authentic and created, and in ways that resist a clear-cut distinction between the two, I suggested that Belle reads to write herself, and writes to read herself.

The desire that had guided her pen in the love letter will undergo change in her epistolary fictions. For while it is still desire that is the operative principle of these texts, now it is problematized and estheticized differently. Where desire in the love letter had been a jewel of yearning, in her fiction, it is the rough stone, the prickly irritant, the frequent cause of despair. It is desire that structures—or sometimes more correctly destructures—the plot, and speaks through objects, shaping time and chronology. It is desire for the other, for the self, for a home, for a place to belong. Desire, unconscious and unspecified; desire awkward and diffused; desire unreturned and overturned; desire lucid and illogical, playful and playing safe, pleasure-giving and pleasure-stealing; desire searching, reaching, disappointed, forced back on itself or liberated into nothingness, lost in space. But always desire, just as it is always desire that propels the reading of a text.

If her love letters showed a heightened sense of drama, contrast, and light, her fictions, those minimalist glimpses of isolated detail, reveal in their discontinuities, dissolves, and indeterminacies, a slow-moving, almost monochromatic quality. This is not the ecstasy of desire, but its opposite. For this desire, never fully dominated or equally reciprocated, is displaced onto the spaces of her fictions and revealed in such spatial *structures d'ensemble* as location (centers, thresholds, and borders); relative position (inside, outside, and the marginal); direction (horizontal, vertical and diagonal); convergency and divergence; and the opened and closed (rooms, doors, circles). Hence she develops her stories of desire through the real and metaphoric spaces of the home (*Mistress Henley*), the gameboard ("Cécile"), the theater of illusion and allusiveness ("Caliste"), and various motifs of displacement in the trips, shortcuts, detours, and routes, conjoined with the contingent (*Lettres Neuchâteloises*).

Spatial Desires

Much of the female adventure played out in the slight intrigues of Isabelle de Charrière's graceful fiction involves, on the one hand, a questioning of woman's space and its liminality, and, on the other, a quest by women for space. Her spaces are both outer (physical) and internal (psychological), domestic and public, tangible as in geography, or intangible but no less real as in class, culture, role, tradition, history. Space may be conceived as positive or negative, visual and structured, or invisible and referenced only by its absence. Space may be either explicit or implicit, having actual or implied frames, limits, margins, and borders, or it may exist in the spacelessness of the nonfinito; it may be opaque or transparent, penetrable or impenetrable. But however it is figured, space is used in Charrière to narrate desire, both erotic and non-erotic, at the same time that it reveals women's social condition or experience, and encodes her vulnerability.[14]

The architecture of space in her fiction testifies to her belief that women exist on the borders in eighteenth-century society, whether they reside in England, France, Germany, Holland, or Switzerland—all countries where she had lived and that figure in her fictions. To be sure, the geographic spaces or locales that Madame de Charrière chooses for her stories—Hollowpark in England, or Neuchâtel or Lausanne, or a Westphalian village—provide only limited local color, largely through the foreignness of naming. The real center of her attention is on the individual women who live as displaced persons or in dislocation in these spaces against a variety of national backdrops. They are uprooted or unrooted—either émigrées or foreigners *en passage*, orphaned or living far from their families, perhaps even "unclassifiable," like Caliste, who belongs to no class or level of society.

Those who are attracted to mythobiographical interpretations may be inclined to see in Isabelle de Charrière's spatial choices her own particular sense of disconnectedness. She was, after all, a Dutch woman married to a Swiss, living in his country, and writing in French, her adopted language since her childhood days with a French nanny. Moreover, the quality of her life, as recounted both in her voluminous personal correspondence and by her biographers, underscores her sense of separateness or aloneness, neither of which should be considered as synonymous with loneliness.[15] What Charrière experiences in her own life is something akin to existential solitude, as proposed by one biographer when he describes her as "like one moving in an empty room."[16] Once at age twenty-two, she had characterized herself to Constant d'Hermenches as "une créature déplacée," by which she seemed to imply she was not "right in her skin." She had, she indicated to him, often wished to be male, for only then—and one might surmise, only with the greater freedom men were granted to determine their space—could she truly exploit her talents and intelligence.[17] Though none of her young heroines, most of whom were also in their twenties, expressed this same desire, we readers might link the microstructure of the genderized spaces of the epistolary fictions in which the female protagonists moved with the macrostructure of sexual politics in eighteenth-century society. For what we see repeatedly is that space is read by Charrière as the artistic measure by which to reveal the thwarting of female desires. Spaces are closed down or opened up along fault lines or crevices or cracks, in order to represent ways in which women's lives are tenuous.

LETTRES DE MISTRESS HENLEY

> Women, realize the source of your pleasures and the foundation of your glory! You are Mothers and Mistresses of the family . . . that is your Empire. Your principal honor is to maintain proper order and harmony: it is in your home that you must establish happiness.
>
> —*Manuel de la toilette & de la mode*, 1776

> It has passed into proverb that it is particularly the woman who makes the happiness or unhappiness of the home.
>
> *Annales de l'Education du sexe, ou Journal des demoiselles*, 1790

Traditionally, women's space is in the home, that place that conjures up images of peacefulness, coherence, fulfillment, and safety. Indeed, it would be difficult to overestimate the power and appeal of the notion of "home" for women in the eighteenth century and its bearing on their ideas of femininity and identity, since women, themselves—even those who might be considered feminists—emphasized its importance, reiterating constantly that it was the single domain in which their ministrations determined the quality of life. For a woman writer to expose the fallacy of this myth in her novella, for her to paint the illusion of woman's domestic power through the portrayal of the empty, strange, negative spaces that she occupies in her own home, is a bold challenge to both gender and cultural ideology. But that is precisely what Madame de Charrière does in *Mistress Henley*, which tells the tale of loss and deprivation and of physical and psychological alienation, conjoining the motifs of speaking, silence, and space, as she writes the sadness of woman's destiny within the home.[18]

Written as a ripost to Samuel Constant's short story, *Le Mari sentimental*, in which the husband is driven to despair and ultimately suicide by his carping wife, *Mistress Henley* begins with an account of the wife's reading of the Constant story and how as reader she links the text of imagination to the realities of her own life (Letter 1).[19] Certain that Constant's text can be made to speak in her place to a husband who never seems to hear, she reads him the story. But those elements that impressed her heart and represented a clear analogy with her pain, create in her husband, the male reader, a quite different effect. He shows only a kind of tolerant wistfulness, and, she reports, "I saw him first smile, then sigh." Hence, the two Henleys make different readings of the same text, just as they do of nearly everything subsequent that occurs in their own lives.

The disjunctiveness that exists between their readings, as between their desires, will be transmuted, in Mistress Henley's account, onto the spaces of the home in which she is an awkward interloper. For she had come as a young bride, led by her widowed husband to his home, already complete with servants, furnishings, traditions, and even a little daughter. In this domestic scene, Mistress Henley is an outsider, a fact of which she is daily reminded not only by the servants, who object to the changes she wants to bring, but by the very portrait of Monsieur Henley's first wife, which hangs over her bed, if not in outright disapproval, at least as solemn witness to the second wife's often gauche and futile attempts both to retain her own identity and impress some portion of it on her new surroundings.

The ineffectiveness and weightlessness of Mistress Henley are in complementary relationship to her lack of roots and family connection, for she is an orphan, whose only relative is an aunt living in London. Anxious to feel grounded, overeager to please and to be useful as the wife, mother, and mistress of the manor, she is repeatedly ineffective, a body who is no*body* in her husband's home. She has no rank, despite *his* name, no autonomous identity, no effective space of her own; her words, like her actions, are weightless, and physically and psychologically, she always ends up "giving way," moving aside, retreating back into herself or to her room where she will write another letter. This room, however, is not the positively encoded "room of her own," but merely the provisional refuge, where she pens letters to her friend that tell of her pain and feelings of emptiness, and of a sickness that seems to be more than anything else—in a cruel irony since she is writing from within the very walls of her own home—a kind of homesickness, a theme revisited in *Lettres de Lausanne* through the female protagonists, Cécile and Caliste.

As her dissolving identity grows into self-effacement, Mistress Henley shows how superfluous and transparent she feels. For her relationship to the space in which she lives has become wholly tenuous, and ultimately she yields not only to every other person but to every *thing*, including inanimate objects. Initially desirous of cutting down a tilbury bush that blocked the view of the countryside from her window, she cedes even this desire because she is unable to arrogate to herself the right to impose her will on either the social or physical landscape in which she lives; clearly, her consent to an *obstructed* view signals a significant psychological retreat. Examining close up the leaves of a tree, the purposeful industry of insects, Mistress Henley is in awe before "this busy, animated universe." The vastness of the natural world fascinates and overwhelms her, because in its design and vigor it is so unlike her world in which she neither belongs nor has a purpose.

In despair because of the emotional distance that keeps her a stranger in her husband's heart as in his house, she cries out at one point, "If you were jealous, I would see you at least feel something, and I would be flattered; I would believe that I mattered to you; I would feel that you feared to lose me." And she even pleads that "the injustices of a jealous man, the excesses of a tyrant would be less upsetting that the apathy and aridness of a sage" (Letter 4, 284). But her complaints are to no avail; her tears, like her kisses, possess for Mr. Henley only a kind of transitory extravagance, like the bubbles of a bath, amounting to nothing more than vaporous trifles that leave no trace. Her existence is so diminished that it becomes like "the residue of an echo," according to one particularly apt description.[20]

Sorrowfully aware of her transparency for her husband, deeply wounded to be "so outside his feelings, so excluded from his thoughts, so useless, so isolated," she writes one last letter to her female friend and correspondent, evoking her sense of futility. Choosing to reason by exclusionary apposition, she writes, "My situation is truly sad, or I am a person without reason or virtues," to which she adds the pendant, "Everything I feel is either absurd or Mr. Henley is without feeling and hard." Having inarguably demonstrated the sadness of her situation and given proofs of her own mental and moral resolve, she has also ipso facto proven that Mr. Henley is insensitive and hardhearted, but she studiously refuses to articulate that conclusion, leaving it instead to her reader—both the internal correspondent and the external public readership—to make a proper reading. All she says is that unlike the weak and harassed husband in "Le Mari sentimental," she will not make the proactive choice of suicide, for she is carrying a child, a sacred trust; but, on the other hand, if all her desires for fulfillment as an individual, a wife, a stepmother, and mother-to-be continue to be blocked, she may with the passage of time simply and inevitably cease to exist. Trivialized into nothingness, she proposes to actualize in terms of space what she suffers psychologically.

Is the tragic story of this novella an indictment of eighteenth-century marriage or simply the story of one ill-arranged marriage despite everyone's best intentions? Is the subtext that of woman's repression or of woman's resistance to her repression, as argued by those who suggest that it is through her writing that she resists the codes and forces that shackle her? (One might, however, object that if it is the latter, she is left too hopelessly forlorn at the end.) Is Mistress Henley the psychologically abused wife or the willing victim? For is there not evidence that Mistress Henley, like Emma Bovary, is victimized not only by others, but by her own romantic notions about life? It is not easy to reach a single, absolute conclusion because, in typical fashion, Isabelle de Charrière provides fodder for both sides of an issue. It is the reader who must decide. In her own contemporary society, reader reception broke neatly along gender lines, as Madame de Charrière is quoted as recalling. Her short story, she said, caused a split in Genevese society. "All the husbands were for Mr. Henley; many women were for Madame. . . . Never had fictional personages had so much the air of having existed, and I was asked for explanations."[21] In other words, her story received precisely the same sexualized reading as had Samuel Constant's, dependent on the gender of the reader. In that respect, we arrive back at the beginning, with Mistress Henley pointing out how differently she and her husband had read the Constant story. I am therefore tempted to propose that while the story is certainly "about" more than reading—more than a metacommentary—the very idea of reading is, nonetheless, a very potent figure.

In mapping the desire of Mistress Henley to be, but showing her at every intersection as becoming less and less, Charrière inevitably arrives at the point at which her character's voice must trail off in the silence of empty space at the end of the page. We do not know whether Mistress Henley triumphs over reason or unreasonableness, for she, like other heroines in Charrière, is left—with her desires intact, but unanswered—in limbo. For an author such as Isabelle de Charrière, who wished to open and not resolve, being in limbo—suspended, as in *Mistress Henley*, in a sort of spacelessness, between two worlds or two mind-sets—was perhaps, after all, a fitting spatial marker for woman's unrequited desire to be and to be understood.

LES LETTRES NEUCHÂTELOISES

If the female condition in *Mistress Henley* is estheticized as transparency or a floating weightlessness, in the *Lettres neuchâteloises*, it will be mediated in art through the narrative or descriptive device of the slippery path, the icy road, leading to the accident, that is, the contingent event: the mishap or fall, both physical and moral. For this novel, reminiscent of those of Jane Austen in which very little seems to happen, Madame de Charrière chooses a canvas of small dimensions, the town of Neuchâtel, and with great delicacy spins a gossamer web of intersecting relationships, as three young people make the perilous journey from adolescence to maturity. Narrative space is structured by a series of chance encounters or accidents, meetings at community musical performances, and social gatherings and balls, all of which are recounted in letters by the three main characters: Marianne de la Prise, the daughter of a minor aristocrat whose fortune is nearly exhausted; Henri Meyer, a young German in Neuchâtel doing an apprenticeship; and Julianne C., the pretty seamstress who left her village to ply a trade in town. In this simple triangle and with a handful of events barely etched on the surface of the ice, Madame de Charrière evokes the many ways of precariousness. The heroine, Mademoiselle de la Prise, is losing her anchored position in society because of dwindling family resources, Henri has only a marginal foothold because he is a foreigner, and Julianne, despite her pretty face, is doomed to tumble because of her low birth. Fortune, nationality, and class, all accidents of birth in the eighteenth century, are rungs of vulnerability on the spatial ladder of advantage and disadvantage.

To intensify the notion of the arbitrary and accidental, the author sets the scene in a winterscape of icy paths and slippery routes. Using two interactive structuring motifs—accidents and money—she links them from the very first scene. One day soon after his arrival in Neuchâtel, Henri comes to the rescue of the servant girl, Julianne, who, her arms full of packages, slips in the muddy street, soiling the garment she was delivering to the house of Mademoiselle de la Prise. Henri insists on accompanying Julianne to help explain to her employers what had happened, and, on taking his leave, in a gesture of sympathy, gives her an *écu* for her misfortune. With this initial incident, both the contingent and the concrete are activated and inflected with ambiguous and unambiguous erotic content.

Later in the story, in another chance encounter with Julianne and in a further show of expansive but inappropriate generosity, Henri makes her a gift of a gold cross she is admiring in a store window. This token is treated by her mistresses as the sign that she is a "loose" woman, and has become involved in the commerce of trinkets in exchange for sex. Unable to persuade them differently and too proud to be called guilty when she believes herself innocent, Julianne leaves their employ, certain that with pluck and hard work she can succeed by herself. However, in a cruel turn of fate brought about by the false accusation, she will now fulfill her former employers' expectations. Rather too boldly for a young woman on her own, she seeks out Henri, to enlist his help in getting firewood for her new lodgings. And there in her room, rather to the surprise of both (if not to the reader), they end up engaging in sexual relations, on this and one other occasion. Embarrassed, though for different reasons, neither refers directly to this incident in their letters, despite Henri's promise of complete openness to his boyhood friend and correspondent. When Julianne writes to her aunt, some time after the event, she does so referring only allusively to possible repercussions from having met Henri. "His name is Mr. Meyer," she informs her aunt, "I know his name now; but what good does it do to know it?" adding portentously, "I haven't seen him for five weeks; I wish I'd never met him (Letter 17)—a clear invitation for her aunt to read between the lines.[22]

In explanation for the five-week silence, we learn that, in the meantime, Henri has met and been wholly taken with Mademoiselle de la Prise, who, he vows, will become his "pretty guardian angel," preserving him, presumably, from further "accidents." It is on his subsequent relations with Marianne de la Prise, their awakening awareness of one another, and desire that the story turns. Through a fortuity of quite another character, more appropriate to their class standing as opposed to Julianne's, Henri and Marianne will meet not on the muddy street in a chance encounter, but on the platform of a concert hall where both have been invited to participate in a musical ensemble. Nonetheless and despite the properness of the cultural milieu, Madame de Charrière will contrive to write the collision of eros and propriety in their first face-to-face meeting. In this scene, she evokes sexual emotion (attraction, embarrassment, and agitation) through the precipitant contraction of sexual and spatial proprieties by means of a mediating object that draws Marianne and Henri together in an intimacy that leaves both shaken. This object is none other than the aforementioned garment that Julianne had been delivering. In writing to his friend, Henri evokes the meeting in these outwardly neutral terms, "I saw a young woman, rather tall, elegant, and well dressed, mount to the stage. . . . I recognized the dress she was wearing as the same one I had, as delicately as possible, picked up from a muddy street" (Letter 4). The juxtaposition of a piece of feminine apparel that he had rescued with the muddy street suggests nothing so much as woman, sex, and moral lapse. For her part, Marianne gives a reading of the scene to her friend, Eugénie de Ville, communicating both its emotional and erotic latency: "In passing by him to go to sing, I looked closely at him; he too looked at me: I saw that he recognized my *dress*. As for me, I recognized him as the man who had *gathered it up*; and we were so lost in contemplation of one another that I let my music sheets *fall* and he *forgot* his violin. He *blushed*, I *blushed*, too, but I really don't know about what" (my italics, Letter 15) No words are exchanged, only looks, but both are aware that an illegitimate intimacy already exists between them.

What they do not say but what the reader knows is that in any system of the female, the dress is a constructed sign that represents and presents female sexuality as it simultaneously dresses and undresses the parts of the body. Here the dress that Marianne is now wearing against her skin, and with which Henri had previous physical contact, becomes a mediator of desire, suggesting an intimate connection or relationship that had indeed occurred (with Julianne) but not between the two of them (Marianne and Henri). In a society in which proprieties are paramount and the rules of polite commerce inflexible, Madame de Charrière has provocatively collapsed the distance between strangers, leaving them both flustered and anxious. It is scarcely any wonder that the two young people meeting for the first time should be so hotly embarrassed, since they already feel physically acquainted through an item of feminine apparel. For Henri, the dress serves as a cognitive reminder and a tactile memory of the intimacy he had shared with the pretty seamstress. This dress, which carries for him erotic import, is now worn on the body of Marianne. For her, to wear against her skin a dress that had been held, possibly caressed, by this stranger, is a troubling collapse of proprieties. In the odd but urgent logic of erotic attraction, both young people may feel that Marianne has been ambiguously undressed although she is fully dresssed. Thus, through erotic prolapse, Madame de Charrière seizes the agitations of desire, while never veering from propriety.

The second erotic signifier that she uses to collapse space is the more banal one of money. If in her other novels, often characterized as texts of "feminized" allusion, delicate form, and barely sketched intrigue, the reader is surprised by a "masculine" insistence on the numbers—on land assets, revenue income, annuities, pensions, dowries, inheritances, wills, and so forth—here hard sums are not mentioned, but their necessity to survival is nonetheless clear, in proof of the principle enunciated in *Les Lettres de Lausanne*, "in this world, money is good for everything" (Letter 4).[23] Nearly every encounter Henri has with Julianne is colored by the passage of money, from the initial *écu* to the gift of the golden cross, to the sum he offers after sleeping with her the first time, to the final deal that is cut when the uncle comes to his rescue, promising—in what is supposed to be read as generosity—to see Julianne through her pregnancy, provided she relinquishes to him all rights to her child. Between the classes, money and privilege segregate, and life for poor women like Julianne will always be a struggle in an unfair world. In writing to her aunt, she bitterly refers to the privileges of the well situated and excuses her own behavior by objecting that she had not been "to all their schools or pensions, and hasn't learned to read their fine books." Her desire, she states, for finery cannot be fulfilled as easily as can that of her wealthy mistresses who get everything they want from mothers or husbands, and not, as she must, from young gentlemen who inevitably ask for something in return.

But money will also play against women of higher class standing in *Les Lettres neuchâteloises*, even within family spaces and the sentimental economy. Marianne is the adored daughter of a retired officer in the service of France who, through rash generosity and ill planning, has squandered his fortune so recklessly that he is now in the position of being unable to provide his beloved child with an attractive dowry and hence any options as she comes of marriage age. Yet one almost suspects that the old gentleman, impotent financially and unfulfilled emotionally by a wife—who while still beautiful is portrayed as unresponsive, and inhospitable—may have unconsciously arranged the matter so that he can keep this precious daughter at his side until his death, an event apprehended as not too far off, given the poor state of his health. Projecting onto the daughter all his desire, he sublimates it into a sentimentality, of which both Diderot and Greuze might well have approved, and which seems only to increase as his fortune and hence her prospects of a happy future, are diminished. Deprived of social standing because of her father's spendthrift irresponsibility, the daughter now is further emotionally blackmailed by a loving father (as Cécile in *Lettres de Lausanne* will be by her mother). In an uncharacteristic and lachrymose scene for Madame de Charrière between daughter and father, observed by Henri and some other guests, Marianne weeps at her father's feet when he, unlike her cold and practical mother, seconds her romantic idea that love suffices and that marriage should be based on feeling, even if the young couple must beg on the streets to survive. The mirroring of romantic notions held by father and daugher suggests a common temperament that permits her to excuse his profligacy, both financial and emotional, and to accept, however unhappily, the fact that when he dies she will be dependent on the charity of others, perhaps needing to become someone's lady-in-waiting.

Monsieur de la Prise is not the only deficient parent in Isabelle de Charrière's fiction, for both William's father and Caliste's mother in *Les Lettres de Lausanne* also set about to deny or rob their children of happiness, the first by playing on the son's guilt and the second by "selling" her daughter to a man enraptured of her. While there is nothing in the author's own life to suggest that she had been victimized by parental pressures, the recurrence of the theme in her fiction points to her concern with the ways parents impinge on children and cause their difficulties, in conjunction with how society likewise constricts the individual's desires and dreams and limits freedom. In other words, there is blame to spare.

Ultimately in *Les Lettres neuchâteloises*, Madame de Charrière has Marianne transcend her oedipal attachment to her father—hence liberating herself from his potentially crippling idolization—by falling in love with Henri, a young man of no great fortune, but of some industry and promise. By novel's end, no bans have been published, but an affectional relationship between the two young people has been established, ironically facilitated by Marianne's active but discreet agency on behalf of Julianne, which has meant wresting from Henri some acknowledgment of his responsibility toward Julianne and her unborn child. This is, of course, an important indication of the female's willingness (or necessity) to overlook the flaws of a potential partner, a subject visited likewise by Madame Riccoboni in her *Lettres de Juliette Catesby*. Hence, while no closure is reached, Marianne's journey from adolescence to maturity, unlike Mistress Henley's or Julianne's, has been successfully completed, for she has surmounted the obstacles of female vulnerability and kept her footing, not by escaping female space but by agilely and creatively becoming mistress of the contingent event that has characterized it.

Reading Desire into Art

These fictions, in which the intrigue is relatively slight, and expression is characterized by reserve and silence, are, in my view, remarkably modern experiments in writing desire. Madame de Charrière feels no inclination to cater to the reader's desire that narrative space be neatly blocked out, that the corners be crisply turned by events, or that the characters be finely chiseled by the author and clear in their knowledge of themselves. Instead, her narration moves superficially if gracefully on the surfaces. Yet in what Jean Starobinski has called the allusive signs and nearly imperceptible indices,[24] in the reserved expression of the protagonist, the indirection of event, indeed, in the very blanks or silences of the text itself, Madame de Charrière sketches not only feminine desire but female psychology. To be sure, the psychology that interests her, like the text it produces, is neither linear nor explicit, but rather elusive, offering intimations of feeling and meaning for the reader capable of reading spatially. What Charrière does in her novels is to present the surface as a dancing line of water, in which the ripples become the suggestion that there is more at stake, that the eye must be drawn down below the surface, that vision is involved not only with wide focus but with deeper levels.

For Madame de Charrière, the premises of art, like human desire itself, are based not on clearly defined states and goals, but on currents that flow into and out of one another, with no necessary beginning or end, never being, but always seeking to become—like her novels, her characters, her self. She excels in evoking those psychological movements toward change or slow metamorphosis that are not themselves change, but are the processes of change and desire. Hence the frequency in her stories of journeys that offer motion but rarely an endpoint; hence the open-ended sentence, the *points de suspension*; and hence the nonfinito of her *dénouements* that are so frequently not endings but unendings, openings into spacelessness. To become the ideal reader of Madame de Charrière's fictions is to enter this space of the ellipsis, to participate in the elusory quest, to understand that perhaps the true object of her desire is art, itself.

LES LETTRES DE LAUSANNE

Published in 1785 and 1787, the two parts of this epistolary novel (henceforth named after their principal characters, "Cécile" and "Caliste") are typically "unified" by critics through apposition, juxtaposition, or balanced antithesis.[25] Sometimes described as different sides of the same coin of female destiny, the two parts have likewise been thought to reveal the struggle at the center of Charrière's thinking in the dichotomy between idealism and materialism. Another way of viewing this bifurcated novel is as two more stories of desire, but a single, converging reading of the failures of desire. Whether it is the passionate, erotic desire of Caliste or the implosive, pre-erotic desire of Cécile, neither female will be the object of desire, according to her wish. In each case, it is, furthermore, the inadequate, even anemic, desire of the male that characterizes the relationship, as he, unlike d'Hermenches, refuses to be her ideal reader/lover.

In a story told through her mother's letters, Cécile's desire is largely chimerical and inchoate, since she is caught between the inappropriate goals of insipid suitors and the suffocating concerns of a mother who wants too much to make her daughter happy. In the end, as she prepares to join her mother on an ill-defined journey into an unknown future, Cécile's plaintive voice betrays not only her disappointed romantic hopes, but also a kind of emotional interruption in her development, as she moves into a state of suspended animation. In a coda to the interrupted saga of Cécile left-in-narrative-limbo, two years later, Charrière publishes "Caliste." As told through William's letters to Cécile's mother, Caliste's story is an admonitory tale, not only about the inadequacy of male commitment, but about desire itself. Hence, against the portrait of overactive maternal desire (perhaps even maternal narcissism) in "Cécile," Charrière counterposes underproductive romantic desire involving a deficient hero and a needful heroine. While the beautiful Caliste yearned throughout her life for acceptance and total commitment, William as the pessimistic romantic is unable to engage with the "text" of Caliste. But in the act of putting into words the story of the woman to whom he could not commit, William is forced to reread himself and confront his inadequacies, including inadequate desire that now metamorphoses into regret for what was not and cannot be. In the face of loss, he cannot even finish his own story, and in wordless despair, abandons his pen as he had abandoned Caliste, dispossessing her in death as in life of positive affect on him, and consigning her to the space of a painful and bad memory.

An examination of the two stories will illustrate how Charrière creates a reading of desire that reveals its sorrows and disappointments.

"Cécile": Desire Checkmated

The motif Madame de Charrière chooses to represent Lausanne society, in which parlor games are such a central part of social interaction of the town bourgeoisie, is the chessboard, which appears in a number of scenes, as the young Milord Edouard endeavors to teach Cécile how to play both at this game and at life. Most of the mother's letters to her female correspondent in France describe evenings spent at home with her daughter in the company of an always changing society of young men, who are in Lausanne to study or for apprenticeships, and who, some assiduously, some less so, pay court to the young woman in her drawing room, around card or board games. As the mother describes these evenings and their games, the reader is drawn to comparing the relationship between adversaries in games of skill or chance with those that men and women play out on the figurative chessboard of society, in a series of strategic moves and defenses.

Cécile's story, recounted by her mother, reveals the double drama of a young woman moving out of adolescence and into adulthood, assailed by uncertain desires that are marked stylistically by the number of her sentences cast as interrogatives or left incomplete, trailing off in dots and dashes, punctuated by confusion. "What is happening in me? What did I feel?" "What makes me feel ashamed?" "What am I crying about?" she asks her mother at one point (p. 47). Showing female adolescence not as a period of rebellion and confrontation, but as a puzzling set of questions, Charrière reveals the enigmatic quality of desires in conflict, first in her young heroine and then in a striking and original problematic of the mother–daughter relationship.

As she is portrayed in her mother's letters, Cécile is attractive without necessarily being pretty, she is natural, good-tempered, alternatively reserved and delightfully direct. She is the single beloved object in the life of her widowed mother, who, mistress of only a small fortune and restrained by her position in society from supplementing it with any kind of work, worries about Cécile's chances of finding a suitable mate. "Poor Cécile! Whatever will become of her?" she writes to a woman friend in the first of her seventeen letters, which will subsequently show that the answer concerns a parent-child relationship as much as question of finding her a suitable partner in marriage.

As becomes clear, the mother is not concerned uniquely with getting her daughter married, but rather both with ensuring her daughter's happiness and not losing her privileged position in Cécile's affections. It is for these reasons and because she is convinced that women are mere pawns on men's game boards that she wants not only to defend her daughter against that danger, but to remove her from the playing field. Fearful that Cécile will be hurt in the games that advantage men such as Milord Edouard, who flirts but does not commit himself, or the unhappily married cousin who lets himself be carried away by passion one evening and rashly embraces Cécile, or the stolid and rather unpassionate Bernois who could provide any woman a materially pleasant life but little else, the mother proposes an alternative vision of happiness. In a reprise of the Demeter-Persephone myth of mother–daughter passion, Charrière's mother suggests to her daughter that the emotional bond with a mother who serves as friend, teacher, and consoler will be more reliable than any romantic relationship with the opposite sex.[26]

Ironically, however, as Cécile is saved from Edouard's inadequate desire, she risks being consumed by an overabundance of desire, in the form of mother-love.[27] In changing the equation of woman's devotion from "everything for a *man*" to "everything for one's *daughter*," Madame de Charrière shows that an excess of desire is as potentially damaging as an insufficiency of desire. Maternal love should be no excuse for raising a child without volitional independence, and, in the effort to do good, she ends by restricting her daughter's chances for happiness. For while the mother considers that the possibility of motherhood compensates for the inevitable disappointments of marriage, by "protecting" her daughter from such a union, she also deprives the young woman of *her* opportunity to experience motherhood.

There can be little doubt that Isabelle de Charrière was fascinated with the influence of parents on their children and with the process of separation on the part of both child and parent.[28] Parents do not play neutral roles in her novels, for they are either forcefully absent or vigorously present. Obedient children such as Caliste and William are exploited by their parents—the first for money, the second through moral blackmail and parental guilt-tripping of the adult child, whereas daughters such as Marianne and Cécile are at risk precisely because they are adored. The problem with Cécile's mother (who, much like Isabelle de Charrière, is an intelligent, opinionated, but also sensitive woman) is not that she does not care enough for her daughter, but that she cares too much. In her anxiety to protect and help her daughter, she denies Cécile her own experiences and forces her to pass too rapidly from adolescence into maturity, and thence into a depressed middle age.

When the mother speaks of a woman's duties and of virtue, she is encouraging restraint and goodness, and self- and sexual denial, as well. In this respect, the reader will certainly cast a wary eye on the mother's long cautionary tirade (pp. 47–53), occasioned because Cécile had permitted Edouard to kiss her hand, following a lover's quarrel, and condemn the mother for bringing out her heavy artillery. The event, after all, hardly required the firing of moral salvos, such as "a girl who is rash rarely becomes a prudent and wise woman" and "she who has not resisted her lover before marriage is rarely faithful to him afterward." The point is that the mother's motives are ambiguous at best and seem based in a youthful error of her own.[29] At worst, she is inhibiting her daughter's growth, robbing her of the freedom to make independent choices and experience on her own terms a relationship with a man. Indeed, we might charge that the mother implicitly asks her daughter to sublimate her own awakening sexuality and recognize that only in female solidarity with a mother, who alone offers unchanging love, can she find happiness. But in doing so, she is foreclosing on her daughter's options by painting the world as black and all men as insincere, self-centered, unfaithful, just as Madame de Chartres had with her daughter in *La Princesse de Clèves*. If such maternal admonitions are not malevolent, they are at least tainted, equivocally motivated, and reveal more than anything else in the mother a kind of weakness, or the fear of losing her daughter, or possibly even of seeing her daughter realize greater happiness than she has.

What is so extraordinary about this story is that while it is the tale of Cécile's coming to age, it is just as much the story of a parent–child relationship that is possibly unique in early literature for the levels and complexities of the emotions involved. It stands in stark contrast to other tales, like that of Caliste and William in Part II, or Manon and Des Grieux, or Julie and St. Preux, in which the drama turns on *paternal* inflexibility and the *patriarchal* virtues of honor, chastity, and steadfast resolve. The single message that this mother aspires to give her daughter is one of support and unconditional love, regardless of the choices her daughter makes. Thus she tells Cécile, "If it is possible, take advantage of my advice; but if you don't follow it, don't hide from a mother who loves you." For what is there to fear? "My reproaches?—I would not make any; they would hurt me more than you," she assures her. "Loss of my devotion?—I would perhaps only love you more should you be unhappy, and if you ran the risk of being abandoned by everyone." Nor would she die of unhappiness if Cécile made bad choices on her own, for the mother says, "I would try to live and to prolong my life in order to soften the sorrows of yours" (53).

Unconditionally devoted to her child, a mother, she believes, is capable of creating not just life but also the gift of happiness.

In the end, with mother and daughter in decampment, embarking on an undefined journey for an undetermined duration and a location that may only initially be that of her correspondent's home, Madame de Charrière shows her two characters having become transients in the futile attempt to reformulate desire. Is leaving the chessboard of Lausanne on which they have been checkmated a liberation or a retreat? Is it a positive step or a step into nothingness? In the nonfinito of the denouement, we are left as uncertain as Cécile. Our readerly desire for resolution remains as unanswered as the character's desire for happiness.

"Caliste": Relegated to the Space of Memory

The central question for Caliste, as for so many of Madame de Charrière's heroines is "Where do I belong?," which, once again, poses the dilemma of woman's desire in terms of space. The story, with its souvenirs of *Adolphe* (1816) by Charrière's friend, Benjamin Constant, with whom she embarks at age forty-seven on an affair of the heart and mind, puts on the scene a young woman, Caliste, whose past as a kept woman makes her forever unworthy in the eyes of society. William, the narrator who is writing to Cécile's mother in reference to his cousin's (Milord Edouard) inability to commit himself unequivocally to Cécile, loves Caliste but is incapable of bucking the moral prejudices of his father who had objected to marriage between his son and the young woman in these terms: "I shudder at the idea of a daughter-in-law in front of whom I would not dare speak of chastity, of grandchildren with whom I could not promote chastity without making their mother blush" (Letter 21, p. 99). Though William weakly yields to his father's wishes, he continues to see Caliste, but despite strong physical attraction, they struggle against sexual desire and do not consummate their love. William, however, grows increasingly frustrated, suspicious, and even ill tempered with Caliste. Finally when he leaves her for some unnecessary mission proposed by his father, Caliste agrees to marry a man willing to ignore her past (though ultimately not her unrequited love), and William submits to his father's demands that he marry a golddigger by the name of Lady Betty. Sometime later, William and Caliste, both unhappily married, meet by chance one evening in the same theater where Caliste's career had begun. On the playbill that night is "The Fair Penitent," the play from which she had taken her name and identity years before. Convincing herself that their presence together in this fateful theater is a sign, Caliste proposes, in an outburst of passion, that they run off together, pleading with William: "Have you not obeyed your father enough? . . . Let us live our real feelings. Whom will we be hurting? My husband despises me and no longer wants to live with me, and your wife doesn't love you anymore!" (132) But William cannot make up his mind to act, a fact Caliste understands even while it crushes her, for while she wants him to cease resisting her, she knows he cannot do otherwise. Retracting her plea, she confesses, "Until now I have been only unhappy. Let me not become guilty. I could accept my own errors, but not yours; I would never forgive myself to have lowered you to that point. Oh! How unhappy I am and how much I love you!" (133).

Caliste accepts, as Jean Starobinski has said, to judge herself as she is judged by dominant morality,[30] not because she is masochistic or unenlightenened, but because she loves William despite his shortcomings—perhaps even because of them. She is entrapped by his self-imposed constraints and his inability or unwillingness to repudiate his father. Yet if William is immobilized by the guilt his father places on him and by his own weakness, Caliste is trapped by her past, and she waits in vain to be rescued. Instead, scenes with William always end with him closing the door, pulling back into a space barred to her. In the end, denied the object of her desire, she succumbs to illness, leaving behind at least three men—William, his father, and her husband, who will, only now, give her a space to which to belong—in the sadness of their memories.

Like Constant's Ellénore, Caliste is a victim of a past she has not chosen and of a cast of characters who range from her own mother to the men she had loved who all let her down, sometimes despite their love. She is victimized in turn by the ambition and greed of her mother who "sells" her to Lord L***, and then by this very same man when he fails to marry her even though, or perhaps because, she becomes his mistress; she is the victim of William's indecisiveness and his father's prejudices, and of her husband's foolish and wounded pride. Her life is a series of losses—first, of her mother's love; of her own name when she becomes "Caliste"; of her honor and reputation when her protector Lord L*** dies; then she loses William; followed by loss of her unborn child through miscarriage when she learns of William's marriage; and finally, she loses her husband's love and esteem. Empathizing with others who have suffered loss, who are treated as life's casualities, she makes it a point to provide care and education for them, these orphans of society, so that they at least might have a chance at life and a place to belong.

Though the story bears her name, it is nonetheless true that the woman herself is denied within it, since, told through William's letters, she is never granted her own voice. (Of course, the same thing happened in "Cécile" in which the young woman is presented through a proud but conflicted maternal voice.) Furthermore, the reader perceives Caliste for all her attractive characteristics—intelligence, talent, sensitivity—as unanchored, floating, uncertain, for she has no name, no roots, no titles, no space of permanence or respect in society. Indeed, the space ascribed to this person, like that of so many Charrière heroines, is that of the approximate, the undefined. All we know of her previous existence is that she was a daughter of honest extraction, but had the misfortune of having an exploitative mother who had fallen on hard times and decided to take advantage of her daughter's beauty and talents by committing her to the role of actress. "She had her theater debut in the role of Caliste, in "The Fair Penitent," says William. "In leaving the theater, a man of some importance spoke with her mother about her, buying her, for all intents and purposes, and the next day they left for the Continent" (89). "Caliste," he explains, "was the name that remained hers due to the role she had played to great acclaim the first and only time she appeared on stage." Hence Caliste is a fabrication, an invention, whose birth occurs in a theater, on the stage, within the notion of illusion. She is born in the spectator's desire, crossed with her own, and in a place that cannot be duplicated in the real world. If the woman without a name becomes Caliste through illusion, is it any wonder that Caliste, the woman, feels both lost and an enigma in society? With her borrowed identity from the space of illusion, she exists only provisionally and with the acquiescence of her male supporter. When he is removed or removes himself, she ceases to be—or to be only in his memory. Caliste may be society's feminine ideal, for she is beautiful, seductive, passionate, yet virtuous and vulnerable. But, ironically, she is not only exploited by men, but also spurned by them. Because of her personality and her situation in society, she is a particularly needy character, which perhaps explains why she is clearly so overwhelming to men who find it easier to deal with her through displacement—as a memory, even as a memory of how badly they treated her.

Because the story of Caliste is both romantic and darkly melancholic, one might argue that it casts a more positive light on the limbo in which Cécile had been left, suggesting some hope for her future. But it is hard to justify that optimism, given the depressed state that characterizes Cécile and her mother's considerable guilt and agitation about whether she has made the right choice in leaving Lausanne. Both stories relate the same disappointments and disillusionments accompanying desire and point to Charrière's conviction that it is desire (nonsexual as much as sexual) that stands at the center of all human endeavor. As the inescapable condition of our lives, desire is also the necessary mediator of all reading.

CONCLUSION

In this respect, one might speculate on how Charrière participates in the debate over reading for pleasure and the pleasures of the text.[31] The answer, I believe, is that while she represents desire continually, she also displaces, intellectualizes, and estheticizes it, thereby expanding the ways in which desire intersects with reading pleasure. This may be clearer if we recall how desire functions within the epistolary form itself as disappointment and disillusionment. Clearly, none of her epistolaries of fiction is truly an exchange between equal partners (nor, indeed, were her love letters to d'Hermenches), thereby immediately undermining the standard of ideal erotic desire. Instead, reflecting the inadequate or mismatched quality of most desire, her epistolaries (except for the polyphonic *Lettres neuchâteloises*) are single-person narratives, thereby mirroring the imperfect quality of exchange in most desire. Mistress Henley receives no letters from her correspondent and scarcely seems to need any, for her words spill forth on their own without any exterior liberating mechanism. The letters in the first half of *Lettres de Lausanne* are likewise one-sided, *about* Cécile but not *by* Cécile, written by a mother who never seems to realize that she may be too attached to her daughter. In the second half, the same technique of one-sidedness is employed when it is the guilt-stricken voice of William who tells the tragic story of Caliste and his inability to have attached himself more to the woman who loved him. Over and underattachment are two sides of the coin of desire. Even in *Lettres neuchâteloises* in which desire is mediated through space and objects, everyone is a victim of desires that do not mesh, lines that do not coincide, planes of comprehension that while parallel are destined to remain separate and nonconvergent. Ironically, it is precisely at the moment that desire becomes loss, disappointment, sorrow, and uncertainty that it can be turned into an artistic object and constitute a new kind of pleasure in reading.

The argument that I would like to make is that Isabelle de Charrière is changing the grounds on which a notion of reading for pleasure is founded, thereby producing what might be called an alternative to the Rousseauistic ideal of reading in which readers are expected to emerge from their reading inspired to virtue and goodness through sentimentality. Reading in that way would have, according to Panckoucke, a liberating effect on the reader, bringing freedom from his or her own alienated life and leading to a new social and personal ideal. Such an ideal of reading also obviated the problem that has always been implied by reading for pleasure. For if the reader puts down the book morally and individually "improved," impelled toward virtue, *douce amitié*, and piety, then the reading of novels could be considered both a redemptive and ennobling activity.

Charrière, on the other hand, takes a different approach to the question of reading through desire and for pleasure. What she does is to reformulate the reader's pleasure and presumptive "redemption," to be realized not through sentimentality, but through the ability to intellectualize and estheticize desire into a work of art. Between the immature, romantic reading that wants the page of fiction to be a palimpsest for life, and the virtuous and sentimental reading that Rousseau proposes, Isabelle de Charrière offers a third path and a new kind of erotics of reading, one concerned not with *what* but with *how*, not with story but with means. For her, the pleasure of the text of fiction derives from a kind of *volupté intellectuelle* achieved by reworking desire and estheticizing it in images and the minimalist structures of a text. Hence, her fictions strive to offer a different kind of reading experience whose pleasures will be neither in sentiment nor what Labrosse, speaking of the effect produced by Rousseau, called an *érotisme d'âme* (literally, an eroticism of the soul),[32] but rather an *érotisme d'intellect.* In the alchemy of Charrière's art, the reader will find pleasure in how imprecision, nondirection, and the unarticulated take shape and provide not emotional but intellectual and artistic pleasure. One might even suggest that this kind of intellectual eroticism resists more gracefully the vagaries of time and the changing of reading tastes, since for many readers the quivering filaments of yearning, muffled desire, and loss within Charrière's slight fictions carry more contemporaneity than the outsized sentimentality of *La Nouvelle Héloïse.*

The notion of desire that leads Cécile to feel that she must abandon the novel is based on the cultural fallacy of the romantic that maintains that reading for pleasure and the pleasures of reading are exclusively erotic activities. As long as she believes this, she will, indeed, be the Unrequited Reader. But if she and other immature readers can outgrow their narrow expectations about reading and desire, as Charrière's fictions show, they will find their pleasure greatly increased when they arm themselves with the resources of art, which will permit them both to reassess reality and rethink the very project of desire.

FIVE

READING RAPE IN THE CULTURE WARS OF THE EIGHTEENTH CENTURY

MARIE-JEANNE RICCOBONI, 1713–1792

> Rape. (1) Act of sexual penetration committed on another by violence, constraint, or surprise. . . . (2) Action of transgressing a law, rule, etc. (3) Action penetrating into a forbidden place.
>
> —*Le Petit Larousse*

In the April 1751 issue of *Nouveau Magasin français*, Madame Leprince de Beaumont includes the strange case, adjudicated earlier that year, of a Monsieur de Penne, who, at age twenty-six, had fallen passionately in love with a young girl, the Demoiselle de Bisès, fifteen years his junior. He married her when she was only eleven years old, promising, however, not to consummate the relationship until she was "nubile." His brother, a monk, did not feel so constrained. Finding the young girl too tempting a morsel, despite his vows of chastity, or unable to resist an act of ultimate sibling rivalry, he dressed in Monsieur de Penne's nightshirt one night, crept into her bedchamber, and raped her, thereby robbing his brother of what the French language delicately calls "*les prémices.*"

At first suspected of having broken his word, Monsieur de Penne was finally able to prove his innocence, but then regarded with horror the union he had contracted with the young girl. Wishing to separate from her, he took the case to court. Normally, under a 1730 law, a rapist—typically called a "seducer" in early French law—could be condemned to death unless the woman agreed to marry him, but since, in this case, the child-wife was too young to have become pregnant and, furthermore, a marriage would have required that the monk take leave of his religious vows, no one seemed anxious to bring about such a conclusion.[1] Instead, the judge ruled that the only viable solution was to dissolve the marriage, in order to leave Monsieur de Penne free to remarry. Should he wish to provide the young woman with a dowry of whatever amount his "generosity" might dictate, he would be making a fine gesture, according to the judge, but the deprived husband was in no way bound to do so, given the fact that the value of the "goods" of which he had taken possession through the marriage contract had been nullified by his brother's act of dispossession.

We do not know the outcome of this affair, but Madame Leprince firmly declared that in her view Monsieur de Penne had no choice but to establish a reasonable dowry, because while innocent of the crime against the girl, he was, nonetheless, its original cause. Focusing on the violation and defilement of an eleven-year-old child, victimized by a series of men—husband, brother-in-law, and judge—who treat her as a commodity with a market value, Madame Leprince is offended that the girl is being treated like spoiled goods, to be disposed of as efficiently as possible. And she fears that if the girl's family does not take pity on her, the young victim will have no other choice but to retreat to a convent where she will be buried for the rest of her life.[2]

The de Bisès case goes to show that the real issue for the judicial system in the eighteenth century was the alienation of a man's legitimate property. Hence, the law treated rape, as it had since feudal times, to be a *property* offense, or theft, perpetrated against men, because only men owned property. It is precisely the same concern that Beaumarchais takes up in his 1784 "Le Mariage de Figaro," where the primary focus is on the dispossession of male rights. Beaumarchais's criticism, directed against the aristocracy, is predicated on the view that Figaro has been defrauded of his right to be the first to have sexual relations with his young bride by the Comte d'Almaviva, who lays claim to his *droit du seigneur*. Thus while the playwright contributed to growing demands for a more democratic society by forefronting issues of class equality, he did not extend his concerns to gender equality in the fullest sense of the word. The primary issue for him, as for the judge in the de Bisès case, was not so much the violation of a woman's body by an act of rape, but the despoliation of another man's rights. In a class-driven society, Beaumarchais sides with the commoner, Figaro, against the aristocracy, while ignoring the plight of the woman.

The case of the rape of the Demoiselle de Bisès and its subsequent judicial adjudication, lacking in appropriate moral and social justice, forms the backdrop for this chapter, both because it highlights the different ways that the sexes have "read" literal rape and because the figurative rape of the reader (in the sense of transgressing on the contract between reader and writer) is the primary bone of contention between Madame Riccoboni and Choderlos de Laclos, who engage in an argument regarding the function of literature in culture, in general, and the purposes of reading in particular. For Riccoboni, the heart of the issue is that Laclos uses the novel to subvert the reader and the reading process, undermining a basic premise of the contract between writer and reader concerning the realistic portrayal of society and fictional characters, and alienating both the reader and textual authority by the overwhelming presence of irony. Thus Riccoboni objects not only as a woman and as an author, but also as a proponent of affective response reading or "reading with feeling," as Susan L. Feagin defines the role of emotional response in reader appreciation and in eliciting value from a work.[3] Laclos, on the other hand, as an early modernist, appears to view literature and reading as a game, an entry into the ludic, in which playfulness is the primary principle and ultimate objective and in which the relationship between reader and writer is based on notions of gamemanship. Diametrically opposed in terms of their esthetics and ethics of reading, both writers participate in the culture wars of their century on the pages of their novels through the interlinked structures of reading and rape.

In order to provide background to the literary, reading, and sexual wars, conducted on the pages of letters exchanged between Madame Riccoboni and Laclos following publication of *Les Liaisons dangereuses* in 1782, I propose first to look at the structures and thematics of reading within her 1759 novel, *Lettres de Milady Catesby*, then to study in detail the rape scene and how Madame Riccoboni rewrites it to produce a different reading. My ultimate objective is to show how reading, in a veritable *mise-en-abyme*, structures both the story within the text and captures the essence of the argument between these two worthy writers who represent different sides of the cultural divide.

SCENES AND IMAGES OF READING

Let us begin by looking at how the very topos of reading shapes the text and grounds the principles of the epistolary universe in fiction. Our first assertion must be that reading is the sine qua non of epistolary fiction, since it is only by letters sent, received, and read that the story progresses.[4] Consequently in any epistolary novel, relations between characters are necessarily dialogic, as each person becomes the literal reader of the written texts of the other, rather than merely the figurative reader of the other's acts, or the seer–reader into the heart of the other. As Nathalie Ferrand reminds us, the epistolary is the only subgenre of fiction in which the protagonists must be readers. And they will spend inordinate amounts of time at the literate activities of reading and writing, since letters are their single way to stay in contact with those not present and to get knowledge about events that take place elsewhere.

Within a text, actual reading can be used in a variety of ways and for a variety of purposes. Descriptions of a character's reading may be utilized by the writer to confer value, especially when describing what is read or how much time is spent reading. Which texts an author proposes, how the characters engage with them, for what purposes, at what point in the story, are all elements that typically provide important information.[5] We know, for instance, that few characters of the eighteenth century are ever cast as readers of the periodical press, but that the novel or the poem often plays a role. And we also know that the incorporation of the notion of recommended reading, as well as the use made of *lectures de formation*, may be straightforward or satirical, depending on how the character exploits the text. Scenes of reading as a public activity may reveal how the textual contents affect listeners differently, and may expose the secrets or vulnerabilities of characters. Joint readings by a male and female can be employed to illustrate shared tastes or to represent a form of chaste couplings in which reading is a kind of protosexual activity. In the epistolary, nearly everyone is a reader of everyone else in the salon, but, even in private, one person may be subjected to being read when another individual does a kind of suprareading of text being created under his very eyes. These, then, are some of the multiple ways in which I would like to look at how Madame Riccoboni uses reading as a revealing motif or internal structure in her novel.

Like many women writers, she assigns to reading a particularly important and positive role in establishing character. Hence, she has Juliette Catesby refer early on to the "useful readings" that she and her friend Henriette had engaged in and that have cemented their friendship (Letter 12), and she has Juliette indicate that she had sought solace in books and music during the two years of her unhappy marriage to a much older husband whom she did not love (Letter 14). Such signs of reading carry positive resonance for the external reader, who identifies with Juliette in good part because of a shared pleasure in reading. Moreover, a heroine who luxuriates in books is automatically cast by the external female reader as someone like herself, cultured, serious, "different," possessing the taste and intellect to be attracted to activities of the mind. This "reading motif," then, confirms the worthiness of the heroine.

When Juliette engages in a shared reading with Milord d'Ossery, he "proves" *his* worthiness by being responsive to the pleasures of reading together and in revealing unusual sensitivity to the text. For he reads "like a woman," with his heart and feelings, as Mademoiselle Catesby points out in Letter 14 in which she reviews for Milord Carlile the history of her love for d'Ossery. Describing a scene that takes places in a delightful garden in which she and d'Ossery were reading together the story of tender lovers cruelly separated, Juliette makes it clear that their cognitive processes of thought and their imaginations are similarly *warranted*, resulting not only in a shared esthetic, but also a chaste but reciprocal sexual response.[6] "Our reading led us to reflections in which our feelings were the primary matter," she says, evoking the erotic but innocent quality of their interaction. This is not a reading of seduction (*la lecture de séduction*) in the usual sense of the eighteenth century in which any lesson—and particularly *la leçon de lecture* in a novel—carries with it the often ironic potential to combine pedagogy and seduction. Instead, deeply moved by the story of sad lovers, Juliette and d'Ossery, as exquisitely sensitive readers, identify physically and emotionally with the text. "The book fell from our hands, our tears were mutual, and struck by I know not what fear, we gazed upon one another," she remembers. "He passed an arm around me, as though to hold on to me; I leaned toward him, and breaking the silence *at the same time* [emphasis added], we cried out together, '*Oh, how unhappy they were!*'" (Letter 14, p. 56).[7] This simultaneous ejaculation of words reveals not only the extent to which Juliette and d'Ossery are perfect soul mates, in spiritual and physical symbiosis, but also how reading is a surrogate-sexual activity through their mutual susceptibility to the story of unhappy lovers. Reading together is for them a way of displacing onto the book, whose story is of sexual desire, the real sexual energy that flows between them. It is, furthermore, an activity that permits them to experience perfect moments of mutuality in reading that will never be duplicated in life.

This is so because the preromantic d'Ossery will be a disappointment, either too weak or too overbearing. Whether it was Riccoboni's silent intention or not, d'Ossery frequently assumes the "woman's role" by taking to his bed when he receives the disturbing news of Jenny's pregnancy in order to avoid having to see his fiancée (Letter 14, p. 63), weeping inconsolably (Letter 14, p. 65), and falling dangerously ill, in an unmanly reassertion of body over mind (Letter 14, p. 71). If he does not plead a migraine, as does Sir James when rebuffed by Juliette (Letter 17, p. 82), or suffer from vapors and faint, as does Sir Henry when he, too, is refused by the heroine (Letter, 24, p. 106), Milord d'Ossery nonetheless reveals a quality of sensitivity more normally associated with fragile females than with the privileged male, whom Juliette, in a moment of anger, compares to Milton's crafty and supple snake (Letter 9, p. 29).[8] Yet he can also become domineering, as he does in the final scene of the novel, when he is presented as the suprareader.

In that scene, Juliette pens a letter to Henriette, while d'Ossery stands behind her and reads the words she writes. She therefore must compose her letter under his watchful gaze, while his very presence as reader permits him to exercise censorship over her words. In that sense, Madame Riccoboni creates a visual image of the unspoken power relations between reader and text, as between the reader and the producer of text (to say nothing of the relations between the sexes). Will Juliette write her text differently because of the presence of a reader who may wish her to say something other than what she wants? Will she be able to say enough so that another reader, Henriette, can read between the lines? Similarly, this scene of d'Ossery as the monitoring reader of Juliette suggests a mirrored image external to the novel in which there is an invisible suprareader—the public—whose existence is always felt by the writer.

In these complex reading relations, we have an external reader (ourselves) of a text being created by an internal reader/writer (Juliette), in the presence of a an overseeing reader (d'Ossery), and addressed to an intended reader (Henriette). Unsurprisingly for a writer who is known for the fineness of her psychology, Madame Riccoboni would seem to be illustrating through the metaphor of reading how she construes human relations in the world. Not only do we read texts of every kind, ranging from the written to the visual, but we also "read" other people's motives and behavior, a moment in time, or a mood. Through reading we identify with and differentiate ourselves from other identities; in reading others, we arrive at our idea as to how we want to be "read" by others. Yet considering the filters through which a text must pass, it is likely that an author or a letter writer within a text will be subject to what might be called an overreading. This happens in two ways in Madame Riccoboni's novel: first with d'Ossery as suprareader, and next with their friends who, believing they can read into hearts, arrange a marriage between Juliette and d'Ossery that the narrative had not seemed to prepare.

Hence, we see that human interactions in Madame Riccoboni's novel are predominantly figured through models of reading, from educative reading that builds and confirms personal and moral character; to passionate reading as a substitute for sexual activity; to at least two kinds of overreading by the couple's friends and by d'Ossery himself. Having demonstrated the value she places on actual reading as a metaphor for human interaction, let us now turn to her reading of rape. For it is the question of rape, both literal and figurative, that gets to the heart of the argument between Riccoboni and Laclos and their diametrically opposed notions of the external reading act.

REWRITING RAPE

Interestingly, the rape, which is recounted in an interpolated letter from d'Ossery to Juliette in her Letter 35, has been interpreted quite differently by modern critics. In his preface to the novel, Sylvain Menant sides with d'Ossery and offers the conventional male reading of the episode as a single, moral lapse.[9] Riccoboni scholar Joan Hinde Stewart characterizes it as a "passing infidelity."[10] Susan Snaider Lanser calls it, as I do, a rape.[11] Such differing views are due, I believe, to how Madame Riccoboni *naturalizes* the act of rape, making it not an extraordinary occurrence, but a disturbingly ordinary one. Nowhere in the text does she use the word "rape" to discuss this scene, but neither does she write of "seduction." Instead, Madame Riccoboni shows in unambiguous terms, despite d'Ossery's subsequent rationalizations, that what occurs is a sexual assault. In fact, in a remarkably modern way, she underscores the compound nature of the rape, which is neither exclusively about power, as contemporary feminists have argued, nor about sex, as sociologists used to maintain. Rather, and regardless of how much he wants to dismiss it as mere "forgetfulness," d'Ossery's act is a crime of sex *and* aggression, perpetrated on a young and vulnerable girl, only a few years older than the Demoiselle de Bisès.

By choosing an ordinary man, neither seducer nor immoral rake, to commit the rape, and by revealing how society is in complicity with him, the author underscores both the commonplaceness of rape and the dubious foundation of her society's ethics. By insisting on the multiple ruptures caused by the act of rape, nullified neither by the man's protestations of good intentions nor by his subsequent marriage with the victim who dies in childbirth, Riccoboni emphasizes the psychic and social damage produced by sexual violation. Furthermore, unlike her male counterparts who suggest an erotics of rape, she refuses to turn the reader into a voyeur or to figure the woman, in Susan Lanser's expression, as a secret to penetrate.[12] Instead and in every respect, Madame Riccoboni rewrites the drama of rape and in the process shatters several myths: that "manly excess" arises from nature or instinct and must therefore be forgiven; that force is erotic; and that only bad men commit rape. An examination of how she "marks" the actual rape scene will support these points.

Spatial Markers

Madame Riccoboni's rape scene occurs in the rambling country manor of young Montfort, a friend of d'Ossery's from university days, who is hosting an evening of drinking and general camaraderie with his male friends. D'Ossery has accepted Montfort's invitation somewhat reluctantly for he has become secretly engaged to Juliette and feels that there are other priorities in his life than drinking and making merry. As his feelings of estrangement from the group of men grow, he seeks to extricate himself and leaves the room in search of the garden. But immediately he becomes lost, going from an ill-lighted vestibule to a number of connecting rooms, and finally a *cabinet* in which, by flickering candlelight, he glimpses a woman's form, that of Miss Jenny, the young sister of his host. Earlier she had, at her brother's request, made a brief and uncomfortable appearance in the assembled company. When d'Ossery enters and surprises her in the *cabinet*, there is no sense, either on his part or hers, that she has been sought or cornered. But in her nervousness, caused by the unexpected confrontation with a man she hardly knows, she makes an incautious movement that extinguishes her candle, the only source of light.

Unfamiliar with this room, even though it is her home ("these quarters were almost as strange to her as to me," says d'Ossery in his letter), Miss Jenny attempts in the total darkness that engulfs them to find the bell to summon the servants. But the room is enveloped in complete blackness, and they are like two bulls in a china closet, crashing into furniture and each other in their attempts to find the bell-chain. Miss Jenny is young and unsophisticated, and their predicament elicits from her the gleeful laughter of a child—laughter which d'Ossery subsequently claims, disoriented him. Typically, of course, mirth is not erotic, but here, according to d'Ossery, it has the extraordinary effect of freeing his libido. Her peals of laughter both enflame and unsettle him: "A respectable girl appeared to me at that instant as a woman offered up for my desires. . . . An impetuous impulse overtook me. . . . " And in an instant the dastardly deed is done. There is no seduction, no pleasure, no love, but simply a blind, physical urge, and the domination of the female by the male. When the act is over and with Miss Jenny sobbing in the background, the moon suddenly throws enough light into the room to reveal the location of the door, and he realizes—too late—that he has commited a deplorable act.

At this point, we might recall that in the typical boudoir seduction scene of literature and art, the single requisite structural prop is the opening, passageway, or door that simultaneously carries sexual, psychological, and ideological import. Conventionally, the door is a structural signifier, a specially inflected challenge for the male who must penetrate and transgress it. Sometimes, as in Fragonard's "Le Verrou," the door is slyly imbued with ambiguous implications (is the woman fighting against an unwelcome intruder, or is she as eager as the swashbuckling man in tights to throw the bolt in preparation for a night of passion?), while at other times, as in *Les Liaisons dangereuses*, the door becomes a part of the drama. For instance, Madame de Merteuil conducts the most important of her business behind closed doors; Valmont breaks down one door in a scene staged to deceive a wronged husband, he kneels in front of another door to peep through its keyhole at Madame de Tourvel praying for strength to resist her passions, and he maneuvers Cécile into aiding him to get a duplicate key to her bedroom.

The door may also hold political and ideological significance at the same time that it insinuates sexuality. In a 1988 New York production of *Le Mariage de Figaro*, for instance, the set designer used doors to suggest a provocative relationship between psychology and ideology. In that modernized and Americanized production, Beaumarchais's play was situated in the Manhattan luxury high-rise, the Trump Towers, well removed from the lowly world below. Describing the feeling she wanted to create, the set designer emphasized the fact that the play is characterized by a large number of doors and connecting rooms, all of which are key to the progression and development of the action, and likewise to the "feeling" of Beaumarchais's play, which is about relations—connections or disconnections between the classes, as well as relations between the sexes. To situate the action in an encapsulated world, such as pre-revolutionary French society, and likewise in a contemporary luxury high-rise apartment, is to choose a world of privilege, yet with the presence of servants to highlight underprivilege. The clash between the two is particularly well symbolized in the politics of doors—who has the right to enter when, where, and how—and the attempts, within the lord's manor, by members of the servant class to gain entry to all doors and thereby rewrite the rules of class accession. If Madame Riccoboni's use of the obscured door is less political, it is just as psychologically important for what it says about her male character's moral confusion and subsequent attempts at self-exculpation and escape.

In her country manor, which in no way resembles the spatial puzzle and erotic stimulus of the labyrinth, such as Vivant Denon proposes in his comic short story of lust and immorality, "Point de lendemain," Madame Riccoboni forsakes another seduction scene convention from libertine literature: the implicit fourth wall, filled by a reader–voyeur. Her reader remains outside the text, perceiving the *cabinet* and its furnighings as unfriendly, angular, obstructionist. The scene itself is encoded from beginning to end as absence, loss, expiration: of love as of virginity, of reason as of passion. What transpires in her *cabinet* is an undoing, a disfiguration, an ending and not a beginning. Which is, of course, precisely the story of the subsequent forced marriage between d'Ossery and Miss Jenny—the young woman having become pregnant as a result of the rape. By refusing to evoke the erotic pleasure and equivocation of the conventional boudoir and its implicit fourth wall at which the *lecteur–voyeur* sits perched at the keyhole, Riccoboni's text makes it impossible to turn rape into an erotic reading.

Hence she reveals her conviction that authorial choice solicits a certain kind of reading, which likewise leads her to dismiss the argument made by Laclos in his two ironic prefaces that novel-reading in general is dangerous to the morals of young and vulnerable women. For her, it is Laclos himself who turns rape into an erotic joke. He is the one responsible for making it impossible to perform both an "ethics of reading," as represented by J. Hillis Miller, and a "reading with feeling" in Susan Feagin's sense, because of his pervasive use of irony that obscures the meaning of every act and every character.[13] Since for Riccoboni, the project of reading, like the project of writing must have two purposes: to please and to be useful," she believes that the writer's goal is not to encourage conspiratorial winks, but responsible writing.[14] For that reason, she will not play to the reader's inflammable imagination by presenting an erotically charged atmosphere or a cynically sophisticated antihero, but rather a typical *cabinet*, an innocent and noncomplicitous victim, and a male who does not sneeringly boast of giving Jenny Montfort "what she wanted" or "deserved," but who plaintively—and self-incriminatingly—pleads fleeting and uncontrollable "instinct."

In that sense, Madame Riccoboni seeks to recuperate the reading of rape, to reveal its prevalence, and to bring novel-reading back to the goal of usefulness. Because she objects to the violence that libertine literature does against both the woman in fiction and the woman reader who is invited to watch herself being degraded or worse yet, made complicitous with her own degradation, Ribboconi seeks a reading that combines ethics and feeling at the same time it disavows female victimhood, even while recognizing the limitations on woman's absolute autonomy. It is from that particular perspective that another more nuanced interpretation can made of the novel's hasty and surprising conclusion, one that focuses neither on authorial contrivance nor on catering to the prejudices of an eighteenth-century public.

Endings and Feminist Irony

Arguably, it is not only by rewriting rape and offering a strong heroine, but by exposing the double standard that prevails in society and mounting a pointed if not scathing critique of marriage that Riccoboni produces an ending at once ironic and feminist. The marriage at the end of the novel does not represent a moment of triumph for her woman protagonist; it is not the fairy-tale conclusion to a rocky and prolonged courtship promising a happily-ever-after future. Instead, this marriage has been arranged and carries all the negative baggage of any arranged marriage, even if these two individuals already know one another. Society had wanted this marriage and cast a blind eye to d'Ossery's misdemeanors and a deaf ear to Juliette's objections. Society had been eager to reinsert male privilege into the contract and to reaffirm female acquiescence. But Madame Riccoboni does not surrender her heroine to these prejudices. While Juliette may indeed love d'Ossery, she no longer harbors rose-colored illusions about him. As he stands over her exulting that she is now his wife and bears his name, Juliette is shown to retain the power of the pen and the presence of mind to wield it for her own purposes. By thus nuancing the scene, the author writes a denouement that is realistic rather than romantic, open rather than closed, and ironic precisely because in ostensible resolution it has not resolved everything.

Such an interpretation is consistent both with her beliefs about right reading and her latent feminism. Because in the figurative sense, Riccoboni "reads" rape differently from eighteenth-century law and society, and because she believes that reading, in literal terms, should be enlightening and perhaps even uplifting—which does not likewise imply that the stories told are naive—she presents a subtle argument that supports a feminist interpretation of this novel despite its apparently unfeminist ending. For, in presenting two implicit theories of male sexuality—one essentialist and the other constructionist—she in effect demonstrates in her novel the idea of female superiority in terms not only of being the moral sex, but also in possessing the capacity to create openings for herself even under the watchful eye of the male reader. Hence, while Madame Riccoboni does not ignore woman's vulnerability and shows her female protagonist ultimately accommodating herself to a conventional marriage, she also has her prefigure in the last scene of the novel a new relationship between reader and writer with distincly subversive impulses. Having reclaimed the pen, Juliette uses it to bear witness to the primacy of her tenderness for Henriette. Far more than merely an elegant expression of friendship, Juliette's words demonstrate her own autonomous will and her refusal to be controlled by the man, the suprareader, who hovers behind her.

Many readers who miss this have wondered exactly who Juliette has become by the last pages of the novel. Is she still the acerbic and delightfully opinionated critic who rails against male baseness, pride, and ingratitude and who compares men to the snake who diverts a woman's attention in order to spring his trap (Letter 9)? Is she the same outspoken combatant of the unjust sexual contract, the one who told Milord Carlile, "I am your equal and I accept no distinctions between creatures who feel, think, and act similarly" (Letter 14, p. 46)? Why has she married this man whom Madame Riccoboni had been at pains to show as so inadequate in terms of rational motivation, so flawed even in his honor, so lacking in taste that he names the child he fathered through rape after Juliette? (Strikingly, Madame Riccoboni did not arrange a convenient miscarriage for the abused Miss Jenny, precisely because she aims to show how shameful acts produce nothing but shameful consequences.[15]) Why does Riccoboni have her protagonist become a victim of society's willing accommodation of male privilege? Playing on variants of the verb to forget (*oublier*)—d'Ossery's plea of having momentarily "forgotten himself" versus Juliette's ironic phrase that his cowardly silence will be her "*préservatif* [emphasis added] against his sex" (Letter 10, 32) and allow her to forget him—the author does not subsequently make the moral argument by which *forgiving* takes over from *forgetting*. Instead, the reader, who had every reason to believe, prior to the last few pages, that Madame Riccoboni's novel would continue the tradition of refusal first set down in the *Princesse de Clèves* and let Juliette forgive but refuse a marriage with d'Ossery, is initially taken aback by the actions of the female protagonist who could, after all, have been permitted to demonstrate magnanimity of spirit while retaining her authority.[16] But whereas Juliette had been infuriated by Miss Jenny's double victimization, first as a victim of rape and than as the martyred young wife; whereas she had been incensed that d'Ossery had caused the premature death of a young woman while ostensibly doing the "honorable" thing by marrying her; outraged that he would seek to excuse his behavior by pleading to a mere error in judgment; and adamantly and inalterably opposed to all he had done and represented, now Juliette marries him.

Is it forgiveness, acceptance, or resignation on the character's part? And is it surrender to reigning literary conventions involving reader expectations on the part of the author, as Susan Lanser proposes?[17] Riccoboni is never explicit on what takes place in Juliette's heart between letters 36 and 37, and from Saturday to Sunday, when her icy resolve against d'Ossery apparently melts away. But in the sudden changes of the last pages of the novel, we see Juliette's friends conspire to make her forget that d'Ossery has sinned against one woman and raped another. Betrayed and diminished by her friends, Juliette, the formerly spunky protagonist, so reminiscent of Jane Austen's heroines, Elizabeth Bennett of *Pride and Prejudice* and the Dashwood sisters of *Sense and Sensibililty*, is poised to be reabsorbed through marriage into the social order of the double standard. When d'Ossery announces to

Henriette, that "Mlle Catesby is no more," having been replaced by Madame d'Ossery, he is not only using gallant language, but is in essence reasserting male dominance, codified in law and the marriage contract and blotting out the woman's name and rights. As a consequence, if the external reader has felt sympathy for Juliette, who had struggled to have her intellect rule her conduct, while demonstrating the spectacle of her heart waging its war against reason, importantly that friendly sympathy does not extend to d'Ossery, who in this final scene persists in trying to impose his views and position on the woman, only this time not through physical violation, but by an attitude of "regulatory" love. In consequence, Lanser has argued that from the moment the husband appropriates her voice, Juliette is silenced and loses control over both her story and her correspondence with Henriette.[18] But is this so?

While certainly only the most blindly romantic reader can conclude that Juliette's marriage represents a truly happy ending, I would propose that this is part of Madame Riccoboni's steely-eyed critique of the double standard and the status quo. For the marriage just negotiated has been constructed on *terra infirma*. Juliette's quarrel with d'Ossery is much deeper than a mere lovers spat, and by forcing a reconciliation leading to marriage between them, her friends assume moral blinders, becoming co-conspirators of the sexist ethos that diminishes the seriousness of rape. Certainly we cannot deny that Juliette's feelings for d'Ossery are complexly motivated, or that part of the story's intent may be to reveal her pridefulness.[19] But we may also remember that Juliette had written to Henriette in Letter 23 (prior to d'Ossery's full confession) of her desire to be able to tell him, "I perhaps still love you, but I no longer respect you . . . the constancy of my feelings is not a proof that I believe you worthy of my commitment" (103). Even into the last scenes Juliette expresses moral anguish, etched in the words she writes to Henriette: "Milady d'Ossery [Miss Jenny] is dead. Her husband is guilty," followed by the questions, "Is he still guilty? Or is he not? There is the troubling dilemma" (169). And if he is still guilty, how long must his crime be held against him? It is a problem as current today as centuries ago.

In trying to explain how the marriage came about, Juliette writes that she had been subjected to a *conjuration* directed against her, and that her will had been *overcome:* "In truth, I was married off so quickly that I truly believe the marriage is worth nothing," she says (174). At this point Madame Riccoboni seems to be marshaling irony and feminist impulses to cast doubt on the wisdom of giving in to the demands of the heart and of society. To underscore that point, the author endows d'Ossery with a newly invigorated voice and has him write with triumphant egotism, "Is there still a Milady Catesby in the world?" and then exult, "She is *mine*, forever *mine*. There is no more Miss Catesby; she is *my* wife, *my* friend, *my* mistress, the happy spirit who gives *me* back all of which *I* had been deprived" [emphasis added]. It could not be clearer that this man sees his new wife as a thing *he* possesses, for *his* happiness, which had unjustly been denied to *him*. By juxtaposing d'Ossery's trumpeting with the muffled voice of the new bride demurely reticent, Madame Riccoboni dramatizes the double standard through language and brings the reader to question the quality of this marriage and, more broadly, marriage as an institution in the eighteenth century.[20]

Furthermore, at the same time that she makes a strong *external* indictment of the double standard that places women at such a disadvantage while pardoning the excesses of the other sex, Madame Riccoboni sets about to propose an *internal* liberation of her heroine. Rejecting the convention by which the woman either agrees to forget the past or resigns herself to the culture and sexual wars of society, the novelist advances a new tactic through her female protagonist. In the final letter of the text, following d'Ossery's self-congratulation on his "ownership" of Juliette, it is Juliette, herself, who seizes the pen and writes the closing words of the text.[21] Outwardly illustrative of the newly married couple's oneness, the letter-writing scene signifies something quite different. For they are not the single entity to which d'Ossery had referred and they do not think and speak with one voice and set of expectations, as Riccoboni shows. If d'Ossery is the triumphant male, ostentatiously beaming and benevolent, his prerogatives as husband/suprareader permit him to police and censure his wife's words either through his mere presence or an overcherishing attitude. Which means that Juliette must maneuver some freedom for her own self under the overseer's eye. That she lays claim to self-expression, that she refuses to let her voice be subsumed in his, that she is not silent, are enormously important acts. Indeed, one might even suggest that this image could be read more broadly in terms of the history of female authors in eighteenth-century France, writing in the shadow of men, but telling their own stories, composed for and communicating with their female readers. It is almost as though Riccoboni is saying that married women and female writers like Juliette must practice a form of positive creative deceit, and learn how to negotiate being at once "connected to" others and autonomous, under the watchful eye of a society that reads them and seeks to, but does not, control their texts.

Through the illustrative metaphor of reading and a kind of delicate feminist irony, Madame Riccoboni's novel deals perceptively and realistically with issues of voice and violence, authority and autonomy. Her position in the end, if not dramatic, is that we live in relationship to one another, and that while that very fact may mute the force of women's voices, it cannot be allowed to silence them. If so much about the hurried ending of the novel had seemed to suggest her heroine's capitulation, except—importantly—that Juliette continues to write, her female protagonist is not by any matter of means utterly dominated. There are hopeful signs that she has begun to integrate disappointment and difficult knowledge into her life without abandoning herself to bitterness and anger, and that she understands the challenge of mediating between the "I" of her essential individuality and the "we" of marriage. And she does, after all, have the last word.

It is with regard to the ending, which is decidedly not romantic, with the female protagonist moving toward rational integration of her new role, while defending her self from being completely appropriated, that the story is more than "simply" a sentimental novel. Indeed, by ending as she does, Madame Riccoboni proposes that her novel be approached through fusing two theories of reading. On the one hand, the reader is asked to "read with feeling," and on the other, she is invited to do so from within an understanding of the double standard and its sociopolitical implications. Hence while Madame Riccoboni could rewrite the actual rape scene, she could not rewrite the larger social contract and the sexist psychology of a society that accommodates rape but not full female autonomy. However, at the same time she does not abandon her heroine either to social or literary convention, but sketches out a way for her to continue to discover and to reaffirm an identity in-process.

By having chosen rape and not seduction as the dramatic focus and by writing a male protagonist who is irresolute, flawed, and unable to control himself—a neat turn in the war of the sexes revealing the *man* as victim of his physiology and sexuality[22]—Madame Riccoboni brings the reader into dialogue with the larger issues of moral society concerning relations between the sexes. At the same time, she offers an insightful but non-melodramatic portrait of the real causes for women's disappointments in love, having to do with social expectations and gender prejudices. Thus, I would argue that for Madame Riccoboni, the novel—especially the woman's novel—carries considerable potential for simultaneously investigating and commenting on the sociological, sexual, and sentimental structures that impact women's lives. In this manner, her novel breaks out of the confines of mere sentimentality, and suggests that woman's sensibility precludes neither rationality, nor a critical view of the social structures. Indeed, as Nancy K. Miller has argued, women's novels of the eighteenth century, despite their appearance as innocuous sentimental tracts, often contain critical discourse about social morals and manners, an observation that if true places them within the important tradition of the rise of realism in the novel.[23] Ironically, it will be on those very grounds of a lack of realism that Madame Riccoboni will base a part of her charge against Choderlos de Laclos in their brief and elegantly barbed correspondence, following the publication of his novel in 1782.

LITERARY AND SEXUAL WARS: THE RICCOBONI-LACLOS CORRESPONDENCE

When the sixty-eight-year-old Madame Riccoboni takes on the forty-two-year-old author of *Les Liaisons dangereuses*, she never states that it is the culture of rape in Laclos's work that raises her ire. But there can be little doubt that precisely this conviction motivates the icy nature of her prose. Whereas she had written of a single rape to show its effects on typical individuals and underscore how social prejudice silently accommodates it, she probably felt that Laclos wrote from within a moral climate that generalized rape as the principle of all social interaction.[24] Moreover, by making a portrait of rape so appealing—even if appalling—his novel perpetrated a sort of figurative rape on the female reader, which put it at variance with the purposes of literature and reading, according to Madame Riccoboni, who believed that especially because women live in greater isolation, their novel-reading will have a stronger effect on them. Indeed, she would second Rousseau who had written, "When one lives in isolation, one meditates more on what one reads; and when there is not much outside to counter it, the reading has a much greater effect internally."[25] Because women do not live in the public sphere, and thus have less opportunity to come in contact with ideas and with others, their domestic reading is all the more important in helping them to make choices about their own lives and to live with greater awareness.

In this sense, one can argue that Madame Riccoboni's critique of Laclos's novel constitutes an early feminist theory of reading, for in her reaction to *Les Liaisons*, she underscores the importance of gender and her own response as a female reader, and exhibits an underlying concern for the political dimensions of reading and gender.[26] Hence, she frames her objections first "as a woman," next as a "French woman," and finally as a "patriot concerned with the honor of her nation." She feels personally offended by the portrait Laclos offers of Madame de Merteuil because he has shown that a highly intelligent, rational woman is in essence a moral monster, "une vile créature," one who consciously uses her mind to master nature and who grounds her behavior on a set of "black principles" (Letter V).

In addition to an implicit clash over ideologies of gender, the correspondence between Laclos and Madame Riccoboni can be plumbed for their different notions regarding reading and the purposes of literature. In fact, in this brief four-week exchange of letters, these two successful eighteenth-century writers reveal diametrically opposed esthetics and philosophies, which illustrate not only fundamentally different worldviews, but also antithetical ideas about the role of private and domestic reading. For Laclos, the pleasures of reading are located in the intellect and in notions of the subversive, while for Riccoboni, reading should act on the reader's emotions and involve questions of value deployment and personal discovery. Because of their basic difference about why one reads and/or why one should read, their two texts—despite a similarity in subject matter—embrace different goals and solicit entirely different readers.[27]

For Laclos that person will be the sophisticated ironic reader who, familiar with the rules of the game and the conventions of the high-society sport of love, finds literary pleasure in the notion of the intellectual, regulated, disciplined world of *ludus* (the Latin word for game), as identified by Roger Caillois, and in which calculation, contrivance, and ingenuity are the main ingredients.[28] This reader will enjoy playing the game of reading, weighing the moves of the different players and following their complex strategies within the network of competing codes and conventions, contracts and compacts.[29] This is the reader for whom "dangerous" means "exciting" rather than "peril," and who wishes to be intelligently entertained. Like Laclos himself, this literarily sophisticated reader is not above poking fun at the conventions of literature, including the "dangerous liaison," and the prejudices of naive readers.

Riccoboni, on the other hand, rejects the ludic as the central principle of reading, because for her such a stance is unproductive, governed as in *Les Liaisons* by a set of rules she finds offensive. There is, in her judgment, no "win" for women in reading Laclos's novel, no payoff in a superior understanding of the issues raised, since in the end the reader learns nothing useful by reading how all ideals are undone or compromised and how everyone or everything is tainted. "So much depravity irritates and does not instruct," she protests in Letter V. The cheating and lying within the text, the bargaining and negotiating games in which bluffing and dissembling prevail, not only between in-text players, but also when perpetrated by the writer on the reader, are authorial strategies condemned by Riccoboni, since they work together to prevent the reader from coming to a positive, enlightening reading. "One cries out on each page, 'that cannot be!'" she criticizes, underscoring the error of exaggeration and lack of realism against which she, as reader, reacts. Negative instruction will further undermine the reading process, she objects, especially when the reader learns from Laclos's text not to trust—neither others, nor the author, who produces a text saturated in irony, through every word and line and page. Unable to form consistent patterns of meaning, the reader is further abused, she might argue, by a writer who teases with him (or her), much as did Valmont with Cécile, not so much in the flirtatious sense of offering and then refusing, but in the malicious sense of treating the other as a plaything, manipulating, exploiting, violating—in other words, "raping."

Indeed, it is the irony of Laclos's text—about women, about sexual assault, about meaning—that bothers Madame Riccoboni who objects to the precarious nature of any system of authorization and the indeterminacy of all knowledge—certainly of all useful knowledge—in *Les Liaisons*. For Laclos's stance on the sexual wars, as on the culture wars, is to ironize them by setting in discourse characters who represent opposing poles and end up destroying each other. She, on the other hand, rejects absolutely the ironic mode as one that does not have the ability to touch hearts and thereby to render the reading "useful." Since her objective is to reveal the effects of real acts on real people, meaning both the sociology and immorality of rape, she seeks to make an affective impact on her reader. Therefore, she exposes the woman's obvious worth, coupled with her victimization, showing a Miss Jenny, much like the Demoiselle de Bisès, abused by men—brother, rapist, husband—and by a society that operates by a diminished notion of what it means to be honorable and to be dishonored.

Since she situates reading within a structure that seeks to affect and to enlighten, and since she aspires to have her reader read with feeling, rather than for pleasure, she bases her appeal to the reader's heart on situations and characters that are easy to identify with and wholly believable. Hence, she adheres to the principle of realism in character and in story, avoiding the extraordinary, unlike Laclos. Objecting to his portrait of extreme depravity in Merteuil and Valmont, who are, in her view, created with absolute disregard for truthfulness and realism, she writes, "One doesn't have to be warned about characters who could not possibly exist," thereby underscoring a double violation of esthetic laws and of women. For, she asks, how can he claim to like women, when he offends them all by his unrealistic image of woman as personified in Madame de Merteuil (Letter V). Making an early feminist reading of his novel, she in essence objects to it on the grounds that it represents a violation against women and against the reader, an opinion shared by another female writer, Madame de Genlis, who referred to *Les Liaisons dangereuses* as "that infamous work" and called it "execrable in its principles."[30] "One finds in it neither invention, nor characters, nor new or faithful portrayals of the world," Genlis wrote, thereby reiterating the criticism of a lack of realism made by Madame Riccoboni. Furthermore, both women might agree that since the objective of the reading act is to confer value and confirm worthiness, Laclos had not only made vice too attractive in his protagonist, but also perpetrated a symbolic rape on all French women, defaming them unjustly and indiscriminately.

Remarkably, nearly all of Madame Riccoboni's objections to Laclos's novel were forecast as early as 1759 in the discourse on writing in Letter 15 of *L'Histoire de Milady Catesby* in which Juliette reviews a book received from her friend Henriette. Through the protagonist's words, Madame Riccoboni presents her view of responsible writing, whose same arguments, twenty-five years later, form the basis for her indictment of Laclos's novel. Convinced that reading is key to self-enlightenment, she believes that a writer has a responsibility to present a moral work of art, which means that fiction must emphasize the ethical dimensions of human relations. Her objective is to expose "the real and simple truths of the heart" that speak to the soul and open it to feeling (Letter 4).[31] "I would like people to write from a more disinterested motive than that of showing off mind and spirit," she has Juliette say (79), adding, "Is it not better to raise the spirit than to pull it down?" Believing that the writer serves the reader by writing the story with empathy rather than *esprit*, Madame Riccoboni attacks Laclos specifically on those grounds in their letter exchange, for she equates "esprit" with superficial cleverness, which does not appeal to the best in human nature. Juliette had said, "The writer who wants to make his ideas useful must help us take advantage of the seed of good that lies within us." People need to feel that virtuous action is a choice and when they make the right one for the right reasons they deserve credit. "To attribute all our good actions to vanity or self-love is to rebuff the heart." Thus, as early as 1759 and through Juliette, who objects to those who call themselves *moralistes* and who set themselves up as "scrutinizers and judges of the soul in order to vilify and to demean its most noble operations," Madame Riccoboni sets forth the very same esthetic and ethical position that nearly a quarter of a century later informs her criticism of Laclos's novel. Fully cognizant of the arguments raised by authors who justify an attitude of cynical pessimism because that is what they "see" in society, Riccoboni's Juliette had objected, "Talking to us only of our weaknesses is like saying repeatedly to an unfortunate person that they are to be pitied. If you can't help, why make their misery even clearer to them?"

In his letters, Laclos defends himself by saying that painting depraved manners is one way of combating them. After all, he argues, showing vice at its most seductive and charming is to expose most decisively its machinations and thus to be "useful" to one's reader. Using third-person attribution to speak of himself (similar to the stance he takes in the two prefaces to the *Liaisons*), Laclos writes, "In sum, Mr. De L. did not at all seek to wrap vice invitingly," arguing that he had merely painted it with all the charms it so often wears, and that his intention had never "for a moment been to lessen the feelings of horror vice must always inspire" (Letter II). His defense is not especially inspired—which does not, of course, mean that it is wrong. But it is his attitude—a kind of cockiness while pretending to take their exchange seriously—that has offended critics like Madelyn Gutwirth.[32] For by adopting an attitude of ostensible obeisance to cultural conventions and proprieties while showing clear presumptiveness about his rights and superiority, Laclos embraces the rhetorical position of the master vis-à-vis an inferior. What makes it worse is that he has even been accused of plundering women's texts for his *Liaisons*, thereby raising the specter of perpetrating a literary rape.[33]

Thus if he continues to correspond with Madame Riccoboni, it is not so much to argue the issues with an opponent whom he does not find fully worthy, as to prolong the game. Very much in the elegantly wicked mode of Valmont, Laclos phrases the arguments in his letters to Riccoboni with the same recourse to ironic apposition and the same quality of rudeness behind double-edged civility that he had used in the service of his fictional *corrupteurs*. Taking ironic aim at his correspondent, he promises that when his readers become tired of the woeful images of society in his book and wish to become acquainted with all the "charms" that a writer might endow on sentiment and virtue, he will invite them to read "Ernestine, Fanny, Catesby, etc. etc. etc." (Letter II). Naturally, to refer to the corpus of his correspondent's considerable writing career in terms of "etc. etc. etc." is scarcely to give much weight to her or her works, a point Madame Riccoboni cannot ignore, and that causes her own brand of specious civility. Opening her next letter by feigning to be flattered, she writes, "You are very generous, Sir, to respond with such polite and flattering compliments, so wittily expressed, to the liberty I dared to take in attacking the principles of a work whose style and details merit so many words of praise" (Letter III). Obviously, her words, like his, can be read through the valence of a double register, signaling insult through the formulae of *politesse*.

At bottom, what offends Madame Riccoboni in Laclos's rape/seductions is the interplay of power and lust, mediated through the voyeuristic gaze of the reader/spectator, and resulting in the constantly repeated story of conquest and defeat.[34] Indeed, as her letters suggest, her antagonism derives from what she deems the global dispossession and disparagement of the female in his novel, leading to the perpetuation or justification of the violence done to women in society. To understand why she reacted in that way to both the social climate of rape and the rape of the woman reader in *Les Liaisons*, it is instructive to remember how every rape in Laclos is a staged event—simultaneously high-spirited and cruel as with Cécile, paradoxical as with Merteuil's reverse-rape of Prévan, and both theatrical and repugnantly sentimental as with Madame de Tourvel, who is permitted short-lived bliss before consigning herself to near-madness and death.

Unlike Madame Riccoboni, who situated her rape scene, as we saw, in an erotically neutral space, Laclos sought out the most transgressive and shocking locales: a young virgin's bed or a woman's own home, so that, in the latter case, Valmont can dispossess both the woman and the "space" of the husband—consistent with patriarchal society's notion that rape is essentially a crime of property. Moreover, Laclos insists on inflecting his scenes with (for many women readers) repellent ambiguity on the part of the female character, since the defeat of the woman is accompanied in the seductions of both the *Présidente* and Cécile not only by their complicity, but also their ultimate acquiescence, including, in the case of the young girl her own involuntary arousal.[35] To thus color the rape of a young girl, it could be argued, is the outworking of a particular male fantasy that perpetuates the myth that every woman really wants to be possessed or dominated sexually and that the man simply should persevere despite the female's protestations, since she will surely (as Laclos shows with all the women bedded by Valmont) enjoy the experience and, moreover, "be the better for it." Which is precisely the argument that Madame de Merteuil raises to quell Cécile's initital shame: now she can feel more like a woman—that is, according to how a *man* thinks a woman should feel.

In sum, the narrative and esthetic choices regarding rape on the part of the two writers could not be more striking. In Madame Riccoboni's rape, there was no willful premeditation, no artfulness, no erotically encoded spaces. There is no ironic ambiguity, as in *Les Liaisons*, and neither her male nor female characters use their sexuality consciously as a way of degrading and controlling the other sex. I have speculated that what she had wanted to reveal was the very commonality of rape as an act committed not by a cunning rake or magnetic seducer impossible to resist, but by an average man of average impulses and powerful little honor. So, while in Laclos, rape is a complicated, premeditated, and complexly motivated act, edging toward being rationalized or justified, in Riccoboni the rape is an opportunistic event, related in its barest essentials, by a man who is not proud, but ashamed. Furthermore, by having d'Ossery accuse himself to Juliette from whom he seeks forgiveness, Riccoboni creates a set of narrative relations not present in *Les Liaisons*. Not only is the relationship between addressor and addressee different than in Laclos, where the intent of the addressor is nearly always to prove him or herself and often to incite arousal in the addressee, but also the relationship between the internal reader and the letter is changed, since the text embracing the female gaze (which d'Ossery adopts) seeks to solicit sympathy rather than admiration. Finally, there is no suggestion in her work that rape is merely seduction misunderstood—as it was codified in ancien-régime law.[36] In the culture wars of prerevolutionary France in which sexual relations figure predominantly, both the male judicial system in society and the code of the libertine text in fiction had in essence re-raped woman through her devaluation in law and text. It is this conviction that in 1759 had persuaded Madame Riccoboni to write her novel and twenty-three years later to object to Laclos's.

READING RELATIONS AND CULTURE WARS

Although it might be possible to dismiss the Riccoboni–Laclos debate as simply a continuation of the age-old battle of the sexes, to do so would both diminish the dynamic and complex ways sex and gender operate on culture, and suggest that the subject "woman" is conceivable only in relationship with men. To accept the latter would be like saying that there was no specific "woman question" in eighteenth-century France, which strikes me as fundamentally wrong. At different points in their creative lives, both Laclos and Riccoboni were convinced that such a question was key to creating a more just social contract to govern "enlightened" times. Riccoboni's views on the subject need hardly be reviewed again, and students of the eighteenth century will recall that Laclos was to write in "De L'Education des femmes" that all women were oppressed in contemporary societies and would leave their condition only by a social revolution. Obviously in *Les Liaisons*, he had not yet reached that point, or, at least, his intentions as a novelist did not embrace such principles. Whereas for Madame Riccoboni, Laclos is completely wrong both in his assumptions about women and in his use of the novel. For he had not made the novel a tool of change, she believed, but had merely exploited his talents in order to playfully and cynically portray, if not justify, libertinism. In fact, for her, his novel represented that part of the cultural divide that did damage to women by engaging in a facile "war" of slander against them. Hence, she felt obliged to do battle not in another skirmish between the sexes, but against the broader context of dominant cultural attitudes in politics and ideology, law and education, religion and ethics that demeaned women, and hence weakened the body politic. It is in that sense that the sharp divisions between Riccoboni and Laclos could be cast as a "battle of the books," involved with diametrically opposed notions of both reading relations and the function of literature, and illustrating the role that text and gender play in the "culture wars" of the eighteenth century.[37]

Writing for an audience largely of bourgeois readers and specifically for a rising female reading public whose consumption of novels would, in Elizabeth Eisenstein's view, lead to a variety of domestic dramas (since now "home" and "family" were endowed with educational functions),[38] Madame Riccoboni invited her reader to look upon the novel as a legitimate site of ongoing education. In the *Lettres de Milady Juliette Catesby*, she would expose the reader not to a new fiction of escape, but a realistic story of disappointment and disillusionment, which did not, however, lead to self-destructive cynicism or moral abandon. In the literary culture wars of eighteenth-century France, which set two ideals in opposition—libertinism and sentimentality—and tended to dismiss female novelists as capable of writing only lesser, sentimental works, Madame Riccoboni would strive for a third position, combining both psychological and social realism, in demonstration of her conviction that literature could not please if it was not real and will not instruct if it is not realistic.

In this sense, Madame Riccoboni participates in the same literary and cultural climate as Jean-Jacques Rousseau, who, in fact, stands as the shadow presence in her correspondence with Laclos and against whom the latter had conceived his novel. Indeed, one simply cannot read *Les Liaisons dangereuses*, especially not its key prefaces, saturated in literary and social irony, without evoking the novelist of *La Nouvelle Héloïse*. For it is Rousseau's epithet, "I saw the manners of my time and I published these Letters," drawn from his preface to *Héloïse*, that is selected by Laclos, the brillant and ironic imitator, for his own title page. Indeed, to read Laclos's two liminal texts, the "Avertissement de l'éditeur" and the "Préface du rédacteur" without placing them in apposition to Rousseau is to miss the rich and creative strikes that he makes against literary convention and popular cultural and reading practice. This is so because Rousseau's preface is generally viewed as an important statement on the reading relations between author and reader and a demonstration of why he was so profoundly to transform the novel. Yet Laclos takes every one of Rousseau's principles and either inverts them in his text or treats them ironically. Madame Riccoboni, on the other hand, embraced those principles, even before Rousseau published them, in proof of the fact that she shared with him a similar esthetic of sensibility and critical assessment of society. Believing that sexual and reading relations occupy common ground and pose potential risks for women, and concluding that Laclos had perpetrated a violence against his readers through the dangerous combination of perverse characters, "esprit," and the "grâces de style," she conducted her criticism of Laclos on exactly the same grounds that Rousseau had set forth. To wit: Rousseau had emphasized that fiction must imitate life; the writer must try to make the reader read in the right way; the novel must be grounded in realism but carry the reader to idealism; the reader should come to value his own *vie intérieure* through the portrayal of that of the main character; the novel must appeal through everyday detail and not through luxury; there must be an emotional exchange between reader and writer, as between reader and the printed word.[39] Riccoboni subscribes to every one of those principles that for her constitute the desiderata of all reading encounters.

So, it is not only the result of a twenty-five year age span between Riccoboni and Laclos (she could have been his mother) and the opposing literary ideals of sentimentality and libertinism that account for the differences between them. But also their adherence to completely different concepts of reading relations. For whereas Laclos takes an ironic view of reading and rape—casting both as games of violation and subversion, from within a framework of complicity between male and female, reader and writer, and places emphasis on the ludic and intellectual, and on power relations within libertinism—Riccoboni focuses on recuperating the reading of rape, to show it not as sport or a theory of human interaction, but as a moral, social, and cultural problem. Her concentration on the double standard shows that what is at issue for her are the two opposing notions of virtue and honor that reign in society, applied differently to the sexes. What she aims to demonstrate is the inherent injustice of the different treatment of the sexes, yet also women's superior capability to deal with disappointment and disillusion. Employing a narrative structure of univocal female epistolarity, through which male voice at first *penetrates* (in d'Ossery's various interpolated letters, most notably in Letter XXI), and then *vainquishes*, with his trimphant "She is *mine*" letter (recalling Valmont's "There she is finally vanquished . . . she is mine, utterly mine" CXXV), one might suggest that Riccoboni unwittingly uses a narrative structure that imitates a figurative rape. Yet she also endeavors to have her heroine persevere with the pen.

As a woman inspired by Enlightenment ideas of culture in which fiction has a social and educative role, she rejects Laclos's exploitative uses of reading and writing through characters in fiction who consciously choose their readings in order to gain mastery in confrontations with others, or who write letters and contemplate memoirs for their own nefarious purposes and to manipulate the internal and external reader. Those are not the worthy purposes of an enlightened individual, in her view, but of an anti-Enlightenment mentality in which both writer and character seek renown. Laclos, after all, had been quoted as saying that he wanted to create a work "that left the usual route, got itself talked about, and had an impact in the world" long after his life. And Madame Riccoboni acknowledges, "All Paris rushes to read you, all Paris is talking about you." But she adds her own barb, saying, "If it is happiness to keep the inhabitants of this vast capital so occupied, then do enjoy such pleasure. No one could savor it as much as you" (Letter III). For her, however, the writer should have a nobler objective beyond seeking to entertain through a wicked sense of humor. One can speculate that her more sober view of literature comes from having to practice her art as did Juliette, from within the constraints of dominant culture, even while writing against them. Such is the meaning that might in fact be ascribed to Madame Riccoboni's final image of reader and writer, as the suprareader looms over Juliette while she writes her letter to Henriette who, as the intended internal reader, is silently charged to model an empathetic reading that will be reproduced by the external reader. In this sense, Riccoboni's text acknowledges the presence of the "male reader" in society and in literary production, but endeavors to reach beyond, under his very eyes, to another reader. Hence she moves the culture wars, in which the violation and violence of sexual relations have played such a large role against women, to a different cultural level in which new kinds of strategies and smaller but courageous examples of self-definition will be proposed to women through reading and writing.

Ultimately, Madame Riccoboni endeavors to make both the project of fiction and the function of reading serve to enlighten the reader not by denying the realities of woman's social existence, but by proposing the means of overcoming the appropriation of her voice and her absorption into the man she marries. Reading, which is cast as a sexual substitute *within* the novel, is offered as the means by which the external female reader can process disappointing relationships with men and tap into a core of strength within herself. In rewriting both the scene and the meaning of rape, and in underscoring the abhorrent double standard that reigned in her society, Madame Riccoboni's novel, through the metaphoric interplay of rape and reading, makes the case for responsible fiction as for responsible sexuality.

SIX

BOOKS, SEX, AND READING IN THE FAIRY TALE

GABRIELLE-SUZANNE BARBOT DE VILLENEUVE, 1685–1755

JEANNE LEPRINCE DE BEAUMONT, 1711–1780

> Continuing her promenade . . . she entered another gallery. . . . It contained an enormous library. . . . Her great taste for reading was going to be easily satisfied in this place
>
> "La Belle et la Bête," Madame de Villeneuve

READING FAIRY TALES

Ironically, the fairy tale has been maligned by individuals as different as Jean-Jacques Rousseau and feminist scholars, who, improbable as it seems, do, however, agree on one thing: tales of the marvelous should be unrecommended reading for little girls. While Jean-Jacques bases his judgment on the reckless quality of the imagination, feminist critics have emphasized gender bias and inequitable modes of socialization and have implicitly accused women writers of the fairy tale of compliance with the patriarchal structures of ancien-régime France. Joining with Rousseau, Félicité de Genlis railed against the genre, insisting that fairy tales have very little educational value: "There is almost not a single one whose subject is truly moral," she opined, "love becomes the entire interest: everywhere one finds a princess loved and persecuted because she is beautiful, and a prince, handsome as the day, who loves her to death."[1]

Insipid, harmful, an arm in the arsenal of patriarchy, according to feminist critics who agree with Genlis that it keeps women too focused on love and marriage, and who accuse the fairy tale of teaching little girls sacrifice and submission to males and to the state, the *conte de fées* has nonetheless proven itself to be enduring for untold readers, both children and adults, when so many other texts from the past have disappeared. That it was a form that flourished well into the Enlightenment period is all the more surprising, given its antirationalist roots and emphasis on fairies and works of magic. But as I will seek to show in my discussion of "La Belle et la Bête," the fairy tale is not only representative of Enlightenment idealism concerning virtue and the educability of human beings, demonstrating the conviction that words and stories can instruct readers, but it is also an unexpected source both internally and externally for a discourse on books and reading. Remarkably, in a genre with oral roots, the written book has, as Gabrielle Verdier has shown, considerable internal presence in the fairy tale.[2] In fact, in "La Belle et la Bête," books and reading play a primary role in both establishing and validating character and developing narrative progression. At the same time, externally, issues of reading are germane, because the reader's very experience with the fairy tale engages with the way reading has been theorized as game-like by Michel Picard in *La Lecture comme jeu*.[3] For if the literary reading is characterized by elements of play and gaming, such an assertion would seem to be especially true in the purest form of literary play—the fairy tale, which is a kind of school in reading, in which we first learn about connotative values and guessing, the symbolic world and illusion.

The fairy tales of early France are a literature of the imagination, coming from the seventeenth and eighteenth centuries, but speaking to all ages.[4] Over time, they have been subject to a variety of interpretive approaches from the psychoanalytic, to the semiotic, the sociocritical to the feminist. In the late twentieth century, scholarship of the fairy tale focused on sexual, historical, and political readings that indicted the genre for reaffirming the worst aspects of patriarchy and becoming part of the problem surrounding women's lack of social progress. Jack Zipes, for instance, lamented the dark side of fairy tales and suggested that women writers unwittingly used it to express "male needs and hegemony" rather than their own.[5] For him and others, the fairy tale either peddled the myth of romantic complementarity and taught little girls to be submissive, obedient, and self-sacrificing, or it misled them into believing they could change life even when social forces are loaded against them. Thus fairy tales were characterized not as innocent and charming trifles, but as Lewis Seifert has paraphrased the case, "profoundly influential tools for reproducing patriarchal constructions of female identity."[6] For example, feminist scholar Karen E. Rowe determined that fairy tales reward girls when they accept a notion of virtue based on passivity, dependency, and self-abnegation, in return for which the girl "gets" to marry the prince.[7] Female readers, she says, will "readily identify with the prettily passive heroine whose submission to commendable roles insures her triumphant happiness" and "dissociate from . . . portraitures of feminine power, defiance and/or self-expression" (218) because they are cast as negative.

Such ideological readings, while fascinating, pose risks. For they appear to derive from notions that suggest that a reader necessarily identifies only with characters of their own sex; that the value system of the fairy tale is always frontloaded against females; and that reading is dangerous when it does not teach "positive" role models according to the critic. Moreover, women from earlier centuries who wrote such stories are judged to be either complicitous with patriarchal society or blind to its failures vis-à-vis women.[8] What is problematic about this kind of criticism is that it presumes to know how *all* readers read and are affected by a text through an overly simplistic notion of identification; it does not recognize that values in the fairy tale are not as categorically sexed or absolute as generally assumed; and it appears to equate reading with sterile and repugnant indoctrination (about which the critic may have no concern if the teaching were "right"). While granting that the fairy tale certainly does have didactic purposes and sometimes does wear sexist blinders in the hands of certain writers of the ancien régime who were not primarily concerned with giving women new social or political roles, I feel compelled to offer some counterarguments to the heavy artillery that has been brought against a genre whose intentions are deeply situated in presenting ritual patterns of challenge and triumph.

When critics claim that female readers will identify only with examples of inactive and vulnerable heroines and will internalize romantic patterns and learn to accommodate themselves to the cultural myths of patriarchy, they seem to be wearing their own blinders *and* denying my reading as a child. Furthermore, they ignore the fact that the lessons of the fairy tale are broadly applicable to both sexes, since the instruction is of a general nature, concerned with universal values such as honesty, patience, and courage. In fact, vices and virtues are not systematically sexed in the fairy tale, and in the recurring patterns presented by the fairy tale, the child reader can learn from *both* sexes how to prevail through physical and mental resourcefulness. The sins and character flaws of pride, cruelty, selfishness, dissipation, irrationality, passivity, and indiscretion are indictable in either sex; it is not just girls who are taught obedience, prudence, and modesty, and not only boys who learn the value of action, industry, and reason.[9] A study of Madame Leprince de Beaumont's collected fairy tales in *Le Magasin des enfants* will reveal, for instance, that the preponderance of her protagonists are males and that they learn lessons of humility and sacrifice just as often as their less present female counterparts.[10]

Ironically, when critics disqualify the readings of many female children who are delighted and energized by the adventures and exploits of successful and active protagonists of *either* sex, they seem to want to legislate both imagination and the reading act. By reducing the reader exclusively to his or her sex, they assume that every reader reads noncritically and palimpsestically, identifying only with members of his or her own sex rather than with individual strengths of character. Yet even young readers can be discerning, and not easily won over to protagonists who are insipid or sit on their beds and wait to be saved. What captures the imagination of many young readers is the hero or heroine who is, as they see themselves, active, intelligent, curious, and above all, creative and ingenious, able to outwit both adults and evildoers. When the main character proves her mettle and demonstrates both guts and guile, grace and intellect—as Beauty does—the child is ratified in her own capacities. That the female protagonist also wins the prince and the material riches that come with becoming his wife is like the frosting on the cake—it's a nice final touch, but the main course is what came before. After all, even the young reader, who can recognize patterns, if not the literary vocabulary that describes them, knows that by the time Beauty or Cinderella enters the palace the fun is over and that the fairy tale will respect its conventions.

The "happily-ever-after" ending is so formulaic, in fact, that even the child may consider it dull, because, like the reader of the modern romance, this child may not so much read for the ending as for the pleasure derived in getting there. Such a reader makes the journey into a fictional or Lilliputian world where things turn out in optative fashion, or as they "should," and in making that voyage, alongside the protagonist, learns about ideal personal empowerment not often duplicated in real life. Popular culture critic Janice Radway has argued that despite the romance's apparent preoccupation with heterosexual love and marriage, the real impetus that inspires female consumers of the romance is not the romantic wish to find a life partner, but the ritual wish to be cared for, loved, and validated.[11] Similarly, one might say that while the fairy tale seems to embrace the single ending of heterosexual love and marriage, its primary interest is in demonstrating the prerequisite of developing moral character in order to achieve happiness—however it might be defined. Hence, for both genres, the happy ending is part of the convention but not the essential driving force, since, as Bruno Bettelheim writes, the real motivating factor of the reader derives from another more fundamentally psychological and deep-seated need in human nature for stories about validation, achieved through small and large triumphs in the course of a life.[12]

Furthermore, just as these tales do not carry a single, unified message of gender, so their individual moral lessons are frequently multiple, and, not infrequently, less than translucently clear. For if the fairy tale encourages honesty, it also accepts certain kinds of guile; if it calls for open generosity in relations with others, it warns against naiveté; if it teaches against selfishness, it shows realistically through myriad examples how selfish characters can charm and wheedle and often gain their way. In addition, while the fairy tale warns against appearances, improvements in physical appearance may be a part of its internal reward system.[13] And while it preaches meritocracy and reviles ambition, its values are often upwardly mobile.

The point, then, is that if the fairy tale as a genre is less than unified in terms of its internal psychology and the presentation of its own value system, it follows that viewing it through the single lens of female victimization will give an overly narrow reading. With the objective of reorienting the focus, I propose to examine one fairy tale, "Beauty and the Beast," to suggest how it can be read, like the very rose that launches its dramatic and psychological conflict, as containing a more varied discourse on gender than is often proposed. For like that same rose whose delicate petals and sharp thorns simultaneously denote beauty and the wherewithal to defend the self, so this fairy tale carries a double discourse, on the one hand being a simple story of "the route to the palace," while on the other, offering a portrait of female agency founded on *the book* and the craft of reading. Through the fairy tale and its internal discourses on books and knowledge, the practice of reading is shown to be about both recovery and discovery, thereby functioning as a key Proustian metaphor in which reading is represented as a "lens" through which a whole horizon of experience, real or possible, becomes magically recoverable, and in which reading leads to self-discovery.[14] In that the actions of the external reader are mirrored and ratified within the text by the internal reader, *reading* becomes the central metaphor.

BEAUTY AND THE BEAST

Though Madame de Villeneuve and Madame Leprince de Beaumont tell essentially the same basic story in their versions of "Beauty and the Beast," their two tales are significantly different in terms of length and detail, esthetic imagination, and depth of psychological and sexual inquiry. To begin with, Madame de Villeneuve's 1740–1741 version is composed of a 109-page first part entitled "Histoire de la Belle et la Bête" and a 76-page second part called "Histoire de la Bête," relating how and why a prince had been turned into a beast.[15] Madame Leprince de Beaumont, on the other hand, distills the essence of the story into the seventeen-page tale that has become the best known version and the one that Jean Cocteau used as the point of departure for his 1946 classic film.[16] Eschewing the ample and even quasibaroque contours of her predecessor—the rich and exotic detail, side plots, *surprises à tiroir*, semi-erotic dreams, and remarkable system of female governance in the universe of fairies—Madame Leprince seeks to appeal to the imagination through evocation rather than detail. Her choice is explained in part because she intends her tale for children for whom she destined *Le Magasin des enfants*, rather than the adult salon women readers of her predecessor.[17] Thus, she merely sketches female psychology and sexuality with a delicate pen, while Madame de Villeneuve constructs a highly charged discourse of female desire and produces the most extended erotic reverie written by a woman in the eighteenth century. In fact, the presence of this discourse, coupled with the elaborate female power structure, make her text one of the richest examples of female imagination in the ancien régime, and one that challenges the notion that the fairy tale is sexist, capable only of reproducing and ratifying patriarchal constructions of gender identity.

In the following pages, my purpose will be to demonstrate that despite its ostensibly simple form and message, the fairy tale, as construed by these two female authors, is not only as a celebration of imagination and an invitation into a magical domain, but the presentation of an alternative social contract in which women have powerful roles, for good and for bad. We will explore this idea by examining how books and reading function in the fairy tale text, and how reading, books, and sex, which constitute female empowerment, become entwined.

In the Universe of Fairies: Female Power

First, however, it is necessary to consider the special nature of female agency in the fairy tale. Fairies are, of course, a convention of the genre. But while Madame Leprince introduces a single good fairy into her story, Madame de Villeneuve creates an elaborate power structure with a Queen of Fairies, a Council of Fairies, and a General Assembly—a veritable supernatural *cité des dames*, or "order" of women, sometimes equated with a feminized utopia. Furthermore, not only do fairies have all the governing roles, but power is singularly vested in female words. In fact, the power of fairy speech is such that it effectively undercuts the notion that woman's utterances are mindless, useless chatter, with no ability to affect anyone or anything. On the contrary, female speech in the fairy tale is exceptionally valorized. In their roles as counselors and legislators, fairies are the ones who determine what happens, and by their prophetic speech acts, it is they who cast spells and transform a person into an animal or a pumpkin into a royal carriage.[18] In "La Belle et la Bête" a good fairy predicts to the merchant that his daughter will do him honor and save his life; a bad fairy condemns Belle to marry a monster; another good fairy helps turn that monster into a prince. Hence, far from being diminished, female speech—as prediction, condemnation, or facilitator—carries real power both in their own *cité des fées* and when they travel among "real" people.

With a foot in both worlds, the real and supernatural, fairies have a single charge: to participate in the lives of mortals. Toward this end, they voyage widely on earth, and, depending on their inclinations, accomplish great acts of goodness and justice or mete out devilish punishments. In the "real" world, they are motivated by the communal ideas of providence and industry, and seek, within the limits of their own personalities, to make things better. They are attracted to the plight of victims, but earthlings must always show that they deserve a fairy's attentions and must work industriously to profit from her power, teachings, and gifts. Those gifts are of several kinds, some lasting only for a limited period, others with strings attached. Typically, there are few "blanket" gifts of happiness or virtue or pleasure, and sometimes the gift resembles a punishment, as, for instance, when the good fairy of Madame Leprince's "Le Prince Fatal et le Prince Fortuné" gives *le don* (the gift) of hardship to the young Fatal.[19] Such an apparently harsh gift can be a blessing in disguise, since it is wholly in keeping with a guiding principle in fairy-tale psychology that individual and moral character is developed through trials and tribulations and that real happiness and success come from learning how to meet obstacles. Not everyone, however, is capable of learning the lesson, as Madame Leprince shows in one highly unusual fairy tale, "Joliette," whose female protagonist is incapable of using her gifts to moderate her flaws. Having the attributes of beauty, grace, health, and intelligence, Joliette still manages to make a muddle of her life because she is an inveterate gossip. When her special fairy, at wit's end, suggests that Joliette could repair her fault by accepting to become deaf and blind, the character refuses. But the flaw continues to grow unabated, finally bringing triple death: of the husband she loved, her mother, and herself. Remarkably, for a fairy tale, murder, suicide, and sadness constitute its ending.

What is perhaps most interesting about the bevy of fairies who populate Madame de Villeneuve's version of "Beauty and the Beast" is that many of them are extremely prone to the same flaws as mortals.[20] In fact, neither sprites of the woods, nor always wise philosopher-queens, her fairies tend to resemble flesh-and-blood women—those who try to be sincere friends and give good counsel, but are themselves imperfect creatures and emotionally vulnerable. Subject to the frailties of vanity, ambition, and self-centeredness, these fairies can become consumed by their own needs, resulting in behavior that is unfair, deceptive, nasty, and vengeful. Fairies who are spurned by a mortal man may, then, commit acts of blackness, because, like human beings, when they are blocked particularly in affectional desires, terrible powers can be unleashed.[21]

As we recall, both kinds of fairies impact the lives of the two principals of "La Belle et la Bête" in key ways. Belle is, in point of fact, the daughter of a fairy, who had fallen in love with the King of Happy Island (*l'île heureuse*). But later, when the fairy-mother is denounced and condemned to prison for having broken fairy law by marrying a mortal, a bad fairy (now trying to win the heart of the king who cares only for his baby daughter Belle) spirits the baby into the forest where she plans to kill her. Baby Belle is rescued only with the arrival of a good fairy, disguised as a bear, who scares off the bad fairy and saves the infant by sneaking her into the crib of a baby who had just died in the home of its wet nurse. Later, of course, as a young woman imprisoned at the Beast's palace, Belle will be helped by a good fairy who will assist and encourage her through her dreams.

The story of the prince and his fairies is somewhat less complicated, though with a wickedly scandalous twist. Soon after his birth, his father dies, leaving the queen to tend both to affairs of state and to the baby. When her country is attacked, she does not hesitate to march off to war, much like a

Joan of Arc at the head of her armies, and to leave the baby prince in the care of a fairy who is her good friend. But delayed for years in battles that are endlessly renewed, the soldier-queen returns after an absence of fifteen years, only to learn to her horror that the fairy has turned into a despicable old hag who has fallen in love with her young charge, and that she is insisting on marrying him. When both the prince and the queen refuse what they consider to be a very unnatural match, the fairy settles the score and gets her revenge by making the prince who spurns her as ugly as she is. He is now the Beast, and the condition for his disenchantment is that a beautiful young girl fall in love with him despite her certainty that he intends to eat her. It is, of course, through the intercession of a good fairy, who sends Belle her dreams and sometimes speaks to her from them, that Belle ultimately becomes the one who can break this spell.

What this story shows is that fairies often become rivals or rival power brokers, pitting their supernatural skills one against the other. However, within fairy law, as presented by Madame de Villeneuve, there are rules that determine the exercise of power, so that all-out battle is never an option. A good fairy cannot, for instance, undo the spell cast by her malevolent sister, nor can she countermand an older fairy until she has put in 1000 years of service, which constitutes her *vétérance*, similar, perhaps, to a colossally extended internship or pre-tenure period. Instead, she must wait for creative opportunities to checkmate her adversary or undo an evil spell. In Villeneuve's story, the good fairy will disguise herself as a monstrous female bear in order to steal Baby Belle away from a fairy who intended to suffocate the child. And she will set into action a long chain of events that makes it possible to liberate the Beast from the evil spell of the bad fairy, first by changing a summer day and a forest route into a blinding snow squall and next by making Belle's father seek refuge in the château where the Beast lives.

But if, through the emphatic use of fairies, Madame de Villeneuve validates female agency, she does not at the same time set about to create a utopian female universe. The model of communal governance that she creates is so loose, despite the presence of a queen (who is primarily a figurehead, without substantive powers over her sisters), that while it is largely democratic, it also borders on the chaotic, with each independent fairy simply enjoined, rather than forced, to obey unwritten laws. It could in fact be argued that rivalry among fairies is one more example of patriarchy at work, setting woman against woman in a politics of divide and conquer. But it may also simply reveal the author's realistic judgment that in any society, even an all-women one, there will always be good and bad. Unlike the female utopias of her British sisters, which tend to be replications of heterosexual society founded on rules, coercion, and surveillance,[22] Villeneuve's fairy world, which is motivated by the ideas of community and good works, tends to enforce strict law only when the evidence of wrong doing appears incontrovertible. Thus, based on testimony found in *le grand livre*, Belle's fairy-mother is found guilty of having ignored the law that forbids marriage to mortals, and the *Assemblée* must find her guilty and punish her. Their act is not illustrative of inadequate female solidarity, but of blind justice, though later the sentence will be overturned through appellate action backed by new evidence.

Thus, while Madame de Villeneuve is clearly envisioning some kind of matriarchy in her *cité*, what is so refreshing about this fairyland is that she does not present an idealized, perfect vision of female governance. Hers is no island of women who know only how to be excellent or are moral amazons. And relations among her fairies are not necessarily better than relations among real-world women. There are fairies of excellent heart who use their power for good, and there are others who know only how to abuse power. Some fairies are just as foolish and vain as Belle's sisters, just as self-interested as a male sovereign, just as weak-willed as any mortal.[23] In the balance of power, the breakdown of good versus bad fairies is roughly equal in numbers if not in effect, since the principle of good does ultimately win out. But what such a portrait may reveal is an effort to reconceptualize women's roles and actual power in society without at the same time falling prey to extremist views.

Both versions of "Beauty and the Beast" were written in mid-century, at a time when liberal ideas were gaining a foothold and new thinking about the social contract was taking hold. So, it has been natural for literary scholars to ask whether the fairies are role models of female power, educative examples of how women would practice power, or even subversive commentary on the real status quo of ancien-régime society. One argument says that the role of fairies should be likened to arbiters of the salon, while another suggests that their speech and power represent a counterdiscourse or compensation intended to privilege women who were mistreated or undervalued in society. Lewis Seifert, for instance, has argued that in view of the harsh attacks against women in the period 1690 to 1715, female writers may have been especially desirous of creating extraordinary destinies for women in their fairy tales, by giving them roles they would never have in society. This argument of "just" recompense says that if men hold most power in society, women should be granted power in the storybook world.[24] Hence, the portrait of female characters, fairies, and queens controlling their own destinies as well as those of men; hence the promotion of women through portraits of those who are nurturing and protective and come to the aid of the disadvantaged; and hence, too, the stories of female agency that brings about marvelous, supernatural events, along with the triumph of moral justice and personal justice.

We might give the final word on the subject to Marina Warner who has suggested that while disadvantaged in society, women writers were able in an ostensibly naive genre, and through their own wit and cleverness, to communicate a sense of purpose and identity to other women. Adopting a botanical metaphor, she says that these women used the fairy tale to "set their own seedlings and plant out their own flower."[25] This image of cultivation can be further elaborated in "La Belle et la Bête" as *self*-cultivation and its result, self-empowerment, accomplished not through any wave of the magic wand, but by warranting women as readers and as keepers of knowledge and history through *the book.*

BOOKS AND LIBRARIES IN THE FAIRY TALE

Significantly, three out of four versions of "Beauty and the Beast"—the two original texts and two films (Jean Cocteau, 1946, and Disney, 1992)—include a key scene featuring Belle and the library.[26] Indeed, for both Madame de Villeneuve and Madame Leprince, one of the first ways in which the Beast wins Belle's gratitude is by making her the gift of the library. In visiting the apartments of the Beast's palace, Villeneuve's Beauty happens upon a music room and then "an enormous *bibliothèque*," which delights her, for the author says, "She liked to instruct herself, and since the move to the country . . . had been deprived of this sweet pleasure." The unhappy uprooting from city to country had taken place when the father lost his fortune, which had also necessitated selling his library. Now upon seeing these books, Belle realizes that her great love of reading was going to be easily satisfied in this place and would keep her from feeling boredom and solitude. The same scene is repeated in Madame Leprince, who had written on the very first page of her story that, to the disdain of her sisters, Belle "used the better part of her time to read good books." The fact that the author includes this detail even in her very economical text is proof of the importance she gives to activities of the mind in her female heroine. Subsequently, as Belle moves through the palace and enters the apartment destined for her, she is amazed to discover its great magnificence. But, the author continues, it is the sight of a great *bibliothèque* that pleases her most.[27] Importantly, what gives such pleasure is not a display of jewelry or personal finery, but rather objects of learning and culture. "She opened the *bibliothèque* and saw a book on which were written in letters of gold: Desire, command; you are here the lady and the mistress." She, like the external reader, will open the book in what has been described as a "gesture of hope toward a space of promise," in an action that implies either a "quest for information or the desire of a dream."[28] This is the promise of the book, this is the promise of reading for women. In the book and in reading, women will access enlightenment and through them be empowered.[29]

The library scene is reenacted by female writers throughout the eighteenth century, as, for instance, in Madame de Graffigny's *Lettres d'une Péruvienne* (1747), also carrying certain fairy tale-like properties. In an episode that doubles as the material reality of the character's own ultimate self-realization, Zilia receives the gifts of space and knowledge in both a literal and figurative sense. At some twenty pages from the end of her story, the gift of property ownership becomes both Zilia's reward and the end of her personal journey. There she recounts the trip to a country house in the company of Déterville and his sister Céline and their gift to her of the house.

Zilia experiences this scene of transfer of ownership as though entering a dream, and everything underscores its fairy-book quality, from her description of the house as an *enchantement*, to her whimsical questioning of Céline about whether the absent owner might be a fairy, to the exquisitely served meal by nearly invisible servants, and the charming music emanating from a nearby room. The storybook aura continues outdoors in the art and symmetry of the gardens, with the appearance of a group of poetic and musically talented peasants bedecked in flowers, which they offer to Zilia along with the keys to the house. In the requisite scene of taking possession, Zilia moves through the rooms of the property, "intoxicated with joy," scarcely registering all the wonders, until one room in particular compels her attention. "The only place where I stopped," she says, "was a rather large chamber surrounded by a delicately worked grille that held countless books of all colors and all forms, in admirable condition; I was in such a state of enchantment that I hardly thought I would be able to leave without having read them all" (Lettre 35).

One might argue that this room, unlike the following one, the temple of the Sun, which is a kind of Incan boudoir with its mirrors and paintings evoking simultaneously both her roots and some feminine essence, represents a claim to culture through the library.[30] To enter this new privileged estate, not as a guest or an interloper, but as the owner, is to hold the keys and to possess the self. Hence, Zilia's experience of property ownership, involved with both book and place, is a textual metaphor for the intellectual proprietorship that she and other eighteenth-century heroines, including Belle, seek. The library and its books are part of the Enlightenment dream of women, and every time they are refused to her, the pretensions of the *siècle des lumières* are open to challenge. For there is nothing universal about reason if women are excluded from participating in the exchange and transference of knowledge. Borrowing the words that sociologist Todd Gitlin has used about the Enlightenment, one might say that both the library and the Enlightenment are best understood as "an aspiration, an invitation, a commitment to a process that aims to bring about understandings that do not yet exist."[31] In this sense, the fairy tale and its embrace of books and knowledge for women are part of the process.

Within the fairy tale, the reading motif functions in several ways, as Gabrielle Verdier observes. First, it legitimates a character by making her a *héroine–lectrice* (in the same way Madame Riccoboni had done in *Lettres de Juliette Catesby*, we might recall), thereby distinguishing Belle from her less serious and less worthy sisters. Second, books connote knowledge as in a storehouse of written words—for instance, with the wizard's book of secret recipes and potions, or with the written record, the chronicle, the annals of a people and a time. Hence the book itself is an object of value handed down from sorcerer to sorcerer, and generation to generation, while at the same time the use of books within the fairy tale serves a third function, which is to mirror the external reader in a positively encoded double structure of reading.

In Villeneuve, the Beast, who had been a handsome prince turned into a beast by a bad fairy whose amorous advances he had resisted, uses books to pass the time—I would read, I went to the theater," he recounts. But it is primarily women who are associated with books. After the bad spell is cast on the former prince, a good fairy appears to offer her aid, seeking counsel in a book she carries in her pocket: "Then she drew from her coat a book and after making a few mysterious footsteps, sat before a table and read for a considerable time, with such seriousness of purpose that it made her perspire" (153). Reading, we understand, carries with it its own rites, but also since this is a book of magic, the fairy must follow certain practices in order to enter into the secrets of the book. Her act of reading requires close attention, indicated by the beads of perspiration produced by her mental activity. The book she reads may be like a miniature encyclopedia or reference book, a scientific treatise or lab manual of equations and problem sets. It is a sourcebook or handbook of collected data, precepts, and principles that she needs to penetrate in order to find a solution to the problem at hand, that of aiding the unjustly bewitched prince. Since one fairy does not have the power to undo the spell of another one, the good fairy must find a way of negotiating through the evil spell, while achieving her own objective. She cannot simply wave a magic wand and obtain the result she wants, but she can strategize a way out of the problem with the help of a text.

The second usage of the book is as *le grand livre* or *le livre général*, that weighty tome at fairy headquarters where the fairies gather for periodic counsel whenever the fairy queen commands their *assemblée*. This book has a double function in the fairy tale, used both on behalf of woman and against her, depending on the reader. *Le grand livre* is not a book of law to consult for how the community must be regulated, but rather a book of true history, in the platonic, ideal sense, in which events are not mediated through any lens of interpretation, but are faithfully and accurately recorded. This *grand livre* is described as one "in which what we do is engraved automatically at the very moment our act takes place" (176). It is, thus, like a photographic snapshot, recorded by some unknown power, transliterated into words, and representing an exact and authoritative accounting of all fairy actions on earth. But it can be misread, or read for evil purposes, as well as for good ones. When the bad fairy (*la fée gouvernante du prince* who had been rejected by him) opens the pages of *le grand livre* to expose the actions of Belle's fairy-mother who had fallen in love with the king of *l'île heureuse* and broken fairy law by marrying him, she is seeking proof to damage a sister in the eyes of the community. The bad fairy realized the power of the book and knew that "in opening *le grand livre*, she would find an important subject" (178) that she could read to suit her purposes. With malice aforethought, "she showed the entire assembly what had been happening for two years, by reading it aloud in a clear voice." Her reading of one scene becomes the overwhelming proof of disobedience, and Belle's fairy-mother is stripped of her rank and condemned to imprisonment in the fairy universe.

But the book can also be read differently, more wholly, telling a different story. The narrating good fairy, the actual sister of Belle's fairy-mother, will practice different reading skills. Following the partial, misleading reading that had convinced the *assemblée* to act against Belle's mother, and that produced further complications of intrigue and countermoves by the good fairy, the latter ultimately insists that *le grand livre* be read in context and that the entire story be known. Recounting how she had seized the tome, she says, "I used against our cruel companion the same arms that she had used against us, and I opened *le grand livre*" (200). By good fortune, she opens the book to the scene in which the bad fairy discredits herself by casting her evil spell on the prince in a fit of pique because he spurned her advances. The good fairy now finds in the book the argument she needs to liberate her sister. "In presenting them the book" (202), the good fairy, like a lawyer, lays out the evidence and wins her case. "After which, closing the book," she hastens to earth to oversee the final turn of events that free the prince from his spell through marriage with a virgin. Thus, the "moral" is that the reading depends on the reader's intentions, experience, expectations, talent, and truthfulness. Though not theoretical in any developed sense, such scenes of reading suggest early considerations on the variables of reader response, or even that, as Shoshanna Felman has said, "reading is a rather risky business whose outcome and full consequences can never be known in advance."[32]

The final use of the book made by Madame de Villeneuve is the written text as archival record of female history and legacy, an especially appealing invention. In concluding her story of the Beast, the narrating fairy says, "The queen and mother of the prince did not fail to have this marvelous story inscribed in the archives of the empire and in those of the *île heureuse* in order to transmit it to posterity" (214). This book will be a part of the permanent collection both in the fairy universe and in the realm of the soldier–queen (the Beast's mother). It will be the archival record to consult for the full and accurate historical act, and it is likely to become a tool of empowerment especially for future women readers who will read it to learn from and to remember their past. In underscoring the book as a legacy for women, by women, and of women, Madame de Villeneuve would seem to be revealing latent feminism with regard to the production and consumption of the text, implicitly posing the question: if women and books belong together even in the fairy tale, should not women and books be given their rightful place in a new sexual and social contract? Her successor, Madame Leprince, who earned her living as the weaver of tales and the teacher of young girls to whom she offered private lessons in French, penmanship, arithmetic, geography, history, and letter writing—as she advertised in the February 1751 "Avis de l'Auteur" of her *Nouveau Magasin français*—would heartily agree.

Sex and the Single Girl in the Fairy Tale

As I have been suggesting, the dominant metaphor that flows throughout Madame de Villeneuve's version of Beauty and the Beast is one of reading—reading books, but also objects and others, reading beneath the surface, penetrating down to the real meaning, integrating reading into life. And because her story is so deeply invested in portraying the erotic, we see once again how reading and sex are deeply entwined. Writing for adult readers, rather than for children, Madame de Villeneuve narrates and ratifies female desire, painting the sexual awakening of a young maiden and revealing the conflicting emotions that bedevil her, as she confronts her own ambivalence and apprehension about sex. In creating this striking portrayal of a young woman's erotic birth, Madame de Villeneuve breaks new ground, doing so with style and taste, as she gives full rein to the power of her imagination in descriptive passages of luxuriant inventiveness and the development of a subconscious that reveals itself in the recurrent erotic dreams of her heroine.

Just as Michel Tournier in an essay, "Le Vol du vampire," presents textual consumption as an erotic encounter and privileges bodily emotion and sensation as key parts of the reading process, so does Madame de Villeneuve through multiple representations of "reading" in her fairy tale. All the tale's mimetic acts of reading—between subject and object, reader (Belle) and text (dreams and the portrait of *le bel inconnu*)—are mediated by desire that is activated by the reader's eye. Entering into the sensually spectacular *cabinets* in the Beast's castle, as into her nakedly erotic dreams, Belle sees and reads simultaneously, in demonstration of the coextensive pleasures and dangers of viewing and reading.

In a series of scenes, replicated in every version, but especially inventive in Madame de Villeneuve's, Belle visits the vast expansiveness of the Beast's palace, discovering with every opened door—much like an advent calendar—the rich exotica of the palace, dazzled by splendors she never suspected existed. One room is filled with mirrors and paintings, another with musical instruments, a third with an immense library, where she will be able to lose herself in one of her favored activities. Yet another *cabinet* houses tools and an appealing work area for the creation of all kinds of crafts. There is a room with an aviary, teeming with rare birds that serenade her, and parrots of all kinds and colors who can speak and sing and recite verse. And there are acrobatic monkeys, honored by her visit, who become her ladies-in-waiting and pages, eager to aid and accompany her, while others, decked out in theatrical garb, perform as though they were in a play, while parrots speak the words. In yet another room, with the optics of the marvelous, there are windows that offer a bird's-eye view onto the "real" world: the *opéra-comique*, *la foire Saint-Germain* and its puppet shows, the Tuileries where all of Europe mingles; the spectacle of *le beau monde* visiting Paris boutiques; colorful card-players who lose and make money, even—inexplicably—the last revolt of the Janissaries of the Ottoman Empire.[33] Through the "marvelous" vision provided by these theatrical windows that are a rupture or breakdown in the laws of physical optics, as of the forbidden erotic, the visitor/reader becomes the voyeur of wonders and displaced sexuality. As Belle glides through the palace—quite literally in Cocteau's vision—entering an exotic narrative of the fantastic that beckons and disturbs in alternately appealing and problematic ways, she both reads and is read in a kind of double and symbolic reading.[34]

The magic of these sensually articulated scenes permits the author's protagonist to see and hear everything and everyone, while remaining a silent observer, in much the same position as the external reader. The effect is to illuminate the semi-erotic pleasure afforded by the position of secret spectator—and reader—able, through the special powers of magic, to "spy" on others. It is the same pleasure referred to by Roland Barthes as "the tiny private scene, in which I can easily take my place,"[35] and arises from the dream of the child to see into a miniature and off-limits adult world, and from the reader's voyeuristic desire for sexual knowledge and acts. Hence Villeneuve's text becomes an experience in sensual reading in which the very act of reading is a process of sensual probing.

The visit into the exotic *cabinets* prepares Belle for a series of erotic dreams that begin immediately after her arrival at the enchanted palace. In a first dream, she is at the edge of a canal that reaches far into the horizon, when a shadowy but handsome young man appears, offering compliments and reassuring her that in this new milieu she will be appreciated as never before. Using dulcet tones, he entreats her to read deeply into the mysteries that surround her. "Use your powers of penetration," he pleads, "to separate the real me from appearances that disguise me." And he beseeches her, saying, "I love you tenderly, you alone can make my happiness in making your own" (69). Paying her constant courtship, imploring her with sweet praise and adoring eyes, he promises to fulfill all her dreams, offering her "fêtes galantes." The pleasure or *trouble* that Belle experiences in the presence of the *bel inconnu*, either through the portrait or in her dreams, demonstrates the notion that reading is not only a desiring activity, with desire both emanating from a text and being generated onto it, but that it is a double contagion.[36] For, standing in front of the life-size portrait of the chevalier in a gallery of paintings, Belle feels that the figure "seemed to look at her with such tender attention that she blushed, for it was as though this painting had testimony of what was in her mind" (72).

The *bel inconnu* is, of course, the very man unjustly imprisoned in an animal skin and mentality, the handsome young man, the one Belle does not see in the beast with whom she lives. Since part of the spell cast on the Beast forbids him to speak on his own behalf, a strategy must be found to circumvent the interdiction, and at the same time Belle must come to understand and accept her affections. Hence, the employment of the dream strategy in which the *inconnu* shows himself to be sensitive, charming, desirable, and very much in love. He is the ideal lover, completely unlike the Beast, who does not know how to speak or charm a woman and who, in a ritual repeated daily, bluntly asks her for sex (though in Madame Leprince's version, he will phrase his question with more gallantry, "Would you like to be my wife?"). Of course, Belle refuses, but every day the dull creature persists in the ritual, thereby keeping alive the issue of sex and the potential of sexual violence.

Madame de Villeneuve's adult version is frank in describing the pleasure that Belle derives from her dream reveries or "songes agréables," referring to the "sweet pleasure" that she procures in collusion with "her nocturnal lover," and showing how reading and sexual pleasure are interrelated. Even in her waking hours Belle's thoughts turn toward *le jeune homme inconnu* and she is eager to invoke him. When she happens upon his figure in the portrait of one of the galleries, she feels herself penetrated by his eyes, and will subsequently seek out the portrait to renew the experience. At other times, she solicits sleep for the purposes of pleasure, for she had found that her sleeping hours are the sweetest of all, reminding us of Baudouin's woman reader (Figure 2), whose reading of the novel had set her off to erotic sleep. Belle is eager to be left alone, even in the middle of the day, so that she can call up another pleasurable interlude. Commenting on her character's ardor for the erotic dreamlike state brought on by reading or having been read by the *inconnu*, Madame de Villeneuve exclaims, "How pleasant her sleep was!"

Clearly, Belle is in the grasp of an erotic obsession, something that we see in no other version of "Beauty and the Beast," in which the psychological landscape is never as rich and troubling. Here, her dreams become a part of what Peter Brooks has called the forepleasure of reading, the creation of a "dilatory space" through which we seek delayed gratification.[37] The erotic reveries of Belle's sleep or dreamy wakefulness give shape to her subconscious mind, revealing the processes of maturation and the female's readiness for erotic and sexual experience.[38] But it is not without conflict. For, while she passes her days in the Beast's palace in so many delicious pastimes, they always end with an interview with the creature who never fails to ask whether she would like to sleep with him. With each passing day, Belle becomes concerned that the Beast's desire for sex is growing stronger than his self-control and that the threat of sexual violation looms before her. At the same time, her desire for *le bel inconnu* is rising to new heights, and it, too, contains the eventuality of physical sex. Delayed gratification is, of course, an important fairy-tale lesson, but as the urges of sex become more powerful, they threaten to overwhelm and destabilize the equilibrium that had been established between eros and chaste desire in her dreams.

Increasingly, her reading relations with the portrait and her dreams become struggles to give herself to them or be appropriated by them, much as Barthes has discussed the image of coupling as a metaphor for reading relations. As her dream texts develop, she feels threatened by their aggressive nature, especially when the *bel inconnu* appears ready to do violence to the Beast. Frightened by the hypnotic power of the text, coupled with a magnetic draw to it, she feels destabilized. As Belle's dreams become more and more troubled, impending violence causes a near-murder scene involving both *le bel inconnu* and the Beast, subsequent to Belle's complaints concerning the Beast's constant imprecations. At the moment when a dagger appears in the hand of the *bel inconnu*, as he prepares to kill the Beast, Belle cries out, "Stop, cruel one. Do not offend my benefactor" (91). To which the *inconnu* objects, "Then you no longer love me if you take the side of this monster who is opposed to my happiness." It takes all of Belle's strength in the dream to try to explain that while she loves *le beau chevalier*, she cannot forget her deep gratitude to the creature. "I owe everything to the Beast," she tells him, "he foresees my desires; he was the one who made it possible for me to know you, and I shall give myself to death rather that have you do him the least harm" (91). Caught in the vise of desire for one and debt toward another, it is clear that Belle cannot reconcile her emotions and free either her mind or body.

The reading of her dreams evokes another major image within the text: that of the prison motif. A reiterative structure of the text, the imprisonment theme represents both physical realities in the fairy tale and a mental and emotional climate. Belle is a virtual prisoner in the Beast's domain, despite the freedom within it granted to her; and the Beast is imprisoned because of the bad fairy's evil spell in a skin and character that are not his own; *le bel inconnu* inhabits a painting from which he cannot escape, though from which he can speak (at one point, he pleads with Belle, "free me from prison," 84), which leads Belle to conclude that he, too, may be a real but hidden prisoner of the Beast's. Furthermore, in an emotional sense, while Belle is initially the willing prisoner of dreams in which she takes so much pleasure, when the Beast and the *beau chevalier* become locked in a battle to erase the existence of the other, she finds her dream reading frightening. And with her allegiances split, and her *amant* refusing to join her in her waking hours, she concludes that despite the delights and riches of the enchanted domain, "this palace is like a prison that wants to become my tomb" (90).[39]

All the images and structures of imprisonment are figures from the psyche of the young woman, who in coming to the Beast's domain, enters an unknown psychic territory, and is being called on to negotiate new feelings. Her dreams, which both protect and impel her forward, admit a certain provisional pleasure, but, ultimately, they are overwhelmed by more demanding tensions. Unsettled during her days because she yearns to see her family, and at night because she must do battle against the *bel inconnu*, who threatens the Beast and her peace of mind, and torn between love and sexual attraction and her strong feelings of love and responsibility, Belle suffers from emotional distress that begins to affect her health. She must return home. She must reconcile her feelings.

The trip back to the father's house, granted with the Beast's reluctant permission, ultimately produces a kind of reconciliation of the contradictions that beleaguer Belle, for now even her father encourages her to marry the Beast, whom he describes as a "generous monster." In view of the Beast's many attentions and liberalities, the father concludes, "when next the Beast asks you if you want to sleep with him, I would counsel you not to refuse." The argument seems troublingly close to an equation of sex for material pleasures, though the father adds, "It is more advantageous to have a husband with an agreeable character than to have one whose only merit is his handsome face." Pursuing his argument, he says, "How many young women have been forced to marry rich beasts far more beastly that the Beast, who is a beast only by his face and not in his feelings and actions?" (103). Belle objects that good-heartedness is not reason enough to form a union. The Beast, after all, is dull-minded, boring, incapable of conversation. But in her father's house, unable to conjure up her nocturnal lover, Belle begins to recognize that other feelings, aside from primarily erotic ones, could be the decisive factor in making a marriage. Exhausted by her internal battles over desire and responsibility and passion and love, Belle finally agrees to marry the Beast as beast, because she does love him, with affection and gratitude and respect, though not with the physical attraction that marks sexual love.

Hence, it is with some trepidation, despite her fraternal feelings for the animal-groom, that Belle envisions her wedding night in Madame de Villeneuve's text, the only one to script the scene in which Beauty and the Beast share a bed. Underscoring the ambivalent nature of her heroine's feelings toward this unusual husband and the imminent act of sex once the wedding has taken place, the author acknowledges Belle's apprehension, accompanied by resignation. But in a rapid change of pace, Madame de Villeneuve introduces comic relief by relating that among Belle's concerns at this capital moment is the fear that with his monstrous weight, the Beast will crush their bed. However, when the giant monster joins her in bed, hardly making a dent in it and promptly begins to snore, her feelings quickly run the gamut from astonishment to gratefulness to tenderness. The monster's intentions were, she now realizes, pure; he did not want to commit a physical act with her, but rather, quite literally, only to sleep with her (hence, perhaps, that awkwardly phrased question in Madame de Villeneuve's version: "Would you like me to sleep with you?" "Voulez-vous que je couche avec vous?"). If physical violation or loss of virginity or even rape had been the unspoken threat throughout the tale, it is now revealed as unfounded. Ultimately, the physical marriage will be consummated at the point when the Beast is metamorphosed into a prince—perhaps, in a delicious turnabout, *his* reward precisely because he had been able to sleep chastely next to Belle.

His metamorphosis is required not only because the evil fairy's spell has been broken through the agency of Belle's freely given love, but also because however kind or loving the Beast may be, he is still a creature who belongs more in the animal kingdom than in the world of man, and the writer feels an obligation to end the story in a union that will neither shock the reader's proprieties, nor condemn the young maiden to an unnatural relationship.[40] Belle's intercession is key to the restoration of beast to man, but in conjunction with a Christian subtext that can also be seen in this fairy tale, it is motivated not by sexual passion, but by a love built on gratitude, respect, friendship, and familiarity. Subsequently, her reward for the gracious generosity of that kind of love will be the complement of sexual love, as well.

The inscription of reading in Madame de Villeneuve's fairy tale about sexuality is powerfully present. There are stories within stories, mediated readings, "dangerous" readings, reading as a validating activity, and reading as a protosexual or priming activity. In the count-counterpoint of book, sex, and knowledge, vision is the primary sense and reading the dominant mode by which subjectivity is constituted and understanding is achieved. The "lessons" of the fairy tale are about more than virtue and moral action; they are also about the pleasure of reading and becoming a good reader.

CONCLUSION: READING ENCHANTMENT IN THE ENLIGHTENMENT

The 1786 edition of *Le Cabinet des fées* is a treasure-trove of more than 600 fairy tales written, translated, or adapted by men and women during the fairy tale's golden age in seventeenth- and eighteenth-century France.[41] The fact that so many of these tales have entered the reader's canon, regardless of national origin or century, demonstrates their universal and timeless appeal. The collection, arising out of Enlightenment idealism and speaking with the voice of hopefulness, tends to be optimistic about the future, suggesting that human beings can be educated to improve themselves and that happy people will build strong communities and just societies. But like the Enlightenment itself, fairy tales will only illuminate the possible, without promising anything.

Understanding how a fairy tale includes a discourse on reading and opens another on how we read may at first seem surprising. But it is less so when we recall the double purpose of fairy tales—to enchant and to enlighten. For as Gaston Bachelard has said in *Poétique de la rêverie*, the mind needs the unreal and its imaginary projections and idealizations as a way of staying mentally balanced, while at the same time the reader needs to be stimulated and ratified in his or her cognitive activities.[42] This is as true of the child reader as of the adult. For while we are raised on reading fairy tales, those early experiences continue to impact our interpretive reading, as we move through the successive stages of being readers, outlined by reading theorists.[43] Matei Calinescu has observed that "earlier phases in the development of a reader are not definitely left behind but are continuously and diversely subsumed under the new modes of reading" (94). And C. S. Lewis explains, "I now enjoy fairy tales better than I did in childhood: being now able to put more in, of course I get more out."[44]

These remarks have direct application to the two versions of "La Belle et la Bête," one intended for children, and the other for adults who access the child reader that survives in our adult reading. Madame Leprince wrote simply, summoning the imagination of her reader, child or adult like Jean Cocteau, to visualize and act on the dream. She called for a reading of symbolic play and fantasy that could be performed again and again by the same reader. Her text reminds us how a child learns to deal with the mechanics of a linguistic system, and to make sense of the processes of a written page, looking for narrative patterns and symbolic meaning in objects like the rose, the mirror, the key.

Madame de Villeneuve, on the other hand, writing for adults, tapped into *reading as a memory*. Like all writers of fairy tales written for adult readers, Villeneuve appeals to the experience of reading as a child, or what Charles Grivel has called those "quasi-hypnotic reading experiences from long ago."[45] She takes us on the trips of reading we enjoyed as children, with the same sense of wonder and creativity, into a second reality or a free unreality. These are the pleasures of reading, but now grown-up, whose symbolic contents pertain to erotic sexuality. The game-like aspects of reading—the riddles, enigmas, and puzzles—are still present. But this is not reading as mere playing, but as game, or playing disciplined by game, in Michel Picard's distinction.[46] It is reading that has an integrative role, incorporating both fantasying and intellectualizing.

In the end, perhaps there is nothing really so incompatible between the Enlightenment and the fairy tale, since while the story of the latter is about enchantment, its purpose is quite clearly enlightenment. Furthermore, through both the enchantment and enlightenment of the fairy tale, the reader, whether old or young, learns about the power of the mind, a truly major Enlightenment preoccupation. That the mind is constructed and enriched by reading is, as we have just seen, just one more of the fairy tale's embedded lessons.

SEVEN

THE PERIODICAL PRINT PRESS FOR WOMEN

AN ENLIGHTENMENT FORUM FOR FEMALES

> Men who will not grant women the ability to think well enough to write are going to exhaust their satirical pens against us. A woman . . . Journalist . . . that's not possible. . . . Well, just as there is no male genius, nor female genius, why would we not write as well as you Messieurs Satirists, jealous of our glory?
>
> —Madame de Beaumer, *Le Journal des dames*, March 1762

> Make yourselves Men, because are we not Men when we think as well as they do?"
>
> —Madame de Beaumer, *Le Journal des dames*, March 1763

In an encounter with one of the first female journalists to wield a pen in France, the censor François Marin describes a scene involving Madame de Beaumer as follows: "She appeared this morning in my chamber," he writes, "a large hat on her head, a long sword at her side, her chest (where there is nothing) and her behind (where there is not much) covered by a long culotte, and the rest of her body in a worn, narrow, black habit. Questioned about the disguise, she replied that since she ran her paper alone, relying only on herself, she dresses thus for reasons of economy and to be admitted to the orchestra circle to review the latest play for 20 sous."[1]

In that short and colorful description, Marin evokes the full array of issues—sartorial, spatial, and sexual—faced by the woman who "took it into her head" to become a journalist. To practice her profession with equal rights and on equal grounds, Madame de Beaumer must have entry to a particular male preserve—in this case, the *parterre*, which is the equivalent of the locker room for the twentieth-century woman sportswriter. But because it is exclusively a male domain, she is forced to present herself as a man. Hence the cross-dressing, complete with a man's hat and habit and even a sword, at once emblematic of male anatomy and the pen, both male preserves. To exercise this quill, the female journalist must unsex herself. But at the same time that she does so in an almost comic display of cross-dressing, she is ridiculed by Marin for her inadequacies as a woman lacking in a specific set of feminine attributes. For him, the attempt by Madame de Beaumer to become an independent businesswoman and journalist is tantamount to an unseemly assault on social and sexual conventions, and her choice of costume only serves to make her a strange and suspicious figure of hybridic sexual identity.

If most female journalists of the eighteenth century did not dress in pants and wield a sword, they did, like Madame de Beaumer, confront the same obstacles, financial and sexual, as they sought to create a new forum for females. The story of the development of the female periodical press, together with the development of a targeted female readership, constitute an important and intriguing chapter in the history of women's reading, for this is the first time that women readers are identified as a specific interest group and market. By subscribing to a woman's periodical, a woman joins a new community, and in the collective "we" of the female press—featuring, as Madame de Beaumer says in her opening issue in March 1761, "All that bears witness to the talent of Ladies," while "men's works will be given a lower rank"—she will gain new rights and recognition not previously enjoyed. Furthermore, this reader will have the opportunity to converse with other women, not just in Paris and the provinces, but throughout the French-speaking world, as the editor grandly asserts. For the first time in a public forum, this woman reader will participate as a full partner in a conversation at the national level, and her voice will be heard and honored.

In assessing the importance of this press, we will see that it is not so much the positions advanced that makes it revolutionary—indeed, the editors are almost never concerned with political governance—but rather the fact that it legitimizes women as a specific interest group and authorizes the process of sex-based identity building. By giving women a vehicle in which both their concerns and speech are valorized, this press, which was read by women of the bourgeoisie and the upper classes, becomes a participant in the widening Enlightenment by raising female consciousness and validating women's concerns. A key player in combating the censorship of women's voices and bringing them into the national conversation, the female periodical press might even have led to the establishment of women's clubs in the revolutionary years. For it supported an activism on the part of its women readers that is the natural result of its primary objective: the ultimate empowerment of women.

BRIEF HISTORY OF THE PRESS IN FRANCE

To understand how eighteenth-century women's periodicals figure in the larger picture of the history of the press in France, we may recall that the general press is usually dated to 1631 and the founding of the *Gazette de France*. During the course of the next 150 years, periodicals of all stripes were published, though most proved ephemeral, managing to print only a prospectus and an issue or two before folding. Nonetheless, by 1787 there were at least 139 journals, as identified by Jack Censer (out of more than 1000 titles between 1745 and the revolution) that had enjoyed a lifespan of at least three years,[2] thereby fulfilling the standards by which a periodical is defined: (1) having a relatively stable presentation under the same title, (2) demonstrating a real or intended periodicity, (3) revealing a concern with recent information. Among these journals are weeklies and dailies, some of which are well known, such as the *Journal des Savants*, which published between 1665 and 1792; the *Journal de Trévoux*, the official organ of the Jesuits, appearing from 1701 to 1767; the *Mercure de France*, dating between 1724 and 1791; the *Année littéraire* begun in 1754 by the antiphilosophe Fréron (whom Voltaire delighted in skewering in chapter 22 of *Candide*); *Le Pour et le contre* of Prévost (1733–1740); and of course, the *Correspondance littéraire*, directed by Grimm from 1754 to 1773 and whose publication spans the period 1753 to 1813.[3]

In terms of readership, it is extremely problematic to try to prove very much about the size and makeup of the audience for each publication, but Jack Censer does venture to suggest that whereas in the 1740s, approximately fourteen long-lasting periodicals had a circulation of 15,000, by the 1780s over eighty publications had a circulation of about 60,000 copies (11).[4] The total readership, however, may have been much larger than the number of subscribers, first because reading materials were often exchanged between friends and family members, and second, because journals could be read without being purchased in reading rooms or clubs. Some historians have suggested, therefore, that every issue might have had between four and six readers, and that the real audience could, in effect, have been closer to 240,000 to 360,000 out of a total population of 26 million. While those figures are small by modern standards, they are certainly not inconsiderable given the size of the reading "notability" in the eighteenth century, a group that included all those, both noble and common, who had the education and financial resources to become readers. Censer has assembled data that show that women provided between 15 and 20 percent of the subscribers to Fréron's *Année littéraire* during the period 1774–1776 and to the *Mercure de France* for 1756.[5]

As for the individuals who produced this press, some 400 journalists are listed by Jean Sgard for the period 1600–1789, and dozens of others continue to be discovered.[6] Historians of the press recognize that the term "journalist" is a loose one and does not imply only those who wrote. Since clear distinctions between various press jobs or functions did not exist in this early period, the word "journalist" has merely become standard nomenclature for anyone who wrote, edited, or published journals. In fact, for many smaller publications, the same individual might perform all those tasks. Further complicating the task of identifying journalists is the fact that many correspondents worked anonymously, and, in addition, editorial practice tended to be lax in crediting contributors by their full name. Nonetheless, Jack Censer has begun sketching out a fascinating profile of the personal, social, and educational backgrounds of journalists in the eighteenth century. Studying some sixty-six journalists (among which, four women), he says that two-thirds of the journalists had middle-class backgrounds, coming neither from the powerful nor lower ranks of society; that they were substantially educated for the times; that many were intellectuals with previous careers as teachers, writers, clergy, translators, librarians, and archivists, who had taken up journalism for financial reasons.[7]

The journals themselves, of course, do not represent anything like the slick, special-interest press we know today, characterized by an overarching editorial vision and focused identity. On the contrary, the press in the eighteenth century often belies a lack of developed professionalism, and is hampered by uncertain or inadequate editorial vision. Consistent editorial practices are not a strong point. For instance, both appearance and point of view may change from issue to issue; authorship attribution is frequently in question, and it is unclear in a single issue what is written by the editor and what was contributed by unnamed writers. Nor was the press always able to respect its own periodicity. Frequently editors used the pages of their press to remind readers that delays in publication were out of their hands, the fault perhaps of a printer or the postal system. The vagaries of censorship were, of course, also a potential problem, for even with the *privilège* or *permission* to publish, and the support of a royal patron who lent his or her name to the enterprise, problems could still arise.[8]

In consequence of these various factors, we often have the impression that a journal was run if not "by the seat of its pants," at least by a very informal set of rules and conditions. Of course, it is possible that the very informality or lack of established practice provided openings for women journalists who sought to write outside the conventions of belles-lettres and to address a primarily female audience. The latter is an important point, for as historians Nina Rattner Gelbart and Suzanne Van Dijk have shown, there would emerge in eighteenth-century journalism a self-conscious search for women readers by male and female journalists, alike.[9] If for some, the woman reader represented just another market for their journal, for others she was the whole reason for their magazine.

WHAT CONSTITUTES THE FEMININE PRESS?

Jean Sgard has identified some nineteen journals from the eighteenth century that can be characterized as for or about women, or fashion, and that represent a feminine press.[10] A careful consideration of these journals, however, raises the need to ask for further clarification on the standard by which to judge what should be called the feminine press. It could be argued that the decisive factor is subject matter—for instance, a concentration on beauty, health, fashion, childcare, or home economy implies a press for women—regardless of the sex of the authors, while another standard would be that press written and directed by women for a female readership. In terms of the eighteenth century, when journals did not have a single, consistent publishing and editorial history, it is probably best to define the feminine periodical press as that which identifies itself specifically in a statement of purpose as being destined primarily, if not exclusively, to a female readership. Thus, a journal such as the *Cabinet des modes*, which, like all early fashion magazines, was always edited by a man, is certainly a part of the feminine press, as well as the *Journal des dames*, edited by both women and men throughout the two decades of its history. Both, of course, were read primarily by women, as were undoubtedly *Le Courrier lyrique*, edited by a woman with the help of a man, *Le Nouveau Magasin français* produced by Madame Leprince de Beaumont, and several anonymous publications including *La Bibliothèque des dames*, *La Bibliothèque des femmes*, and *Le Glaneur du Parnasse*, which appear to have been penned by men. Then again, female authorship does not necessarily imply that a journal should be considered a part of the feminine press, as, for instance, the *Journal de Monsieur*, edited by Madame La Présidente d'Ormoy, but whose focus is on broad, general subject matter.

I am, of course, interested in the press that specifically seeks a female readership, and, primarily that part of it written by women, since it alone carries the specific discourse of virtue or the politics of virtue that I have identified. However, the "other" feminine press is not without interest, since the mediated image of woman in prescriptive literature and its traditional model of female socialization provide an excellent foil against which to study the press created by women. Thus, before taking up the discourse of virtue within the female-authored press, it is useful to briefly review examples from the male-authored press.

MALE-WRITTEN PERIODICAL LITERATURE FOR WOMEN

Declaring themselves the friend of *les femmes* and openly preaching to women with regard to every aspect of physical, moral, and intellectual behavior, the anonymous but probably male writers of journals such as the *Bibliothèque des femmes* (1759), the *Glaneur du Parnasse* (1759), the *Bibliothèque des dames*

(1764), and C. S. Walther's *Manuel de la toilette et de la mode* (1770–1780), reveal in their publications a considerable subtext of paternalism and paradox with regard to sex. Some do little more than establish or reflect a system of hierarchies and fixed sexual complementaries. Though all these works are secular in nature, they still invoke the divine plan of Nature in justification of their view of relations between the sexes. The *Manuel de la toilette* conveys its belief that relations between the sexes have been set down by "the word of God" and are exercised through "the power of husbands," whose authority over a wife is "as natural, as reasonable, and as broad as that of fathers over children" (4e Partie, 1773, 80). A writer in the *Bibliothèque des dames* says in 1764, "Man and woman are made for each other. It is in the very intention of Nature and the goal of society that they please one another" (225). The author further declares that men can live more easily without women than vice versa, which is why women must please in order to receive from man "le nécessaire." "The supremacy of man is founded on physical strength; that of woman on the art of pleasing" (227). Man is the protector, woman the companion. The woman who pleases a man "demonstrates virtue, itself," the writer says, "How fine it is for her to be able to say in all sincerity: I was born to make the happiness of a man, by which I fulfill my role in the order of nature and society!" (232)

A modern reader perusing these pages concerned with relations between the sexes, cannot help wondering about the author's primary concern. Is it with women or the salvation of men? For the writer gives every appearance of wanting to perpetuate the status quo and double standard of sexual relations, while sugarcoating the message for women, seducing or guilt-tripping them into becoming selfless heroines who carry personal responsibility for the moral condition of others. In the *Manuel de la toilette et de la mode*, a conduct book appearing in serial form for almost ten years, the principal motivating force for bringing women to virtue is through guilt. Hence, by emphasizing female culpability and worthlessness and conducting intense criticism of woman, the author tries to lead her toward a new ideal of "domestic heroism," arguing that her happiness depends uniquely on what she gives her husband and children. In article after article, he offers a model of female behavior and socialization whose purpose is "the right and proper integration of women in the world in which they live," consistent with the universal and timeless dictates of nature. Assuming that women are incapable of discovering "nature's plan" by themselves, he lays it out for them in such articles as "Règles de conduite pour le dix-huitième siècle," "Le Governement domestique," "Leçons et maximes pour le beau-sexe," and "De La Beauté des grâces."

Casting women as fundamentally different, if not necessarily worse than men, he preaches the precepts of traditional virtue, including obedience, resignation, and pleasing men. And, while decrying beauty, he shows that it is the single, surest means of woman's "authority," thereby laying down a beauty and fashion culture that would, arguably, become the basis for all the other inequalities that women face.[11] Hence, while ostensibly committed to helping women discover the bases of new female authority, he in fact contributes to their anxiety and possibly weakened self-esteem. By promoting feelings of guilt and shame, and by refusing to recognize the authenticity of independent desires in a woman, he links female happiness to sacrifice and self-abnegation. The risk, of course, is that as women renounce their wishes, interests, pleasures, hopes, and ideals to cater to the needs of husband and children, they actually end with less individual identity and have less authority. At the same time, a contemporary reader may suspect that the motives of the conduct book writer, who practices such a commanding eye and disciplinary prose, pontificating and promoting female guilt, may in actuality derive from his own need to seek through women his own "redemption." Curiously, the real subtext of the conduct book may be not the amelioration of women, but of men.

To be sure, there is doubt as to whether these texts really should be considered a part of the periodical press, despite their actual or intended periodicity. Such is not, however, the case with another journal, *Le Cabinet des modes* (1785–1792), the premier fashion magazine of the period, which features beautiful fashion plates in pastel colors.[12] Appearing with regular periodicity—even as the revolution breaks out in the summer of 1789—the *Cabinet* is a particularly fascinating specimen of the suppleness with which fashion can mold itself to the dictates of politics, using changes in the power structure as the inspiration for inventing new forms of self-adornment. Written primarily but not exclusively for women, by several successive male editors, the *Cabinet* goes through three different stages. During its first years, it is unabashedly devoted to fashion and carries the facile maxim, "Boredom is born of uniformity." Then, during the early revolutionary years, the journal embraces patriotism by linking fashion to politics. And, finally, in its last years, it becomes more culturally oriented, concentrating on reviews of plays and books.

In the opening issue of 15 November 1785, the male editor of fashion and fashionableness began by declaring, "The Capital of the French Nation has long been regarded as the source and model of taste in the Arts of pleasure and usefulness, as in Productions of the mind." Tapping into traditional nationalism, he says that "all the Peoples of Europe are eager to pay daily tribute to our Fashions, our Inventions, and our Industry." He further contends that the practice of luxury is really a form of benevolent charity that women should feel good about practicing, for, he argues, "luxury returns . . . to the poor person that which inequality made him lose." In consequence, the embrace of luxury—that is, fashion and fashionableness—represents, in his view, a kind of patriotic commercialism with a trickle-down effect for the classes and includes commerce, manufacturing, the arts, and even agriculture. Later, during the revolutionary years, the *Cabinet* would repeatedly restate the idea that fashion concerned patriotism as much as it did elegance, both of which, it implied, were the female's responsibility. Indeed, according to one writer, the fair sex "seems to have been born for no other concern. . . . Any other role . . . seems to us to be in total opposition to the views of nature" (20 May 1787).

In view of such rhetoric, it is easy to understand why these journals, though primarily about women, never really became a forum for them. With their language and vision belonging to men, such journals have a tendency to practice a top-down power structure, putting the female reader in the role of receiver or pupil, and the male writer above her as guiding teacher. The true *journaliste de femmes*, on the other hand, was eager to transform that relationship into a *participatory* one, in which reader and writer would enjoy a relationship *in dialogue*.

A New Kind of Press for, by, and about Women

Who, exactly, were the female journalists who dared to enter the public arena of a still unformed profession that contracted with readers to provide a "useful and entertaining" product on a regular basis? To begin with, they were by necessity businesswomen, since journalists had to be able to handle all aspects of publishing, from financial arrangements, to securing royal patronage and obtaining the *privilège* or *permission*, to marketing the journal, dealing with printers, and even, on occasion, delivering the published volume to the bookseller or postal authorities. Second, while they were generally minor characters whose names are nowhere near as familiar as those of the celebrated *salonnières*— Madame Du Deffand, Madame de Geoffrin, Mademoiselle de Lespinasse, Madame D'Epinay, the *only* female names traditional history has bequeathed to us—they actually had the potential to have greater impact on far more women than their sisters in the salon. Among the successful and unhonored women journalists are Adélaïde Dufresnoy of the *Courrier lyrique* and the three editors of *Le Journal des dames*— Madame de Beaumer, Catherine Michelle de Maisonneuve, and Marie Emilie de Montanclos. Each of these women belongs in any full history of women's writing. To ignore them in favor of remembering only the *salonnières* does both them and women's history a considerable disservice in that it ignores the ways in which new kinds of connections between women were being forged. Journalists, after all, sought to engage a far wider and more diverse group of women from Paris and the provinces in debate and conversation. They used their periodicals to validate a wide range of women's voices, perhaps, we might judge, because with the rise of democratic ideals, the idea that conversation was limited to a select few in a closed salon was antithetical to the (revolutionary) remaking of society.

At times, we scholars have wanted to set the *salonnière* against the *journaliste*, or one century against the other, in terms of which women acted more "subversively" and courageously. Thus, while it is certainly true that women's issues never enjoyed much political legitimacy in the male-oriented ancien régime, to laud seventeenth-century *salonnières* for subverting patriarchy through focusing salon conversation on a radical reexamination of love and marriage, while charging that their sisters in the eighteenth century had lost the power to set the agenda, seems disputatious to me.[13] Likewise, to dismiss the seventeenth-century *salonnière* as a *précieuse* and a snob in order to give the eighteenth-century journalist her due is unnecessary.[14] These kinds of arguments overlook the essential: that is, both the *salonnière* and the *journaliste* were power brokers of conversation, the real distinction being *where* those conversations took place and with whom. On the one hand, in the private salons, people talked with their peers in the intellectual elite; while, on the other, in the pages of the periodical press, they exchanged views with people they did not know from throughout the nation. What happened was that with the growth of democratic ideals, what formerly could transpire only in the private salons of a privileged cultural and intellectual elite was now being relocated. As the mantle of public discourse was enlarged, there was an inevitable relocation of discourse from the private salon to which the few were invited, to the more inclusive pages of the periodical press. The salon, which, as Dena Goodman says, offered a convergence between female and philosophic ambitions,[15] no longer was the only arena in which women could play a role in important conversations. It had, indeed, been an early and key stage in women's participatory history with men, but the female periodical press, focused on women, would represent the first "feminist" conversation/outreach to a wholly new community—that of female readers.

As Elizabeth Eisenstein has written, the periodical press displaced the pulpit, in terms of mobilizing a population and, when that happened, a change in the relationship between the *communication system* and the *community structure* became possible.[16] Information now passed in printed rather than in aural form, which would have a significant impact on the restructuration of the public sphere. Eisenstein argues that as a consequence, the notion of what it meant to belong, as well as what it meant to participate in public affairs, was changed. Paradoxically, although a reading public was more "dispersed, more atomistic and individualistic," to use Eisenstein's words, it also led to the establishment of new forms of group identity that would compete with traditional and strongly class-separated identities.[17] In this sense, the female periodical press became a leveler and unifier, reaching out to a broader audience and also connecting women through its sex-specific focus.

To be sure, there is a long-standing debate on the relationship between the extension of a print culture and the spread of democracy. Eisenstein makes the valid point that a print culture may do no more than extend the spread of conservative ideas,[18] a judgment reiterated by Joan Landes who has accused the *Journal des dames* of merely participating in the restructuring of morality as a category of private or individual rather than communal life.[19] But Eisenstein also emphasizes that the expansion of a reading public—in the present case, a female reading public—has the potential to create a new class of women of letters, as readers and writers. Thus, I would submit, that with the birth of a feminine periodical press that joined women's voices and interests throughout the nation, the distinctions between private and public space began to be modified, becoming both more fluid and more complex. In the interplay between journalist and reader, as between reader and reader, women in different parts of the capital and throughout the nation and abroad were encouraged to see themselves as part of a community of interrelated interests, having their own history and a future that demanded both continuity and change.

CREATING A FEMALE FORUM

My argument that a female forum was being created does not depend on suggesting that the periodical literature produced by women is necessarily a faithful reflection of the "average" woman's hopes or aspirations in the eighteenth century. Nor am I trying to argue that women journalists, any more than women writers in general or the *salonnières* in particular, are "typical" women, or that their thinking is representative of eighteenth-century female mentality. What I am suggesting, instead, is that for the first time women had a vehicle that permitted, and indeed required, them to think in new ways about themselves. On page after page of this press, a call was being sent out for women to become informed, to participate in debate, to speak their mind. The objective of the editors was to create a bond with their readers by articulating matters of interest to women and giving them the opportunity to express themselves. Some, like Madame Dufresnoy, offered a free subscription to anyone who sent her a dozen contributions, while others, such as Madame de Beaumer, explicitly privileged women's works, past and present, and emphasized her desire to make known female exploits and expertise in all fields of endeavor.

It would be overstating the case to say that female editors focused on setting a full pro-woman agenda in their periodicals, or to assert that they saw themselves first as feminist activists and secondarily as journalists.[20] But it is, nonetheless, true that their journals often carried a competing and alternative discourse for women, at significant variance from the model widely accepted in the mainstream. This does not mean that they sought to destroy or undermine or subvert the government. In fact, there is relatively little political commentary in their journals, presumptive evidence, it would seem, that they did not link the end of women's subordination to specific legislative matters.[21] In January 1766, the editor of the *Journal des dames*, Madame de Maisonneuve, explains the absence of political news in her periodical by asserting that it is more important to discuss morals and manners than politics, which are, in her view, only the phenomenon of the moment. So, unlike the more militant women who penned the *cahiers de doléances* or the *réclamations* in 1789 and the immediate revolutionary years, women journalists did not tend to formulate their aspirations in terms of specific economic or political demands—political rights (citizenship, voting, representation), legal rights (equality before the law, property, and inheritance rights), or economic concerns (control of dowries and fortune, or the right to work and conditions of the workplace).

Instead, they challenged the status quo and an unfair social contract as they argued for greater respect for women, their minds and talents. Thus, in addition to a variety of subjects proper to the cultural interests of a well-off female readership—history, book and theater reviews, verse, anecdotes, and so forth—the journals addressed with striking frequency five main woman's issues: (1) problems of female self-image, (2) lack of public recognition and fair reception of women's minds and works, (3) the necessity for better female education, (4) issues of marriage, and, to a lesser extent, (5) motherhood. To be sure, the trajectory of women's voices in these various periodicals was sometimes uneven. There was never total unanimity among the different editors, even of the same journal, on questions of feminine psychology, female education, marriage, and maternity. Nor did the journals reveal the same attitudes toward social or political problems. Surprisingly, some issues were not even treated at all, such as the question of divorce, which, at that period, could be defined as a feminist issue.[22] Or the question of *la vocation forcée*—that is, forcing a young woman into the convent against her will, which was a hot-button issue in other periodicals.

In pursuit of its goal to create a forum for women, the editor strove to adopt a tone of intimacy with her reader, as though in face-to-face conversation. This is a far different approach from the male editors of publications like the *Bibliothèque des dames* or the *Bibliothèque des femmes*, whose tone could veer from condescendingly paternalistic to silly and embarrassing paeans of praise of the fair sex. Obviously, the fact that women editors spoke from the common experience of their sex and were able to address their readers as *we* rather than *you* had the benefit both of establishing less psychological distance between editor and reader, while developing the reader's confidence in herself and the journal. On occasion, the idea of an open forum could lead to surprising results, as both Mesdames de Maisonneuve and de Montanclos discovered when writers wrote in to object to their advocacy of the second sex. For instance, in February 1764, Madame de Maisonneuve published a letter from a reader who took issue with the editor's feminism, saying, "Do you absolutely insist upon imposing laws on us? Do you not know that women in general do not like to write?" in apparent disregard for what she was doing herself. "To maintain that we can distinguish ourselves in Literature is to leave the sphere that belongs to us. Mind and knowledge are the prerogatives of men." Provided that her words are not ironic, we may speculate that if the editor included this dissenting voice, it was to encourage other women to step forward and state their opinion. To silence the protester would be, Madame de Maisonneuve may have concluded, to repeat the sins of patriarchy: to muzzle dissent, while disarming and diminishing the dissenter. The legitimization of the female cause required respect for the views of others; thus, to maintain the integrity of their enterprise, which was to give voice to women, Madame de Maisonneuve had to prove her openness to dissent. It is likely that it is this very spirit of dialogue and exchange that contributes to, if not accounts for, the extraordinary success and longevity of the *Journal des dames*, which published for more than twenty years.

Such a new mode of discourse was welcomed by many women readers—witness their letters of appreciation—for they felt marginalized or forgotten in other national forums. They were far more accustomed to being treated or written about as had Monsieur Du Rozoi, a royalist and Madame de Beaumer's unlikely collaborator during one period at the *Journal.*[23] Taking up the argument of the so-called warring extremes of female nature, Rozoi had said that woman is "a sweet, agreeable and affable being, kind, and religious, and at the same time hard, difficult to deal with, proud, cruel, impious; sometimes a god who merits our Praises . . . sometime a Tyrant . . . she shines in society, charms in love, bores in marriage, is prostituted in the theater, crushed in Cloisters" (July 1762). Women editors, on the other hand, were united in their desire to combat such an image, and so in their writing set themselves the task of leveling the playing field. They wanted women to be reintegrated into the center, to identify themselves as belonging to and having rights, including the right to speak in the cultural mainstream, in which, the journalists insisted, both male and female voices had to be heard. Consequently they used their journals to create an ambiance of tolerance, accessibility, and support for women, in order to counteract their exclusion elsewhere. But they certainly did not seek to validate everything women said or did. In fact, their own criticism of their sex is anything but timid. They are contemptuous of females who continue to want to make their way in society by seeking men's indulgence or by using a pretty face or nicely turned ankle to advance their interests. Such women forget, the editors warn, that those charms will tarnish and disappear.

We might think of the role of editor as that of facilitator who used her journal as a platform for women's conversation. Most typically, she set herself the task of combating diminished self-esteem of those women readers who had let themselves believe that they were an inferior sex or that they would defeminize themselves by acts of speech or publication of their words. It is to such female readers that the journalist directs her commentary, challenging them to create their own discourse in which they will no longer be victims of others' rhetoric and dependent on men's ideas.

What I would emphasize, then, with regard to the feminine press, and what is truly remarkable is that despite all manner of obstacles and prejudices, women *did* succeed in founding their own journals or in taking them over from men, managing and financing them, and dealing, as need be, with censors and booksellers and sometimes even the police.[24] Though they risked personal humiliation, loss of reputation, ruined health, and financial failure for their "deviant"—or defiant—stands against dominant gender ideology, these women journalists also believed in, and bore witness to, the Enlightenment idea of free speech in their journals. And, in so doing, they both proposed a new model of female behavior and became role models for others. That they should have been successful in their enterprise, even though few journals in those years lasted for much more than a handful of months, with a great many never making it past a first issue or prospectus of lofty and impossible ideals, is persuasive evidence that there was a ready reading market for woman-oriented papers that did not, like the *Cabinet des modes*, for instance, depend exclusively on women's interest in the frivolous or in fashion. For that journal, written by men for women, and presenting an image of the feminine that is largely negative in its assumption of her frivolousness, stoked woman's pride in terms of her physical attractiveness alone. Rationalizing both its own existence and woman's exploitation on the grounds of economic nationalism and patriotism, the *Cabinet* proposed a view of women that the feminine press by women determinedly set itself to counteract.

THE JOURNALS OF THE FEMININE PRESS

Of the fewer than twenty periodicals of the eighteenth century that have been classified by Jean Sgard as belonging to the feminine press, I propose to look more closely at four in particular: the *Spectatrice* (1728–1729), written anonymously; the *Nouveau Magasin français, ou, Bibliothèque instructive et amusante* (1750–1751) by Madame Leprince de Beaumont; the *Courrier lyrique, ou Passe-temps des toilettes*, edited by Madame Dufresnoy during the period 1787 to January 1789; and, finally, the longest lasting of all feminine periodicals, the *Journal des dames*, published with some interruptions over a period of nearly twenty years (1759–1779) by nine editors, three of whom were women. These journals have been chosen, either because they are excellent examples of the debate that resides within eighteenth-century women's writing over sex roles and women's relationship to the social order, and/or because they have unusually long publication lives for periodicals of the eighteenth century, proof that they must have appealed to quite a few readers. In the following discussions, I will also attempt to characterize the quality of either their sexual or gender discourse.

The *Spectatrice* (1728–1729) and the Sexualization of Signature

The earliest paper expressing a feminist ideology in a sustained way is the *Spectatrice*, which appears for a year (28 March 1728 to 5 March 1729) and is written entirely by a single individual. Composed of one long weekly essay, detailing the author's moral and social philosophy, as well as offering harsh judgments on both men and mankind in general, this journal minces few words as it condemns condescending treatment of women. To be sure, we do not know for certain who the author of the *Spectatrice* was, or even if, as claimed in the opening pages, this person was a female. Certainly the author's contention that she disguises herself in men's clothes so as to be able to safely roam the streets at night and practice her trade as a *spectatrice* would be unconventional behavior for a woman, although, as we saw with Madame de Beaumer, cross-dressing could open up certain realms of society.[25] Perhaps the *spectarice's* reference to male disguise is poetic license; perhaps it was never intended to be accepted as an authentic claim. Or perhaps there *was* an unusual woman in the 1720s who, in the style of Restif de la Bretonne and his *Nuits de Paris*, became an early "philosopher night-owl."

Another possibility, of course, is that the author may have been male but identified and sympathized with women, somewhat like the infamous Chevalier d'Eon who felt more in tune with the female sex than his own.[26] If that is the case, then the *spectatrice* is not engaging in actual transvestism, but a kind of surreal parody. But regardless of the *spectatrice's* sex, which unlike d'Eon's cannot be established, by wearing or adopting male dress in order to freely circulate in society, the author replicates the sense of alienation experienced by women in a society governed by males when she must become male in order to access certain structures (or, as Madame de Beaumer had said, "Faites-vous Hommes"). To this demonstration of sexualized access will be added the vexing issue of sexualized signature, which occurs when readers judge preemptively the style, contents, and significance (or authority) of a text, according to the sex of the author's name. Such sexualized polarities undoubtedly explain why many writers in the eighteenth century sought to remain anonymous or have their identity reduced to a letter and a series of asterisks.

Some critics doubt that the *spectatrice* was female, largely because, like historian Suzanne Van Dijk, they believe that no woman would describe her own physical unattractiveness as the writer does. Moreover, some have argued, cross-sexed authorship or the adoption of a feminine pseudonym was seen by some men as a great joke. Van Dijk quotes the antiwoman critic, Fréron ("What folly, a woman who sets herself forth as a great mind!"), who suggested that some men would willingly take on a feminine pseudonym because such authorship offered them the opportunity to write "like a woman"—that is, with the freedom to be superficial.[27] Without rising to the bait that Fréron offered, we can say that though the *spectatrice* does indeed emphasize in herself a certain sexual equivocation, her text is neither lightweight nor innocuous and hence does not, by Fréron's definition, appear to be written "like a woman." On the contrary, her journal articulately and often even elegantly stands in support of women. In that respect, it is totally unlike other texts by men pretending to be women, particularly those *faux cahiers féminins* of the revolutionary years that sought to engender in the reader negative feelings about women, sabotaging them through unwarranted exaggeration, prudishness, or licentiousness.[28]

Indeed, the arguments about sexual relations that the *spectatrice* mounts are both remarkable and modern, particularly when she calls for a more androgynous ideal or declares at one point that if she were the sovereign, she would establish a "Sénat de femmes" and a "Colony for Scorners of Women" over which a woman would rule. Moreover, we are struck by the author's expression of acute sensitivity to the experience of the woman who is both exceptionally bright and physically disadvantaged—plain, even ugly, and lacking in grace—but possessing an intellect superior to most others in her immediate society. This may be one of the earliest references to a complex problem that all women face and which Carolyn G. Heilbrun has identified as "the process of becoming, or *failing to become, a sex object*" (my italics).[29] To have one's value determined by how attractive or unattractive men find her is an injustice, but it is even more painful to be judged an inadequate example of one's own sex, lacking in femininity and desirability. No wonder that the *spectatrice* wants to move beyond sex and gender.

Subsequently in the text, the *spectatrice* refuses all the conventions that weigh on women—to be coquettish, marry well, to practice forbearance when married off to an inadequate husband. In speaking of "the yoke of marriage" and her distaste for a husband who would insist on seeing himself as her "Seigneur" or "Master," she objects that if she were married, she would no longer be able to "play the philosopher"—that is, to think for herself and have a public existence—for, as a married woman, she would be limited to being the *spectatrice* only of a single private household and family. And she adds that nature had not given her the "feminine and heroic patience" necessary to undertake marriage on those terms. "To be obliged to carry an insignificant little man wherever one goes," she writes, "seems to me the most humiliating misery that has fallen on women" (1 April 1728). While in other examples of the feminine press, the harshness of these sentiments is never reflected to the same degree, there is often the same sense of bitter injustice about the gendered expectations of women's lives.

In the final analysis, it is undoubtedly immaterial whoever or whichever sex wrote this fascinating document of female disentitlement. Perhaps the *spectatrice* was not the "honest woman" she says she was, perhaps she did not live in a room in a neighborhood of working-class people; and, if she was a woman, very likely she did not roam the streets incognito. All this may be a fiction, it may be a bit of poetic license that permits the author to take up specific topics. But it scarcely matters, because what is important is the authenticity of the argument made within the text for female equality and recognition. Few others would argue, as this author implicitly does, that if justice is to be had, gender boundaries must be blurred and traditional and absolute male and female oppositions discarded.

It would be fascinating to know how readers of the eighteenth century viewed this work. What we do know is that crossing sexual boundaries, whether through cross-dressing or authorship, was viewed with suspicion in the eighteenth century, even as it is so often today. A large portion of the public is comfortable only with clear distinctions of sex. In terms of the eighteenth century, if the writer of the *Spectatrice* were a female, she discredited herself by her methods (acting as a man) and expressing sentiments inadmissible to her sex; if the writer were male, he undermined his credibility by giving serious attention to the disenfranchised in the female population. In either case, the eighteenth-century reader might have concluded that the writer revealed confusion about sex and about categories that were articles of faith. If growing numbers of people in ancien-régime France were on the verge of challenging the lack of freedom that characterized individual lives, the rights they claimed for individuals did not also include those of uncertain or changing or flexible sexual identity. Cartesian logic called for clear categories of thought and of sexuality, and anything less disqualified the argument. Certainly for a writer in the 1720s to cast doubt on the notion of unequivocal difference between the sexes was a courageous, if ultimately self-defeating, stand. But what should particularly arrest our attention is that both the equivocal figure of the *spectatrice* and the rhetorical figure of the cross-dresser underscore how the problems of access, authority, and authorship have characterized so much of sexual history.

Le Nouveau Magasin Français (1750–1751): The Compatibility of Virtue and Satire

Two decades later, when Madame Leprince de Beaumont opened her journal, she made no attempt to hide her sexual identity, saying to her reader, "It is useless that I disguise from you my Sex," for, she continued sardonically, the negligence of style, the lack of organization and the caprices of her text would automatically lay bare the truth. "No more is needed," she writes tongue-in-cheek, "to reveal a female Author and worse yet, a Frenchwoman." Madame Leprince de Beaumont knew that potential readers might be predisposed against a magazine edited by a woman who necessarily carried less authority than a male. Men, she felt, would certainly ask her, "How did you ever take it into your head, as a woman, to produce a Magazine?" And she imagined that they would advise her to take up more appropriate and "womanly" activities such as coiffures, pompons, and feathers. So, in the *avertissement* of her first issue, she preempted their objections with this categoric response, that would be repeated like a leitmotif by other women throughout the century: "Speak as you like, *Messieurs*. But be forewarned that I would better compose a Book . . . than be concerned about where to place a Ribbon" (January 1750).

Offended that men would automatically dismiss her ideas because of antiwoman prejudices, she charged that males were "unjust legislators," and accused them of claiming for themselves despotic power. "They maintain," she expostulates, "that submission must be our lot, and that we are incapable of anything but sewing and spinning" (January 1751, 39). This conventional image of the woman wedded to her needle and thimble, a staple in the sex and gender argument of difference, is a pivotal and emotionally charged one for feminist journalists, who want to change not only the instrument, but also the meaning and reception of women's work. In her third issue, Madame Leprince publishes a letter, ostensibly from a reader, charging her to become women's "Knight" and to redress the wrongs that men have done to their sex in that "multitude of brochures appearing today whose only objective seems to have been to lower our sex . . . imagining in us vices we know nothing of . . . exaggerating our weaknesses." Couching her argument in the familiar terms of the inadequate education given to women, the letter writer (or Madame Leprince herself) continues the attack against men, saying, "If our talents had not been limited to learning to wield a needle; if we had been educated to use the pen with ease, men would not tear us apart with impunity, and we could expose to the light of day their faults and ridiculous habits, in order to avenge ourselves of their slander and frequent calumnies" (March 1750). There is ample evidence that that is precisely the task that Madame Leprince de Beaumont sets for herself in her periodical, as she seizes the quill and discards the needle.

According to Madame Leprince, the problem with "women's work"—those so-called natural occupations of sewing, darning, and embroidery, presumably assigned by Nature, and ratified through practice everywhere in the world—is that it is both dreary and mind deadening. In an ironic phrasing of the condescending and misogynistic "male" argument against women, Madame Leprince has a man telling women that females have been given just enough intelligence to be able to devote themselves to the most boring tasks of housework, but not enough to realize how really boring it is (June 1750). With malicious delight, she has him say, "the organs of your body are so arranged that you have precisely enough intelligence to please," but "your brain being softer than men's cannot in truth retain the subjects given to it." However, he adds, "it is thanks to this happy default that we owe the vivacity, pleasantness, and variety of your conversation." And, then, demonstrating how man arrogantly presumes that women are there to serve his psychic and physical needs, Leprince has him say, "and what would happen to men, if in those moments when they come to find relaxation from their labors at the side of a pretty woman, they found her instead buried in meditating a problem of geometry." Thus Madame Leprince hoists the man on his own petard. Later, in a further demonstration of her privileging of women, she will even argue that the Creator, reaping the benefits of practice, did a much better job when he came to creating woman (January 1751).

Such satires reveal that Madame Leprince de Beaumont used her journal in part to conduct a polemic against male presumptiveness. This was certainly not her only goal, as it seems to have been in the *Spectatrice*, but it is possibly the most interesting part of her thirty- to forty-page monthly journal. Initially the *Nouveau Magasin français* seems to have been intended as a periodical for a general readership, containing a variety of articles dealing with scientific or medical matters, verse, book reviews, excerpts from works by Voltaire and others, along with literary news. Increasingly, however, it became a vehicle for Madame Leprince de Beaumont's own moral views, which she cast in the thin fiction of letters or stories sent to her. Of course, as with many early periodicals, it is often difficult to assign authorship with absolute certainty, but since, stylistically and ideologically, these "outside contributions" resemble everything else in the journal, I am inclined to assume that frequently Madame Leprince wrote the entire journal herself, a truly prodigious undertaking.

While unremarkable at first glance, many of the tales that fill so many pages of the periodical in fact grow out of a philosophy that is, curiously, both sentimental and feminist. Centerpiecing difficult relationships and posing some serious questions about the quality of marriage, Madame Leprince de Beaumont shows male characters who are inconstant and ungenerous, weak-willed and incapable of controlling their passions, whereas the women are patient and constant, perhaps unhappy, but in command of their emotions. As for marriage, the author sees it as always potentially problematic for women. Herself briefly and unhappily married in her early thirties, she would later remarry with more success in a second union that produced six children. But in her writing, she suggests that even when marriage begins with passion, it will evolve into something else, and she is nagged by the question of whether esteem can ever really replace love. Traditional in that she believes it is a woman's duty to bring out the best in her husband by setting him an example, and by forgiving him his sins, she takes this position not because she accepts that a wife has no other choice, but because she is convinced that woman is made of stronger moral fiber. Having fought prejudice herself and having achieved, often with great difficulty, some degree of success in journalism, literature, and education, Madame Leprince de Beaumont knew what it was to have to earn her own living. Thus she preaches the virtues of virtue-redefined to her sex, demonstrating through her own life that women are capable of intelligence, hard work, patience, and independent decision-making.

In the final analysis, she proves in her journal that satire and virtue are not incompatible. Being virtuous does not mean being innocuous, kindly disposed toward everyone and everything. She, like all the other women in this book, is persuaded that virtue has nothing to do with silence, and everything to do with intelligence, integrity, and industriousness. Madame Leprince de Beaumont is not picking a fight with men, but appealing to women to believe in themselves.

The *Courrier lyrique et amusant* (1785–1788): Badinage and Virtue

Poet, dramatist, translator, novelist, and short story writer, Adélaïde-Gillette Billet Dufresnoy (1765–1825) was, acccording to Michaud's *Biographie universelle*, an extraordinary woman. She married at age fifteen and became the editor of the *Courrier lyrique* in her early twenties, making her literary debut with two plays in the late 1780s. Young, rich, beautiful, and eager for literary fame, she was one of the "femmes à la mode" prior to the revolution, which would subsequently impoverish her before her thirtieth birthday and force her to seek new protectors each time there was a change of government. A woman who spent her life working and writing, she would later, when her husband became blind and was no longer able to perform his functions as court clerk in a small town in Italy, take over almost all his responsibilities, appearing on his behalf and assisting him by writing his judgments and keeping files in order. But the chapter of her life that focuses our attention at this point occurs when she is only twenty-two years old and involved in the publication of a periodical.

Fully cognizant of men's long history of mocking "le beau sexe Auteur," Madame Dufresnoy advised women in the *Courrier lyrique* to ignore male ridicule and seek within themselves their own happiness and pleasures (15 November 1787). Demonstrating that she will not be frightened by male calumny, she publishes a piece written by a male author in which she is cast as "a woman with little sense" who "has decided to play the savant and to write a rather pitiable Journal that she announces under the title of Amusing. . . ." Attacking her "unwomanly" pretensions as a woman editor—a risible notion, her critic sneered—he wrote, "The Public willingly forgives her the desire to deceive, provided that she dispenses us with having to read her." But with resolute self-confidence, Madame Dufresnoy goes right ahead and keeps publishing.

Being pro-woman will not mean, however, that she is also necessarily "feminist" in her editorial approach. In fact, in designing her journal for both women and men, she shows a considerable tolerance for lightweight material that often takes a bantering tone with regard to relations between the sexes. Apparently her approach was successful, for a year after the first issue, she doubles the size of her bi-monthly to sixteen pages for which she charges fifteen *livres* for subscribers in Paris and sixteen *livres* eight *sols* for the provinces.[30] Typically, the first part of the magazine was composed of songs (*chansons*, *vaudevilles*, *romances*, *ariettes*, *contredanses*) and accompanying music, devoted almost exclusively to love and bearing such titles as "L'Alphabet des amants," "L'Instant favorable," even "Les Adieux de Mme de Tourvel à M. de Valmont." Often gallant in tone, these songs sometimes reveal a certain pathos and social realism, as, for instance, in "Les Suites d'une erreur," by a Mlle Victoire B***, in which the young woman, pregnant and abandoned by her lover, laments the irony that her present misfortune had arisen from what had been a moment of happiness. "Did I have to become a mother, to enjoy your favors?" (15 June 1785) she complains to the god of Cythera.

A poet herself, Madame Dufresnoy regularly publishes her own verse, as well as that of Madame de Genlis and Madame de Montanclos. Michaud judged her poetry very favorably, singling out her erotic poetry, which, in his view, placed her in the first rank of women poets of France. In addition to verse, Dufresnoy devotes a great deal of space to book reviews and theater news and reviews, and shows herself to be a demanding critic, unhesitant about stating her negative judgment of much of the theater then being produced in Paris.[31] At one point she complains: "Will Authors never cease to give the Public the kind of Plays that are nothing but disconnected scenes? Will they finally deign to realize that it would be better to make a single good Comedy or a good Comic Opera in the course of their lives, rather than produce a multitude that have neither sense, nor wit, nor reason" (1 April 1787)

Perhaps what is most interesting about this journal is its taste for the colorful anecdote, that ubiquitous staple of eighteenth-century journalism. The large number of amusing or piquant anecdotes is striking, revealing something both about reading tastes and about the society, its sense of humor and approach to problems. While it may be impossible to argue that these anecdotes have feminist underpinnings or import, it is certainly true that the majority relate in some way to issues of gender or sexuality, which suggests that Mme Dufresnoy was not in the least hesitant about including such material in her journal. To laugh at sex was not, she felt, a blemish on her virtue. Thus she relates these yarns with relish and pleasure. One concerns a peasant father on his way to the parish church, his just-born twin daughters in his arms. A friend joshes with him, saying, "I suppose they are still virgins," to which the new father replies, "For the first-born, I'm pretty darn sure; but for the other one, I'm not about to give any assurances" (1 September 1788). On another occasion, she includes the following witticism: "A bride said to her husband who was leading her too quickly to the altar: 'For pity's sake, let's take it a bit slower; or I could have a miscarriage'" (16 December 1788).

Frequently these stories make multiple appearances in a variety of print sources, as with the apparently true story of the marriage of two men that was published in the *Cabinet des modes* in the 10 May 1787 issue and then six months later (15 November 1787) in the *Courrier lyrique*. Eighteen months after the marriage of François Suire and Marie Besson, it was ascertained that the latter was a male. Apparently Marie Besson had been brought up as a girl and believed it, and François—either very tolerant, or a closet gay, a bisexual, or simply a man who loved another person—wished to remain married to Marie. Though public officials had dissolved the marriage, the two were allowed to remarry, a decision applauded by both the *Courrier* and the *Cabinet*. If the ratification of same-sex marriage appears surprising, especially given the fact that the public was uncomfortable with expressions of indeterminate sexuality, it is all the more striking that a woman like Madame Dufresnoy deemed the reinstatement of the same-sex union a desirable denouement.

One can provisionally conclude that at least for Madame Dufresnoy the primary issue was a loving relationship and commitment to one's partner. She did, after all, use the pages of her journal to celebrate her own happy marriage of love, and she applauded what she considered to be a positive change in public opinion promoting *mutual* fidelity by both husbands and wives to their wedding vows. But under closer scrutiny and with regard to society as a whole, that provisional answer seems problematic. How are we to square society's apparent tolerance for a same-sex marriage with the virulent defamations of character directed at individuals who did not act according to gender or sex? A man who acted like a woman was excoriated, as was the woman who acted like a man. Such individuals were nearly always attacked in their very sexuality, as *dénaturés* or "contrary to nature," sexually undesirable, monsters of unclear or bisexuality.[32] Effeminacy in a male or manliness in a female suggested to many in eighteenth-century society not only moral weakness or a corroded character, but something sexually repulsive as well. So, why was the public ready to bless a marriage between two men?

There is no easy answer to the question. Some would say that the determining factor is class, others that it depends on whether those involved are public or private personages, while still others would point to more complicated issues of nurture versus nature and the sociopsychological dimensions of sexual identification.[33] Gary Kates has proposed that in the case of the Chevalier d'Eon, the diplomat and spy who at age forty-nine was forced by reasons of state and politics to present himself as a woman, the key issue is one of sex versus gender. As Kates shows, d'Eon felt great sympathy for females and perhaps even identified himself as female, but, in a patriarchal culture, the idea of a man becoming a woman and therefore losing status was out of the question. Moreover, in his view, the story of the Chevalier proves that while people in eighteenth-century France could do what they wanted in their sexual lives, in their public lives they needed to respect social conventions regarding gender. Since d'Eon was a public personality and a diplomat and representative of the French nation, he could not be permitted to live ambiguously. He could not be allowed to straddle the fence: wear the military uniform of France and "feel like a woman." If d'Eon did little to squelch the rumors of his sexual identity, and indeed seemed to feed them, while at the same time refusing to submit to a physical exam, the public could hardly feel sorry for him or cast him as a victim when he was obliged to "become a woman" as the condition for his return to France. It seems safe to say that in his case, politics and contagious hysteria over sex (even his mother seems to have reported that her child was a female) determined that d'Eon live as a woman.

Marie Besson, on the other hand, had been raised to think he was a woman. And since François Suire is happy to accept him as a wife, no one is being misled, nor are there any political issues at stake. Furthermore, Marie Besson can be permitted to be whatever he had been raised to think he was or wanted to be, because he is a simple peasant. If the marriage of Suire and Besson was accepted and even applauded, it was because privileged members of society were willing to let the unprivileged do as they wished, as long as both expressed satisfaction with the arrangement. In the case of the two men united in marriage, there are no political interests at stake. If Besson, a male, wanted to be a female, he could. If Suire, a male, accepted to be married to another male who acted like a female, that was fine. Neither was a public figure and both could return to living in total anonymity.

One may well conclude that for a woman like Madame Dufresnoy, who is very traditional in her own marriage and politically conservative, the most important issue is a married relationship based on love and respect. Using the pages of her journal to celebrate her own heterosexual marriage, while at the same time supporting the homosexual marriage between Suire and Besson, suggests in the final analysis that the discourse of virtue could easily coexist with a surprising tolerance, at least for the lower classes. The success of her journal, which combines critical commentary on the arts with lightweight badinage, would further suggest that, for many readers in the eighteenth century, it was a pleasing combination.

THE *JOURNAL DES DAMES* (1759–1774)

Begun in 1759 by a male editor, the *Journal des dames* would be the most successful women's periodical of the eighteenth century, publishing under nine different editors and lasting until 1774. As a general statement, one could characterize this periodical under all its editors as pleasant and useful reading, whose purpose was to keep women abreast of the latest literature by offering long résumés and sometimes excerpts from new works. There were also *pièces fugitives*, curious anecdotes from past and present, gleaned from sources at home or abroad; poems; letters from readers; sometimes songs and fold-out music, accompanied by diagrams of dance steps. On occasion, there were also advertisements for beauty products (how, for instance, to deal with both freckles and smallpox scars, which were seen as equally disfiguring), and other publicity notices for midwives, schools, and various courses of instruction. In addition, there were reviews of books on health, childbirth, teeth, skin, hair care, and aging, though mostly this section contained synopses of fiction or plays, without a great deal of critical apparatus, since the apparent objective of the "review" was to summarize or present a digest of contents rather than an evaluative judgment.

The three periods of female editorship constitute about eight years of the nearly twenty-year span, and each woman marks her tenure as editor differently. The first woman editor of the *Journal* was the colorful individual, Madame de Beaumer, whose editorship lasted from October 1761 to April 1763. An educated and energetic woman, she was unmarried and lived simply in the *quartier du Temple*. Like the author of the *Spectatrice*, she apparently occupied the margins of society, which may explain why she often used harsh and direct language in speaking up for the oppressed and disadvantaged—among whom she counted the female sex. A combative advocate for women, she could scarcely repress her irritation with men's traditional disparagement of women's capabilities. "How happy I would be to be able . . . to avenge [my sex]," she wrote in her opening issue, "of this injurious idea still held by certain barbarians amongst our citizens who have such difficulty in granting us the ability to think and write!" (October 1761). She derides the vertical notion of authority in society that keeps women in an inferior position, and fulminates over men laying sole claim to the roles of soldier, politician, and savant, and arrogating to themselves the professions of writer, thinker, historian, and journalist, leaving women with nothing, or making sport of those few who do try to assume other roles. Women, she insists, were made "to understand reason as well as men," adding in ironic gibe that they even have the honor of seeing men lose their reason over a woman.

In a striking exchange with a letter-writing reader, Madame de Beaumer rejects categorically the concept of authority that excludes female voices, just as language itself had done by giving masculine gender to certain nouns, thereby requiring the addition of a sex-specific adjective to convey the break from the norm, as in a *woman author*. Furthermore, objecting to the virtual disappearance of the woman who is collapsed into her husband's title made feminine—"Madame la Présidente, Madame la Conseillère or Madame la Maréchalle," the editor's correspondent asked, should one not also, then, logically say "mon femme"? She insisted that Madame de Beaumer should feminize "auteur" into "autrice" and "editeur" into "editrice," a point the editor concurs with, because she feels that men have stolen the means of language and exploit it to their own advantage (February 1762).

For women to have been discussing their exclusion from language more than two centuries ago, to have shown how certain words such as *tout le monde* (everyone) or *la jeunesse* (youth) or *on* (the third person singular pronoun) or *l'homme* (man) had taken on restrictive meanings and most often designate only males, reveals a sophisticated awareness that is strikingly modern.[34] For what in effect they were recognizing is how language has been used to exclude women. Yet because there is only one language to which all are privy, and one standard of quality by which to judge, Madame de Beaumer counseled women to appropriate the voice of men and emulate their work and study habits as well as their language: "Make yourselves Men," she said, "because are we not Men when we think as well as they do?" (March 1763)

Speaking like a man, however, will present problems for her, with the censor and others who were unable to accommodate a "strong" female voice. Increasingly harassed by difficult *censeurs* and growing financial problems, Madame de Beaumer needed a way out. Finding a young man named Du Rozoi to take over the journal temporarily, she managed to save the magazine and appease the censors, though at the same time took the risk of compromising its voice. In fact, in the last issue that carries her name, the question of voice comes back in an ironic way, as there is an almost comic reversal of gendered voices, with Madame de Beaumer continuing to speak "as a man," and Du Rozoi writing in a flowery and affected style. One would have thought that gender reversal would have been problematic to the censors, suggesting the image of a topsy-turvy world, but apparently a foppish man was considered less threatening that a mannish woman laying claims to the prerogatives of the other sex. Ultimately, the censors were pacified, the *Journal des dames* continued to publish, Du Rozoi disappeared, and a new and wealthy female editor took over.[35]

Madame de Beaumer's successor, the well-connected and socially ambitious widow, Catherine Michelle de Maisonneuve, would be equally committed to the concept of a journal for women, but less acrid in her confrontations. A savvy businesswoman, she edited the *Journal* from April 1763 to July 1768, uniting the promotion of women with rallying calls to female readers to adopt a politics of virtue. Using her "Nouveau Prospectus" to insist that there is "no real difference between the two sexes," despite "all the foolishness" that Rousseau had written about the female sex, she exhorted women readers to help show that "you can be amused and pleased . . . other than with calumny, slander, and frivolousness" (May, June, July 1763).

In her October 1765 issue, she charges that "men have become the dispensers of celebrity, and they have agreed to keep it for themselves. . . . After having taken all the honors and freedom for themselves, they decided to make the Universe agree that brilliant talents were not appropriate in virtuous women, and that fame was not made for them." What she is pointing out is that by stipulating that female virtue depends on silence and invisibility, men had effectively disciplined women to believe, in the words of a letter writer to the *Journal*, that "a modest silence must be the lot of our sex."[36] The pernicious effect of this warped judgment has been, she continues, to poison "the days of most women who have tried to break free," and to smother "from birth an infinity of quality production that women could have produced."

More typically, however, under Madame de Maisonneuve, the *Journal* takes a cajoling tone, as she backs an ideal of what might be called "heroic femininity," through which she conducts her attacks not on the power structure, but on the attitudes that feed bifurcated and hierarchical thinking about the sexes. Her audience is, after all, primarily composed of relatively well-off women of leisure and means, who, in the time-honored phrase, sought in their reading to be both instructed and amused. Madame de Maisonneuve specifically targeted this group when she chided her reader to bring together the ideas of femininity and knowledge: "Couldn't one place a writing table next to your vanity table?" she sweetly and pointedly asks (May 1763).

As we know from Madame de Maisonneuve's repeated statements, the improvement of female education in the broad sense of culture and knowledge is one of the purposes of her journal. In pursuit of that goal, she discusses with her reader serious issues—inoculation against smallpox, the case against luxury, moral authority as opposed to authority legislated by law (January 1766), and so forth. Hence, she fulfills her part of the bargain or the challenge she had made to women in her "Nouveau Prospectus" of May 1763 to prove to men that women are eager to engage in reading that is serious and enlightening. Interestingly, and in demonstration of her belief that authority comes not through bombast or by aggravating the differences between the sexes, Madame de Maisonneuve puts out a hand to men by claiming that they, too, are often disadvantaged by inadequate education. Reviewing a book by Madame Riccoboni, she says, "I don't believe that men are as guilty as Madame Riccoboni seems to think; I am convinced that their education, even if much more extensive than ours, is almost as defective" (July 1765). Of course, that might just be a nice way of lodging a complaint.

This quiet authority that she endeavored to take was also the approach adopted by the third and last woman editor of the *Journal des dames*, Marie-Emilie de Montanclos (1736–1812), the Baronne de Prinzen (or Princen) by her first marriage and Madame de Montanclos by a second marriage. She was at the helm of the journal from January 1774 to May 1775 when ill health forced her to relinquish the reins of power. Beginning her editorial stint as Madame de Princen, she was to become Madame de Montanclos a few months later in a second marriage that was not particularly happy and quickly ended in a legal separation. Thus, like her two predecessors, Madame de Princen edited the journal primarily as a single woman and, also like them, was childless, although she would speak glowingly about motherhood in the *Journal*.

Implicitly agreeing with Madame de Maisonneuve that the best politics was one that muted the language of contention, she devoted the efforts of her editorship to encourage in women a code of conduct that mixed feminine gallantry, graciousness, and resolve. She had taken over the *Journal*, she confided, not in search of personal glory, but to win recognition by men for women. "It is not I who want to shine," she writes, "but it is I . . . who want to force men to give to women the justice they have so facilely refused [us]." The way to do this, she believed, was first to instill in women a sense of their own worth, by calling on them to be broadly educated and practice the kind of virtue that was neither submissive, nor weak, nor obedient to men or social prejudice. The virtue she preached would be founded in knowledge and compassion, and confidence in oneself. In this way, a woman would acquire authority through virtue, which in Montanclos's discourse is synonymous with women's duties. Indeed, during her editorship, the *Journal* includes much more advice to women about their duties and responsibilities than under previous editors. Women's duties, she writes, include those of religion, being a good citizen, a faithful wife (even when marriage is contracted less for joy than in fulfillment of duty), and a tender mother. In illustration of her beliefs, every month she wrote a "Vie de femme" in which she presented a great woman whose life story illustrated virtue and courage, moral knowledge, and recognition that a woman is not in a position to command others until she has learned to command herself. Only in that way will she be able to fulfill her responsibilities and hence achieve happiness, according to the editor's philosophy.

Though Madame de Montanclos exercises restraint over her language and would never want to appear to be a "mannish" woman in act or speech, her dignified affirmations of belief in women are nonetheless rooted in a firm sense of the injustices done to the female sex. Objecting through her own example to the prejudice that commands women to modest silence, she adopts a politics that is both cleverly conciliatory and effective. Hence, she supports the royal family, dedicating her work to Marie Antoinette, and dialogues *with* men, while pursuing the same goal of recognition for women, as combatively promoted by her more contentious predecessor, Madame de Beaumer. Madame de Montanclos may talk of a woman's pen as having scant force and precision, though much delicacy and *douceur*, and she may say that women write out of "a need of the heart and not the mind," but her words serve more as shields by which to deflect society's antifeminism or suspicions. For she is also inordinately proud, as a woman, to have successfully kept aloft the *Journal* and to possess opinions that are firm, well-grounded, and capable of rivaling any man's. Let men squabble over power, she implies; women should seek authority. "Our sex knows," she writes in August 1774, "how to arm itself with the seriousness of analysis," and because it does, it is "on an equal footing with its rival sex." Never shrill, she speaks in conciliatory tones, but she will not budge from her purpose of celebrating "the virtues, genius, good works and talents of a Sex that has been for the other what the iron is to the stone that strikes it" (January 1774). In fact, the single image that may best describe her editorship is that of the proverbial hand of steel in the velvet glove.

THE FEMININE PRESS: FEMINIZING THE SOCIAL CONTRACT

Clearly, the female editors of the feminine press are seeking to sketch out a new ideal for women, one in which they take active responsibility for the quality of their lives. Setting virtue, not men, as the new object of their desires, and looking for support among the members of their own sex,[37] female journalists used the pages of their journals to develop a discourse of virtue that arose out of a definition that emphasizes not so much moral excellence or goodness or righteousness; not chastity, innocence, or purity; not devotion and sacrifice and renunciation—though at various times and in different contexts it might include all these elements and qualities—but rather a definition that insisted on virtue as an enabling force, a potency, possessing the efficacy and the inherent power to produce results. Virtue would be an instrumentality, the union of reflection and choice; it would be a stance, a politics, a psychology totally different in character than in the precepts of conduct manuals or in handbooks of Christian piety written by men. In women's hands, virtue was intimately linked with the ultimate objective of what today we call female empowerment and what more traditionally is identified as respect or authority.

The virtue that female editors featured in their journals and encouraged their female readers to emulate would be neither submissive nor groveling, nor would it allow women to play up feminine vulnerability. The women of the periodical press were not attracted to the notion of persecuted virtue. Females were not weak, they were not natural victims, and they should not reduce themselves to hoping that men would protect them. Men, moreover, were not the makers or breakers of happiness, for it was woman herself who had that power and responsibility. As Madame de Beaumer said, "It is yourselves who are the arbiters of your destiny" (December 1761). In common with other editors of the female press, she sought to instill in female readers a firmer sense of their own worth and capacities. True, women journalists would point up woman's oppression, her "chains," her status as second-class citizen, but not, as male commentators had done, to arouse pity, but to impress her female readers about the reality of their situation and persuade them that they had the right to insist that it be changed. The virtue these journalists promoted arose out of an ideal of enlightened wisdom, justice, and humanity toward which women should aspire. Their virtue involved courage and generosity of heart, and was concerned with *honnêteté* toward oneself as well as toward others. Their virtue permitted belief in and pride of the self, which is why they dedicated their journal "to the glory of a sex that has always been undervalued."

All of which is not to say that the female editors of the feminine periodical press refused to think of women as being in relationship to men. Indeed, the whole question of relationships is very much in evidence in their periodicals in the articles and poems and songs on love and marriage. But by emphasizing woman's rational powers and her ability to found her attractiveness on something other than beauty and charm, women editors such as those of the *Journal des dames* sought to buttress women's self-esteem and propose a new basis on which to form relationships with men.

In their work as journalists, they often had male collaborators or assistance: for instance, Madame Dufresnoy of the *Courrier lyrique* worked with Monsieur de Murville, and the three woman editors of the *Journal des dames* also each had the collaboration of men—Madame de Maisonneuve and Mathon de la Cour, Madame de Montanclos and L. S. Mercier, and Madame de Beaumer and Du Rozoi, although to be sure the latter was more or less forced on her. They did not banish male contributors, even if Madame de Beaumer did conspicuously promise to privilege contributions from women. Madame de Maisonneuve made a special point of enlisting men's help on her journal, and, as much as she promoted women's concerns, Madame Leprince de Beaumont devoted a significant number of pages to publishing scientific papers or addresses given by men. Most of the women editors liked Voltaire, many applauded specific aspects of Rousseau, particularly his ideas on childrearing, although they were offended by the potential of misogynist content in his writing. Curiously, however, none referred directly to the infamous, at least to twentieth-century feminists, Book V of *Emile*.

The women editors for the most part were not antimarriage or antifamily, even though several of them were or had been unhappily married. On the contrary, they wanted to see the institution of marriage revitalized, for this was part of their program of a return to virtue, which they identified as not only key to the improvement in women's condition, but necessary in the badly corrupted moral fiber of the nation. As proof that the public was ready to change, Madame Dufresnoy reports with pleasure on the enthusiastic reaction of a theater audience to *Le Préjugé à la mode*, in which the husband rejects "the false principles of the century," which make him "inconstant by set purpose rather than by intention," and returns to his wife, amorous and hereafter constant (March 1787). To be sure, the anonymous author of the *Spectatrice* rails against "the yoke of marriage" because "for most men, a wife is a woman engaged and enlisted to take care of the [domestic] details they scorn" (May 1728), and Madame Leprince de Beaumont, sounding a very modern note in the mid-eighteenth century, says that marriage brings "in its wake cares, problems, anxieties. There is a house to take care of, children to raise." And she adds, perhaps in reference to the *double* yoke of sexual fidelity, "The habit of pleasure [soon] diminishes pleasure itself" ("L'habitude de jouir diminue le prix de la jouissance," June 1751). She prints a letter from a reader in the September 1750 issue whose complaint is that "there is no doubt that many women have not at all found in marriage the sweet comforts and satisfaction for which they had hoped." Perhaps they will have love or friendship, she says, but not "esteem," and it is that they most desire. But she also points out, like most writers of either sex at this time, that it is "social custom" that prevents individuals from contracting reasonable marriages based on mutual respect, if not love, and that condemn both parties to playing roles they may not desire. For her part, Madame de Maisonneuve laments the fact that the establishment of a *foyer* is done with so little care, observing that "it is certainly very strange that the most important thing for the life of a woman, being the choice of her future, is nearly always decided by chance." She cannot understand mothers who sympathize with criminals condemned to ten years of prison, but obstinately commit their own daughter to such unsuitable husbands that they themselves would have preferred death over marriage to the man (Fall 1763).

None of these women writers scorns love, though the *spectatrice* does see it as a trap and finds that it is humiliating for women to be dependent on men. In her estimate, women are more willing to be tolerant of men's weaknesses than men are of women's, since "women are more made for men than men are for women" (7 May 1728). All the writers publish love poetry and all seem to laud the marriage of real partnership. Many journals receive letters from women anxious not to lose their husbands, but fearful that it may be inevitable. Madame Leprince de Beaumont has a mother point out to her unhappily married daughter at one point that "from the moment of marriage, the reign of men begins and ours ends" (February 1750). Madame de Beaumer receives a letter from a wife who wonders how best to keep her husband from straying and wants to know if there is any "magic" by which a woman can make a husband who demands faithfulness from his wife be equally faithful to her (December 1761).

The female editors do not conceive of their roles so much as dispensers of lovelorn advice as of presenters of a general philosophy. They most emphatically do not want women to immolate themselves in marriage, to be constantly required to sacrifice their needs and desires to those of a master, and to harden themselves, as the *spectatrice* says, to domestic miseries and the insensitivity of a husband. Yet even if marriage should be unsatisfactory, most female editors still counsel women to be virtuous, for they remain convinced, at least in print, that the practice of virtue is the best choice for women—not only in the hope of a better afterlife or because divorce is impossible—but because it will make the woman feel stronger and better about herself. Even Madame de Beaumer counsels virtue to the woman unhappily married, arguing that "even the most scoundrel of men pays tribute to [woman's] virtue" (December 1761). Moreover, she suggests that the faithlessness of husbands may be the fault of wives. If a wife is unhappy with her husband, she should realize that it is up to her "to captivate and subjugate him through feelings." In striving for virtue, she will find the way of satisfying her husband, assures Madame de Beaumer, a surprising conclusion for a woman who claimed no illusions about how the majority of men see the majority of women.

In October 1761, she publishes a strongly worded letter from Madame de *** to Mlle de *** in which no words are minced regarding male disdain for women: "From the bottom of their soul, they look upon us as beings who are inferior to them; they make sport of us; we are ranked along with their pleasures. . . . Let us take full cognizance of this unhappy truth: war and peace are made without us." For this reason, the writer exhorts women readers to take themselves more seriously, saying, "let us use our vanity less to look in our mirrors and instead look inside ourselves with clear vision." Promoting a new idea of gender relations, removed from the single role of sexual attraction, she counsels women to seek out "male friends who instruct us . . . and not insipid worshippers who use the little smarts they have received from nature to try and seduce us." And then in an interesting use of the word, concludes, "I await this revolution with impatience."

Female journalists had perhaps not initially conceived of their journals as designed to fulfill the emotional needs of their readers, but the letters and contributions they received tended to show that this is what their female readership especially valued. Evelyne Sullerot observes that as the feminine press developed in the nineteenth and twentieth centuries and became more bourgeois, it tended to become more and more practically oriented, with recipes and home economy hints increasingly replacing the theater or book review columns.[38] Readers wanted periodicals to provide useful information that would help in their daily lives; they wanted advice on how to live their lives, how to make the most of themselves, and how to achieve happiness. In fact, says Sullerot, the feminine press has always been intimately concerned with questions of *devoirs* and *droits*. Behind every discussion or meditation, whether on marriage, morality, maternity, love, or religion, there is always the preoccupation with "shoulds," what women should and should not do, what the role of women and her responsibilities should be at any particular time in history. At the same time, Sullerot points to the concern in the feminine press with women's rights, moving first from women's right to literacy, to her right to equal education, to remunerated work, equal salary, and finally her right to divorce.

Certainly the feminine press of the eighteenth century is concerned with rights and responsibilities. But I would identify the "right" that focused the editors' interest as being primarily the right of women to respect. In this quest, they propose to their readers a politics of rational virtue, rejecting the old definition of virtue as necessarily giving rise to guilt and self-sacrifice, and involving chastity, obedience, and pleasing the opposite sex. Instead, they insist that real virtue means being self-aware and courageous, energetic and committed, proud of oneself and eager to meet the challenge to excel. It is through the exercise of this new virtue that they promise that women can achieve authority. As Madame de Montanclos says, "It is so fine to enjoy one's own esteem! And when we women have arrived there, we'll soon have the esteem of men, as well." Thus, she exclaims, let us women speak, write, and sound "the sacred name of virtue" (February 1774).

CONCLUSION: WHAT DID THE FEMALE PERIODICAL PRESS ACHIEVE?

To answer this question, we must begin by acknowledging that the very fact that a feminine press exists is already a notable achievement. That a press for, by, and about women could succeed in a century so frequently driven by the dual principles of patriarchy and paternalism is a tribute, first, to the resourcefulness and talents of the female editors, and second to the female readership that supported it financially, emotionally, and philosophically. In publishing their journals, the editors advanced the cause of women, identifying women as a distinct interest group, and giving them their own platform in a new form of print literature. This was a considerable innovation in the cultural milieu, for henceforth a female readership became a market to be tapped, and women's reading became a sociable, *collective* practice, even when readers lived far apart. To be sure, we cannot prove the influence that this press may have had, and we cannot claim with facts and figures that it touched the lives of thousands of French women. But we also, surely, cannot discount it.

In terms of the history both of the women's movement and women's reading, the feminine periodical press of the eighteenth century has often played second fiddle to other forms of self-expression and reading. This chapter has been an attempt to give the print press for women its due, and so I would like to suggest two further points, both of which have a bearing in writing a history of women's reading and writing. Jack Censer has said that during the ancien régime the general press, eager not to get out of step with its readership and apprehensive about displeasing those who occupied positions of power in society, tended not to lead, but to follow public opinion during most of the century. Is this statement equally true for the feminine press? Remarkably, whether one replies yes or no, it seems to me that the answer is positive for women.

If, for instance, the women's press followed and did not lead, it would suggest that enlightened opinion about women's roles in society was generally more advanced in prerevolutionary France than we may have thought. It would suggest that the press for women was simply providing the much-needed opportunity at the national level for women to express themselves. Hence, the creation of a new collective and the collected expression of women's thinking merely coincided in a particularly felicitous way. This is an image that does positive service to women's history and their awareness of themselves. Additionally, it makes women's disappointment with regard to the revolution all the more understandable.

Alternatively, if the female press played quite a different function from the national press—described by Censer as moderate and sometimes even reticent—this, too, would seem to be very much in women's favor. For it would imply that the female editors, much more than their male counterparts, took the lead (and with it the risks) in courageously opening their pages to women and offering to engage in democratic dialogue with their readers. Even if their objectives were more cultural than political, they nonetheless represented a challenge to standard practice and the status quo of gender relations. These women's journals of ideas may not have directly *shaped* public policy in the 1760s and the 1770s, but they were certainly true participants in the public debate and the political and intellectual discussions that were ultimately to describe new directions for the nation. It seems very clear to me that the cultural space occupied by early women's journals is one that deserves its place in the history both of female writing and female reading.

To the second set of questions, did women achieve authority through their press—and an ancillary one, was the politics of virtue an effective strategy—our answer may, however, be less categorically positive. To some extent, the answer to the first question depends on which women we are talking about and who we consider as the audience. Certainly the editors of the press in the eighteenth century did achieve authority with their female readers. But recognition from their male counterparts was not as forthcoming as Madame de Montanclos had promised. Even today, the very idea of a "feminine press" continues to suggest something rather lightweight and not too serious. If women in society have achieved a greater degree of authority than they formerly had, it is not in largest measure because of a female press. Still, having a press for, by, and about women serves today, as it did in the past, as a sort of protected space for a full range of opinion expressed by women. The press for women was never meant to replace the more general press, but rather to serve the interests of a defined group, and to help women reach self-knowledge through self-enlightenment. In that sense, or perhaps more precisely, in terms of the market, it has been very successful. For the female press indisputably succeeded in defining women as an interest group to be reckoned with, and won for them if not the ungrudging esteem of their contemporaries, certainly the respect of many historians today.

In terms of tactics, a politics of virtue is not quite the eviscerated strategy that one might initially judge it to be, but also it is not as dramatic and effective a legacy as some modernists would like. Still, I believe that a strong argument can be made that, given the times and the exclusion of women from mainline cultural discourse and debate, the program of virtue was actually a sophisticated and psychologically astute choice in the struggle for legitimacy. For a politics of virtue would ensure that women's writing in and of itself would not be summarily dismissed, since the subject matter would automatically validate the very act of writing. If women were preaching virtue and virtuous action toward their fellow beings, whether they were talking of female education or marriage or motherhood or patriotism, they could hardly be accused of being immoral. Second, in choosing to phrase both the ideal and their dissent in terms of rational virtue, they could appeal to a variety of women, while at the same time reduce the appearance of threat to established power. These achievements, while perhaps modest, are not insignificant. A press that was in its infancy could hardly expect to do more.

In the final analysis, what is important in establishing the history of women's reading in the eighteenth century and the role played by the periodical press is not whether or how "feminist" it was, but the simple, stark, and dramatic fact that it existed. It was a capital moment in French history to have women identified as a specific market and a legitimate interest group. In a real sense, women made history as they crossed the divide, and sometimes cross-dressed, to practice the profession of journalist and invite all women to enter into a collaboration in which the individual woman would no longer be the subject to be read by others, but rather the reader—and writer—herself.

CONCLUSION

THE "OTHER" REVOLUTION

> If you think about it, reading is a necessarily individual act, far more than writing. If we assume that writing manages to go beyond the limitations of the author, it will continue to have a meaning only when it is read by a single person and passes through his mental circuits. Only the ability to read by a given individual proves that what is written shares in the power of writing, something that goes beyond the individual.
>
> —Italo Calvino, "If on a Winter's Night a Traveller"

In *The Cultural Origins of the French Revolution*, Roger Chartier asks whether books make revolutions and answers by declaring that while books themselves do not make revolutions, the ways they are made, used, and read just might.[1] His assertion that acts of reading can produce profound changes in society—revolutions—is particularly germane to my argument with regard to the "other" revolution of the eighteenth century—the quiet revolution of women's reading. For not only did the eighteenth century see a dramatic rise in female rates of literacy, and a radical change in the way women were encouraged to regard their reading, but women's reading was also to carry emancipatory consequences and impact the social contract, both by enlarging the nation's literate class and posing a possibly unintended challenge to masculine hegemony in matters of cultural authority. The sources of this "other" revolution include the discourses of reading that characterize women's texts from the memoir to the fairy tale, the novel to the periodical press, and that in the aggregate lay the foundation for a new reading culture for females.

A pivotal moment in the history of reading, as in the history of French women, the eighteenth century stands at the midpoint in the Age of the Book. As John Lukacs has said, the age of Enlightenment comes 300 years after the introduction of the printing press and 300 years prior to what he suggests may be the triumph of the pictorial over the written word.[2] At the same time, it is a period coextensive with the growth of democratic ideals embraced by the Revolution of 1789 that will ultimately lead to progressive changes in society, including the triumph of an ideal of universal literacy. In view of these two coinciding developments, the eighteenth century becomes a capital moment and a turning point in culture, both in regard to reading and women. For when women writers legitimized the female reader in their texts, when they conveyed the idea that worldliness and knowledge were not incompatible with femininity, when they encouraged reading books for ethical, esthetic, and moral purposes, and when they laid the groundwork for becoming a "responsible" reader, they were promoting the ideals of a new social contract. But they were also advancing the idea that women's reading even within domestic spaces could have not only useful and practical benefits and improve daily life, but also be a valuable use of their time. Rather than suggesting that women were repressed within the domestic sphere, they thus attributed positive value to the home spaces of the young girl, wife, or mother because that was where her reading and self-enlightenment took place. Moreover, while she might read alone, a woman would not read in isolation, since through the choice of her reading material she could join the larger community of ideas, as well as the community of readers throughout the nation, whose lives, knowledge, and cultural practices would be profoundly impacted by books and the printed page.

To uncover within women's texts a discourse concerned with the construction of a reading culture for women, one that will prepare the climate for the spread of literacy in the next century, is to corroborate the statement that reading has both a sex and a history. It is to acknowledge that reading is at once personal, social, cultural, and historical, dependent on a time and a place and on one's sex. For given the constellation of issues of gender surrounding reading—different rites of passage and protocols for the sexes as well as separate educations, resulting in dissimilar rates of literacy between men and women, the development of divergent tastes, variant criteria of censorship and self-censorship as applied to the sexes—it is clear that a history of reading cannot be studied apart from issues of sex. Most historians and critics, in fact, agree that as a social and cultural practice, reading, like other practices must be examined and reconstructed with the dual lens of history and gender.

This book has told a story about reading and women in eighteenth-century France. It is certainly not the entire story, but rather a chapter within the larger history that may always elude full discovery. There is much about the reading of the past that we do not and probably cannot know, especially if we focus on how people processed their reading.[3] But if we limit ourselves to "listening" carefully to eighteenth-century women and teasing out discourses on reading, or discovering what writers have said about reading at any one point and within a historical framework, we have the opportunity, I believe, to illuminate aspects of the broader culture in ways that invite us to rethink some of our basic assumptions. The story told by the essays of this book builds on but takes a different direction than those written by recent feminist historians of women's writing and culture. For while many of my counterparts have sought to unearth evidence of political or social subversiveness and/or defiance in women's writing from the Enlightenment period, claiming an early prerevolutionary mind-set by women, I have taken the quieter route. Still, I would suggest that when we examine women's *reading* and their notions about reading, we may be inclined to change the story of their *writing*. Rather than seeing in their texts the ubiquitous velvet fist or a politically motivated subversiveness, I would submit that these women's texts are involved less with covert radicalism than with elaborating the case for empowering virtue through "right reading," consistent with the goals of *their* cultural moment.

To politicize the literary production of our foremothers in our terms, to speak of the feminist agendas of eighteenth-century women, or to argue that these women were demanding sexual freedom as an entitlement of female identity, or that they wanted control over their own bodies, or experienced desire as powerful individuals (or, on the contrary, used passionlessness as a power weapon) is to present these women as direct precursors of our own cultural battles. To speak with such a vocabulary is to use the present moment and the politics of contemporary feminism to model in our image the reading and writing of the past. It may be one way of reasserting an unbroken lineage in terms of women's history, but it also tends to dismiss the real differences that exist between the eighteenth century and the present, and between women on different continents.

A particular case in point has been the use of the term "subversive," which in the last decade of the twentieth century enjoyed a substantial vogue in critical analyses of women's narratives from earlier periods. According to many arguments concerning female subversiveness in writing, the woman used her texts to resist covertly in ways that only the twentieth-century critic could uncover. Motivated by a lack of freedom in ancien-régime France and by her very marginality in society, plus the threat of censorship, and growing social disquiet, the woman would write subversive resistances to the social and political status quo into her stories. But how dangerous was it, really, for women to publish? And which women of talent actually lost their reputations by allowing their names to appear on print? To be sure, eighteenth-century women often refer to this fear, but given that hundreds of female-authored texts have been identified, it is reasonable to ask whether their fear was not more a conventional expression of required modesty, rather than an inflexible truth that prevented them from saying openly what they thought. After all, vast numbers of women did publish, even if their works—like men's—were sometimes open to harsh criticism. It was, in point of fact, a censorious age. But it was often also the case that "everyone" seemed to be writing, since the upper classes considered it "good form to be making literature."[4] Certainly, censorship could potentially be very strict—although it was also unevenly and arbitrarily applied—yet we do not hear about women being censored (as opposed to feeling *self*-censored), or sent to prison for their views. Even women's condemnation of society's infrastructure was tolerated, as, for instance, when women writers let their heroines refuse bourgeois marriage, which has been said to serve the purposes of the state in prerevolutionary France.[5] Fear of being socially subversive did not prevent Madame de Graffigny, or Madame de Genlis, or Madame de Charrière from publishing their works, any more than it had Madame de Lafayette or would George Sand. They may have felt vulnerable, but they wrote anyway.

So I would argue that it is not any underlying current of political subversiveness in eighteenth-century women's writing that carries the seeds of revolution, but rather those discourses of reading. For in this carefully elaborated culture of reading, in which both book and reading—available to women in their homes—are arms and tools of change, they received and sent messages about a new female ideal that was to become a legacy of revolutionary potential to women in succeeding generations. In the eighteenth century, women readers were not a majority of all French women, but, as historians tell us, it is often the minority who lead the way to major change. They formed a vanguard who looked on reading as one of the ways by which identity is continually engendered, formed, deformed, and reformed. They knew that reading was not just for entertainment or personal pleasure, but for self-improvement through self-enlightenment, and that it could help them negotiate the thicket of ethical choices and access the esthetic pleasures that enhance the quality of lives. For reading, while it carried responsibilities, was also a gift with the power to forge links and create change.

Some seventy years ago the French anthropologist, Marcel Mauss, set forth a theory of the gift that has particular appeal for discussing the exchange between readers and writers because it proposes a theory of human solidarity giving precisely the sense of lineage and connectiveness that is created between the discourse of reading in women's texts in the eighteenth century and the legacy it makes to the nineteenth century and beyond.[6] Mauss suggests that what is given with a gift is a part of one's nature and substance, and what is received is a part of someone's spiritual esence. Furthermore, a gift that does nothing to enhance solidarity is a contradiction, since in his view there is a built-in reciprocity in any economy of the gift that stipulates that there must always be gifts and countergifts. Extending his theory of reciprocal exchange to literature is, I believe, an eloquent and appropriate way to study women's reading and writing, because as sociologist David Cheal observes, women are the most active gift-givers and attach great importance to making gifts to other women.[7] Cheal was referring especially to life passages and the gifts that nearly always accompany them, but it is no leap in logic to suggest that a similar movement takes place with women's narratives that become legacies capable of invoking creative memory and collective history. Bridging both past and future, reading produces the linkages that bind us across time and continents. And as in the gift economy studied by anthropologists, which entails gifts and countergifts, we in succeeding generations reinvoke the words, the stories heard, the themes sounded, echoing, forming and reforming, reading and rewriting, in ongoing participation in the passage of a culture through reading and rereading.

In the course of this book, I have used the reading glass metaphorically to reveal the construction of a book culture for and by women in Enlightenment France. It has been, I believe, a particularly pertinent choice, because the reading glass is to the book as the book was to women, opening up both a world and wealth of ideas perhaps unsuspected at first glance. Books, of course, are an integral part of the wider Enlightenment dream, and as symbols of culture and objects of personal and intellectual proprietorship, they carry not only prestige but also the promise that the social contract can be remade. When eighteenth-century women embraced the culture of books and set about to extend the culture of reading, they became direct participants in a revolution that would quietly but determinedly and permanently change their society. To tell that story is to remind us of an enormously important and often overlooked chapter in the history of reading, one that by coupling books with women makes women's history more complete.

NOTES

INTRODUCTION: THE READING GLASS AND THE POLITICS OF VIRTUE

1. According to Porée, women under the influence of novels will attempt "openly or in secret to direct royal deliberations, distribute the offices of war, play a role in the management of finances, influence the scales of justice." "De Librus qui vulgo dicuntur romaneses oration" ("Discours sur les livres appelés en langue vulgaire romans"), public address, 25 February 1736 at the Collège Louis le Grand in Paris.

2. Although, as Kate Flint suggests in *The Woman Reader, 1837–1914* (Oxford: Clarendon Press, 1993), 10, Bourdieu employs the notion of cultural capital primarily to consider how high culture functions to conserve preexisting social distinctions and hierarchies, like Flint, I am using it more broadly in the sense of a system of shared and circulating ideas relating to issues of power, knowledge, and access in culture.

3. *The Rape of Clarissa; Writing, Sexuality, and Class Struggle in Samuel Richardson* (Minneapolis: University of Minnesota Press, 1982), 49–50.

4. "La Femme en France aux XVIIe et XVIIIe siècles," t. IV, Livre I, *Histoire mondiale de la femme* (Paris: Nouvelle Librairie de France, 1966). The dichotomic condition of women as both "queens of the universe" and "pandoras to whom are imputed all the woes that afflict human kind" (*Le Glaneur du parnasse*, 1759) has given rise to a critical tradition that has tended to privilege one or the other extreme. Two examples of the first tendency are the Goncourts, *La Femme au XVIIIe siècle* (1882) and Vera Lee, *The Reign of Women in Eighteenth-Century France* (Cambridge: Schenkman, 1975). The second tradition has understandably fed the ire of much feminist criticism. Relatively rare are the studies like that of Linda Timmermans, *L'Accès des femmes à la culture (1598–1715); Un Débat d'idées de Saint François de Sales à la Marquise de Lambert* (Paris: Honoré Champion, 1993), which show how women used the contradictions and limits imposed on them to their advantage.

5. Erica Harth in *Cartesian Women: Versions and Subversions of Rational Discourse in the Old Regime* (Ithaca, N.Y.: Cornell University Press, 1992), 3, has defined the problem confronting intellectual women in the post-Descartes era as a paradox of (in)visibility. On the one hand, females benefited from the argument separating

mind and body (including the notion that reason could be used by either sex), while, on the other hand, it was by their very female body that they were excluded from participating in some of the most important spaces of intellectual production and exchange in the academy, the café, the club, and the pages of the press.

6. *Enlightenment and Pathology: Sensibility in the Literature and Medicine of Eighteenth-Century France* (Baltimore: Johns Hopkins University Press, 1998), 256.

7. The appellation "feminist" is of course an anachronism, since the word "feminism" was not coined until the following century. My use of the word "feminized" is intended to acknowledge this fact, while at the same time evoke the specific quality of virtue that eighteenth-century women were advancing along with the promotion of female self-esteem and respect for women's minds and works.

8. "Le Langage mâle de la vertu: Women and the Discourse of the French Revolution," in Peter Burke and Roy Porter, eds., *The Social History of Language* (Cambridge: Cambridge University Press, 1987), 120–135.

9. *Only Paradoxes to Offer: French Feminism and the Rights of Man* (Cambridge: Harvard University Press, 1996).

10. Anne Thérèse de Marguenat de Courcelles, marquise de Lambert (1647–1733), published in 1727 a collection of four essays under the title *Réflexions nouvelles sur les femmes* that has most recently been republished by côté-femmes (Paris, 1989), 143.

11. David Smith, "The Popularity of Mme de Graffigny's *Lettres d'une Péruvienne*: The Bibliographical Evidence," *Eighteenth-Century Fiction*, Vol. 3, Number 1 (October 1990), 1–20.

12. For what remains to be an important statement of the relationship between the woman reader and the growth of the novel in France, see Georges May, "Féminisme et roman," *Le Dilemme du roman au XVIIIe siècle* (Paris: Presses Universitaires de France, 1963), 204–245.

13. *The Moral Sex; Woman's Nature in the French Enlightenment* (Oxford: Oxford University Press, 1995), trans. by Pamela E. Selwyn. Originally published as *Das moralische Geschlect: Theorien und literarische Entwürfe über die Natur der Frau in der französischen Aufklärung* (Stuttgart: J. B. Metzlersche, 1992). In building her case to show that while women were allotted morality and the domestic sphere, men solidified their claim to political and economic decision-making in the public realm, Steinbrügge indicts the emerging bourgeois capitalist model for systematically excluding women from civil rights and public life. My argument will seek to reenter women's own thinking and beliefs to suggest how, while often critical of society, they were participants in and contributors to the intellectual and emotional climate of the times through their particular promotion of virtue politics.

14. Nancy K. Miller, *The Heroine's Text: Readings in the French and English Novel, 1722–1782* (New York: Columbia University Press, 1980); Joan DeJean and Nancy K. Miller, eds., "The Politics of Tradition," *Yale French Studies* (1988), 75, 40–55; Joan DeJean, *Tender Geographies; Women and the Origins of the Novel in France* (New York: Columbia University Press, 1991); Erica Harth, *Cartesian Women; Versions and Subversions of Rational Discourse in the Old Regime* (Ithaca, N.Y.: Cornell University Press, 1992); Dena Goodman and Elizabeth C. Goldsmith, eds., *Going Public; Women and Publishing in Early Modern France* (Ithaca, N.Y.: Cornell University Press, 1995); Joan B. Landes, *Women and the Public Sphere in the Age of the French Revolution* (Ithaca, N.Y.: Cornell University Press, 1988); Joan Hinde Stewart,

Gynographs: French Novels by Women of the Late Eighteenth Century (Lincoln: University of Nebraska Press, 1993).

15. "Day by Day with Roland Barthes," in Marshall Blonsky, *On Signs* (Baltimore: Johns Hopkins University Press, 1985), 101.

16. "Cartésianisme(s) et féminisme(s)," *Europe* 56 (October 1978), 73–86.

17. *Becoming a Reader; The Experience of Fiction from Childhood to Adulthood* (Cambridge: Cambridge University Press, 1990). Appleyard believes that most theoretical models of the reading process underestimate its complexity, failing to acknowledge both the search for images by which we give perspective to experiences and the dynamic interplay of communal and personal values and codes, which are produced when reader, text, and world come into dialectical relationship (182–187).

18. "La Lecture: Une Pratique culturelle," conversation entre Roger Chartier et Pierre Bourdieu, *Pratiques de la lecture*, ed. by Roger Chartier (Marseille: Rivages, 1985), 218–236, 230 and 235.

19. In his 1758 *L'Ami des femmes, Ou La Philosophie du beau sexe* (nouvelle édition augmentée, 1774), for instance, Boudier de Villemert attempts to advance himself as a partisan of the idea that "the mind has no sex" at the same time that he insists on denying women the study of the "abstract sciences and thorny research issues whose details could weigh down their spirit and snuff out the finesse at which they excel." Cited by Maïté Albistur and Daniel Armogathe, *Histoire du féminisme français du moyen âge à nos jours* (Paris: des femmes, 1977), 187.

20. Jean-Marie Goulemot, *Forbidden Texts: Erotic Literature and Its Readers in Eighteenth-Century France*, trans. by James Simpson (Philadelphia: University of Pennsylvania Press, 1994), 56–57. In the second chapter of this work, Goulemot describes the role of writings by S. A. Tissot (*L'Onanisme, dissertation sur les maladies produites par la masturbation*, 1760) and D. T. Bienville (*La Nymphomanie ou Traité de la fureur uterine*, 1771) in the birth of sexual pathology and the linking of "wicked" reading to sins of the flesh. For further commentary on issues of the sensible body, see Anne C. Vila, *Enlightenment and Pathology; Sensibility in the Literature and Medicine of Eighteenth-Century France*, and Lindsay Wilson, *Women and Medicine in the French Enlightenment: The Debate over "Maladies des Femmes"* (Baltimore: Johns Hopkins University Press, 1993).

21. *De La Santé des gens de lettres* (Geneva: Slatkine, 1981), 183–184. Originally published in 1766 in Latin and 1768 in French. Quoted from *Enlightenment and Pathology*, 327. Even in America as late as 1873, Harvard Medical School Dr. Edward Clarke could write in *Sex in Education* that too much reading had an inhibitory effect on reproduction of the species, since limited vital energy would be wasted on books instead of on essential bodily functions. See Carroll Smith-Rosenberg and Charles Rosenberg, "The Female Animal: Medical and Biological Views of Women and Her Role in Nineteenth-Century America," *Journal of American History* (60), September 1973, 339–342.

22. "Préface de Julie, ou Entretien sur les romans," *Julie, ou La Nouvelle Héloïse*, éd. de René Pomeau (Paris: Garnier, 1960), 750.

23. "Readers Respond to Rousseau," *The Great Cat Massacre and Other Episodes in French Cultural History* (New York: Basic Books, 1984), 241.

24. *Oeuvres completes* II, *La Nouvelle Héloïse*, Lettre 18, 2eme Partie (Paris: Gallimard, 1964), 261.

25. The distinction between "aesthetic" and "efferent" readings is made by Louise Rosenblatt in *The Reader, The Text, The Poem: The Transactional Theory of the Literary Work* (Carbondale: Southern Illinois University Press, 1978).

26. For general works on reading in the eighteenth century, see *Livre et société dans la France du XVIIIe siècle* (Paris and The Hague: Mouton, 1975), 2 tomes; Henri-Jean Martin and Roger Chartier, eds., *Histoire de l'édition française.*, Vol. II: *Le Livre triomphant, 1660–1830* (Paris: Promodis, 1984); Robert Darnton, *Edition et sédition: L'Univers de la littérature clandestine au XVIIIe siècle* (Paris: Gallimard, 1991); (in English: *The Forbidden Best-Sellers of Pre-Revolutionary France* [New York, W.W. Norton, 1995]); Roger Chartier, *Lectures et lecteurs dans la France d'Ancien Régime* (Paris: Editions du Seuil, 1982, 1984, 1987) (in English: *The Cultural Uses of Print in Early Modern France*, trans. by Lydia G. Cochrane [Princeton, N.J.: Princeton University Press, 1987]; Roger Chartier, *Pratiques de la lecture* (Marseille: Rivages, 1985); Roger Chartier, *Les Usages de l'imprimé* (Paris: Fayard, 1987); Roger Chartier, "The Practical Impact of Writing," *A History of Private Life (Passions of the Renaissance)*, Vol. III (Cambridge: Harvard University Press, 1989), 111–159; François Furet et Jacques Ozouf, *Lire et écrire: l'alphabétisation des Français de Calvin à Jules Ferry* (Paris: Editions de Minuit, 1977), 2 tomes. For history leading up to the eighteenth century, see H. J. Martin, *Livre, Pouvoirs et société à Paris au XVIIe siècle (1598–1701)* (Geneva: Droz, 1969). In his *Le Triomphe du livre: Une Histoire sociologique de la lecture dans la France du XIXe siècle*, tr. de l'anglais (Paris: Promodis, 1987), Martyn Lyons contextualizes analysis of nineteenth-century book trade by useful retrospectives onto the preceding century. While there is no monograph that exists on women's reading in France during the Enlightenment, works by Kate Flint, *The Woman Reader, 1837–1914* (Oxford: Clarendon Press, 1993), which discusses British women readers of the nineteenth and twentieth centuries, and Elizabeth A. Flynn and Patrocinio P. Schweickart, eds., *Gender and Reading: Essays on Readers, Texts, and Contexts* (Baltimore, Johns Hopkins University Press, 1986) are useful for tracing both the tenacity and widespread nature of society's gender prejudices against female readers in general.

27. Mornet, "Les Enseignements des bibliothèques privées (1750–1780)," *Revue d'histoire littéraire de la France* XVII (1910), 449–492. For a critique of the use of such inventories, see Darnton's prefaces in *Edition et sédition : L'Univers littéraire clandestine au XVIIIe siècle*, trans. as *The Forbidden Best-Sellers of Pre-Revolutionary France.*

28. *Nouvel Armorial du bibliophile, Guide de l'amateur des livres armoriés*, t. I (Paris Emile Rondeau, 1890).

29. Albert Cim, *Les Femmes et les livres* (Paris: Boccard, 1919), 4. Cim, who bases a great deal of his book on a nineteenth-century work by Ernest Quentin Bauchart entitled *Les Femmes bibliophiles de France (XVIe, XVIIe, et XVIIIe siècles)* 2 vols. (Paris: Damascène Morgand, 1886; réimpression, Slatkine Reprint, 1993), divides his study into two parts: "Femmes bibliophobes" (a term coined by George Sand, he says) and "Femmes bibliophiles." In this last part, he lists and discusses women, many of whom are members of the royal family and other titled nobility, as well as abbesses, who appreciated books either for their contents or for their value as objets d'art.

30. After this manuscript was complete, I learned of Sandrine Aragon's *Des Liseuses en péril: Les Images de lectrices dans les textes de fiction de* La Prétieuse *de l'abbé de Pure à* Madame Bovary *de Flaubert (1656–1856)* (Paris: Champion, 2003).

31. "Quelques lettres inédites sur la *Nouvelle Héloïse*," in M. Launay: *Jean-Jacques Rousseau et son temps* (Paris: Nizet, 1969), 192.

32. *Rereading* (New York and London: Yale University Press, 1993), 105.

33. See, for example, W. Poulet, *Atlas on the History of Spectacles*, 3 vols., trans. by Frederick C. Blodi (Bonn-Bad Godesberg, West Germany: Wayenborgh, 1978 [vol. I], 1980 [vol. II]; Astrid Vitols, *Dictionnaire des lunettes: Historique et symbolique d'un objet culturel* (Paris: Bonneton, 1994); A. Bourgeois, *Les Besicles de nos ancêtres* (Paris: A. Maloine, 1923); Benjamin Milder and Melvin L. Rubin, *The Fine Art of Prescribing Glasses Without Making a Spectacle of Yourself*, 2nd ed. (Gainesville: Triad, 1991); and articles in Diderot's *Encyclopédie* on *lunette*, *loupe*, and *lorgnette*.

34. All references to illustrations in this paragraph can be found in Poulet's *Atlas*, vol. II, pages 372–373, 486, 472, and 196–197, in order of their presentation in my text.

35. *Enlightenment, Romanticism, and the Blind in France* (Princeton, N.J.: Princeton University Press, 1987), 11.

CHAPTER 1: FEMALE READERS AND *L'ESPACE DU LIVRE*

1. (Paris: Baccard, 1919).

2. Quoted in Cim, *Les Femmes et les livres*, 211.

3. *Mémoires*, V (Paris : Ladvocat, 1825), 95.

4. *The Crafty Reader* (New Haven: Yale University Press, 2001), 81.

5. *Rereading* (New Haven: Yale University Press, 1993), 92.

6. Most of these arguments take off from Jürgen Habermas, *L'Espace public: Archéologie de la publicité comme dimension constitutive de la société bourgeoise* (Paris: Payot, 1978), trans. by Marc B. de Launay from the German, *Strukturwandel der öffentlichkeit: Untersuchungen zu einer Kategorie der bürgerlichen Gesellschaft* (Neuwied and Berlin: Hermann Luckterhand, 1962).

7. Dorinda Outram, "'*Le Langage mâle de la vertu*': Women and the Discourse of the French Revolution," in Peter Burke and Roy Porter, eds., *The Social History of Language* (Cambridge: Cambridge University Press, 1987), 120–135; Joan B. Landes, *Women and the Public Sphere in the Age of the French Revolution* (Ithaca, N.Y.: Cornell University Press, 1988); Dena Goodman, "Enlightenment Salons: The Convergence of Female and Philosophic Ambitions," *Eighteenth-Century Studies* 22 (Spring 1989), 329–350; Joan DeJean, *Tender Geographies: Women and the Origins of the Novel in France* (New York: Columbia University Press, 1991); Erica Harth, *Cartesian Women: Versions and Subversions of Rational Discourse in the Old Regime* (Ithaca, N.Y.: Cornell University Press, 1992).

8. *Women and the Public Sphere in the Age of the French Revolution*, 2.

9. "'*Le Langage mâle de la vertu*'": Women and the Discourse of the French Revolution."

10. " '*Le Langage mâle de la vertu*'": Women and the Discourse of the French Revolution," 129.

11. See also Bonnie G. Smith, *Ladies of the Leisure Class* (Princeton, N.J.: Princeton University Press, 1981).

12. See especially chapter 1, "Gender and Discursive Space(s) in the Seventeenth Century" in *Cartesian Women*, 15–63.

13. *Cartesian Women*, 58–59.

14. *Women and the Public Sphere in the Age of the French Revolution*, 65.

15. Outram argues that Madame Roland practiced contorted self-censorship while in the salon, though when she was imprisoned in the place of her husband, she would be forced to recognize her own failure to achieve respect and political participation. Incarcerated with women of easy virtue, Madame Roland was offended to be treated not like a political prisoner, but rather a "fallen" woman. Outram suggests that when the sentence of death was carried out a few weeks later, Madame Roland was both chastised and permanently silenced for acting as though she could rewrite the rules of women's space, even while outwardly accepting the space of female domesticity, "Le Langage mâle de la vertu'": Women and the Discourse of the French Revolution," 126–127. It is, however, also possible to argue, as I do in chapter 2, that in fact Madame Roland is not silenced, since the very publication of her *Mémoires* ensures—ironically, far more than had she lived—that her "voice" continues to be heard.

16. Elizabeth Eisenstein, *The Printing Press as an Agent of Change: Communications and Cultural Transformations in Early-Modern Europe*, 2 vols. (Cambridge: Cambridge University Press, 1979). Eisenstein also makes the important point that transformations in communication structures impact both public and private life. For the former, these changes put into question what it means to participate in public affairs (whether directly and in physical contact with others, or vicariously, reflectively, and alone), while in the private domain, the quality of reading materials—particularly reams of popular and moralistic works—would penetrate family life as no public sermons ever had, I, 132–133.

17. François Furet and Jacques Ozouf, *Reading and Writing: Literacy in France from Calvin to Jules Ferry* (London: Cambridge University Press, 1982), 46. Orig. pub. as *Lire et écrire: l'alphabétisation des Français de Calvin à Jules Ferry* (Les Editions de Minuit, 1977).

18. "Women as Readers: Visual Interpretations," *American Antiquarian Society*, 107 (1998), 339.

19. For this kind of sociology of reading, see, for instance, Martyn Lyons, *Le Triomphe du livre: Une Histoire sociologique de la lecture dans la France du XIXe siècle*, traduit de l'anglais (Paris: Promodis, 1987). Though it is the nineteenth century that focuses his interest, Lyons has many interesting things to say about the background provided by the eighteenth century.

20. *The Cultural Uses of Print in Early Modern France*, trans. by Lydia G. Cochrane (Princeton, N.J.: Princeton University Press, 1987), 219–225. Indeed, the male, whether depicted in his book-lined library or in reverie as he walks in nature with a book in hand, is neither surprised nor embarrassed in his reading. Should the intention be to use reading to produce a sexual response in the male (such as Restif de la Bretonne describes in *Monsieur Nicolas*), the image is blatantly pornographic, minus all the equivocal subtext of the rococo painting, which typically and playfully eroticizes the woman reader.

21. This is the case in an image by Adriaen van de Venne entitled either *Le Lecteur d'épreuves* or *Philosophe au travail*, located in the collection of the Musée Plantin in Antwerp, Belgium, and appearing as the frontispiece in Jan Herman and Paul Pelckmans, eds., *L'Epreuve du lecteur; Livres et lectures dans le roman d'Ancien Régime* (Louvain : Peeters, 1994). I was unable to obtain permission to reproduce the image, but will describe it since it is an example of how an entire library can become an accessory to the presentation of feminine charms. In this book-lined library, a

woman serves three men, two aristocrats and a prelate, who watch approvingly if somewhat sheepishly as she climbs a book ladder to retrieve a desired volume. Dressed so as to reveal her bosom, corsetted waist, a finely turned ankle and impossibly small feet slipped into high-heeled and pointed-toe shoes, she is the dominant figure by her placement in the scene, as well as the center of all three men's interest. But why place the young woman on the ladder, made all the more precarious because of her ample petticoats and high heels? Is it the moral and sexual precariousness of the woman in contact with books that the artist wishes to illustrate? Why surround her by men who stand idly by as she serves their needs but not her own through books? As it stands, this woman does not really belong to the culture of books, and the viewer is hard pressed to see the library as anything but a pretext for viewing a woman, just as some critics seem to feel that reading is a pretext for a woman seeking other pleasures.

22. *Ces Livres qu'on ne lit que d'une main* (Paris: Aliéna, 1991), trans. by James Simpson as *Forbidden Texts: Erotic Literature and Its Readers in Eighteenth-Century France* (Philadelphia: University of Pennsylvania Press, 1994), 30–35.

23. See various discussions in S. A. Tissot, *De L'Onanisme* (1760), trans. as *Onanism, or A Treatise upon the Disorders produced by Masturbation, or The Dangerous Effects of Secret and Excessive Venery*, by A. Hume, M.D., 1766; (reprint, New York and London: Garland, 1985); D. T. Bienville, *La Nymphomanie, ou La Fureur utérine* (1771), 2nd ed. (Amsterdam: M. M. Rey, 1780); P.J.G. Cabanis, *Rapports du physique et du moral de l'homme* (1802) (Geneva: Slatkine Reprints, 1980); Eng. trans. *On the Relations between the Physical and Moral Aspects of Man*, by Margaret Duggan Mora (Baltimore: Johns Hopkins University Press, 1981); P. Roussel, *Système physique et moral de la femme* (1775); P.-V. de Sèze, *Recherches physiologiques et expériences sur la vitalité* (Paris: Fuchs, an VI (1797). For an analysis of their thinking, see Anne C. Vila, *Enlightenment and Pathology; Sensibility in the Literature and Medicine of Eighteenth-Century France* (Baltimore: Johns Hopkins University Press, 1998).

24. See Yvonne Johannot, *Tourner la page: livre, rites, et symboles* (Jérôme Millan, 1988), 154.

25. Conrad Salomon Walther's *Manuel de la toilette & de la mode* was published in Paris from 1771 to 1780. The quote comes from the Seconde Partie, 1771.

26. *Psychoanalysis and Storytelling* (Oxford: Blackwell, 1994), 29–30.

27. In *Absorption and Theatricality: Painting and Beholder in the Age of Diderot* (Berkeley: University of California Press, 1980), 168–169.

28. Interestingly, Isabelle de Charrière will show that the reverse can also occur when she turns the male (the Baron d'Hermenches) into the text of *her* desire by making him into her ideal and vulnerable reader. See chapter 4.

29. Written by Rosalinde and Michel Deville and directed by the latter, the film embraces the pleasures of reading and of words with thoroughgoing playfulness. While the woman reader in the film is called the Lectrice, the word *Liseuse*— the title used by most artists of the eighteenth century for their female reader—is also evoked in its three contemporary usages: bookmark, book cover, and book jacket. That it is a feminine noun that has come to identify these objects illustrates just how much woman, sex, and reading are interrelated in cultural practice.

30. (Paris: Actes Sud, 1986).

31. *La Lenteur*, trans. by Linda Asher (New York, Harper Perennial, 1996) is a libertine fantasy that references Vivant Denon's eighteenth-century tale, "Point de lendemain."

32. "Paul Sutton, "Reading *La Lectrice*," in Michael Syrotinski and Ian Maclachlan, eds., *Sensual Reading: New Approaches to Reading in Its Relations to the Senses* (Lewisburg, Pa.: Bucknell University Press, 2001, 153–165.

33. *Sexuality and the Reading Encounter; Identity and Desire in Proust, Duras, Tournier, and Cixous* (Oxford: Clarendon Press, 1996).

34. *The Cultural Uses of Print in Early Modern France*, 199. See also Michel Marion, "Les Livres chez les Parisiens dans la deuxième moitié du XVIIIe siècle," in Institut d'Etude du Livre, *Les Espaces du livre*. II: *Les Bibliothèques*, Deuxième Colloque (6–7 juin 1980), 31–37. Where and how books are kept—for instance, separating books of piety from a dictionary such as the *Larousse*, which symbolizes republicanism and laity—can be ways of categorizing and dividing knowledge and constructing experience. See *Le Triomphe du livre*, 233.

35. The episode is related in *Mémoires de Madame Roland*, éd. présentée et annotée par Paul de Roux (Paris: Mercure de France, 1986), 309–310.

36. *L'Accès des femmes à la culture (1598–1715); Un Débat d'idées de Saint François de Sales à la Marquise de Lambert* (Paris: Honoré Champion, 1993), 819.

37. *On the Relations between the Physical and Moral Aspects of Man*, 1:242. Quoted in *Enlightenment and Pathology*, 254–255.

38. See *Le Triomphe du livre*, chapter 11, "La Pratique de la lecture: nouvelles orientations," 221–252.

39. Scholes, *The Crafty Reader*, 77. Darnton, "Readers Respond to Rousseau," in *The Great Cat Massacre and Other Episodes in French Cultural History* (New York: Basic Books, 1984), 215.

40. "Rapport sur la nécessité et les moyens d'anéantir les patois et d'universaliser l'usage de la langue française," presented to the National Convention on 16 Prairial an II. See *Le Triomphe du livre*, 25.

41. *Reading and Writing: Literacy in France from Calvin to Jules Ferry*, 11.

42. Jean Quéniant, *Culture et société urbaines dans la France de l'Ouest du XVIIIe siècle* (Paris: Klincksieck, 1978), 57–58 and 115–116.

43. Offering a visual support, Chartier shows a painting by Hubert Robert of Madame Geoffrin at breakfast, being read to by a manservant standing behind her, *The Practical Impact of Writing, A History of Private Life*, III: *Passions of the Renaissance*, trans. by Arthur Goldhammer (Cambridge: Harvard University Press, 1989), 143.

44. "The Practical Impact of Writing," 115, and *Le Triomphe du livre*, 30.

45. *Le Triomphe du livre*, 30. Earlier the Council of Trent (1545–1563) had proclaimed a rule of "holy ignorance" to prevent those who did not know Latin—a majority of nuns and many monks—from directly accessing the Vulgate. See also Calinescu, pp. 80–85, on the history of reading the Bible.

46. *Going Public; Women and Publishing in Early Modern France*, 2.

47. "The Practical Impact of Reading," 112.

48. P. Gasnault, "La Bibliothèque de Mazarin et la Bibliothèque Mazarine au XVII et au XVIIIe siècles," in *Les Espaces du livre*, II: *Les Bibliothèques*, 38–56. Gasnault writes, "Readers had to have a strong constitution: because of fear of fires, there was no chimney; and the library's few account books from the eighteenth century show no outlays for heat or for lighting. This situation was to continue until the middle of the nineteenth century" (52).

49. *Mémoires*, X, 265–266. See also chapter 194 in Léon Sébastien Mercier, *Le Tableau de Paris*, ed. by Michel Delon (Paris: Robert Laffont, 1990), 114–115. For the

early history of the Bibliothèque Nationale, see Simone Balayé, *La Bibliothèque nationale, des origines à 1800* (Geneva: Droz, 1988).

50. *Le Tableau de Paris*, 114.

51. Arthur Young, *Travels in France during the Years 1787, 1788, and 1789*. Edited by J. Kaplow (Garden City, N.Y.: Doubleday, 1969), 97.

52. In 1791, Talleyrand proposed the establishment of a public library in each *département*. The initial collections would come from the confiscated books of the clergy, while the librarians would be the ecclesiastics whom the revolution's anti-church legislation had put out of a job. Jack A. Clarke, "French Libraries in Transition, 1785–1795," in *Library Quarterly* 37 (1967), 366–372. Martyn Lyons observes that criteria used to build the collections of these early bourgeois and philanthropic public libraries tended to be both paternalistic and conservative, principles that likewise determined the construction of edifying book lists prepared for readers. *Le Triomphe du livre*, ch. 9, "Les Bibliothèques et leurs lecteurs," 169–192.

53. Roger Chartier, *The Cultural Uses of Print in Early Modern France*, 209.

54. Rousseau, *Oeuvres complètes*, I, ed. by Bernard Gagnebin et Marcel Raymond (Paris: Gallimard, 1959) 1530 (note).

55. As Darnton explains, the high price of printed materials was driven primarily by the costs of elaborate, artisanal methods of production in which each sheet of paper was made individually, each letter and line of type set by hand by a typesetter with an artistic eye, before being passed on for binding, "Readers Respond to Rousseau," 223–224. Hence, few families would have been able to purchase all the books they read. It is for this reason that Michel Marion writes that books, which were considered to be objects of pride, symbols of culture, and even indicators of social status, were so precious that they were included in wills and inheritances, "Les Livres chez les Parisiens dans la deuxième moitié du XVIIIe siècle," 36.

56. *The Cultural Uses of Print in Early Modern France*, 187–188. One should be aware, however, that like the problem of using signature to establish literacy, the use of inventories of private book holdings, occurring following a death, is an unreliable source of reading patterns or taste. Typically, only reading matter of importance would be catalogued, and of course there is no assurance that the volumes had actually been read.

57. In "The Practical Impact of Writing," 125, Chartier observes that reading silently constitutes a key change, in that such reading is faster, more private, and allows the reader to internalize the subject matter more readily. Similarly, even today, the beginning child reader moves from pronouncing aloud each word to reading silently, which is a sign of intellectual maturity and progress.

58. Rolf Engelsing, *Der Bürger als Leser: Lesergeschichte in Deutschland 1500–1800* (Stuttgart: Metzler 1974). Discussed in "Readers Respond to Rousseau," 249–251.

59. This is Darnton's thesis in "Readers Respond to Rousseau." In the *Confessions*, Rousseau had discussed the necessity of his reader possessing a special sixth sense in order to be in tune with him, saying, "I have always believed that no one could have a strong interest in my *Héloïse* without having a sixth sense, that moral sense with which so few hearts are endowed and without which no one can understand my heart," *Oeuvres complètes*, I, 547.

CHAPTER 2: AUTOBIOGRAPHY AND REREADING

1. In the preface to his *Rereading* (New Haven: Yale University Press, 1993), Matei Calinescu discusses rereading as a "metaphor of haunting" and locates rereading as "a special case in a larger phenomenology of repetition," xi–xii.

2. This is one of the arguments made by Dorinda Outram, "Words and Flesh: Mme Roland, the Female Body and the Search for Power," in *The Body and the French Revolution, Sex, Class and Political Culture* (New Haven and London: Yale University Press, 1989), 124–152. In "Sweet and Consoling Virtue: The *Memoirs* of Madame Roland," *Eighteenth-Century Studies* 34, no. 3 (spring 2001), 403–419, Lesley H. Walker rehearses some of the approaches to Manon Roland. She herself emphasizes what she sees as the masochistic quality of Roland's notion of virtue that views suffering as the means by which one can feel more virtuous. Walker also charges Roland with "stage-managing" her death so that it would be "exemplary."

3. *Inventing the Truth: The Art and Craft of Memoir*, ed. and with a memoir by William Zinsser (Boston: Houghton Mifflin, 1987), 21. Autobiography, on the other hand, follows a "dutiful line from birth to fame, omitting nothing insignificant." The question of what to call autobiographical writing is addressed by Estelle C. Jelinek in *The Tradition of Women's Autobiography: From Antiquity to the Present* (Boston: Twayne, 1986), who considers as nonautobiographical such forms as letters, journals, and diaries, but accepts recollections, reminiscences, and memoirs, xii. Jelinek's essential criterion for determining that writing is autobiographical is whether the author has actually expressed the intent to write a life or to look back over a part of it.

4. Her self-approving auto-portrait (*Mémoires*, 254–255) has led critics to pillory her for lack of modesty and hence of virtue. For instance, Pierre Fauchéry, *La Destinée féminine dans le roman du dix-huitième siècle, 1713–1807: Essai de gynécomythie romanesque* (Paris: A. Colin, 1972) emphasizes that her self-description is located in the "semantic gesture" of both the *vasculaire* and *musculature*, which become revealing signs not only of self-identity and psychological conflict, but also of literary sensitivity. Along this same line, Outram has suggested that the "whole of her bodily history [becomes] the matrix of her plot," 137. In response, one might say that if Madame Roland's objective is to teach and to transcend her own nature, it is hardly surprising that she reveals her essentially sexual nature, quick to arousal and " excited by the most sensitive nerves," since it is precisely against this image of voluptuous nature that she will ultimately triumph.

5. All citations from the *Mémoires de Madame Roland* are to the 1986 edition presented and annotated by Paul De Roux (Paris: Mercure de France), 201. Henceforth, the page number will be given in parentheses in the text.

6. Introduction to *Mémoires*, 14.

7. "In studying metaphysics and the systems of philosophy, exactly the same thing happened to me as when I read poetry; I found myself transformed into whatever character in the drama seemed most like me or whom I most admired. I adopted opinions whose newness or brillance struck me; they were mine until a new or more profound discussion replaced them," *Mémoires*, 256.

8. *Mémoires*, 280. Dorinda Outram reads this entire episode as representing Madame Roland's simultaneous fascination with and conflict over sexuality, "Words and Flesh," 133–134. She even suggests that Manon reveals a "considerable degree of erotic response" in the way she presents the other woman's physical sexuality, while

ostensibly criticizing such ostentatious self-presentation. However, another less negative explanation for the physical presentation of this woman is that Manon is a facile word portraitist and that her *literary* talent determines her choice.

9. "La Lecture: une pratique culturelle," in *Pratiques de la culture* (Marseille: Rivages, 1985), 222–223.

10. The argument is interesting because it suggests that a taste for good reading develops at a young age. Thus, Manon says "Even today I know the names of only two or three [books of questionable morality], and the reading taste that I was acquiring as a child did not incite in me the least temptation to seek out such books" (213).

11. Madame de Graffigny's novel had been translated into seven languages, and went through as many as forty-eight editions in its first forty years, for a frequency rate of 1.2 editions *a year* between 1747 and 1787, thus enjoying its greatest popularity in the 1760s and 1770s when Manon would have been in her teens and early twenties, David Smith, "The Popularity of Mme de Graffigny's *Lettres d'une Péruvienne*: The Bibliographical Evidence," *Eighteenth-Century Fiction*, 3 (October 1990), 6–7.

12. Françoise Kermina, *Mme Roland ou la passion révolutionnaire* (Paris: Académique Perrin, 1976), 403.

13. Like the princess, Manon confesses to her husband the love she has for another man, while promising to remain a virtuously faithful wife. Subsequently, both husbands die—the prince, wracked by jealousy, succombs to illness; while Monsieur Roland, desperate to escape his political enemies and distraught by his wife's emotional betrayal, commits suicide. Yet to charge Manon with emulating literature seems to ignore how literature also copies life.

14. Elisabeth Vigée-Lebrun, for instance, describes the deleterious effect that novel-reading can produce when she refers to the loss of her daughter's affections: "Unbeknownst to me, her old governess, Madame Charrot committed the great wrong of letting her read novels, totally taking over her mind and hardening her against me to the point that all my maternal love was powerless against this dreadful influence," *Souvenirs*, II, 2nd ed. (Paris: des femmes, 1986), 51–52.

15. "Avis d'une mère à sa fille," in *Réflexions nouvelles sur les femmes*, 96 and 99–100.

16. Porée had said, "If novels permit a woman to have dominion over humankind and to rule civil society, what more is needed to ruin utterly her modesty?" *Mémoires de Trévoux*, juin 1736, pp. 1486–1487, quoted in Georges May, *Le Dilemme du roman au XVIIIe siècle* (Paris: Presses Universitaires de France, 1963), 215, note 1.

17. It must be emphasized, however, that *both* men and women effused over this novel. Men like Panckoucke confessed to having shed torrents of tears while reading the novel. See Robert Darnton, "Reader Response to Rousseau," 243–248, in *The Great Cat Massacre and Other Episodes in French Cultural History* (New York: Basic Books, 1984).

18. As Mary Trouille points out in *Sexual Politics in the Enlightenment: Women Writers Read Rousseau* (Albany: State University Press of New York, 1997), to a very large extent Rousseau elicited women's greatest enthusiasm while they were young or unsophisticated. In their later years, many women felt more ambivalence about him. Furthermore, we might also observe, even when they did discover chinks in his armor, they never took these as the reason for discarding his entire corpus.

19. Rousseau refers to the necessity of this sixth sense in the *Confessions*. For the full quote regarding the importance of this sixth sense, see chapter I, footnote 59.

20. While it has become de rigueur to castigate Rousseau for antifeminism, he himself was capable of writing very positive pages about women. In a two-page essay, he says, "Few women who have had the opportunity to rule states and command armies remained in mediocrity; almost all distinguished themselves in some brillant way that is deserving of our admiration." And "due allowance being made, had the injustice of men not stripped women, along with their freedom, of opportunities to show themselves to the world, they could have given more numerous and greater examples of the grandeur of the soul and the love of virtue than we men" (*Oeuvres complètes*, II, 1255). Mira Morgenstern, *Rousseau and the Politics of Ambiguity* (University Park: Pennsylvania State University Press, 1996) makes the long overdue argument that many feminists have been unfair to Rousseau. For an earlier study of the same subject, see Gita May, "Rousseau's 'Antifeminism' Reconsidered," in Samia Spencer, ed., *French Women and the Enlightenment* (Bloomington: Indiana University Press, 1984), 309–317.

21. We should not mistake the recreation of her thought processes from an earlier time, neither the reconstructed doubts and anxieties of the young Manon, nor the rhetorical flourishes and exalted language about "the sublime and delightful duties of wife and mother," with the mature woman. In the fourth cahier, second part, there is one such passage in which she revisits the thoughts of the young teenaged girl who enflames herself with her own rhetoric. Speaking of the "sacred duties" of wife and mother, she exclaims that her young years must be devoted to assiduous preparation for them: "I must study their importance; by controlling my own inclinations, I will acquire the skills to be able, one day, to direct those of my children; in learning the habit of commanding myself, in properly informing and shaping my own mind, I shall be able to make the happiness of those dear ones around me, to surfeit with joy the mortal man who will win my heart, to cause all that surrounds us to reverberate with that same joy and know that it is my very own work" (264). The rhetorical ardor, the clarion call to noble duty, the taming and sculpturing of the self in order to better serve others and achieve one's own glory, the creation of bountiful happiness of the future mate are typical of the romance of youth. This is Madame Roland reading her young self, somewhat tongue in cheek, as she recounts those early rhetorical excesses.

22. See, for instance, Marie-France Silver et Marie-Laure Girou Swiderski, eds., *Femmes en toutes lettres: Les Epistolières du XVIIIe siècle* (Oxford: Voltaire Foundation, SVEC 2000:04) whose seventeen articles probe women's contributions to noncanonical genres such as correspondence, autobiography, memoirs, personal journals, religious writing, pedagogical texts, and historical and philosophical works.

23. For a study on Manon's early letters to Sophie as foundational work for her *Mémoires*, see Brigitte Diaz, "De La Lettre aux *Mémoires*: les fonctions autobiographiques de la lettre dans la correspondance de jeunesse de Mme Roland, 1767–1780," in *Femmes en toutes lettres: Les Epistolières du XVIIIe siècle*, 211–227.

24. Claude Perroud points out that because postal rates were expensive in the eighteenth century, letter writers often took advantage of the trips of friends and acquaintances to have them deliver letters. *Roland et Marie Phlipon: Lettres d'amour, de 1777 à 1780* (Paris: Alphonse Picard, 1909), xiii.

25. Quoted by Paul De Roux, *Mémoires*, 24.

26. "Madame Roland," in *Imagination in Confinement: Women's Writings from French Prisons* (Ithaca, N.Y.: Cornell University Press, 1983), 131–152. In a scathing critique, *Le Moniteur universel* (29 brumaire an II) had editorialized, "The Roland woman, great intellectual that she trumpeted herself to be with her grandiose projects, [but in fact only] a paper-scribbling philosopher . . . was a monster in all respects. Her haughty bearing . . . the arrogant stubbornness of her words, her ironic wit, and the assurance she paraded in her trip from the Palais de Justice to the Place de la Révolution prove that a sorrowful thought never crossed her mind. Yet she was a mother who had sacrificed nature. . . . The desire to be a savant led her to forget the virtues of her sex, and this omission, which is always dangerous, finished by bringing about her death on the scaffold." We can only speculate as to how much more vitriolic the language might have been had the editors of *Le Moniteur* had access to her *Mémoires* before writing their commentary.

27. This incident concerns Sister Agathe, whom she had met during her year in a convent and who could barely repress her strong feelings for Manon. Calling her by the name she attributed to other young nuns whom she would revisit on occasion—*colombes gémissantes*—Manon delicately recognizes that those tender letters from Sister Agathe, accompanied by gifts of sweets and ribbons, were stand-ins for the real but forbidden feelings of love that prompted them.

28. Or, for that matter, strong-willed mothers, as Elisabeth Vigée-Lebrun reveals in her memoirs in the clash with her daughter, Brunette, who wished to marry (and did) a suitor her mother considered too much like her own husband, Jean-Baptiste-Pierre Lebrun, a man of small talent and huge appetites for gambling and prostitutes. Brunette's intended is a man Vigée-Lebrun describes as talentless, fortuneless, and classless (see *Souvenirs*, II [Paris: des femmes, 1984], 48–55), which simply underscores the different criteria of parents and their children who are seeking independence through love or marriage.

29. Manon writes, "at sixteen years of age, reading Buffon's natural history . . . I jumped over without reading whatever dealt with the act of generation, and I glanced at the accompanying drawings with the speed and tremulousness of a person seeing a precipice," 220–221.

30. "Madame Roland," in *Nouveaux Lundis* (Paris: Calmann-Lévy, 1896) VIII, 198–200.

31. Another female intellectual, Belle de Zuylen, had also spoken of the conflict, when she wrote to Constant d'Hermenches, "To be at once virtuous and voluptuous, to sow and find flowers of pleasure in the bosom of duty would be a heavenly joy" (26 August 1764).

32. In her early twenties, Madame Roland had said, "I never had the least desire to become an author" (304), perhaps in reference to a particular time in her life, or in concession to current values, or with a particular definition of "author" as novelist in mind. But when France is, as she says "a vast theater of carnage, a bloody arena in which its children tear one another to pieces" (234), to write is to bear witness and to be virtually assured of having one's text enter history.

33. *Lettres de Mme Roland*, Tome II: 1777–1780, nouvelle série, 157. The letter is dated 16 November 1777.

34. *Le Pacte autobiographique* (Paris, 1975), 45. The complete citation reads, "C'est à ce niveau global que se définit l'autobiographie: c'est un mode de *lecture* autant qu'un type d'écriture, c'est un *effet contractuel* historiquement valuable."

CHAPTER 3: THE ROMANCE AS TRANSFORMATIVE READING

1. *Mémoires* (Paris: Ladvocat, 1825), Vol. III, 87–88. Footnotes referring to the ten-volume set of her memoirs will henceforth contain only the volume number of this edition in Roman numerals, accompanied by ordinal page numbers. Louis-Philippe duc d'Orléans, known as Philippe d'Egalité (1747–1793), is called the Duc de Chartres until his father dies, at which point he takes the name of Orléans and makes his son (the future Louis-Philippe, 1733–1850) the Duc de Chartres.

2. Her biographer, Gabriel de Broglie, *Madame de Genlis* (Paris: Perrin, 1985) considers the *Mémoires* her best work, an opinion seconded by Alice Laborde, who, in the only full-length study of the works of Madame de Genlis, calls them "the most captivating part of her corpus," *L'Oeuvre de Madame de Genlis* (Paris: Nizet, 1966), 227. Béatrice Didier believes that her novels and especially *Mademoiselle de Clermont*, deserve that honor (see her preface to *Mademoiselle de Clermont* [Paris: Regine Deforges, 1977)], 7–33. More recently, Michèle Weil has argued persuasively that the Genlis letters deserve far more attention for the power of their prose and as chronicles of extraordinary times by a woman who knew everyone, "Mme de Genlis épistolière : lettres d'une femme de lettres ou vers une poétique de la lettre féminine ou l'être en lettres," in Marie-France Silver and Marie-Laure Girou Swiderski, eds., *Femmes en toutes lettres: Les Epistolières du XVIIIe siècle* (SVEC, 2000–04), 193–210.

3. Victor Hugo in *Choses vues* (année 1844, le roi Louis-Philippe, 79–82; Paris: Charpentier, 1888). Quoted in Albert Cim, *Les Femmes et les livres* (Paris: Boccard, 1919), 193.

4. In support of that bipolarity, one recalls that she had once said, "it always seems to me less difficult to renounce something completely rather than to moderate oneself" (II, 268).

5. *De L'Influence des femmes sur la littérature française, comme protectrices des lettres et comme auteurs; Ou, Précis de l'histoire des femmes françaises les plus célèbres*, 2 vols. (Paris: Lecointe et Durey, 1826) I, l. Later in this same work, she observes that it is "necessary that women have religious sentiments; those who don't soon become what Ninon [the celebrated seventeenth-century courtisan] called a *femme honnête homme*" (Vol. II, 215)—in other words, a cross-sexed individual, a sexual hybrid, or creature of suspect morality, for mainstream eighteenth-century French society.

6. *Les Souvenirs de Félicité L***** (Paris: Maradan, 1804), 42.

7. For more on the classical syllabus, see François Furet and Jacques Ozouf, *Reading and Writing: Literacy in France from Calvin to Jules Ferry* (London: Cambridge University Press, 1982), 11. Interestingly, Madame de Genlis recommends the same approach in teaching foreign languages: first, the child should learn to speak, then read, then write.

8. In that way she followed advice handed down to women who were enjoined to practice reading and writing as complementary skills. In *Nouvelles Réflexions sur les femmes* (1727), for instance, Anne Thérèse de Lambert strongly counsels the benefits of writing in conjunction with reading. "Write a great deal," she admonishes women, because "by writing you form your style; and you learn your language, which would be a shame for any well-bred girl not to know." On a practical note, she urges women to make written remarks on their readings, for in that way they will impress on the mind better what they have read (Paris: côté-femmes, 1989), 137.

9. For modern pedagogical research on the complementary nature of the two skills, see Donna E. Alvermann and Stephen F. Phelps, *Content Reading and Literacy: Succeeding in Today's Diverse Classrooms* (Boston, Allyn and Bacon, 1994), 197–198.

10. *Adèle et Theodore, ou Lettres sur l'éducation* (Paris: Lecointe et Durey, 1822, 6th ed.), IV, 384–401.

11. In this respect, she is in full agreement with Jesuit teaching, founded on the principle of "guided reading" (*la lecture guidée*) and the elimination of "self-chosen reading" (*lecture individuelle*) for a young reader. For a further discussion, see the Preface to Guillaume-Hyacinthe Bourgeant, *Voyage merveilleux du Prince Fan-Férédin dans la Romancie*, édition critique par Jean Sgard et Geraldine Sheridan. Publications de l'Université de Saint-Etienne, 1992, 16.

12. Madame de Genlis might have been surprised by Jonathan Culler's contention that any theory of reading must recognize boredom as a major theoretical category. In his essay, *Roland Barthes* (New York: Oxford University Press, 1983), Culler maintains that to reflect on boredom is to think about texts and the strategies of reading they may require—an enterprise more theoretical than confessional, in his view (99). It is the same enterprise that Patricia Spacks takes up in her critical study, *Boredom* (Chicago: University of Chicago, 1995), in which she shows how "boredom" was a menace to ethical energy in the eighteenth century and would have an impact on women.

13. Caroline was to die in childbirth at twenty-one, while Pulchérie's marriage was a disaster.

14. In this judgment, she appears to agree with an archenemy of the novel, Father Porée, who railed against the genre in a speech "Discours sur les livres appelés en langue vulgaire romans" (25 February 1736), describing the novel as "a lightweight work of pure fiction whose objective is nothing other than worldly love."

15. Kate Flint, *The Woman Reader, 1837–1914* (Oxford: Clarendon Press, 1993), has said that women who censor their own sex may do so in the hope of gaining greater social and cultural legitimacy for themselves, 10.

16. It is difficult to assess the actual role of religion and how specific tenets or practices determined decisions in her life. Like many women of the period, she considered the convent a refuge from the maelstrom of society. For her, society outside the convent was too often ruled by the passions, in contrast to life behind convent walls in which the spirit of peace and truth reigned. Given the drama of both her life and times, it is not unreasonable that she would speak positively about the "unknown happiness that one tastes in the cloistered life," where free from the vanities of social interaction, a sincere person can come closer to knowing "la félicité suprême" (*Mémoires*, VII, 118). Yet there are remarkably few indications in her writing that show any interest in issues of dogma, unlike her intellectual predecessors in the seventeenth century, described by Linda Timmermans in *L'Accès des femmes à la culture (1598–1715); Un Débat d'idées de Saint François de Sales à la Marquise de Lambert* (Paris: Honoré Champion, 1993).

17. Ironically, it is also that principle that may explain why in her memoirs she eliminates or obfuscates certain of her own actions. In a significant passage, she wrote, "I think that in memoirs in which you have not engaged yourself to tell the whole story, you can and must, out of respect for yourself, pass over in silence serious mistakes that you may have made." To be fair, she does add the proviso, "unless those mistakes are linked to events that you want to report." In which case, she declares,

"you must accuse yourself sincerely and not seek to attenuate your wrongs" (*Mémoires*, II, 161), and she insists that is what she did.

18. *Les Annales de la vertu, ou, Histoire universelle, iconographique et littéraire*, 5 vols. (Paris: Lecointe et Durey, 1825), V, 194–229.

19. *Le Livre des Trois Vertus*, eds. Charity Cannon Willard and Eric Hicks (Paris: Champion, 1989), 61.

20. According to Roberta Krueger, *Women Readers and the Ideology of Gender in Old French Verse Romance* (Cambridge: Cambridge University Press, 1993), chapter 8, 217–252, Christine is conflicted in her response

21. In 1661, Louise-Françoise de La Baume-Le Blanc (1644–1710) came to the court of Louis XIV, who only the year before had made a political marriage with Marie-Thérèse of Austria. Louise was soon noticed by the dashing eighteen-year-old king and became his mistress. In the course of their more than ten-year relationship, she gave birth to five children, two of whom lived and were legitimized. In 1667, she received the title of "duchesse," at about the same time that Louis's amorous interests were turning to the bewitching intriguer, Madame de Montespan. Though he continued to share his royal favors with both women, Louise grew increasingly uncomfortable with the irregularity of her situation. She had always been drawn to the religious life, and in 1674 she left the court to enter the convent of the Carmelites where she took the name of Louise de la Miséricorde. It was in the convent on the rue Saint-Jacques that Madame de Sévigné went to visit the royal mistress-turned-nun, whom she described as "this little violet hiding in the grass, ashamed of being a [royal] mistress, mother, and duchess."

22. Notes are to the 1823 Lecointe et Durey eleventh edition in two volumes.

23. Georg Lukacs, on the other hand, in The *Historical Novel* (Boston: Beacon Press, 1963) calls for the historical novel to probe the processes of history and attempt to uncover the causes for the rise or fall of states.

24. The term is that of Louise Rosenblatt, *The Reader, the Text, and the Poem: The Transactional Theory of the Literary Work* (Carbondale: Southern Illinois University Press, 1978) and describes the effect produced by a reading that has a physical impact on the reader and leads to change in her life.

25. Madame de Genlis does recount one interpolated story in volume II, 121–139.

26. Speaking of her own mother, Madame de Genlis says, "I respected my mother, and my complete submission to her never wavered an instant. I thought it necessary to show her by my attentions, respect, and absolute obedience (until death) what I was not able to give her in intimate confidences." But, "there was in our spirits, opinions, moods, and characters the most singular difference. She was serious, severe, imposing" (*Mémoires*, I, 121).

Interestingly, Madame de Genlis duplicates the pattern with her own children. Her youngest daughter, Pulchérie, expresses ambiguous, if not actually hostile, feelings about her mother when she is a young adult, saying, "She loves us . . . but coldly, without expansiveness, and without ever needing us . . . it's always her mind that acts and speaks, and never her heart," quoted in Gabriel de Broglie, 423. Contemporary family therapists might be fascinated by the long history of frosty mother–daughter relations in Madame de Genlis's family. Félicité remembers her grandmother as "a most unnatural mother" (*Mémoires*, I, 145) who first tried to force her daughter into becoming a nun, keeping her in a convent until age twenty-six, and out of pure meanness refusing the offers of marriage the daughter received, then robbing her of her inheritance (I, 148–156). Once when Félicité accompanies her mother to visit her grandmother, the young girl is shocked that her mother, whom she fears, shows similar fear of *her* mother.

27. The same is true in *L'Histoire intéressante de la duchesse de C*** when the heroine refuses to marry the man she had formerly loved. In this story interpolated in *Adèle et Théodore* (and based on the tale of a real woman whom Genlis met in Italy), an obedient daughter marries the man of her father's choice, even though she is in love with the Comte de Belmire, who also loves her. Though she remains faithful to her husband, when he learns of her love for another man and cannot wrest from her his name, he is overwhelmed by jealousy and locks her in a room in the depths of his country château after staging her death for friends and family. There she remains for nine years, and when at last upon her husband's death, she is liberated, she rejects the idea of marriage with the Comte de Belmire. No longer interested in romantic love, she commits her life to study and meditation.

28. *Reading the Romance: Women, Patriarchy, and Popular Literature* (Chapel Hill: University of North Carolina Press, 1984).

29. In her own life, Genlis separates the body and the mind as two entirely different domains. In fact, until her old age, she is not very interested in recounting her body, though she is eager to put her mind on display. As long as her health is robust, her physical body is of scant concern, and she gives relatively few personal and almost no intimate physical facts about her self. When it comes to treating her own three pregnancies in her memoirs, she does so almost in passing. We learn on the occasion of the first that she is happy to become a mother; during the second, that before she knew she was pregnant she continued horseback-riding with no ill effect; on the third that she had short convalescences, and that she did not breastfeed her children because it was not yet a current practice. In her post-Palais Royal years, we know she had a predilection for a spartan existence of few comforts and was a woman of considerable mental and physical discipline. Undoubtedly because she considers the physical body a mere instrument, she hardly mentions it until the point at which the frailties and unsexed body of old age force themselves on her. Unsurprisingly, she, like many older people, feels that her mind remains as young and vibrant as ever, but that her body is "nothing more than a kind of shadow, having become a sort of lightweight envelope" (*Mémoires*, VII, 75). In her seventies and eighties she has problems of balance and dizziness; she cannot hold her head aright. Her heart beats arythmically and she suffers from nocturnal convulsions. The physical body, once the unquestioned vessel, now focuses her attention only because it no longer obeys the commands of its mistress and seems to present a logic of its own—that of its own degradation. In the last volumes of the memoirs, Genlis does not shy away from revealing and analyzing the body, which is now self-destroying, but in her poignant descriptions of the deprecations of old age, it is as though she is talking about someone else, so great is the disjunction between her mental faculties and the physical body.

30. In perhaps further demonstration of the affinity that Genlis wants to establish between herself and Louise, she makes her character thirty years of age instead of thirty-four, which is historically true, when she leaves the court for the convent. In other words, exactly the same age that Genlis had been when she accepted the Duc de Chartres's gift and committed herself to a new life.

31. Fiona MacCarthy, review of Jo Ann Kay McNamara, *Sisters in Arms: Catholic Nuns Through Two Millennia* (Cambridge: Harvard University Press, 1996), *New York Review of Books*, December 19, 1996, 31.

32. Madame de Genlis portrays a Louis who had no longer been in love with Louise for some time, but who did not want her to bury herself in a convent, preferring that as the mother of five of his children, she continue to live at court as a displaced but respected former mistress.

33. "Le Cercle pédagogique: Un Mode dominant de lecture au début du XVIIIe siècle," in Jan Herman and Paul Pelckmans, eds., *L'Epreuve du lecteur; Livres et lectures dans le roman d'Ancien Régime* (Louvain: Peeters, 1994), 191–199.

34. This is a concept described by Claude Labrosse in *Lire au XVIIIe siècle: "La Nouvelle Héloïse" et ses lecteurs* (Lyon: Presses Universitaires de Lyon, 1985).

35. Michèle Weil, "Mme de Genlis épistolière: lettres d'une femme de lettres ou vers une poétique de la lettre féminine ou l'être en lettres," 193–210, *Femmes en toutes lettres*, says that Genlis can be considered a feminist in that she practiced all the rights of man (210).

36. She had said, "Physically weaker than men, and bearers of children, women are not destined by nature to fight or carry arms; and those who cannot *defend* are not made to *command* and to govern," (*De L'Influence*, I, xxxi). However, she continues, if women were not made to rule or to become involved in politics, their "*supériorité de l'esprit*" will not go to waste, since it can be exercised through their roles as wives and mothers (I, xxxiii).

37. In this respect, she recalls Madame de Lambert who had written, "Truth is the same for everyone; why should it not be equally true with virtue?" "Conseils importants d'une amie," in *Réflexions nouvelles sur les femmes*, 229.

38. *L'Accès des femmes à la culture (1598–1715); Un Débat d'idées de Saint François de Sales à la Marquise de Lambert*, 818.

CHAPTER 4: THE PROJECT OF DESIRE

1. Terry Eagleton suggests in *The Rape of Clarissa; Writing, Sexuality, and Class Struggle in Samuel Richardson* (Minneapolis: University of Minnesota Press, 1982) that reading and writing are always in some sense illicit intercourse, 50.

2. Emma Wilson, *Sexuality and the Reading Encounter; Identity and Desire in Proust, Duras, Tournier, and Cixous* (Oxford: Clarendon Press, 1996).

3. "La Poétique d'Isabelle de Charrière ou la correspondance comme laboratoire d'une oeuvre," in *Femmes en toutes lettres: Les Epistolières du XVIIIe siècle*, textes réunis et présentés par Marie-France Silver et Marie-Laure Girou Swiderski, *SVEC* 2004–04, 173.

4. The entire correspondence—over 159 letters by her hand and 108 from Constant d'Hermenches—is collected in volumes I and II of the twelve-volume complete works of Isabelle de Charrière published by G. A. Van Oorschot, Amsterdam, 1979. For the year 1760, Vol. I shows a single letter from Belle to d'Hermenches. There are 11 entries from her to him for 1762; 6 for 1763; 52 for 1764; 19 for 1765; 15 for 1766; 12 for 1767; 18 for 1768; 6 for 1769; 7 for 1770; 2 for 1771 (Isabelle marries Charrière on 17 February 1771); 6 for 1772; 1 for 1774; and one for 1775. His letters to her and their dates are: 1762: 4; 1763: 1; 1764: 24; 1765: 12; 1766: 15;

1767: 9; 1768: 13; 1769: 6; 1770: 7; 1771: 2; 1772: 8; 1773: 3; 1774:1; 1775: 2; 1776: 1. These indications refer to the total number of entries, but it should be noted that some entries contain more than one letter. We also do not necessarily have all the letters exchanged between the two, since some may have been lost or destroyed.

5. These include the pen, the ink, and paper of her erotic expression, those handmaidens of rapture, so to speak. She transfers onto the letters she receives from d'Hermenches all the value of the absent lover. The sheets of paper that had been in contact with his body, and perhaps carry his scent, are imbued with a sensual materiality and become the new fetishes of erotic stimulation. She is transported by his letters, kissing and using them to fill the void of his physical absence, and to serve as literary and erotic nourishment.

6. She enjoys discussing the art of language with other practitioners such as Benjamin Constant and Isabelle de Gélieu, and writes to her translator, L. F. Huber, "I enjoy myself like a queen when I hold forth on language" (17 March 1794).

7. *Women, Letters, and the Novel* (New York: AMS Press, 1980), 99.

8. Her boldness as a writer, in opposition to the real woman, is something that James Boswell, an erstwhile suitor, did not understand. In 1764, he wrote her a shocked letter in which he reproved her "libertine sentiments" for having said that, even after marriage, she might become another man's mistress if she and her husband did not sincerely love one another. "Ah Zelide!" Boswell reprimanded her, "do you not see that you would reduce yourself to the most despicable of all situations. No, Zelide, whatever men may do, a Woman without Virtue is terrible." And in response to her idea that a husband who does not love his wife need not consider fidelity as a duty: "Fy Zelide! What fancies are these? Is a mistress half so agreeable a name as a Wife? . . . I beseech you never indulge such ideas. Respect mankind. Respect the Institutions of Society. If Imagination presents gay Caprice, Be amused with it. But let Reason reign. Conceal such ideas" (9 July 1764). Clearly what Boswell did not understand was the exciting and creative power of what she calls her "imagination libertine" to speak and to imagine anything—but to do much less. For her somewhat annoyed response to him, see her letter, 27 January 1765.

9. D'Hermenches seems to recognize the literary impulse that underlies her expression, and he will counsel her to be less *romanesque* and to abandon her taste for *intrigues* when she deals with men other than himself. "Forget . . . that you are Sappho" (5 June 1765) he advises her before she meets his friend, the marquis de Bellegarde, a possible marriage partner.

10. Thus, Madame de Tourvel would say "with the reputation you have acquired . . . what woman could admit to being in a correspondence with you? What woman of honor would resolve to do what she feels she will be obliged to hide?" (Letter XLIII). But caught in the grip of a powerful passion, she disingenuously adds, "Yet if I were confident that your letters would be of a kind I could find no fault with, that I could always justify myself in my own eyes for having received them . . . I might be persuaded . . . to [permit] you to write to me from time to time." As she will acknowledge in Letter LXVII, "While you do everything to oblige me to discontinue this correspondence, it is I who goes about to find ways of sustaining it." Of course she does, because despite her willed blindness, as every reader including Valmont knows, she is madly in love.

11. In view of such expressions, we understand why Isabelle and Jean-Louis Vissière entitled their edition of the Charrière-d'Hermenches correspondence *Une*

Liaison dangereuse, correspondance avec Constant d'Hermenches, 1760–1776 (Paris: Editions de la Différence, 1991).

12. Nearly two decades before Choderlos de Laclos's great epistolary novel, Belle's correspondence with d'Hermenches will manifest the same spatial and erotic tension of Laclos's novel, the same motifs of desire and danger, the same ambiguous mixture of innocence and knowledge—though not, to be sure, the same project of destructive seduction. The fact that his novel postdates the Belle–Constant correspondence does not undermine the point because the double structure on which his novel was premised, *le danger des liaisons* and *les dangers de l'écriture*, were both essential parts of the culture of erotic and sentimental relations that reigned in public perception long before 1782. One has only to read eighteenth-century book reviews to understand the extent to which Laclos had merely assembled—though masterfully so—all the themes and *lieux communs* of the dangerous liaison.

13. For example, immediately after finishing one letter on 3 November 1764, Belle begins another the next morning, and yet another the following day, since, in an unequivocally literary judgment, she deemed the earlier one "not interesting enough to be sent alone."

14. For a discussion of the definitions of space as a psychological concept, see Lynn S. Liben, "Spatial Representation and Behavior: Multiple Perspectives," in *Spatial Representation and Behavior Across the Life Span*, ed. by Lynn S. Liben et al. (New York: Academic Press, 1981), 3–36.

15. See C. P. Courtney's biography, *Isabelle de Charrière (Belle de Zuylen): A Biography* (Oxford: Voltaire Foundation, 1993).

16. Geoffrey Scott, *The Portrait of Zélide* (London: Constable, 1925), 190.

17. In her letter of 23 October–6 November 1762, she had said, "You are not the first to regret that I am not a man. I myself have often wished it . . . if I were, I would be a less displaced person than I seem to be at present, and my situation would offer more freedom to my tastes, plus a more robust body would better serve an active mind."

18. Though separated by an ocean and a century, Charrière's heroine has a veritable soul mate in the female protagonist of Charlotte Perkins Gilman's story, "The Yellow Wallpaper." Both stories are written by women from within their rooms, in homes where they live like visitors in inhospitable spaces, explicitly in "The Yellow Wallpaper," because the couple are only summer renters of the house, and implicitly in "Mistress Henley," because the husband expects his new wife to coexist in a room replete with the memories and mementoes of his first wife, his mother, and grandmother. Both stories are related in the first person by women married to men of great seriousness who with kindly despotism control their wives whom they treat like children. The husbands often speak to their wives using condescending third-person address, such as when Mr. Henley says to his spouse on one occasion, "I see that my young wife is as youthful as her headdress and as light as its feathers" (Letter 4), while John calls his wife "little girl" and says "Bless her little heart! She shall be as sick as she chooses." Both wives have been conditioned by society to accept woman's domestic duties, yet in their own homes they are also deprived of the authority that such duties would suppose. Both are even denied woman's so-called natural role of motherhood, since neither has much access to the child who also lives in the house. In "The Yellow Wallpaper," it is undoubtedly on the orders of the husband that the child is sheltered from the mother, and in "Mistress Henley," the wife is made to feel so miserably inadequate that she con-

cedes to probably harming more than helping her husband's little daughter. Deprived of all sense of importance and forced into idleness, both women become ill and suffer from depression. But as each falls deeper and deeper into the abyss—Gilman's heroine becomes mad and Charrière's increasingly immobilized—they nonetheless seem to exercise some revenge on their husbands. Mistress Henley leaves behind a correspondence that, while never directly accusing her husband of self-centeredness and neglect, thoroughly indicts him. In an ironic reversal of traditional sex roles in which "masculine" is strength and "feminine" is weakness, in "The Yellow Wallpaper," it is John in the last scene who faints upon discovering his wife creeping like an animal around and around her room, and it is over his inert body that the wife must pass as she continues her senseless rounds. He, then, becomes in her world the "obstacle" she had been in his.

19. All quotes to the epistolary novels are from Isabelle de Charrière, *Romans* (Paris: Le Chemin vert, 1982).

20. Jenene C. Allison, *Revealing Difference: The Fiction of Isabelle de Charrière* (Newark: University of Delaware Press, 1995), 96.

21. Quoted in Godet's Preface to *Lettres neuchâteloises, Mistress Henley, Le Noble* (Geneva: Julien, 1908), xv.

22. It is interesting that Isabelle de Charrière lets her working-class girl know how to read and write because the possession of those skills suggests how the author values her characters. In opposition, she begins her novel *Sainte-Anne* (1799) by establishing her main character who had fled France during the Terror with the sentence, "She doesn't know how to read! Can you imagine that: She doesn't know how to read!" *Oeuvres complètes*, IX.

23. I am reminded in this respect of another publication of the eighteenth century that also jolts the reader by the decidedly unidealistic and, many would argue, inappropriate insistence on money in affairs of the heart. In 1791 and in response to a sincere desire to implement a revolution in marriage—badly in need of reform, by the account of all contemporaries—one publication, *Le Courrier de l'Hymen*, became an eighteenth-century version of an agency for matrimonial services in which individuals seeking marriage partners could advertise. However, rather than facilitating the marriages of lonely hearts, the journal appears to have fostered the merging of economic partnerships, since in the majority of classified ads, potential spouses clearly and antiseptically announce their own net worth and the financial assets and qualities that they require of a future mate: "young man . . . age 30 . . . seeks young woman between 22 and 28, belonging to a good family, with a taste for business, acceptable furnishings, and at least 15,000 *livres*, that is 1000 *livres* in cash and the rest in income or well placed prospects" (24 April 1791).

24. Quoted in Avant-propos, *Romans*, 8.

25. Though neither the characters nor the action of Parts I and II significantly overlap, it is generally assumed that the second part—at once the tragic story of Caliste and a cautionary tale of William's shameful behavior toward her—serves to ratify the decision made in Part I by Cécile's mother to withdraw her daughter from the inconsequence of Lausanne society and from the desultory nature of men in matters of the heart.

26. In "The Mother-Daughter Plot in Isabelle de Charrière's *Lettres écrites de Lausanne*," 57–102, *Subverting the Family Romance: Women Writers, Kinship Structures, and the Early French Novel* (London: Associated University Press, 2000), Charlotte Daniels places the collapse of the marriage plot against the patriarchal values pro-

moted in the Rousseauian family ideal, and also perceptively discusses Charrière as a reader of Rousseau.

27. See also Katharine Anne Jensen, "Mirrors, Marriage, and Nostalgia: Mother-Daughter Relations in Writings by Isabelle de Charrière and Elisabeth Vigée-Lebrun," *Tulsa Studies in Women's Literature* 19 no. 2 (Fall 2000), 285–314.

28. Isabelle de Charrière never became a mother. She did, however, relate as teacher and confidant to young women, as witnessed in the correspondence of her tender and devoted friendships with Caroline de Chambrier and Henriette L'Hardy. In literature she deals with female friendship, particularly in *Trois Femmes,* in which she casts three very different women in lead roles: the rather cerebral and passive Emilie, who loves virtue; her companion and servant girl, Joséphine, a straightforward and sensual young woman wholly devoted to her mistress; and Constance de Vaucourt, the vivacious and pragmatic widow, who tries to overcome the suspicious nature of her fortune by using it for good purposes. Among these women there exists a bond closer than blood, and though there is a marriage between Emilie and the German, Theobald d'Altendorf, the really meaningful relationship is the friendship between Emilie and Constance, marked by the gift that Constance gives Emilie on her wedding day: a ruby with a "C" and "E" interlinked.

29. Semiacknowledging her own lack of virtue, she says to Cécile, "I won't paint for you the regrets for having too much loved someone who so little merited it, nor the despair of having to blush for one's lover more even than for his weaknesses, or the unhappy surprise, when seeing him more clearheadedly, of having been guilty because of him" (53). Clearly, she is alluding to having given herself to an unworthy man, who, she admits with regret, did not subsequently behave correctly toward her.

30. *Roman et lumières au XVIIIe siècle* (Paris: Editions sociales, 1970), p. 139.

31. For a demonstration of how Charrière's correspondence can be plumbed for reflections on the various literary and esthetic debates of her day, and for her "artisanal conception of the work of art," see Isabelle Vissière, "La Poétique d'Isabelle de Charrière ou la correspondance comme laboratoire d'une oeuvre," in *Femmes en toutes lettres: Les Epistolières du XVIIIe siècle*, textes réunis et présentés par Marie-France Silver et Marie-Laure Girou Swiderski, *SVEC* 2004–04, 165–174.

32. "Quelques lettres inédites sur la *Nouvelle Héloïse,*" in M. Launay, *Jean-Jacques Rousseau et son temps* (Paris: Nizet, 1969), 192.

CHAPTER 5: READING RAPE

1. In the language of the eighteenth century, rape and seduction are not adequately distinguished, so that the crime of rape is often treated as morally unsanctioned seduction. Hence, the rapist is cast as the silver-tongued seducer who has charmed, pleaded, or persuaded the woman to grant him sexual favors, on the explicit or implicit promise of love or marriage, and then has abandoned her, often pregnant. He is frequently the figure of authority—the priest, master, or government official—who has misled a gullible and childlike woman, who was naively complicit—consensual—in her downfall. Given this benign view of rape, perhaps it is not surprising that much eighteenth-century libertine fiction (with the notable exception of Restif de la Bretonne, who narratizes rampant sexual and psychological disorder, including father–daughter incest) plays all acts of sex as seduction and never as rape.

2. Typically, according to Roy Porter, violated daughters were disposed of either by giving them to nunneries or marrying them to their abductor or rapist, a practice intended by law to save the life of the man. Roy Porter, "Does Rape Have a History?" in *Rape*, ed. by Sylvana Tomaselli and Roy Porter (Oxford: Basil Blackwell, 1986). In France, according to the post-1730 law, the death penalty, without obligatory marriage, for a *séducteur* was supposed to be mandatory, but in practice was seldom carried out, according to Léon Abensour, *La Femme et le féminisme avant la révolution* (Paris: Ernest Leroux, 1923).

3. *Reading with Feeling: The Esthetics of Appreciation* (Ithaca, N.Y.: Cornell University Press, 1996).

4. I am indebted to Nathalie Ferrand, "Livre et lecture dans quelques romans épistolaires: *La Nouvelle Héloïse*, *Les Malheurs de l'inconstance*, *Les Liaisons dangereuses*, *L'Emigré*, in *L'Epreuve du lecteur*," 367–377, for many insights into the relationship between reading and the epistolary.

5. In Choderlos de Laclos's novel, for instance, he has Madame de Merteuil parading her reading in preparation for a seduction, in parody of the *lecture de formation*. At other times, the protagonists make intratextual references to themselves through the texts of *littérateurs* and historians. Nathalie Ferrand describes the role of reading in his text by observing that the characters might be divided into two groups: those who read and have been able to master their reading, and those who either do not read, or read badly, or too late (372).

6. The notion of *warrant* comes from Feagin, who develops her argument of personal warrant as it works in the process of reader appreciation in Part Two of *Reading with Feeling*.

7. All footnotes are to *Lettres de Milady Juliette Catesby à Milady Henriette Campley, son amie* (Paris: Desjonquères, 1983).

8. Feagin argues that the development of an appreciation for fiction not only enlarges readers' imaginative capacity but also their capacity for emotional control, *Reading with Feeling*, 239. Whether, however, they respond to actual events in accordance with esthetic response to fiction depends on whether the principle of warrants accessed in literature is overridden in real life, 218. This, one assumes, is what happened with d'Ossery.

9. The edition referred to in note 7.

10. *The Novels of Madame Riccoboni* (Chapel Hill: University of North Carolina Press, 1977), 82.

11. *Fictions of Authority: Women Writers and Narrative Voice* (Ithaca, N.Y.: Cornell University Press, 1992), 29.

12. *Fictions of Authority: Women Writers and Narrative Voice*, 33.

13. In *The Ethics of Reading* (New York: Columbia University Press, 1987), J. Hillis Miller argues that ethics and narration cannot be kept separate, though their relation is neither symmetrical nor harmonious, 2. With regard to Feagin's promotion of "reading with feeling," which cannot be realized in *Les Liaisons*, according to Riccoboni, I am reminded of Dorothy Thelander's critique of the "withering of emotion" in Laclos's novel, *Laclos and the Epistolary Novel* (Geneva: Droz, 1963), 145.

14. Lettre I, "Correspondance de Laclos et de Madame Riccoboni au sujet des *Liaisons dangereuses*," Laclos, *Oeuvres complètes* (Paris: Gallimard, 1951), 686–698.

15. Heroines of the upper classes in women's writing are not usually shown as having been seduced, let alone raped—which is why Madame Riccoboni's Miss Jenny

is such an interesting case. More typically, the upper-class heroine helps a woman of the lower classes who has been raped or seduced, as in Madame de Charrière's *Lettres Neuchâteloises*, in which a disappointed Marianne de la Prise must delicately press her gentleman suitor to "do right by" a young servant girl pregnant with his child.

16. In her feminist reading of the theme of female refusal in epistolary novels [*Women, Letters, and the Novel* (New York: AMS Press, 1980), 31], Ruth Perry argues that the theme of female refusal is often motivated by the female protagonist's protection of her own individuality, Such an argument is borne out with Madame de Graffigny's *Les Lettres d'une Péruvienne* (1747), in which Zilia refuses an offer of marriage by a worthy man who loves her in order to live independently. For an interesting account of how the story evolved in Graffigny's mind, see Vera L. Grayson, "Ecrire son identité: la génèse des *Lettres d'une Péruvienne*" (in Marie-France Silver and Marie-Laure Girou Swiderski, eds., *Femmes en toutes lettres*, 33–40) who argues that the novel became original in plot and tone only at the point when Graffigny rejected François Duvaux's advice to make it a pathetic love story. Another woman who chooses herself over marriage is Madame de Genlis's heroine in *L'Histoire intéressante de la Duchesse de* C*** (see chapter 3, note 27). This novel, which deals with domestic violence and psychological abuse—possible metaphors or precursors of the modern concept of marital rape—is a brief 100-page story concerning a jealous husband who assumes unjustly that his wife is engaged in an adulterous affair and punishes her by locking her in a secret prison for nearly a decade. The story, which Genlis says is based on the real Duchesse de Cerifalco, an Italian duchess, whom she met in 1776 and which is recounted in Volume III of her *Mémoires*, ends with the heroine liberating herself from prison and deciding to reject the offer of marriage from the comte de Belmire, the man she had earlier and chastely loved, in order to live on her own, with her books and writing.

17. Lanser argues that economic necessity could have determined Riccoboni to write a book with a "happy ending" that would easily find a publisher and sell well because while she was openly feminist and had a twenty-five year companionship (possibly lesbian) with Thérèse Biancolelli, she was separated from her husband and was forced to earn her own living, *Fictions of Authority*, 40.

18. *Fictions of Authority*, 30–32.

19. To be sure, the spector of death within the story may also provide some motivation for Juliette's marriage. Miss Jenny had died of consumption, Juliette's own brother is killed in a duel, the wife of Abraham (d'Ossery's *valet de chambre*) had died, and so did Lady Seymour's lover in an accident (114). While all these characters have only a shadowy presence in the story, the effect of their deaths may incline Juliette to seize any opportunity, however tarnished, for a love relationship. In an early letter (Letter 10) in which Juliette quotes Milady Sunderland, who refuses Sir Manly and a life precariously based on passion, Juliette had shown herself critical of Milady for having loved herself so much she was unable to love another: "She enjoyed the admiration of everyone," says Juliette, "but the happiness of no one, not even her own, perhaps" (36). Seeing little to admire in the marriages of women in her environs, Milady Catesby envies neither their dull domesticity nor their conjugal stability, but still dreams of a relationship of love tempered by noble ideals. And that is certainly not what she gets.

20. For recent considerations of the subject, see Olga B. Cragg and Rosena Davison, eds., *Sexualité, mariage et famille au XVIIIe siècle* (Laval: Presses Universitaires de Laval, 1998).

21. Lanser, 39.

22. More typically, woman was considered by moral anthropologists and others such as Diderot in "Sur Les Femmes," to be, first, the victim of a physiology that condemned her to a lifetime of physical dysfunction (menstruation, pregnancy, childbirth, lactation, menopause), and second the victim of men who would betray her trust.

23. Nancy K. Miller, "La mémoire, l'oubli et l'art du roman: textes libertins, textes sentimentaux," in Danielle Haase Dubosc and Eliane Viennot, eds., *Femmes et pouvoirs sous l'ancien régime* (Paris: Rivages, 1991), 238–253. See also Miller's "Cultural Memory and the Art of the Novel," in *French Dressing: Women, Men, and Ancien Regime Fiction* (New York: Routledge, 1995), 69–79.

24. Women are not the only ones to see rape as the operative principle in Laclos. In "Le Lecteur-voyeur et la mise en scène de l'imaginaire viril," *Laclos et le libertinage, 1782–1982*, (Paris: Presses Universitaires de France, 1983), 163–175, Jean-Marie Goulemot asserts that the fictional climate in Laclos' novel reveals an ambiance in which all sexuality derives from an "imaginaire viril" and that "the presence of rape is at the very heart of the amorous practices," 166–167.

25. Rousseau was in fact referring to the difference between country and city readers, but the remark works equally well for female and male readers in terms of their positions in the domestic and public spheres of life. "2e Préface de la *Nouvelle Héloïse*: ou Entretien sur les romans, entre l'éditeur et un homme de lettres," 16 février 1761, *Oeuvres complètes*, II, 19.

26. In her article, "Dangerous Liaisons 2: The Riccoboni–Laclos Sequel," in *Eighteenth-Century Fiction* 9 (October 1996), 51–70, Janie Vanpée argues that against the two models of reading presented by Laclos in his editor's "avertissement" and publisher's preface, Madame Riccoboni's letters advocate a third kind of reading, "as a woman," which is a first step in establishing a feminist reading. I would like to push this conclusion even further.

27. Nancy K. Miller says that while libertine and sentimental novels explore the same territory, the position chosen by the author for telling and judging the social interaction results in different effects of reading. Indeed, she suggests, it is this point of view that constructs different readerships and is at the heart of the creation of esthetic canons, "La Mémoire, l'oubli et l'art du roman: textes libertins, textes sentimentaux," 247.

28. *Man, Play, and Games*, trans. by M. Barash (New York: Schocken Books, 1979), 33.

29. For more on the notion of the ludic, see Matei Calinescu, "The Ludic Dimension," *Rereading* (New Haven & London: Yale University Press, 1993), 138–156.

30. *Memoirs*, IV, 10–12. Few readers today would agree with Madame de Genlis's blanket criticism of *Les Liaisons*. It is therefore all the more amusing to learn from her that one of her fans had somehow managed to confuse the authorship of her very moral and rather dull novel, *Adèle et Théodore*, with Laclos's *Liaisons*. In Volume III of her memoirs, she recounts that a certain M. d'Héricourt, traveling in Italy, received both novels at the same time but without their title pages. Believing that Madame de Genlis was the creator of the *Liaisons*, he wrote to a mutual friend to express his surprise "that a still young woman and teacher of a prince of blood would have the inconceivable effrontery to publish such a work" (180). Presumably, the same work but under the authorship of a male writer would have posed fewer problems for him.

31. "Correspondance," 693.

32. Gutwirth takes Laclos to task for his "reductive misogyny" and tone of condescension in her analysis of the Riccoboni–Laclos correspondence in "Laclos and 'Le sexe': The Rack of Ambivalence," *Studies on Voltaire and the Eighteenth Century* (189), 247–296.

33. In *Textual Promiscuities: Critical Rewriting in the Eighteenth Century* (Lewisburg, Pa.: Bucknell University Press, 2002), Antoinette Sol suggests that Laclos raided *women's* novels, especially those of Madame Riccoboni and Frances Burney. An earlier critic, Laurent Versini, *Laclos et la tradition; essai sur les sources et la technique des "Liaisons dangereuses"* (Paris: Klincksieck, 1968), while acknowledging the derivative nature of the *Liaisons*, emphasized Laclos's superior mastery of the narrative.

34. E. Ann Kaplan in discussing this concept, "Is the Gaze Male?" in *Powers of Desire; The Politics of Sexuality* (New York: Monthly Review Press, 1983), points out that the gaze is not necessarily and literally male, but that to possess and employ the gaze is to be in the masculine position (319). Hence, a female like Madame de Merteuil can appropriate the masculine role and reduce a man like Prévan to the conventionally feminine role as victim.

35. One might speculate whether by introducing Cécile's brief pregnancy, Laclos is implicitly taking up the myth whereby only the woman who reaches orgasm (thus a sign of her pleasure in the sex act, it was thought) will conceive. Though Thomas Laqueur says in *Making Sex: Body and Gender from the Greeks to Freud* (Cambridge: Harvard University Press, 1990) that, by the end of the Enlightenment, medical science ceased to regard the female orgasm as relevant to conception (3), it is still possible that for many of Laclos's readers, the fact that Cécile did conceive was further proof of her guilt rather than victimization.

36. F. C. Green says that while, morally speaking, Cécile was raped, in a court of law, Valmont would come off without a blemish on his character. *Minuet; a Critical Survey of French and English Literary Ideas in the Eighteenth Century* (New York: Dutton, 1935), 425.

37. The fact that I do not capitalize either expression, "battle of the books" or "culture wars," should distinguish my less ambitious intentions from Joan DeJean who, in *Ancients against Moderns: Culture Wars and the Making of a Fin de Siècle* (Chicago: University of Chicago Press, 1997), links the seventeenth century's Culture Wars in France with late twentieth-century Culture Wars in America. Both, she argues, characterize highly divisive periods in which intellectual anxieties over social and intellectual change lead society as a whole to believe that civilization, as we have known it, is coming to an end (6). The woman issue in eighteenth-century France, though divisive, did not lead to society going to war (or revolution) over that question alone. Still, the quality of the literary/woman debate between Riccoboni and Laclos should not be underestimated, since it captures the very essence of how literary factors are symptomatic of social conflict, which is a part of DeJean's argument.

38. Elizabeth Eisenstein, *The Printing Press as an Agent of Change: Communications and Cultural Transformations in Early-Modern Europe*, I (Cambridge: Cambridge University Press), 133.

39. Rousseau's two prefaces to *La Nouvelle Héloïse* are in *Oeuvres complètes*, II (Paris: Gallimard, 1964), 5–30. See Bernard Gagnebin's discussion of them, 1341–1343.

CHAPTER 6: BOOKS, SEX, AND READING IN THE FAIRY TALE

1. *Adèle et Théodore, ou Lettres sur l'éducation* (Paris: Lambert, 1782), I, 139. Her own *contes de fées* were very didactic.

2. "Grimoire, miroir: Le Livre dans les contes de fées littéraires," in Jan Herman and Paul Pelckmans, eds., *L'Epreuve du lecteur; Livres et lectures dans le roman d'Ancien Régime* (Louvain: Peeters, 1994), 129–139. Verdier studied the use of books in the tales of fifteen different writers from the period 1695 to 1760.

3. *La Lecture comme jeu; Essai sur la littérature* (Paris: Editions de Minuit, 1986).

4. For a history of the early fairy tale in France, see R. Robert, *Le Conte de fées littéraire en France de la fin du XVIIe à la fin du XVIIIe* (Nancy: Presses Universitaires de Nancy, 1981).

5. *Fairy Tales and the Art of Subversion; The Classical Genre for Children and the Process of Civilization* (New York: Methuen, 1988), 38.

6. *Fairy Tales, Sexuality, and Gender in France, 1690–1715: Nostalgic Utopias* (Cambridge: Cambridge University Press, 1996), 103.

7. For Rowe's feminist analysis of fairy tales, see chapter 19, "Feminism and Fairy Tales," in *Don't Bet on the Prince; Contemporary Feminist Fairy Tales in North America and England,* ed. by Jack Zipes (New York: Routledge, 1986), 209–226. Other feminist approaches can be found in Ruth Bottigheimer, *Grimm's Bad Girls and Bold Boys* (New Haven: Yale University Press, 1987), Maria Tatar, *The Hard Facts of Grimm's Fairy Tales* (Princeton, N.J.: Princeton University Press, 1987), and Marina Warner, *From the Beast to the Blonde; On Fairy Tales and Their Tellers* (New York: Farrar, Straus, and Giroux, 1995).

8. With regard to the two women writers of this chapter, such criticism is unwarranted, given that they themselves experienced patriarchy at its worst in unhappy marriages, legal separations, and subsequent financial worries. Moreover, neither woman lacked personal or literary sophistication. For biographies of the two writers, see Marie-Laure Girou Swiderski, "La Belle ou la bête? Madame de Villeneuve, la méconnue," in Roland Bonnel and Catherine Rubinger, eds., *Femmes savantes et femmes d'esprit: Women Intellectuals of the French Eighteenth Century* (New York: Peter Lang, 1994), 99–128; and Patricia A. Clancy, "A French Writer and Educator in England: Mme Le Prince de Beaumont," in *Studies on Voltaire and the Eighteenth Century* (201), 1982, 195–208.

9. Being overly ambitious, for instance, is faulted in both men and women. A large number of stories in *Le Magasin des enfants* seek to teach the reader to be happy with what he or she has, but since there are more male protagonists than females, boys are more often on the receiving end of the lesson, as in "Conte des trois souhaits" and "Conte du pêcheur et du voyageur." The reader must also ascertain what exactly a character trait signifies in a particular story. For instance, with regard to curiosity, traditionally assumed to be a negative trait in women though lauded in male characters, we must ask whether it is intellectual curiosity that is being featured or rude curiosity. In her short tale, "La Curiosité," Madame Leprince's Adam and Eve are banquet guests in the palace of a king who offers a splendid array of dishes for their delectation, but forbids them to partake of one covered dish. When the king is not noticing, Eve's curiosity gets the better of her and she convinces her husband to

lift the lid. A tiny mouse escapes, and when the king sees the scurrying creature, he has irrefutable proof that his guests have not understood the basic rules of hospitality. The fault being criticized, through the shorthand of curiosity, has less to do with the probing mind than with inappropriate behavior and bad manners in both sexes.

10. Her 1758 collection, *Le Magasin des enfants*, was reissued in paperback by Philippe Picquier in 1995. In explanation of the title, Elisabeth Lemirre points out in the preface that a *magasin*, from the Arabic to amass and possess, is used in the sense of a place for collecting, transmitting, and nourshing the reader with an *entrepôt d'histoires*.

11. *Reading the Romance: Women, Patriarchy, and Popular Literature* (Chapel Hill: University of North Carolina Press, 1984), 83. Although Radway believes that all popular romance originates in the failure of patriarchal culture to satisfy its female members (149), her conclusion, showing Chodorow's influence, is that despite the romance's apparent preoccupation with heterosexual love and marriage, its real goal is the reestablishment of the union between mother and child (155).

12. *The Uses of Enchantment* (New York: Random House/Vintage, 1977).

13. The most obvious case, of course, is "Beauty and the Beast." If Belle is so admirable because she learns to see past external appearance, why dismantle the teaching by rewarding her with a handsome prince? Undoubtedly it is because the idea of having a maiden wedded to an animal, or only half-man, would be repugnant for most readers even of make-believe. Moreover, of course, the protagonist's condition as beast is not his real state, but rather the result of a fairy's curse—unjust in the Villeneuve version, unexplained in Leprince, and variously motivated in other versions, with some even suggesting that the prince had been made into a beast because he had seduced a virgin and would be disenchanted only when he managed to win the love of another virgin. (It is interesting to note that in a theatrical version by Madame de Genlis, Beauty does, in fact, marry the Beast as beast, perhaps because for Genlis the purpose of the fairy tale is unequivocably moralistic.)

In another tale, "Le Prince Spirituel," Madame Leprince expressly keeps her male protagonist ugly, but she also makes him well educated and wise, so that when a beautiful but unschooled princess (whom he assists to become cultivated) falls in love with him, and a good fairy offers to take away his ugliness, the bride-to-be says no, "I am not concerned that he be handsome; it is enough for me that he be kind." On the other hand, in "Belote et Laidronette," Madame Leprince chooses cruel realism in distinguishing the simultaneous marriages of twin sisters, one of whom is beautiful, the other ugly: "Belote married a young and charming prince who was only twenty-two years of age. Laidronette married the minister of this prince, a man of forty-five years. He had recognized the qualities of mind of this girl and had great esteem for her [despite] her face which did not inspire love in him, and he confessed to Laidronette that he felt only friendship for her" (154).

14. For a further discussion, see Matei Calinescu, *Rereading* (New Haven: Yale University Press, 1993), 96.

15. The Villeneuve tale is in volume 26 of *Le Cabinet des fées, ou Collection choisie des contes des fées, et autres contes merveilleux* (Amsterdam, 1786), 27–214.

16. I have used the Philippe Picquier edition, pages 37–54. For Cocteau's expressions on poetic creation and the filmed image, plus the epic challenge of making a film so soon after World War II, see *"La Belle et la Bête": Journal d'un film* (Monaco: Rocher, 1958).

17. For further on Madame Leprince, see chapter 7 and the discussion of how the pedagogue of virtue and the spinner of fairy tales is equally at home as a satirist.

18. See Seifert's discussion of prophetic speech, *Fairy Tales, Sexuality, and Gender in France, 1690–1715*, 198.

19. This gift of hardship, like many punishments, has a term to it, so that, by the end, all turns out well, since Prince Fatal grows in virtue and fortitude, while his brother, whose life is too easy, becomes lazy and dissolute. Hence, apparent privilege turns to punishment and vice versa.

20. In somewhat comic demonstration of a fairy's own fallibility, Madame Leprince introduces a fairy in "Le Prince Désir" who endeavors to help the prince understand how flattery has blinded him, without recognizing in herself a similar weakness to honeyed words. While ultimately she will be successful in teaching the prince the necessary lesson, the fairy never learns it herself, in proof of the moral that it is easier to see flaws in others than in oneself.

21. In another tale, "Le Prince Spirituel," the narrative conceit used by Mme Leprince de Beaumont is based on a king's rejecting the bad fairy Furie's affections. When a good fairy, Diamantine, arranges a more appropriate marriage for him and promises to defend him against Furie, the latter finds her revenge by making his first-born son ugly. Interestingly, the subsequent story does not return to Furie, for the writer of the fairy tale does not find it necessary to dot all the moral "i's" or teach all the evil parents a lesson, since her objective is not to create a perfectly just and therefore perfectly unrealistic universe, but to show how the abused or unfairly treated can, despite everything, succeed.

22. Female utopian imagination in England gave rise in late seventeenth- and eighteenth-century literature to a substantial number of exclusively female utopias, presented by women such as Margaret Cavendish, Delariviera Manley, Mary Astell, Sarah Scott, and Mary Hamilton. In Sarah Scott's *A Description of Millenium Hall* (1762), for instance, a socialistic commune is created by aristocratic women, who, eschewing marriage and pooling their fortunes, establish a highly regulated domestic economy, in which everyone makes herself useful and agrees to the disciplinary shape of an exclusively female society. As Christine Rees has written in *Utopian Imagination in Eighteenth-Century Fiction* (London: Longman, 1996), most "utopian fiction tolerates a very high manipulation of individual, private lives for public good," 225.

23. One of the groups of weak-willed mortals is mothers and fathers. In the fairy tale, children are often ill served by parents, even well meaning ones, to say nothing of all the truly malevolent or callous parents who populate the fairy world. In fact, far from replicating idealistic visions of happy families, the fairy tale is actually very realistic in its portrayal of neglectful and sometimes even abusive parents. Madame Leprince, for instance, includes many such examples in her *Magasin des enfants*, less to punish the parents or teach better parenting skills, than to show how the child can, despite negative baggage, grow up to be a virtuous and effective adult. One thinks, for instance of "Le Prince Fatal et le prince Fortuné," in which the parents prefer the youngest child and give away their oldest, who will, however, ultimately prevail because he learns through misfortune the value of work. Or of "Aurore et Aimée" in which the oldest daughter is sent away so that people will think that her vain mother is younger. Indeed, in this case, as with Fatal, it is fortunate that the child is brought up by someone other than the parents, for the new caretaker—a lioness-mother or *bergère*—teaches the child to use time meaningfully

through reading, physical exercise, work, and prayer. It is noteworthy that inadequate parents are never punished by Madame Leprince; in fact, they are simply forgotten in the story, as the wronged child goes on to learn perseverance, fortitude, stamina, and steadfastness, precisely the qualities that confer worthiness. See, for instance, "Le Prince Titi," whose foolish and greedy parents love only one of their sons because he, unlike le Prince Tati, resembles them. It is in such cases of parental injustice that the child is helped by fairies in various disguises, who act to provide opportunities. They do not wave a magic wand and make everything okay, but rather extend a hand to the child in need.

24. Seifert, 198. Along this line, Virginia Swain has suggested that the fairy tale of mid-eighteenth century stands at the intersection of two transforming spheres of influence, the private and the public, and offers women the opportunity to engage in a fantasy of liberation. "Beauty's Chambers: Mixed Genres and Mixed Messages in Villeneuve's 'Beauty and the Beast,'" paper at Modern Language Association, Toronto, December 1997.

25. *From the Beast to the Blonde*, xxiii.

26. The library scene is absent only from Jean Cocteau's 1946 classic film in which gender is a less compelling interest than the parable of beauty—hardly surprising, in that his film follows so close on the heels of the Second World War.

27. Since the fifteenth century, the word *bibliothèque* had been used to designate the place where one deposits books. In his dictionary of 1690 Furetière gives three meanings for *bibliothèque*. The first implies a collection of books, the second a building, and the third an anthology, similar to how the word *magasin* is used. In the eighteenth-century fairy tale, a *bibliothèque* is a piece of furniture (see also chapter 1). In Disney, the *bibliothèque* is a public library.

28. Yvonne Johannot, *Tourner la page: livres, rites, et symboles* (Jérôme Millon, 1988), 147.

29. Of all the versions, Disney's asserts most emphatically Belle's qualities of mind. The first time the brown-haired Beauty comes on the scene, she is on her way to the local library, her nose deep in a book. The townspeople consider her to be "different" because she is a reader and consumer of knowledge. When the boorish antihero, Gaston, meets her on the street, he is quick to discredit himself with a misogynist statement about the wrongness of a woman reading, which he underscores by grabbing her book and throwing it down. Like all figures in fairy tales, Disney's Belle is not just a character, but also representative of a particular cultural moment and need. If in the eighteenth century, it was narratively essential that Belle be the loving and forgiving daughter, it was culturally important in America in the 1990s that she be a modern role model: bright, plucky, and ambitious. Neither docile nor submissive, and eager to go beyond the stifling confines of her hometown, Disney's defiant Beauty becomes the contemporary woman who yearns to participate in the dream of upward mobility, and puts into song her wish both to be understood and to leave her "provincial life."

30. For a study of Zilia as cultural critic, see Julia V. Douthwaite, *Exotic Women: Literary Heroines and Cultural Strategies in Ancien Régime France* (Philadelphia: University of Pennsylvania Press, 1992) esp. chap. 2, "The Exotic Other Becomes Cultural Critic: Montesquieu's *Lettres persanes* and Mme de Graffigny's *Lettres d'une Péruvienne*," 74–139.

31. *The Twilight of Common Dreams; Why America Is Wracked by Culture Wars* (New York: Metropolitan Books, 1995), 218.

32. *What Does a Woman Want? Reading and Sexual Difference* (Baltimore: Johns Hopkins University Press, 1993), 5.

33. The Janissaries were members of an elite within the Turkish army established in the fourteenth century and disbanded in 1826 following a revolt against the Sultan. It thus appears that Villeneuve foresees, or reads as might a fortuneteller, an event that will occur more than eighty years after her writing.

34. Jacques Leenhardt has described symbolic reading as "at once internal to the text and nourished by a source exterior to it," "Les Instances de la compétence dans l'activité lectrice," 305, in Michel Picard, *La Lecture littéraire* (Paris: Editions Clancier-Guénaud, 1987), 302–311.

35. *The Pleasure of the Text* (New York: Hill and Wang, 1975), 53. Barthes is explaining the enjoyment a reader takes from novels, biographies, and historical works that represent the "petty details" of daily life, such as schedules, habits, meals, lodging, clothing, or the very materiality "*that once existed.*"

36. Emma Wilson, *Sexuality and the Reading Encounter* (Oxford: Clarendon Press, 1996), 9.

37. *Psychoanalysis and Storytelling* (Oxford: Blackwell, 1994), 29–30.

38. In the *Uses of Enchantment*, Bruno Bettelheim speaks of the fairy tale as a kind of preparation for the challenges faced in life, and he suggests that through the story of Belle, the young female reader is reassured about the sexual requirements that will be placed on her in marriage. In other words, through the edifying spectacle of Belle's ultimate happiness, she discovers that what appears disagreeable (an undesirable husband) can turn out much better than she feared, since love can metamorphose even the worst of beasts into a highly worthy partner.

39. Belle is also the prisoner of other people's expectations and needs. In the family, she is the generous daughter of a weak-willed and ineffective father and the scapegoat of her sisters. From that standpoint, her sojourn in the Beast's world is a kind of escape, ultimately even salvation. Despite her apparent lack of freedom, she leaves behind the disharmonies of family life and learns to function and express her will in a new milieu.

40. As previously observed, only Madame de Genlis has her heroine marry the unmetamorphosed beast. A later version, an American television spinoff in the 1980s, avoids marriage between an ugly man and a beautiful maiden by incorporating its impossibility into the narrative tension. In that version of "Beauty and the Beast," the hideously deformed but wise and just Beast lives beneath New York City—a sort of modern interpretation of the *parc sauvage*. His Beauty is a blond lawyer, and though each loves and respects the other, theirs will be an unrequited love, both because such a marriage defies and shocks convention (which apparently did not bother Madame de Genlis) and because television series have typically been based on the convention of irresoluble romantic tension. Hence, in this story, and despite their love, the Beast can neither live above ground, nor Beauty join him in the underground. Even more important, for all Beauty's love and respect, this Beast will remain ugly. The integration of opposites in pursuit of harmony, an ostensible objective of the fairy tale, will not be achieved in this version because, as a television series, it must reject the closure that comes with the triumphant

marriage of Beauty and the prince and with his reintegration with society and her entrance into his world.

41. In addition to Mesdames de Villeneuve and Leprince, the forty-plus volumes of *Le Cabinet des fées* contain works by the following women: la comtesse Marie Catherine d'Aulnoy (c. 1650–1705), 33 tales; la comtesse Louise de Bossigny Auneuil (1650–1705), 6; Madame Fagnan, 1; Charlotte Rose de la Force (1650–1724), 8; Dame Louise Cavalier L'Evêque (1703–1745), 2; Marie-Jeanne L'Héritier de Villandon (1644–1734), 3; Madame Le Marchand, 1; Dame Catherine Caillot de Lintot, 3; Mademoiselle de L[o]ubert (1710–unknown), 3; Mademoiselle de Lussan (1682–1758), 8; la comtesse Henriette-Julie de Castelnau Murat (1670–1716), 6. In addition to well-known male crafters of the fairy tale, such as Perrault and Caylus, there are also many anonymous stories from *Mille et Une Nuits* and other traditions and countries including India, China, and Turkey, with a large number translated by Thomas-Simon Gueullette (1683–1768).

42. (Paris: Presses Universitaires de France, 1961), 23.

43. J. A. Appleyard, *Becoming a Reader: The Experience of Fiction from Childhood to Adulthood* (New York: Cambridge University Press, 1990), charts five stages in a reader's life: (1) first readings, or being read to, when reading is about fantasizing and pretend play; (2) the seven- to eleven-year-old child who reads to identify with fictional characters; (3) the adolescent reader who begins to reflect on his reading in terms of himself and his own identity; (4) the reader as interpreter striving to articulate a valid interpretation from multiple possible meanings; (5) the fully mature reader who understands that different kinds of reading may be for information, intellectual stimulation, or relaxation, and who in fiction prefers more character-driven than plot-driven stories.

44. Appleyard, 164, and quoted by Calinescu, 94.

45. "Les Premières Lectures," in Michel Picard, ed., *La Lecture littéraire* (Paris: Clancier-Guénaud, 1987), 128–160.

46. *La Lecture comme jeu* (Paris: Editions de Minuit, 1986).

CHAPTER 7: THE PERIODICAL PRINT PRESS FOR WOMEN

1. Related by Nina Rattner Gelbart, "The *Journal des dames* and Its Female Editors," in Jack R. Censer and Jeremy D. Popkin, *Press and Politics in Pre-Revolutionary France* (Berkeley: University of California Press, 1987), 45.

2. *The French Press in the Age of the Enlightenment* (London and New York, Routledge, 1994) 225.

3. As historians point out, the modern distinction between *journal* and *revue* did not exist at the time, which means that the word "journal" should not be assumed to indicate a daily newspaper. Like historians, I use the words journal, press, magazine, and publication interchangeably.

4. The most successful journal for women, the *Journal des dames* (1759–1768, 1774–1778) has been estimated to have had from 300 to 1600 subscribers. Nina Rattner Gelbart places the figure at 300 to 1000 in her *Feminism and Opposition Journalism: "Le Journal des dames"* (Berkeley: University of Callifornia Press, 1987), 33.

5. *The French Press in the Age of the Enlightenment*, 187.

6. See the serialized *Dictionnaire des journalistes*, sous la direction de Jean Sgard (Grenoble: Presses Universitaires de Grenoble, 1976) with its subsequent supplements.

7. See chapter 4: "Eighteenth-century Journalism and Its Personnel," in *The French Press in the Age of Enlightenment*, 121–137.

8. For instance, the *Journal des dames*, which had been publishing since 1764, was refused a *permission* in 1769, when Mathon de la Cour applied, and did not resume publication until five years later. For a short version of the history of this journal, see Nina Gelbart in Jack R. Censer and Jeremy D. Popkins, eds., *Press and Politics in Pre-revolutionary France* (Berkeley: University of California Press, 1987), chap. 2: "Le *Journal des dames* and Its Females Editors: Politics, Censorship, and Feminism in the Old Regime Press," 24–75.

9. See *Feminine and Opposition Journalism*, and Suzanne Van Dijk, *Traces des femmes: Présence féminine dans le journalisme français du XVIIIe siècle* (Amsterdam and Maarsen: APA-Holland University Press, 1988).

10. Sgard, *Inventaire de la presse classique, 1600–1789* (Grenoble, 1978), 32. The titles are: *Amusements de la toilette* (1755–1756); *Amusements des dames* (1759), *Amusements du beau sexe* (1740–1741), *Bibliothèque amusante et instructive* (1753–1756), *Bibliothèque des dames* (1764), *Bibiothèque des femmes* (1759), *Cabinet des modes* (1785–1786), *Courrier de la mode* (1678), *Courrier de la nouveauté* (1758), *Courrier lyrique et amusant* (1785–1787), *Hebdomadaires ou Lettres de Madame* (1750), *Journal de Monsieur* (1776–1783), *Journal des dames* (1759–1777), *Journal des Modes, Magasin des modes nouvelles* (1786–1789), *Mélanges littéraires ou Journal des dames* (1777–1778), *Nouveau Magasin français de Londres* (1750–1751), *Parnasse des dames* (1773), *Spectatrice* (1728–1729). He points out that the use of words such as *affiches, lettres, nouvelles, bibliothèques, recueils, annales, glaneurs, almanach, journal*, and so forth in titles causes much uncertainty in cataloguing. Sometimes a *journal* is a novel or essay, sometimes an *almanach* or *calendrier* is a magazine.

11. There are, of course, other men who understand that beauty can be a trap for men as for women, since the male is so easily ensnared by physical attractiveness. This seems to be the view of Abbé Fromageot whose book, *Cours d'études des jeunes demoiselles*, is reviewed in the February 1777 issue of the *Journal des dames*. He criticizes men for emphasizing the importance of female beauty, which he deems degrading to women, tantamount to treating them like "beautiful flowers whose single purpose is to please the eye."

12. The journal underwent two further name changes: *Le Magasin des modes nouvelles françaises et anglaises* (mid–1788 to the end of 1789) and *Le Journal de la mode et du goût, ou Amusements du Salon et de la toilette* (until early 1792).

13. As argued by Erica Harth in "The Salon Woman Goes Public . . . or Does She?" in Elizabeth C. Goldsmith and Dena Goodman, eds., *Going Public; Women and Publishing in Early Modern France* (Ithaca, N.Y.: Cornell University Press, 1995), 179–193.

14. Gelbart proposes that the salon women, whom she labels *précieuses*, may have been repelled by the "virile pretentions" of women journalists, (*Feminine and Opposition Journalism*, 36). But to suggest that all *salonnières* were *précieuses*, who shunned politics while embracing passion, celebrity, and extravagance, is inaccurate. If such a characterization is correct for a particular variety of *seventeenth-century* woman, it certainly does not describe all *salonnières* either of that century or the next.

15. "Enlightenment Salons: The Convergence of Female and Philosophic Ambitions," *Eighteenth-Century Studies* 22 (Spring 1989), 329–350.

16. *The Printing Press as an Agent of Change: Communications and Cultural Transformations in Early-Modern Europe*, 2 vols. (Cambridge: Cambridge University Press, 1979), I, 131.

17. *The Printing Press as an Agent of Change*, I, 132.

18. *The Printing Press as an Agent of Change*, I, 147.

19. *Women and the Public Sphere in the Age of the French Revolution* (Ithaca, N.Y.: Cornell University Press, 1988), 61.

20. Suzanne Van Dijk and Nina Rattner Gelbart are two historians with differing views of how feminist the feminine press is, with the former presenting an antidote to Gelbart's fascinating, but sometimes overheated, reading of feminist subversiveness in the *Journal des dames*. At the same time, while Van Dijk is absolutely correct to fault sociologist Evelyne Sullerot's *Histoire de la presse féminine française* (Paris: Armand Colin, 1966) for proposing a far too optimistic (and, I would add, extremely sloppy and flawed) conception of women's feminist sentiment, her own conclusions may underestimate the extent to which the very enterprise of woman's journalism represents a challenge to the reigning principles of femininity in the eighteenth century. My contention is that the real interest of the feminine press must be located within the history of women's reading, which is, in itself, a very important chapter in the history of women.

21. The female-authored *Etrennes nationales des dames* is an example of more politicized writing, in opposition to the relatively moderate voices of the women's press that I am considering. Writing in November 1789, a journalist in the *Etrennes* decries men's deficient "systems of equality and freedom" that had forgotten women, leaving them in a "state of inferiority; or to tell the truth, slavery." This publication demanded that women be permitted to serve in the National Assembly, for, it argued that if it was not fair that 23,400,000 individuals be forced to submit to the caprices of 100,000, it was no fairer to continue to exclude from government half of the population simply because of their sex.

22. Other feminist-identified periodicals, such as the socialist-leaning and male-edited *La Bouche de fer*, call for the passage of a divorce law, because, they declare, such a law would be beneficial not only to both sexes, but to the children of unhappy households. Many of the major male thinkers of the age also supported divorce, including Voltaire, Montesquieu, and Diderot. Diderot, for instance, argued that not only is the indissolubility of marriage contrary to the natural inclinations of both sexes, but also that it has deleterious effects on the growth of the population, since unhappy spouses will not be doing their civic duty and making future citizens. See William F. Edmiston, *Diderot and the Family: A Conflict of Nature and Law* (Stanford: Stanford University Press, 1985), chapter on "Marriage and Fidelity."

23. The biographical entry of Du Rozoi (1743–1792) in the *Dictionnaire des journalistes* describes him as a prolix writer, who lived by his pen and was the first journalist condemned by the revolutionary tribunal for his counterrevolutionary ideas.

24. See "An *Editrice* Hides in the *Frondeur* Temple," in *Feminine and Opposition Journalism in Old Regime France*, 95–132, for Gelbart's often fascinating story about Madame de Beaumer's tumultuous editorship at the *Journal des dames*.

25. For a discussion of both gender and the political agenda of cross-dressers, see also Estelle Jelinek, *The Tradition of Women's Autobiography: From Antiquity to the Present* (Boston: Twayne, 1986), 39, who treats British eighteenth-century memoirs by women claiming to have disguised themselves as men. In one instance, Mother

Ross (1667–1739) in *Life and Adventures* (1740) describes being a footsoldier under Marlborough; another, Hannah Snell (1723–1792), relates in *The Female Soldier* (1750) how she adopted the roles of sailor and soldier in order to track down a husband who had abandoned her.

26. Generally characterized as the most famous transsexual in European history, the Chevalier d'Eon (1728–1810) had served both as a diplomat and spy, in the French government, before being officially declared a female by Louis XVI. At age forty-nine, with his career blocked, he offered no resistance to the royal declaration and was subsequently forced to wear women's clothes, living the rest of his life as a female. The public, convinced that he had been born female, was shocked to learn on his death that he was, in fact, a male. In retelling this story, in *Monsieur d'Eon Is a Woman; A Tale of Political Intrigue and Sexual Masquerade* (New York: Basic Books, 1995), Gary Kates refuses to put a psychosexual label on d'Eon, arguing that to do so would be to minimize the deliberate and intellectual nature of the Chevalier's decision to become a woman, which Kates suggests derives primarily from d'Eon's sincere admiration of the fair sex.

27. Van Dijk, "Femmes et journaux au 18e siècle" (175) in *Australian Journal of French Studies* 18 (1981) 164–178.

28. See the discussion in Paule-Marie Duhet, ed., *Les Femmes et la Révolution, 1789–1794* (Paris: Julliard, 1971), 30–32.

29. *Writing a Woman's Life* (New York: W. W. Norton, 1988), 27.

30. As a comparison, Censer points out that *affiches* (those regional publications containing considerable advertising) cost 10 *livres*, political papers about 20 *livres*, and most literary and philosophical journals between 20 and 40 *livres*. Since these prices amounted to considerable sums for families of relatively modest means, it may explain, he says, why periodicals rarely show up in the inventories of the belongings of the poor (189).

31. Most readers would agree with Dufresnoy about the lamentable quality of theatrical plays in Paris in the 1780s, with the major exception of *Le Mariage de Figaro*. The reader will likewise be impressed by the large amount of "borrowing" or piggybacking onto other literary vehicles that had already found success. One example, announced in February 1787, is the play *Saint-Preux et Julie d'Etanges*, which begins with Julie's father trying to force her to marry "Volmar," and receives another bad review by Dufresnoy.

32. Political attacks through one's sexuality were as common in the eighteenth century as they are today. Marie Antoinette, for instance, was pilloried and caricatured by her enemies as a lesbian and worse—an unnatural mother who had engaged in sexual relations that had physically (as well as psychologically) damaged the young Louis XVII.

33. Isabelle de Charrière, for one, had a character in fiction propose to explore matters of sex and gender. In *Trois Femmes* (1797), Constance suggests an experiment to the foster parents of orphaned twin babies, a boy and girl: in exchange for complete financial support from her, the foster parents will raise the children in a sexually nonprejudicial way. The parents are to call the girl Charles and the boy Charlotte, and dress the children in precisely the same way, without distinction to sex. As for their own occupations, the parents are to continue as usual, with the wife doing the weaving, sewing, and knitting, and the husband attending to the tilling of soil and carpentry work. The point of this sociopsychological experiment, claims Constance,

is to see whether once the children reach their early teenage years, "the real Charlotte will knit, be delicate, nice, coquettish and affectionate; and whether the real Charles will take the plane and pickaxe, be straightforward, brave, a little brutal and pugnacious." Or, on the contrary, whether the boy will have the mind and spirit of a girl, and the girl those of a boy, an outcome that would please Constance, who would make the results of her experiment known far and wide, in the hope that henceforth a great deal less would be said about the two sexes having essentially different characters and different aptitudes. If her experiment is less than perfect, it reveals, nonetheless, a concern with how gender is embedded culturally and environmentally in the individual, in distinction with how tradition claims that it derives from essences or nature.

34. Van Dijk, "Journaux des dames et journaux des hommes: La Notion *femme*," in *L'Année 1768 à travers la presse traitée par ordinateur*, présentée par Jean Varloot and Paule Jansen (Paris: Centre National de la Recherche Scientifique), 85.

35. Nina Gelbart deals with this episode in detail in chapter 3 of *Feminine and Opposition Journalism*, 95–132.

36. This is a phrase of Mlle D——in a letter published in the *Journal* in August 1774. She is objecting to the idea that men, jealous of women's eloquence, condemn them to silence in application of the "code of education invented for women," commanding them to "work, meditate, and be silent." The theme of breaking silence becomes ever stronger as each decade of the age of Enlightenment (an ironic appellation for some) passed, and woman after woman found the courage to speak out. Still, as late as 1789, a woman identified only as Madame B***B*** would publish a work in which she wrote, "It is in this time of a general revolution that a woman, astonished by the silence of her sex when it should have so many things to say, so many abuses to combat, so many grievances to air, dares to raise her voice in order to defend the common cause," "Cahier des doléances et réclamations des femmes," in Paule-Marie Duhet, ed., *Cahiers de doléances des femmes en 1789* (Paris: des femmes, 1981), 47–48.

37. The *spectatrice* says, "After all, what difference is it to me whether [men] . . . pay their regards or not to this Work. If they have none to pay, I can do without, and be satisfied with those of women on whom there is a great deal more to count" (March 1728).

38. *La Presse féminine*, 2e ed. (Paris: Armand Colin, 1966), 7.

CONCLUSION

1. Translated by L. G. Cochrane (Durham, N.C.: Duke University Press, 1991), 85–87.

2. "It's the End of the Modern Age," *The Chronicle of Higher Education*, Section 2, April 26, 2002, B9.

3. This is, however, part of the goal of Adrian Johns in his 700-plus page *The Nature of the Book; Print and Knowledge in the Making* (Chicago: University of Chicago Press, 1998), which makes a monumental effort to understand both the commercial production and intellectual, political, and individual consumption of the book and print culture in England.

4. Alice M. Laborde, *L'Oeuvre de Madame de Genlis* (Paris: A.-G. Nizet, 1966), 133.

5. See historian Sarah Hanley's article on "Family and State in Early Modern France: The Marriage Pact," in *Connecting Spheres: Women in the Western World, 1500 to the Present*, ed. by Marilyn J. Boxer and Jean H. Quataert (New York: Oxford University Press, 1987), 53–63.

6. *The Gift: Forms and Functions of Exchange in Archaic Societies (Essai sur le don, forme archaïque de l'Echange*, 1925), trans. by W. D. Halls (New York: W. W. Norton, 1990).

7. *The Gift Economy* (London: Routledge, 1988), x and 7.

BIBLIOGRAPHY

Abensour, Léon. *La Femme et le féminisme avant la révolution*. Paris: Ernest Leroux, 1923.

Albistur, Maïté, and Daniel Argomathe. *Histoire du féminisme français du Moyen Age à nos jours*. Paris: des femmes, 1972.

Allison, Jenene C. *Revealing Difference: The Fiction of Isabelle de Charrière*. Newark: University of Delaware Press, 1995.

Alvermann, Donna E., and Stephen F. Phelps. *Content Reading and Literacy*. Boston, Allyn and Bacon, 1994.

André, Arlette. "Le Féminisme chez Madame Riccoboni," *Studies on Voltaire and the Eighteenth Century*, 193 (1980): 1988–1995.

Appleyard, J. A. *Becoming a Reader; The Experience of Fiction from Childhood to Adulthood*. Cambridge: Cambridge University Press, 1990.

Aragon, Sandrine. *Les Liseuses en peril; Les Images de lectrices dans les textes de fiction de* La Prétieuse *de l'abbé de Pure à* Madame Bovary *de Flaubert (1656–1856)*. Paris: Champion, 2003.

Ariès, Philippe, and Georges Duby, eds. A *History of Private Life* [originally published as *Histoire de la vie privée* (Paris, Seuil, 1986)]. 3 vols. Trans. by Arthur Goldhammer. Cambridge: Harvard University Press, 1989.

Balayé, Simone. *La Bibliothèque nationale, des origines à 1800*. Geneva : Droz, 1988.

Barthes, Roland. "Day by Day with Roland Barthes," in Marshall Blonsky, *On Signs* (Baltimore: Johns Hopkins University Press, 1985) 98–117.

——— *The Pleasure of the Text*. New York: Hill and Wang, 1975.

Bauchart, Ernest Quentin. *Les Femmes bibliophiles de France (XVI, XVIIe, et XVIIIe siècles)*. 2 vols. Paris: Damascène Morgand, 1886; réimpression, Slatkine Reprints, 1993.

Benhamou, Paul. "Popularizing 'Bad Books' in France During the Second Half of the Eighteenth Century." Paper, American Society for Eighteenth-Century Studies, 1996.

Bettelheim, Bruno. *The Uses of Enchantment: The Meaning and Importance of Fairy Tales*. New York: Knopf, 1976.

Bienville, D. T. *La Nymphomanie, ou La Fureur utérine* (1771), 2nd ed. Amsterdam: M. M. Rey, 1780.

Bourgeois, A., Docteur. *Les Besicles de nos ancêtres*. Paris: A. Maloine, 1923.

Braudel, Ferdinand. "Superfluity and Sufficiency: Houses, Clothes and Fashion," chap. 4, *Structures of Everyday Life*. Trans. and rev. by Siân Reynolds. New York: Harper & Row, 1981.

Broglie, Gabriel de. *Madame de Genlis*. Paris: Perrin, 1985.

Brooks, Peter. *Psychoanalysis and Storytelling*. Oxford: Blackwell, 1994.

Burk, Peter, and Roy Porters, eds. *The Social History of Language*. Cambridge: Cambridge University Press, 1987.

Burns, E. Jane. *Bodytalk: When Women Speak in Old French Literature*. Philadelphia: University of Pennsylvania Press, 1993.

Cabanis, P. J. G. *Rapports du physique et du moral de l'homme* (1802). Geneva: Slatkine Reprints, 1980. Trans. by Margaret Duggan Mora as *On the Relations between the Physical and Moral Aspects of Man*. Baltimore: Johns Hopkins University Press, 1981.

Caillois, Roger. *Man, Play, and Games*. Trans. by M. Barash. New York: Schocken Books, 1979.

Calinescu, Matei. *Rereading*. New Haven & London: Yale University Press, 1993.

Censer, Jack R. *The French Press in the Age of the Enlightenment*. London and New York: Routledge, 1994.

Censer, Jack R., and Jeremy D. Popkins, eds. *Press and Politics in Pre-revolutionary France*. Berkeley: University of California Press, 1987.

Chartier, Roger. *The Cultural Uses of Print in Early Modern France*. Trans. by Lydia G. Cochrane. Princeton, N.J: Princeton University Press, 1987. In French: *Lectures et lecteurs dans la France d'Ancien Régime*. Paris: Seuil, 1982, 1984, 1987.

———. ed., *A History of Private Life*, Vol. III: *Passions of the Renaissance*. Cambridge: Harvard University Press, 1989.

———. "La Lecture: Une Pratique culturelle," conversation entre Roger Chartier et Pierre Bourdieu. In *Pratiques de la lecture*, ed. by Roger Chartier, 218–239. Marseille: Rivages, 1985.

———. "The Practical Impact of Writing." In *A History of Private Life*, Vol. III: *Passions of the Renaissance*, 111–159. Cambridge: Harvard University Press, 1989.

———. ed., *Pratiques de la lecture*. Marseille: Rivages, 1985.

———. *Les Usages de l'imprimé*. Paris: Fayard, 1987.

Cheal, David. *The Gift Economy*. London: Routledge, 1988.

Cim, Albert. *Les Femmes et les livres*. Paris: Boccard, 1919.

Clancy, Patricia A. "A French Writer and Educator in England: Mme Le Prince de Beaumont." In *Studies on Voltaire and the Eighteenth Century* (201), 1982: 195–208.

"Correspondance de Laclos et de Madame Riccoboni au sujet des *Liaisons dangereuses*." In Choderlos de Laclos, *Oeuvres completes*, 686–698. Paris: Gallimard, 1951.

Courtney, C. P. *Isabelle de Charrière (Belle de Zuylen): A Biography*. Oxford: Voltaire Foundation, 1993.

Cragg, Olga, and Rosena Davison, eds. *Sexualité, mariage et famille au XVIIIe siècle*. Laval: Presses Universitaires de Laval, 1998.

Crosby, Emily. *Une Romancière oubliée, Madame Riccoboni*. Geneva: Slatkine Reprints, 1970.

Culler, Jonathan. *Roland Barthes*. New York: Oxford University Press, 1983.

Daniels, Charlotte. "The Mother-Daughter Plot in Isabelle de Charrière's "Lettres écrits de Lausanne." In *Subverting the Family Romance: Women Writers, Kinship Structures, and the Early French Novel*, 57–102. Lewisburg, Pa.: Bucknell University Press, 2000.

Darnton, Robert. *The Forbidden Best-Sellers of Pre-Revolutionary France*. New York: W. W. Norton, 1995. In French: *Edition et sédition: L'Univers de la littérature clandestine au XVIIIe siècle*. Paris: Gallimard, 1991.

———. "Readers Respond to Rousseau." In *The Great Cat Massacre and Other Episodes* in *French Cultural History*, 215–256. New York: Basic Books, 1984.

———. "What Was Revolutionary About the French Revolution?" In *The New York Review of Books*, January 19, 1989: 3–4, 6, 10.

Deguise, Alix S. Preface, *Mademoiselle de Clermont, suivie de L'Histoire intéressante de Madame La Duchesse de C****. Geneva: Slatkine, 1982.

DeJean, Joan. *Ancients against Moderns: Culture Wars and the Making of a Fin de Siècle*. Chicago: University of Chicago Press, 1997.

———. *Tender Geographies; Women and the Origins of the Novel in France*. New York: Columbia University Press, 1991.

———, and Nancy K. Miller. "The Politics of Tradition," *Yale French Studies* (1988), 40–55.

Delon, Michel. "Cartésianisme(s) et féminisme(s), *Europe* 56 (October 1978), 73–86.

Diaz, Brigitte. "De La Lettre aux *Mémoires:* Les Fonctions autobiographiques de la lettre dans la correspondance de jeunesse de Mme Roland (1767–1780)." In Marie-France Silver and Marie-Laure Girou Swiderski, eds., *Femmes en toutes lettres* (SVEC: 2000:04): 211–227.

Didier, Béatrice. *Mademoiselle de Clermont*. Paris: Régine Deforges, 1977.

———. *L'Ecriture-femme*. Paris: Presses Universitaires de France, 1981.

Docherty, Linda J. "Women as Readers: Visual Interpretations," *American Antiquarian Society*, 107 (1998): 335–388.

Douthwaite, Julia. *Exotic Women: Literary Heroines and Cultural Strategies in Ancien Régime France*. Philadelphia: University of Pennsylvania Press, 1992.

Dubosc, Danielle Haase, and Eliane Viennot, éds. *Femmes et pouvoirs sous l'ancien régime*. Paris: Rivages, 1991.

Duhet, Paule-Marie, ed. Preface, "Cahier des doléances et réclamations des femmes," 9-19, *Cahiers de doléances des femmes en 1789*. Paris: des femmes, 1981.

———. *Les Femmes et la Révolution, 1789–1794*. Paris: Julliard, 1971.

Eagleton, Terry. *The Rape of Clarissa; Writing, Sexuality, and Class Struggle in Samuel Richardson*. Minneapolis: University of Minnesota Press, 1982.

Edmiston, William F. "Marriage and Fidelity," *Diderot and the Family: A Conflict of Nature and Law*. Stanford: Stanford University Press, 1985.

Eisenstein, Elizabeth. *The Printing Press as an Agent of Change: Communications and Cultural Transformations in Early-Modern Europe*. 2 vols. Cambridge: Cambridge University Press, 1979.

Engelsing, Rolf. *Der Bürger als Leser: Lesergeschichte in Deutschland 1500–1800*. Stuttgart: Metzler, 1974.

Fauchéry, Pierre. *La Destinée féminine dans le roman français du dix-huitième siècle*. Paris: A. Colin, 1972.

Feagin, Susan L. *Reading with Feeling; The Aesthetics of Appreciation*. Ithaca and London: Cornell University Press, 1996.

Ferrand, Nathalie. "Livre et lecture dans quelques romans épistolaires: *La Nouvelle Héloïse*, *Les Malheurs de l'inconstance*, *Les Liaisons dangereuses*, *L'Emigré*," 367–377. In Jan Herman and Paul Pelckmans, eds., *L'Epreuve du lecteur; Livres et lectures dans le roman d'Ancien Régime*. Louvain: Peeters, 1994.

Fletcher, Pamela R., and Martha Roth, eds. *Transforming a Rape Culture*. Minneapolis: Milweed, 1993.

Flint, Kate. *The Woman Reader, 1837–1914*. Oxford: Clarendon Press, 1993.

Flynn, Elizabeth A., and Patrocinio P. Schweickart, eds. *Gender and Reading: Essays on Readers, Texts, and Contexts*. Baltimore: Johns Hopkins Press, 1986.

Fried, Michael. *Absorption and Theatricality: Painting and Beholder in the Age of Diderot*. Berkeley: University of California Press, 1980.

Furet, François, and Jacques Ozouf. *Reading and Writing: Literacy in France from Calvin to Jules Ferry*. 2 vols. London: Cambridge University Press, 1982. Orig. pub. as *Lire et écrire: l'alphabétisation des Français de Calvin à Jules Ferry*. Paris: Editions de Minuit, 1977.

Gasnault, P. "La Bibliothèque de Mazarin et la Bibliothèque Mazarine au XVII et au XVIIIe siècles," *Les Espaces du livre*, II: *Les Bibliothèques*, Deuxième Colloque (6–7 juin 1980) de l'Institut d'Etude du Livre, 31–37.

Gelbart, Nina Rattner. *Feminism and Opposition Journalism: "Le Journal des dames."* Berkeley: University of California Press, 1987.

———. "The Journal des dames and Its Females Editors," in Jack R. Censer and Jeremy D. Popkin, *Press and Politics in Pre-Revolutionary France*. Berkeley: University of California Press, 1987, 24–74.

Gelfand, Elissa. *Imagination in Confinement: Women's Writings from French Prisons*. Ithaca, N.Y.: Cornell University Press, 1983.

Gitlin, Todd. *The Twilight of Common Dreams; Why America Is Wracked by Culture Wars*. New York: Metropolitan Books, 1995.

Goncourt, Edmond, and Jules de. *La Femme au dix-huitième siècle* (1882). Pref. d'Elisabeth Badinter. Paris: Flammarion, 1982.

Goodman, Dena. "Enlightenment Salons: The Convergence of Female and Philosophic Ambitions," *Eighteenth-Century Studies* 22 (Spring 1989) 329–350.

———, and Elizabeth C. Goldsmith, eds. *Going Public; Women and Publishing in Early Modern France*. Ithaca, N.Y.: Cornell University Press, 1995.

Goulemot, Jean-Marie. *Forbidden Texts: Erotic Literature and Its Readers in Eighteenth-Century France*. Trans. by James Simpson. Philadelphia: University of Pennsylvania Press, 1994. Orig. pub. as *Ces Livres qu'on ne lit que d'une main*. Paris: Aliéna, 1991.

———. "Le Lecteur-Voyeur et la mise en scène de l'imaginaire viril dans *Les Liaisons dangereuses*," *Laclos et le libertinage, 1782–1982*, 163–175. In *Actes du Colloque du Bicentennaire des* Liaisons dangereuses. Paris: Presses Universitaires de France, 1983.

Green, F. C. *Minuet; A Critical Survey of French and English Literary Ideas in the Eighteenth Century*. New York, Dutton, 1935.

Guignard, Joannis. *Nouvel Armorial du bibliophile, Guide de l'amateur des livres armoriés*. Tome I. Paris: Emile Rondeau, 1890.

Gutwirth, Madelyn. "Laclos and 'Le Sexe': The Rack of Ambivalence," *Studies on Voltaire and the Eighteenth Century* (1989): 247–296.

Habermas, Jürgen. *L'Espace public: Archéologie de la publicité comme dimension constitutive de la société bourgeoise*. Paris: Payot, 1978. Trans. by Marc B. de Launay from German, *Strukturwandel der öffentlichkeit: Untersuchungen zu einer Kategorie der bürgerlichen Gesellschaft*. Neuwied and Berlin: Hermann Luckterhand, 1962.

Hanley, Sarah. "Family and State in Early Modern France: The Marriage Pact," 53–63. In Marilyn J. Boxer and Jean H. Quataert, eds., *Connecting Spheres: Women in the Western World, 1500 to the Present*. Oxford: Oxford University Press, 1987.

Harth, Erica. *Cartesian Women: Versions and Subversions of Rational Discourse in The Old Regime*. Ithaca, N.Y. : Cornell University Press, 1992.

———. "The Salon Woman Goes Public . . . or Does She?" 179–193. In Elizabeth C. Goldsmith and Dena Goodman, eds., *Going Public; Women and Publishing in Early Modern France*. Ithaca, N.Y.: Cornell University Press, 1995.

Heilbrun, Carolyn G. *Writing a Woman's Life*. New York: W. W. Norton, 1988.

Herman, Jan, and Paul Pelckmans, eds., *L'Epreuve du lecteur; Livres et lectures dans le roman d'Ancien Régime*. Louvain: Peeters, 1994.

Hillis, J. Miller. *The Ethics of Reading*. New York, Columbia University Press, 1987.

Holland, Norman. *The Dynamics of Literary Response*. New York: Oxford University Press, 1968.

Houillon, Henriette. "La Femme en France aux XVIIe et XVIIIe siècles," t. IV, Livre I, *Histoire mondiale de la femme*. Paris: Nouvelle Librairie de France, 1966.

Hugo, Victor. *Choses vues*. Paris: Charpentier, 1888.

Jelinek, Estelle. *The Tradition of Women's Autobiography: From Antiquity to the Present*. Boston: Twayne, 1986.

Jensen, Katharine Ann. "Mirrors, Marriage, and Nostalgia: Mother-Daughter Relations in Writings by Isabelle de Charrière and Elisabeth Vigée-Lebrun," 285–314. *Tulsa Studies in Women's Literature* 19, no. 2 (Fall 2000).

Johannot, Yvonne. *Tourner la page: livre, rites, et symboles*. Jérôme Millon, 1988.

Johns, Adrian. *The Nature of the Book; Print and Knowledge in the Making*. Chicago: University of Chicago Press, 1998.

Jones, Kathleen B. "On Authority: Or, Why Women Are Not Entitled to Speak," 119–133. In *Feminism and Foucault: Reflections on Resistance*, ed. Irene Diamond and Lee Quimby. Boston: Northeastern University Press, 1988.

Kaplan, E. Ann. "Is the Gaze Male?" 309–327. *Powers of Desire; The Politics of Sexuality*. New York: Monthly Review Press, 1983.

Kates, Gary. *Monsieur d'Eon Is a Woman; A Tale of Political Intrigue and Sexual Masquerade*. New York: Basic Books, 1995.

Kauffman, Linda. *Discoveries of Desire: Gender, Genre, and Epistolary Fictions*. Ithaca, N.Y.: Cornell University Press, 1986.

Kermina, Françoise. *Mme Roland ou la passion révolutionnaire*. Paris: Académique Perrin, 1976.

Krueger, Roberta. *Women Readers and the Ideology of Gender in Old French Verse Romance*. Cambridge: Cambridge University Press, 1993.

Laborde, Alice. *L'Oeuvre de Madame de Genlis*. Paris: Nizet, 1966.

Labrosse, Claude. *Lire au XVIIIe siècle: "La Nouvelle Héloïse" et ses lecteurs*. Lyon: Presses Universitaires de Lyon, CNRS, 1985.

Lambert, Anne Thérèse de Marguenat de Courcelles, marquise de. *Réflexions nouvelles sur les femmes*. Paris: côté-femmes, 1989.

Landes, Joan B. *Women and the Public Sphere in the Age of the French Revolution*. Ithaca, N.Y.: Cornell University Press, 1988.

Lanser, Susan Snaider. *Women Writers and Narrative Voice: Fictions of Authority*. Ithaca, N.Y.: Cornell University Press, 1992.

Laqueur, Thomas. *Making Sex: Body and Gender from the Greeks to Freud*. Cambridge: Harvard University Press, 1990.

Launay, M. *Jean-Jacques Rousseau et son temps*. Paris: Nizet, 1969.

Lee, Vera. *The Reign of Women in Eighteenth-Century France*. Cambridge: Schenkman, 1975.

Leenhard, Jacques. "Les Instances de la compétence dans l'activité lectrice," 302–311. In Michel Picard, *La Lecture littéraire*. Paris: Clancier-Guénaud, 1987.

Lejeune, Philippe. *Le Pacte autobiographique*. Paris: Seuil, 1975.

Letzter, Jacqueline. *Intellectual Tacking: Questions of Education in the Works of Isabelle de Charrière*. Amsterdam: Rodopi, 1998.

Liben, Lynn S. "Spatial Representation and Behavior," 3–36. In Lynn S. Liben et al., eds., *Spatial Representation and Behavior across the Life Span: Theory and Application*. New York: Academic Press, 1981.

Long, Elizabeth. "Women, Reading, and Cultural Authority: Some Implications of the Audience Perspective in Cultural Studies," 591–612. In *American Quarterly*, Vol. 38, 4 (Autumn 1986).

Lukacs, George. *The Historical Novel*. Trans. by Hannah and Stanley Mitchel. Boston: Beacon Press, 1963.

Lukacs, John. "It's the End of the Modern Age." In *The Chronicle of Higher Education*, Section 2, April 26, 2002, B9.

Lyons, Martyn. *Le Triomphe du livre: Une Histoire sociologique de la lecture dans la France du XIXe siècle*. Traduit de l'anglais. Paris: Promodis, 1987.

MacCarthy, Fiona. Review of Jo Ann Kay McNamara, *Sisters in Arms: Catholic Nuns Through Two Millennia* (Cambridge: Harvard University Press, 1996). In *New York Review of Books*, December 19, 1996, 31–33.

Mander, Jenny. "Le Cercle pédagogique: Un Mode dominant de lecture au début du XVIIIe siècle," 191–199. In Jan Herman and Paul Pelckmans, eds., *L'Epreuve du lecteur; Livres et lectures dans le roman d'Ancien Régime*. Louvain: Peeters, 1994.

Manguel, Alberto. *A History of Reading*. New York: Penguin Books, 1996.

Marion, Michel. "Les Livres chez les Parisiens dans la deuxième moitié du XVIIIe siècle," 31–37. In *Les Espace du livre*. II: *Les Bibliothèques*, Deuxième Colloque de l'Institut d'Etude du Livre (6–7 juin 1980).

Martin, Henri-Jean. *Livre, Pouvoirs et société à Paris au XVIIIe siècle (1598–1701)*. Geneva: Droz, 1969.

———, and Roger Chartier, eds. *Histoire de l'édition française*. 2 vols. Vol. II: *Le Livre triomphant, 1660–1830*. Paris: Promodis, 1984.

Mauss, Marcel. *The Gift: Forms and Function of Exchange in Archaic Societies* (*Essai sur le don, forme archaïque de l'échange*, 1925). Trans. by W. D. Halls. New York: W. W. Norton, 1990.

May, Georges. *Le Dilemme du roman au XVIIIe siècle*. Paris: Presses Universitaires de France, 1963.

May, Gita. "Rousseau's 'Antifeminism' Reconsidered," 309–317. In Samia Spencer, ed., *French Women and the Enlightenment.* Bloomington: Indiana University Press, 1984.

Mercier, Léon Sébastien. *Le Tableau de Paris*, ed. by Michel Delon. Paris: Robert Laffont, 1990.

Milder, Benjamin, and Melvin L. Rubin. *The Fine Art of Prescribing Glasses without Making a Spectacle of Yourself.* 2nd ed. Gainsville, Fl.: Triad, 1991.

Miller, J. Hillis. *The Ethics of Reading.* New York: Columbia University Press, 1987.

Miller, Nancy K. "Cultural Memory and the Art of the Novel: Gender and Narrative in Eighteenth-Century France," 69–79. In *French Dressing: Women, Men and Ancien Regime Fiction.* New York: Routledge, 1995.

———. *The Heroine's Text: Readings in the French and English Novel,1722 –1782.* New York: Columbia University Press, 1980.

———. "La Mémoire, l'oubli et l'art du roman: textes libertins, textes sentimentaux," 238–253. In Danielle Haase Dubosc and Eliane Viennot, *Femmes et pouvoirs sous l'ancien régime.* Paris: Rivages, 1991, 238–253.

———. "Men's Reading, Women's Writing: Gender and the Rise of the Novel," *Yale French Studies* 75 (1988): 40–55.

Morgenstern, Mira. *Rousseau and the Politics of Ambiguity.* University Park: Pennsylvania State University Press, 1996.

Mornet, Daniel. "Les Enseignements des bibliothèques privées (1750–1780)," *Revue d'histoire littéraire de la France* XVII (1910): 449–492.

Outram Dorinda. " 'Le Langage mâle de la vertu': Women and the Discourse of the French Revolution," 120–135. In Peter Burke and Roy Porter, eds., *The Social History of Language.* Cambridge: Cambridge University Press, 1987.

———. "Words and Flesh: Mme Roland, the Female Body and the Search for Power," 124–152. In *The Body and the French Revolution, Sex, Class and Political Culture.* New Haven and London: Yale University Press, 1989.

Paulson, William R. *Enlightenment, Romanticism, and the Blind in France.* Princeton, N.J., Princeton University Press, 1987.

Perroud, Claude. *Roland et Marie Phlipon: Lettres d'amour, de 1777 à 1780.* Paris: Alphonse Picard, 1909.

Perry, Ruth. *Women, Letters, and the Novel.* New York: AMS Press, 1980.

Picard, Michel. *La Lecture comme jeu; Esssai sur la littérature.* Paris: Editions de Minuit, 1986.

———, ed. *La Lecture littéraire.* Paris: Clancier-Guénaud, 1987.

Porée, Le Père Charles. "De Librus qui vulgo dicuntur romaneses oration" ("Discours sur les livres appelés en langue vulgaire romans"). Public address, 25 February 1736, at the Collège Louis le Grand, Paris.

Portemer, Jean. "Le Statut de la femme en France, depuis la réfomation des coutumes, jusqu'à la rédaction du Code Civil," *Recueils de la Société Jean Bodin*, XII: *La Femme*, 2e partie. Bruxelles: Editions de la Librairie Encyclopédique, 1962.

Porter, Roy. "Does Rape Have a History?" 216–236. In *Rape*, eds. Sylvana Tomaselli and Roy Porter. Oxford: Basil Blackwell, 1986.

Poulet, W. *Atlas on the History of Spectacles.* 3 vols. Trans by Frederick C. Blodi. Bonn-Bad Godesberg, West Germany, Wayenborgh, 1978 (Vol. I), 1980 (Vol. II)

Radway, Janice. *Reading the Romance: Women, Patriarchy, and Popular Literature.* Chapel Hill: University of North Carolina Press, 1984.

Rees, Christine. *Utopian Imagination in Eighteenth-Century Fiction*. London: Longman, 1996.

Reynaud, Denis. "La Lecture de la presse dans les genres narratifs au XVIIIe siècle," 387–395. In Jan Herman and Paul Pelckmans, eds., *L'Epreuve du lecteur; Livres et lectures dans le roman d'Ancien Régime*. Louvain: Peeters, 1994.

Rogers, Adrienne. "Women and the Law," 33–48. *French Women and the Age of Enlightenment*, ed. Samia Spencer. Bloomington: Indiana University Press, 1984.

Romans de Femmes du XVIIIe siècle. Paris: Robert Laffont, 1996.

Rosenblatt, Louise. *The Reader, The Text, the Poem: The Transactional Theory of the Literary Work*. Carbondale: Southern Illinois University Press, 1978.

Rousseau, Jean-Jacques. *Oeuvres complètes*, 4 vols. Paris: Gallimard, 1959.

———. "2e Préface de la *Nouvelle Héloïse*: ou Entretien sur les romans, entre l'éditeur et un homme de lettres," 16 février 1761, *Oeuvres complètes*, II. Paris: Gallimard, 1959.

Roussel, P. *Système physique et moral de la femme* (1775).

Rowe, Karen E. "Feminism and Fairy Tales," 209–226. In *Don't Bet on the Prince; Contemporary Feminist Fairy Tales in North America and England*, ed. by Jack Zipes. New York: Routledge, 1986.

Sainte-Beuve, Charles-Augustin. "Madame Roland" in *Nouveaux Lundis*. Paris: Calmann-Lévy, 1896), VIII, 198–200.

Scholes, Robert. *The Crafty Reader*. New Haven: Yale University Press, 2001.

———. *The Protocols of Reading*. New Haven: Yale University Press, 1989.

Scott, Geoffrey. *The Portrait of Zélide*. New York: Charles Scribner's, 1927.

———. *The Portrait of Zélide*. London: Constable, 1925.

Scott, Joan Wallach. *Only Paradoxes to Offer: French Feminism and the Rights of Man*. Cambridge.: Harvard University Press, 1996.

Seifert, Lewis C. *Fairy Tales, Sexuality, and Gender in France, 1690–1715: Nostalgic Utopias*. Cambridge University Press, 1996.

Sèze, P.-V. *Recherches physiologiques et expériences sur la vitalité* (1797). Paris: Fuchs.

Sgard, Jean. *L'Abbé Prévost: Labyrinthes de mémoire*. Paris: Presses Universitaires de France, 1986.

———. *Dictionnaire des Journalistes*. Grenoble Presses Universitaires de Grenoble, 1976, plus subsequent supplements.

———. *Inventaire de la presse classique, 1600–1789*. Grenoble, 1978.

Silver, Marie France, and Marie-Laure Girou Swiderski, eds. *Femmes en toutes lettres; Les Epistolières du XVIIIe siècle*. Oxford: Voltaire Foundation (SVEC 2000:04), 2000.

Smith, Bonnie G. *Ladies of the Leisure Class*. Princeton: Princeton University Press, 1981.

Smith, David. "The Popularity of Madame de Graffigny's *Lettres d'une Péruvienne*: The Bibliographical Evidence," 1–20. In *Eighteenth-Century Fiction*, Vol. 3, Oct. 1990.

Sol, Antoinette. *Textual Promiscuities: Critical Rewritings in the Eighteenth Century*. Lewisburg, Pa.: Bucknell University Press, 2002.

Spacks, Patricia. *Boredom: The Literary History of a State of* Mind. Chicago: University of Chicago, 1995.

Spencer, Samia, ed. *French Women and the Enlightenment*. Bloomington: Indiana University Press, 1984.

Steinbrügge, Liselotte. *The Moral Sex: Woman's Nature in the French Enlightenment*. Trans. by Pamela E. Selwyn. New York: Oxford University Press, 1995. Orig. pub. as *Das Moralische Geschlect: Theorien und literarische Entwürfe über die Natur der Frau in der französischen Aufklärung*. Stuttgart: J. B. Metzlersche, 1992.

Stewart, Joan Hinde. *Gynographs: French Novels by Women of the Late Eighteenth Century*. Lincoln: University of Nebraska Press, 1993.

———. *The Novels of Madame Riccoboni*. Chapel Hill: U.N.C. Dept of Romance Languages. North Carolina Studies in Romance Languages and Literatures: Essays, 8 (1976).

Stock, Brian. *After Augustine: The Meditative Reader and the Text*. Philadelphia: University of Pennsylvania Press, 2001.

Sullerot, Evelyne. *Histoire de la presse féminine française*. Paris: Armand Colin, 1966.

———. *La Presse féminine*, 2nd ed. Paris: Armand Colin, 1966.

Sutton, Paul. "Reading *La Lectrice*," 153–165. In Michael Syrotinski and Ian Maclachlan, eds., *Sensual Reading: New Approaches to Reading in Its Relations to the Senses*. Lewisburg, Pa.: Bucknell University Press, 2001.

Swain, Virginia. "Beauty's Chambers: Mixed Genres and Mixed Messages in Villeneuve's 'Beauty and the Beast'," Modern Language Association, Toronto, 1997.

Swiderski, Marie Laure Girou, "La Belle et la bête? Madame de Villeneuve, la méconnue." In Roland Bonnel and Catherine Rubinger, eds., *Femmes savantes et femmes d'esprit: Women Intellectuals of the French Enlightenment*. New York: Peter Lang, 1994.

Thelander, Dorothy. *Laclos and the Epistolary Novel*. Geneva: Droz, 1963.

Timmermans, Linda. *L'Accès des femmes à la culture (1598–1715); Un Débat d'idées de Saint François de Sales à la Marquise de Lambert*. Paris: Honoré Champion, 1993.

Tissot, S. A. *L'Onanisme, dissertation sur les maladies produites par la masturbation*, 1760. Trans. in English by A. Humes, M.D., as *Onanism, or A Treatise upon the Disorders produced by Masturbation, or The Dangerous Effects of Secret and Excessive Venery*, 1766.

Trouille, Mary Seidman. *Sexual Politics in the Enlightenment: Women Writers Read Rousseau*. Albany: State University Press of New York, 1997.

Van Dijk, Suzanne. "Femmes et journaux au 18e siècle," *Australian Journal of French Studies*, 1981.

———. "Journaux des dames et journaux des hommes: La Notion *femme*," *L'Année 1768* à travers la presse traitée par ordinateur, présentée par Jean Varloot et Paule Jansen. Paris: Centre National de la Recherche Scientifique, 1981.

———. "Lire ou broder: deux occupations féminines dans l'oeuvre de Mmes de Graffigny, Riccoboni, et de Charrière," 351–360. In Jan Herman and Paul Pelckmans, eds., *L'Epreuve du lecteur; Livres et lectures dans le roman d'Ancien Régime*. Louvain: Peeters, 1994.

———. *Traces des femmes: Présence féminine dans le journalisme français du XVIIIe siècle*. Amsterdam and Maarsen: APA-Holland University Press, 1988.

Vanpée, Janie. "Dangerous Liaisons 2: The Riccoboni–Laclos Sequel," *Eighteenth Century Fiction* 9 (October 1996): 51–70.

Verdier, Gabrielle. "Grimoire, miroir: Le Livre dans les contes de fées littéraires," 129–139. In Jan Herman and Paul Pelckmans, eds., *L'Epreuve du lecteur; Livres et lectures dans le roman d'Ancien Régime*. Louvain: Peeters, 1994.

Versini, Laurent. *Laclos et la tradition; essai sur les sources et la techniques des "Liaisons dangereuses."* Paris: Klincksieck, 1968.

Vigée-Lebrun, Elisabeth. *Souvenirs*. 2 vols. 2nd ed. Paris: des femmes, 1986.

Vila, Anne C. *Enlightenment and Pathology: Sensibility in the Literature and Medicine of Eighteenth-Century France.* Baltimore: Johns Hopkins University Press, 1998.

Vissière, Isabelle, and Jean-Louis. *Une Liaison dangereuse, correspondance avec Constant d'Hermenches*, 1760–1776. Paris: Editions de la Différence, 1991.

———. "La Poétique d'Isabelle de Charrière ou la correspondance comme laboratoire d'une oeuvre." In Marie-France Silver and Marie-Laure Girou Swiderski, eds., *Femmes en toutes lettres* (SVEC, 2000:04): 165–174.

Vitols, Astrid. *Dictionnaire des lunettes: Historique et symbolique d'un objet culturel.* Paris: Bonneton, 1994.

Walker, Lesley H. "Sweet and Consoling Virtue: The Memoirs of Madame Roland," *Eighteenth-Century Studies*, 34, no. 3 (Spring 2001): 403–419.

Walther, Conrad Salomon. *Manuel de la toilette & de la mode.* 1771–1780.

Warner, Marina. *From the Beast to the Blonde; On Fairy Tales and Their Tellers.* New York: Farrar, Straus, and Giroux, 1995.

Weil, Michèle. "Mme de Genlis épistolière: Letttres d'une femme de lettres ou vers une poétique de la lettre féminine ou l'être en lettres," in Marie-France Silver and Marie-Laure Girou Swiderski, eds., *Femmes en toutes lettres* (SVEC, 2000:04): 193–210.

Willard, Charity Cannon, and Erick Hicks, eds. *Le Livre des Trois Vertus*. Paris: Champion, 1989.

Wilson, Emma. *Sexuality and the Reading Encounter; Identity and Desire in Proust, Duras, Tournier, and Cixous*. Oxford: Clarendon Press, 1996.

Wilson, Lindsay. *Women and Medicine in the French Enlightenment: The Debate over "Maladies des Femmes."* Baltimore: Johns Hopkins University Press, 1993.

Young, Arthur. *Travels in France during the Years 1787, 1788, and 1789*, ed. J. Kaplow. Garden City, N.Y.: Doubleday, 1969.

Zinsser, William. *Inventing the Truth: The Art and Craft of Memoir*. Boston: Houghton Mifflin, 1987.

Zipes, Jack, ed. *Don't Bet on the Prince; Contemporary Feminist Fairy Tales in North America and England*. New York: Routledge, 1986.

———. *Fairy Tales and the Art of Subversion; The Classical Genre for Children and the Process of Civilization*. New York: Methuen, 1988.

INDEX